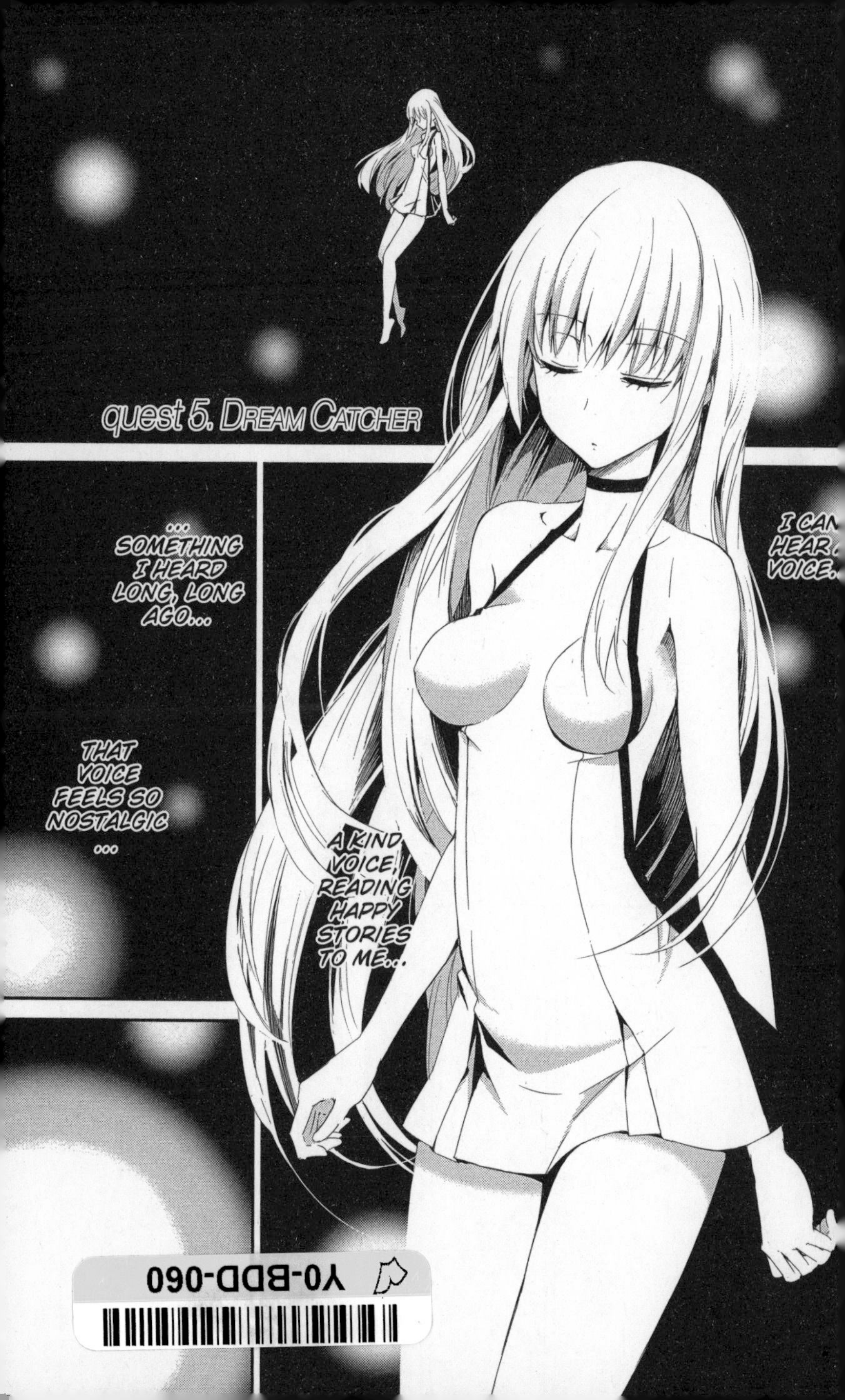
quest 5. DREAM CATCHER
I CAN HEAR VOICE..
A KIND VOICE, READING HAPPY STORIES TO ME...
...SOMETHING I HEARD LONG, LONG AGO...
THAT VOICE FEELS SO NOSTALGIC...

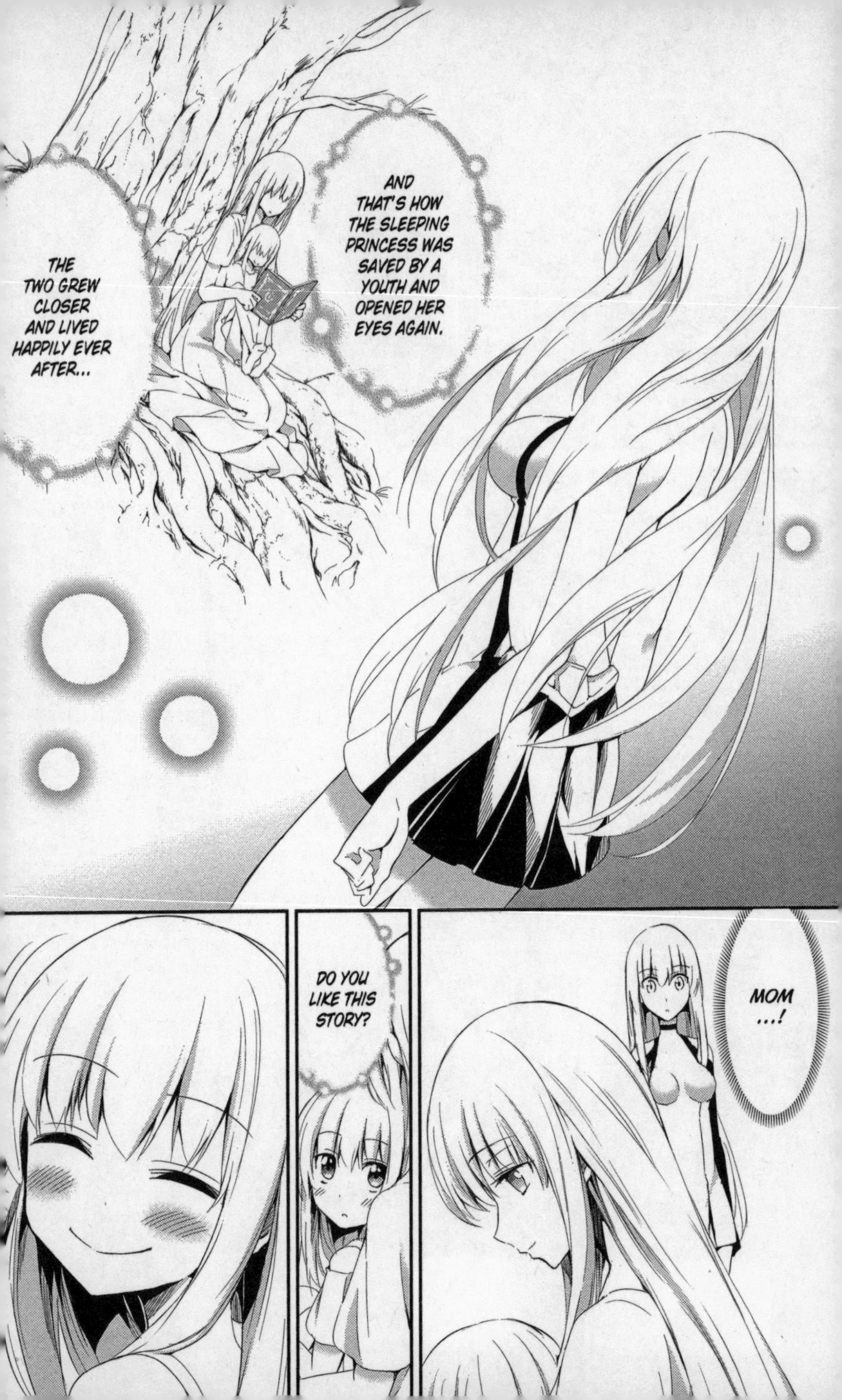
AND THAT'S HOW THE SLEEPING PRINCESS WAS SAVED BY A YOUTH AND OPENED HER EYES AGAIN.
THE TWO GREW CLOSER AND LIVED HAPPILY EVER AFTER...
MOM ...!
DO YOU LIKE THIS STORY?

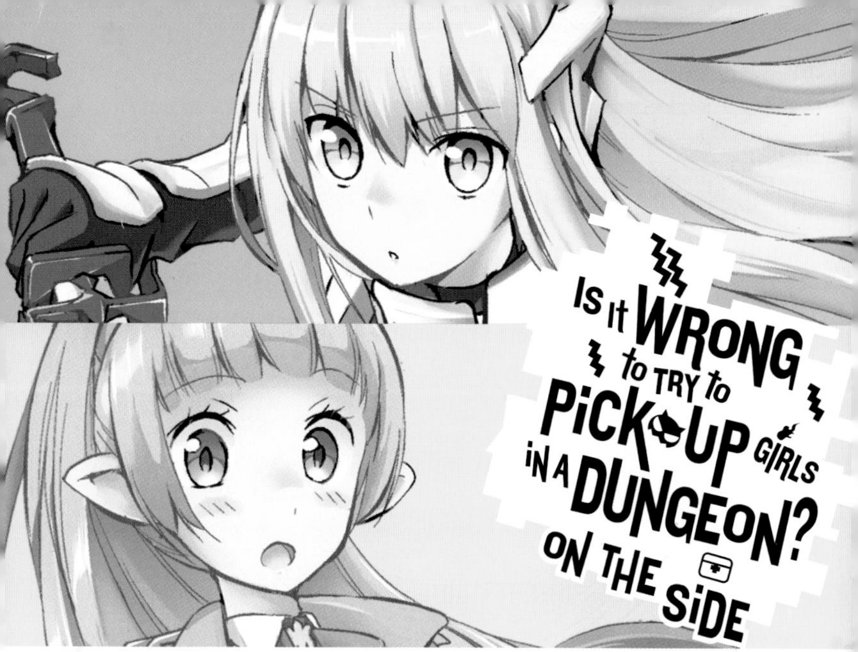

Is It Wrong to Try to Pick Up Girls in a Dungeon? On the Side

SWORD ORATORIA

TAKASHI YAGI
ORIGINAL STORY FUJINO OMORI
CHARACTER DESIGN KIYOTAKA HAIMURA
SUZUHITO YASUDA

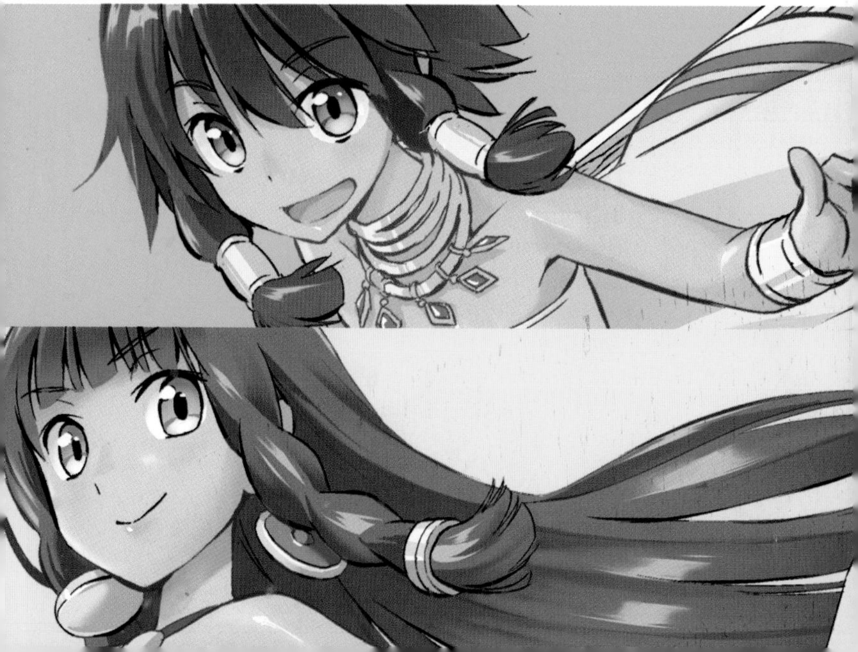

2
SWORD ORATORIA

CONTENTS

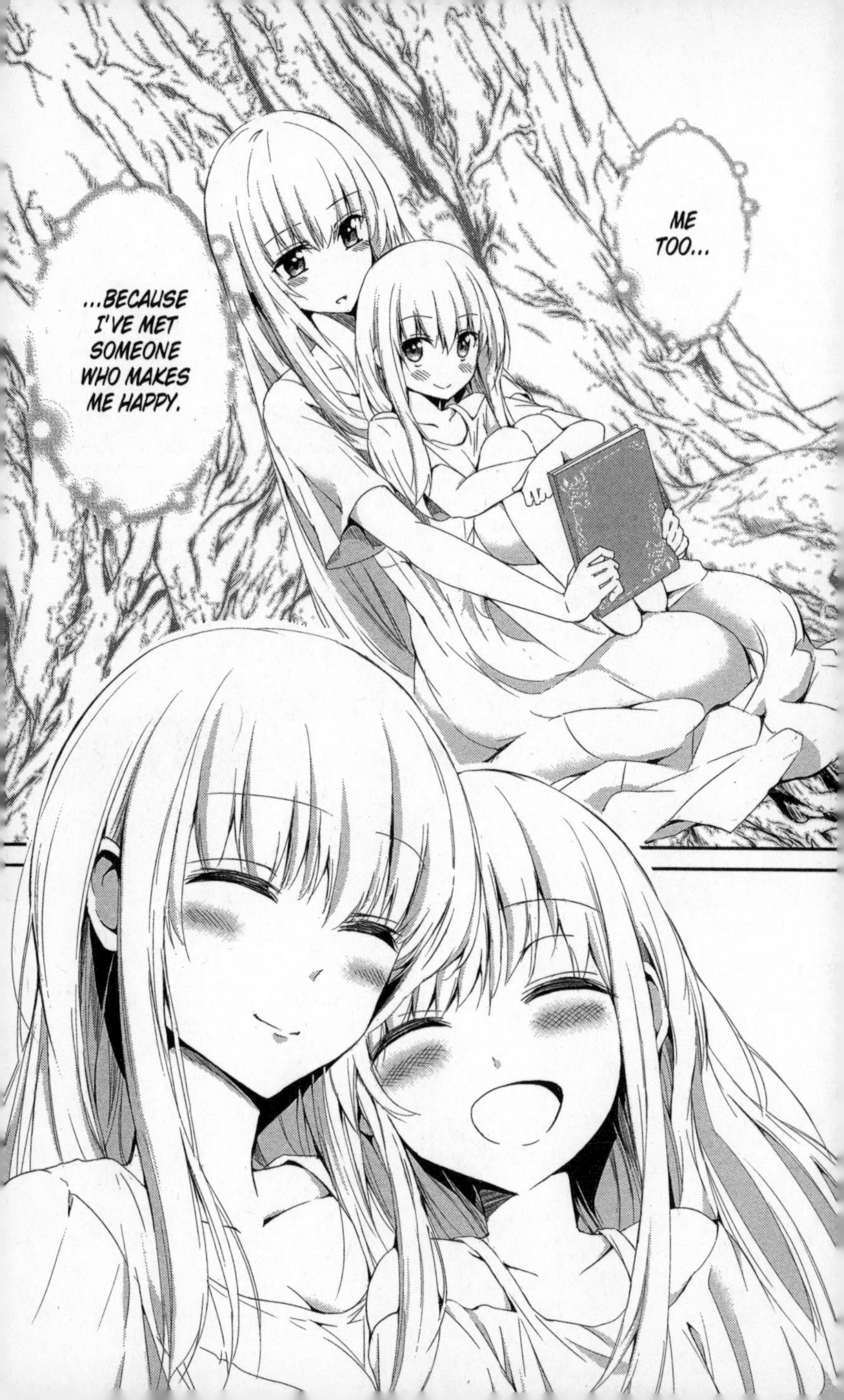
ME TOO...
...BECAUSE I'VE MET SOMEONE WHO MAKES ME HAPPY.

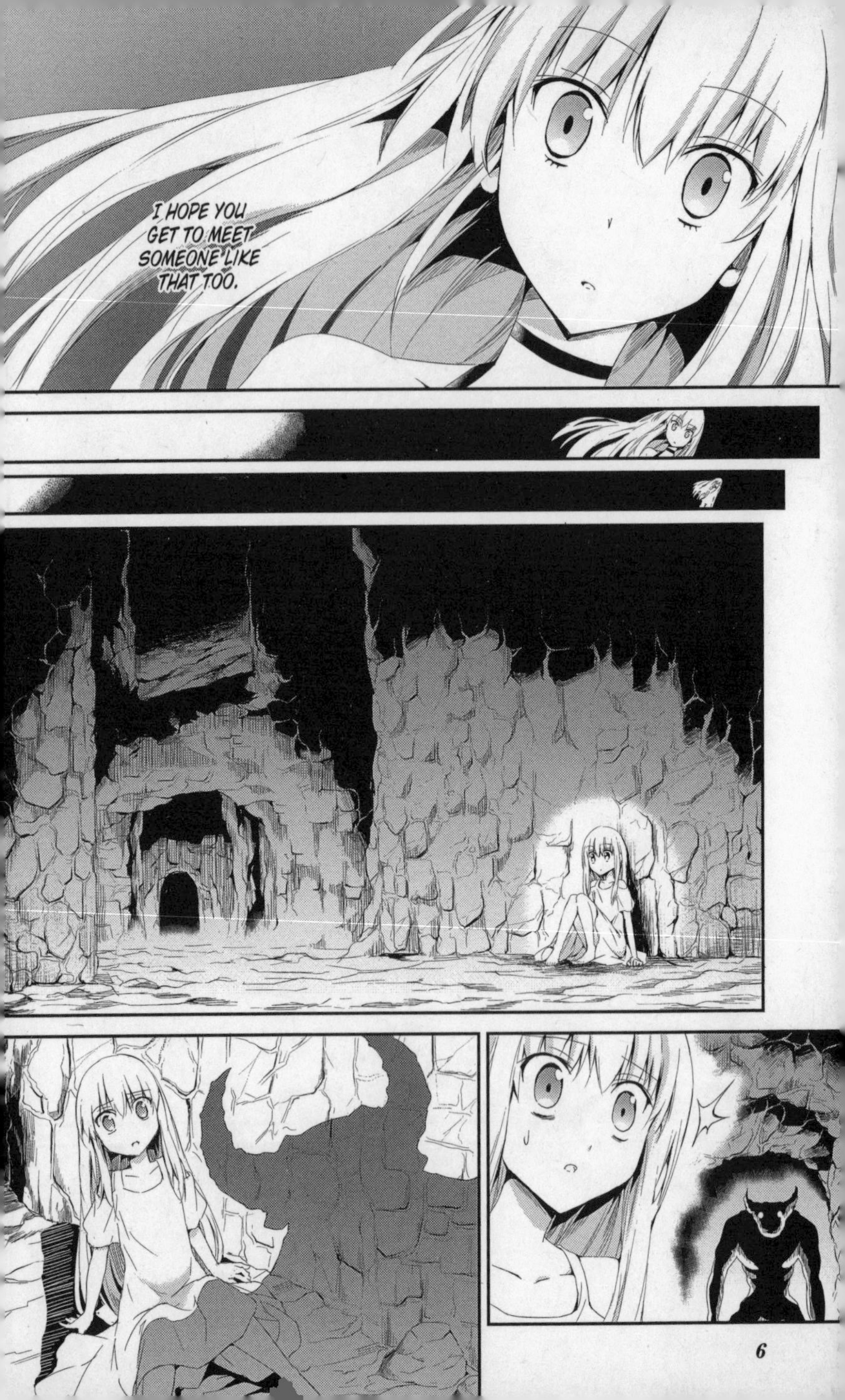
I HOPE YOU GET TO MEET SOMEONE LIKE THAT TOO.

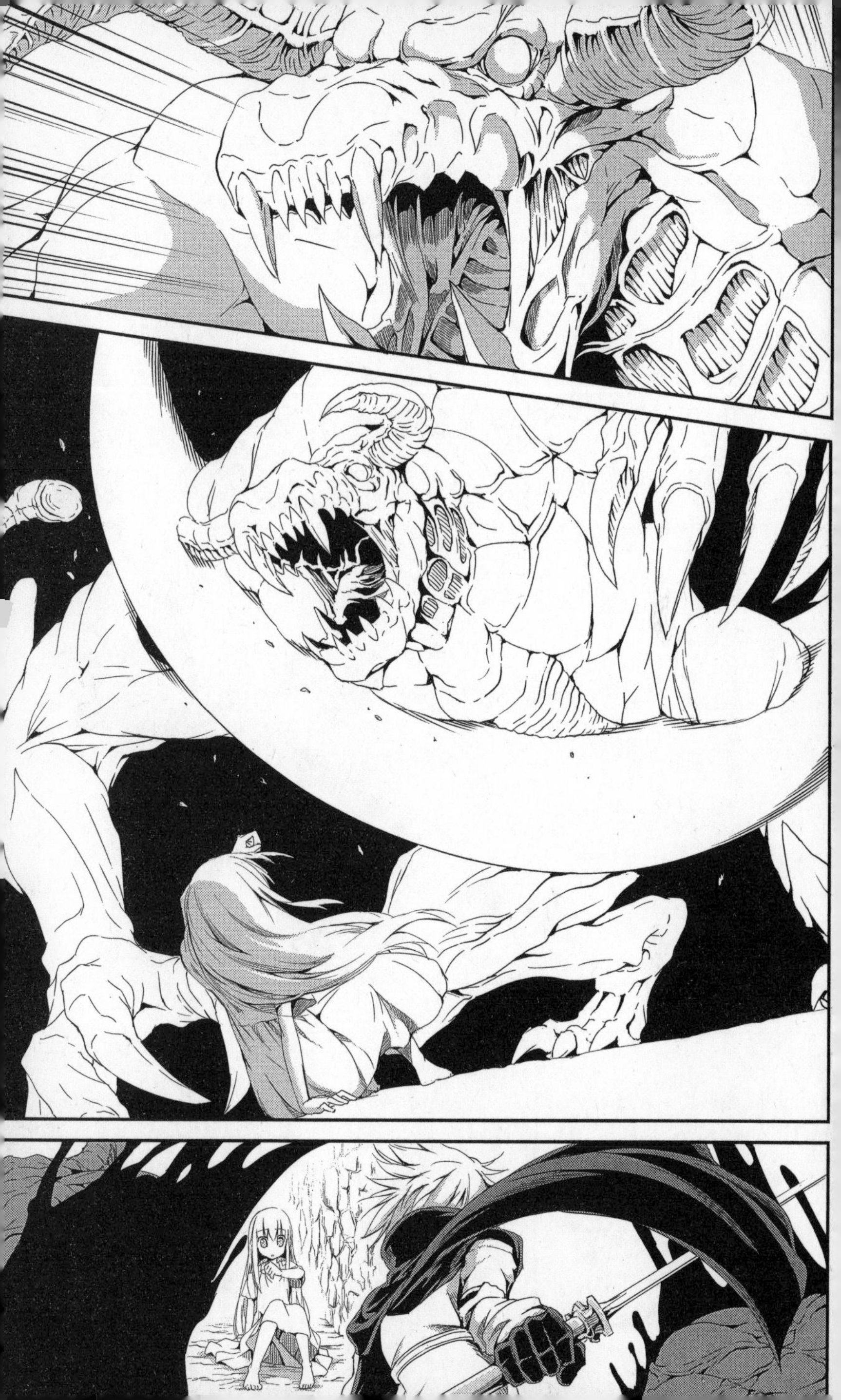

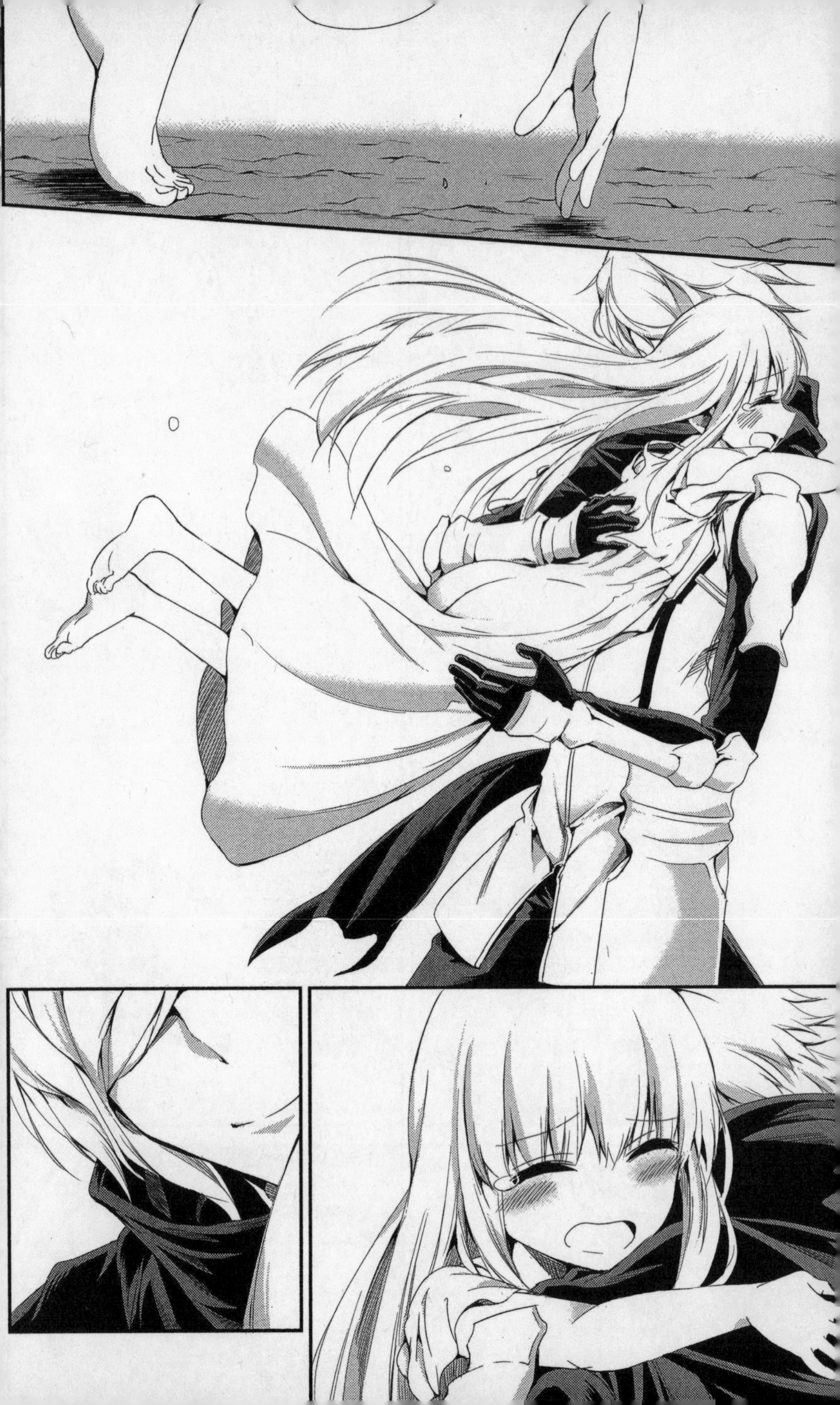

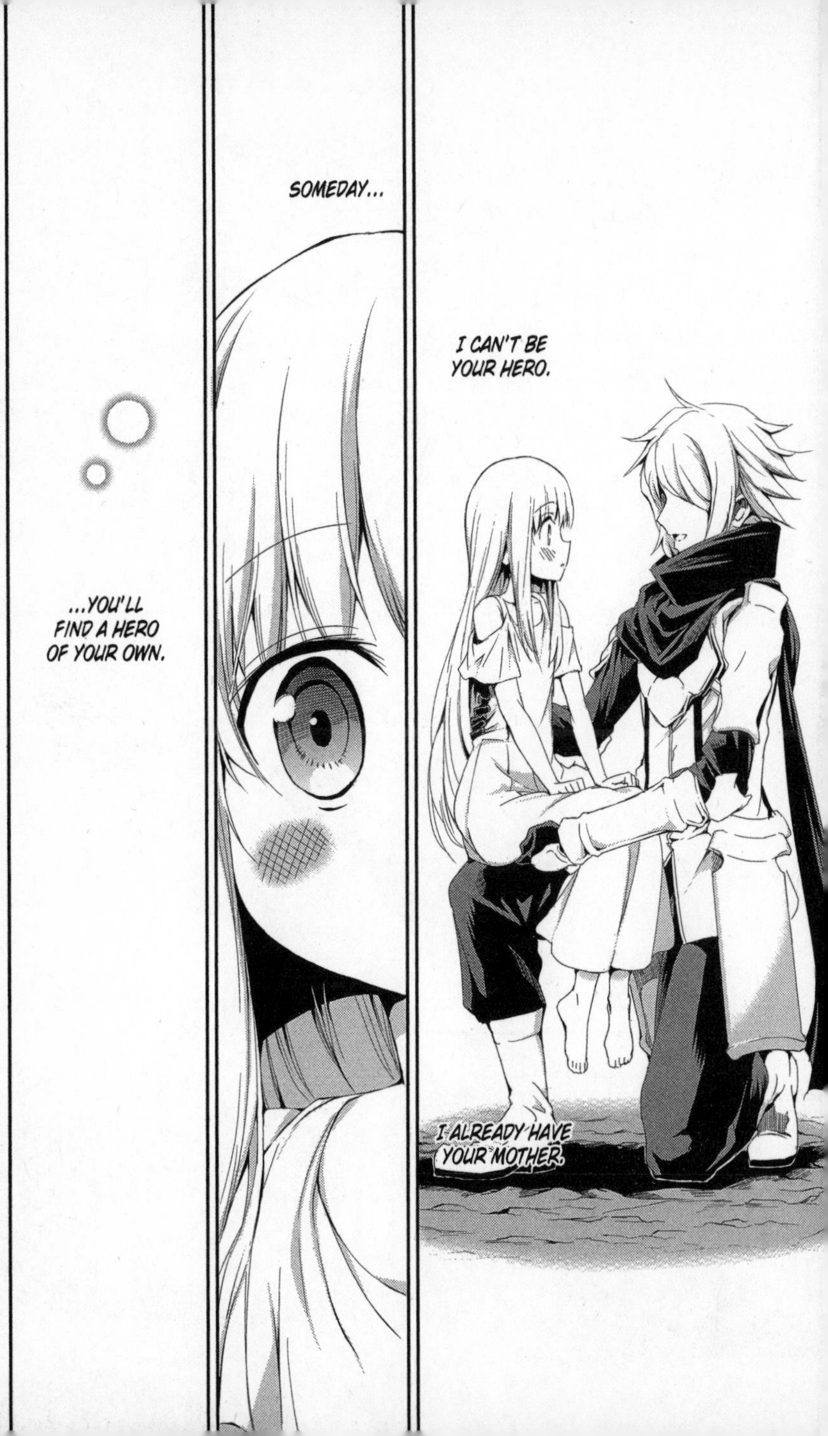
I CAN'T BE YOUR HERO.
I ALREADY HAVE YOUR MOTHER.
SOMEDAY...
...YOU'LL FIND A HERO OF YOUR OWN.

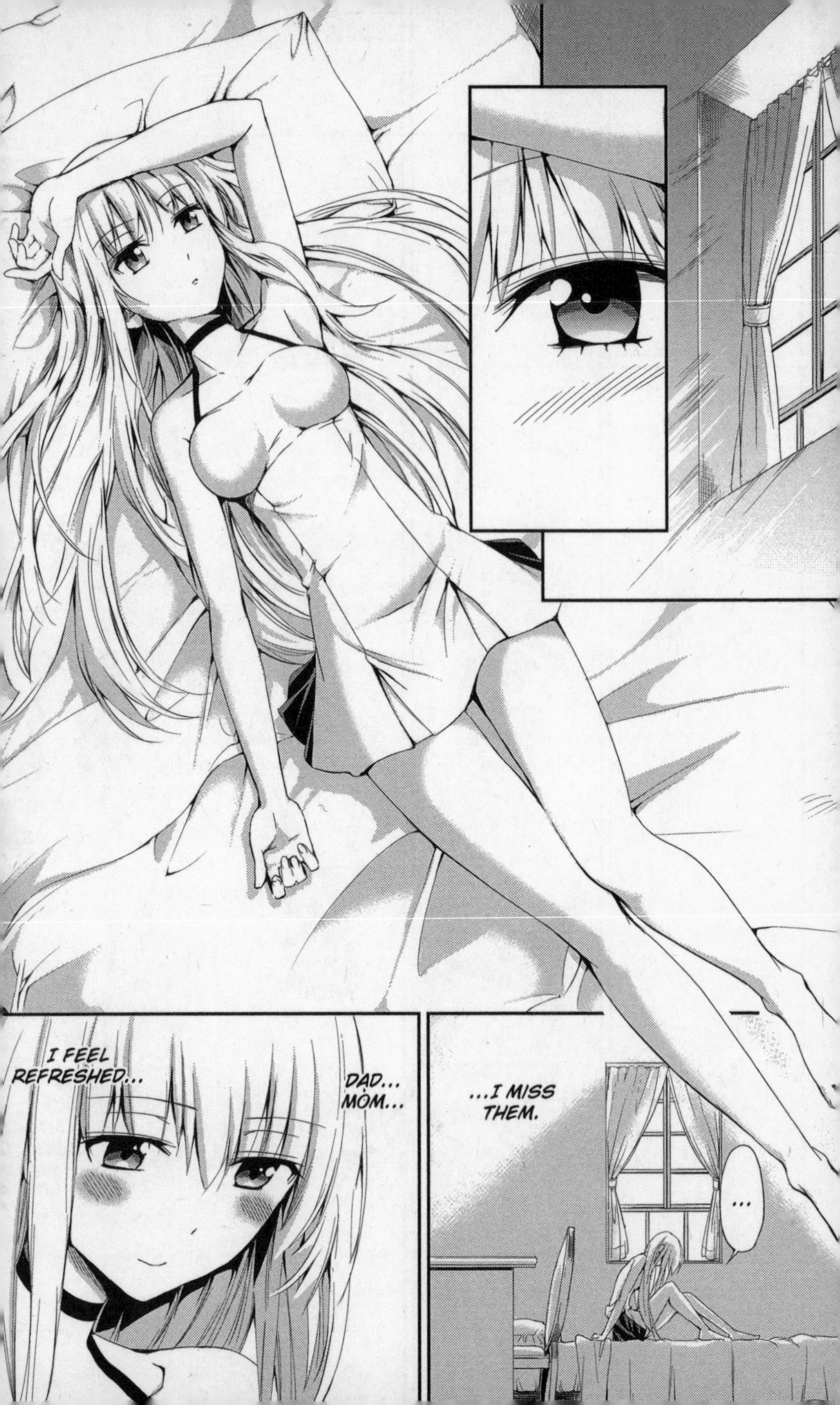
...I MISS THEM.
...
I FEEL REFRESHED...
DAD... MOM...

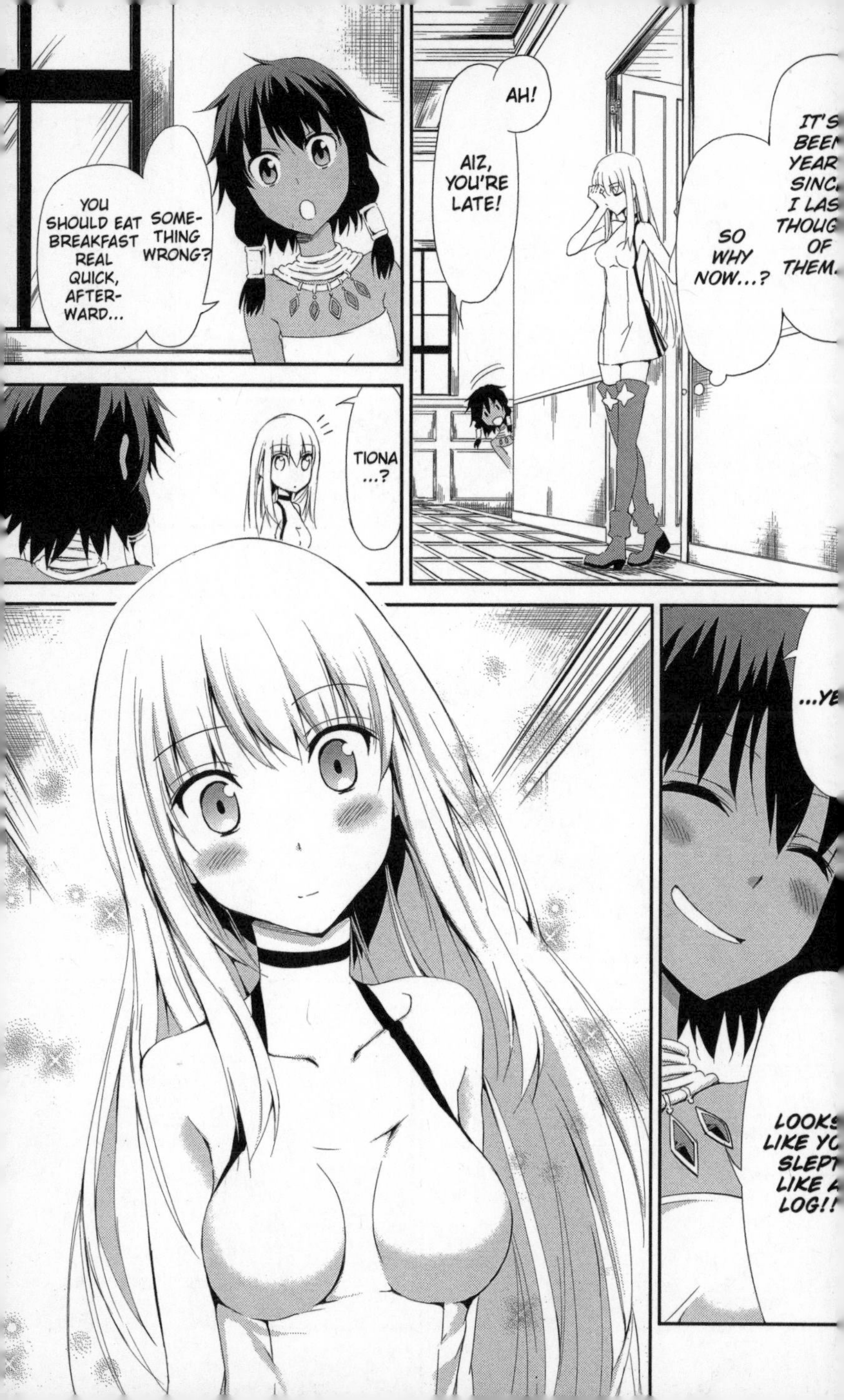
IT'S BEEN YEAR SINC I LAS THOUG OF THEM.
SO WHY NOW...?
AH!
AIZ, YOU'RE LATE!
YOU SHOULD EAT BREAKFAST REAL QUICK, AFTER-WARD...
SOME-THING WRONG?
TIONA ...?
...YE
LOOKS LIKE YO SLEPT LIKE A LOG!!

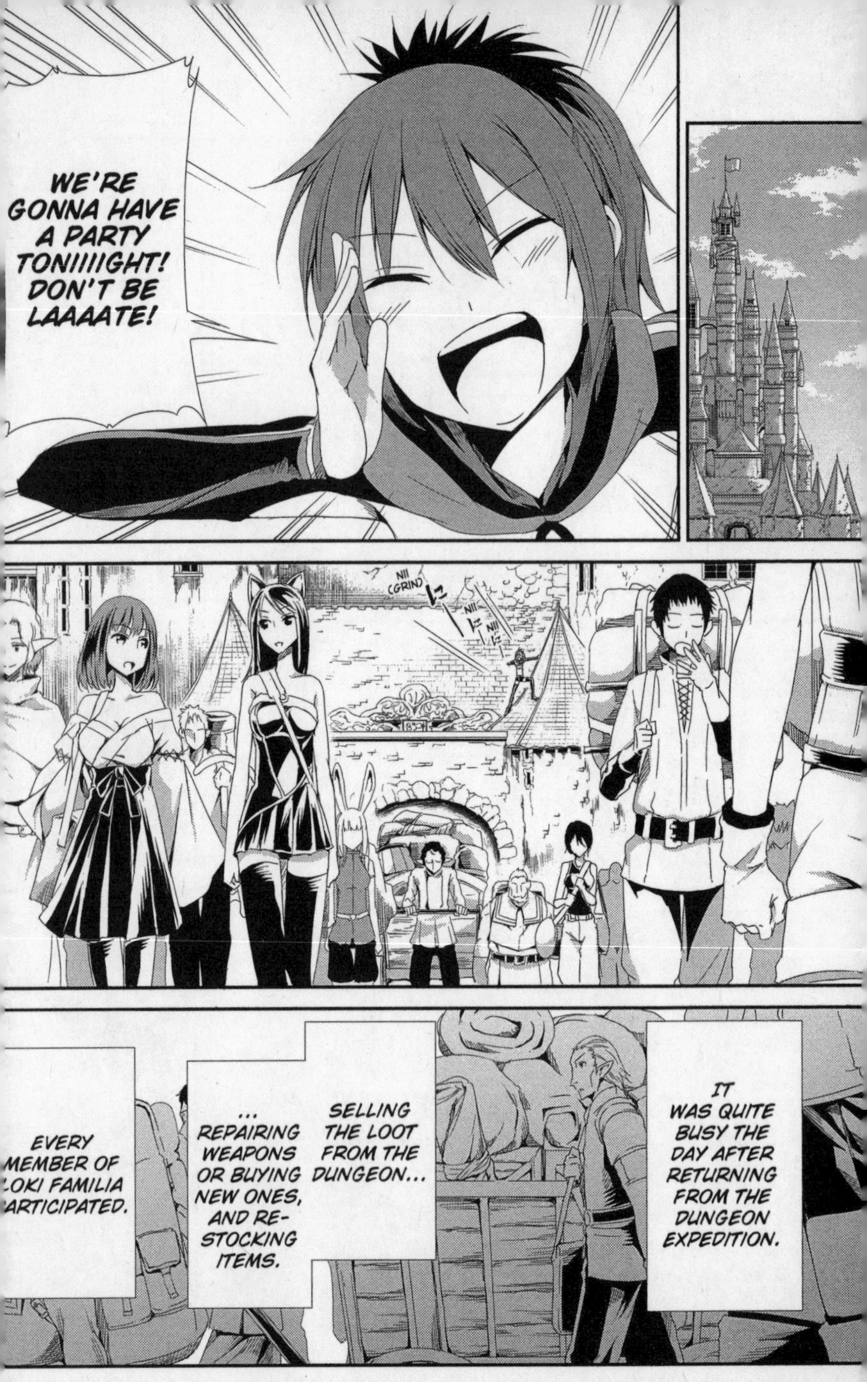
WE'RE GONNA HAVE A PARTY TONIIIIIGHT! DON'T BE LAAAATE!
NII (GRIN)
NII
NII
IT WAS QUITE BUSY THE DAY AFTER RETURNING FROM THE DUNGEON EXPEDITION.
SELLING THE LOOT FROM THE DUNGEON...
...REPAIRING WEAPONS OR BUYING NEW ONES, AND RE-STOCKING ITEMS.
EVERY MEMBER OF OKI FAMILIA ARTICIPATED.

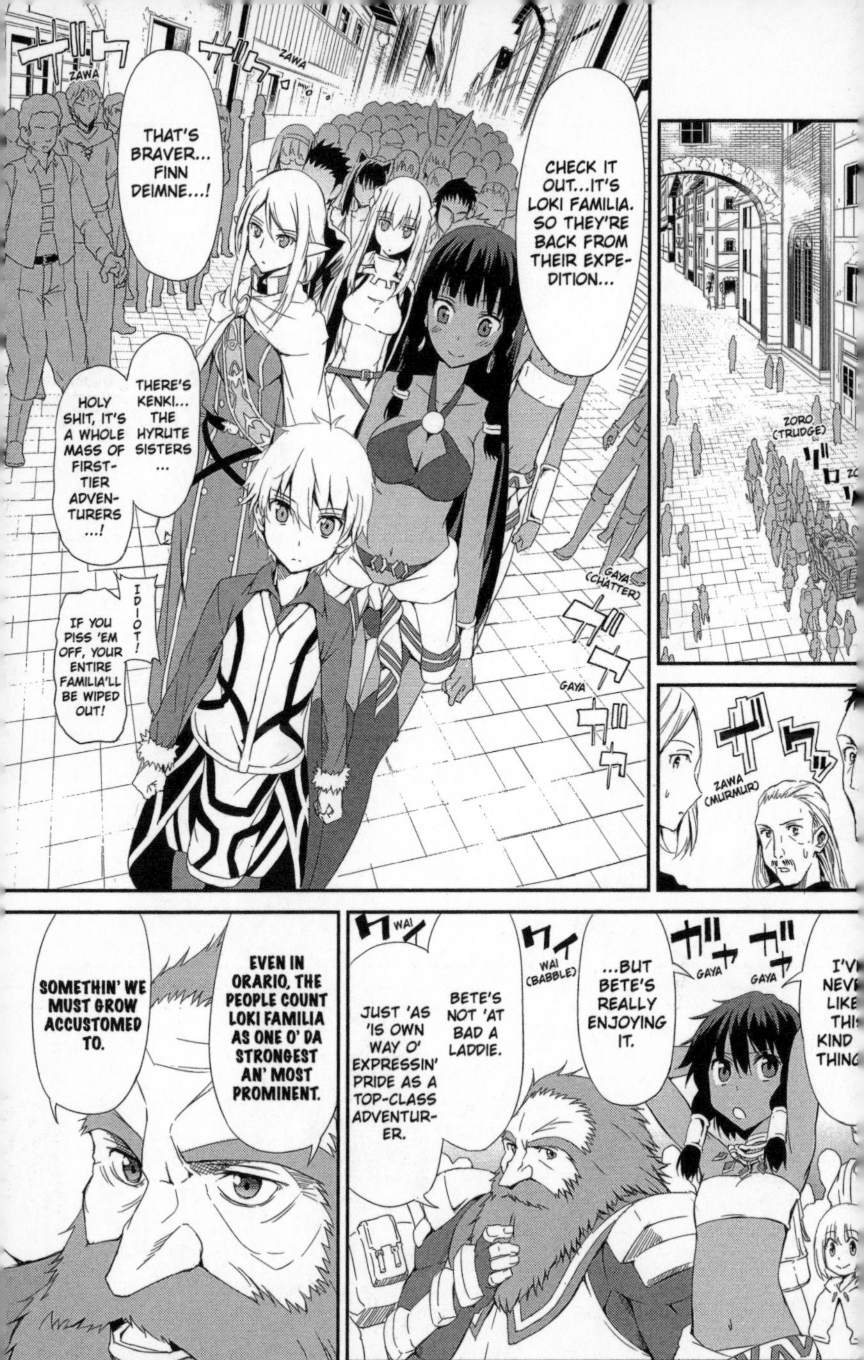
ZORO (TRUDGE)
ZAWA (MURMUR)
CHECK IT OUT...IT'S LOKI FAMILIA. SO THEY'RE BACK FROM THEIR EXPEDITION...
ZAWA
ZAWA
THAT'S BRAVER... FINN DEIMNE...!
THERE'S KENKI... THE HYRUTE SISTERS...
HOLY SHIT, IT'S A WHOLE MASS OF FIRST-TIER ADVENTURERS...!
GAYA (CHATTER)
GAYA
IDIOT!
IF YOU PISS 'EM OFF, YOUR ENTIRE FAMILIA'LL BE WIPED OUT!
I'V NEVE LIKE THIS KIND THING
GAYA
GAYA
...BUT BETE'S REALLY ENJOYING IT.
WAI (BABBLE)
WAI
BETE'S NOT 'AT BAD A LADDIE.
JUST 'AS 'IS OWN WAY O' EXPRESSIN' PRIDE AS A TOP-CLASS ADVENTURER.
EVEN IN ORARIO, THE PEOPLE COUNT LOKI FAMILIA AS ONE O' DA STRONGEST AN' MOST PROMINENT.
SOMETHIN' WE MUST GROW ACCUSTOMED TO.

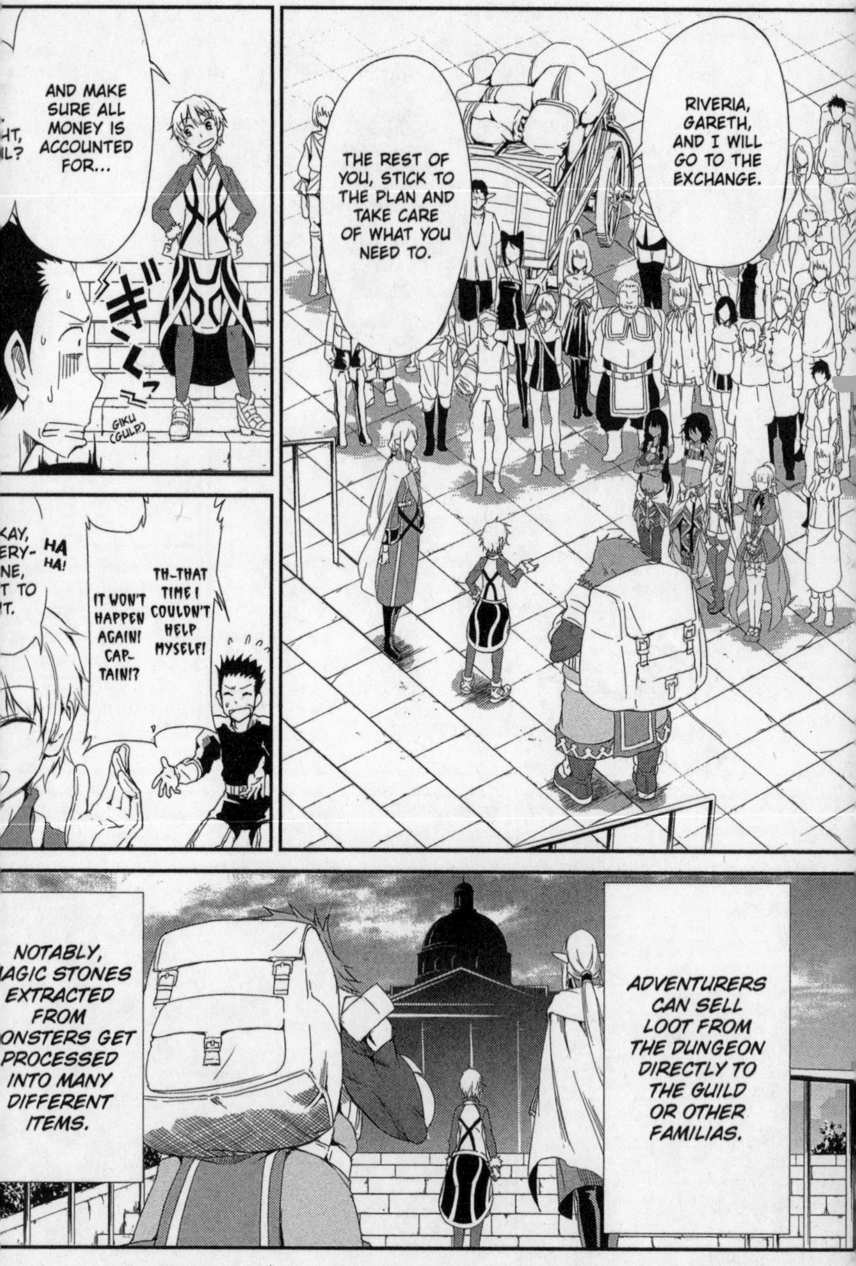
RIVERIA, GARETH, AND I WILL GO TO THE EXCHANGE.
THE REST OF YOU, STICK TO THE PLAN AND TAKE CARE OF WHAT YOU NEED TO.
AND MAKE SURE ALL MONEY IS ACCOUNTED FOR...
GIKU (GULP)
HA HA!
TH-THAT TIME I COULDN'T HELP MYSELF!
IT WON'T HAPPEN AGAIN! CAP-TAIN!?
ADVENTURERS CAN SELL LOOT FROM THE DUNGEON DIRECTLY TO THE GUILD OR OTHER FAMILIAS.
NOTABLY, MAGIC STONES EXTRACTED FROM MONSTERS GET PROCESSED INTO MANY DIFFERENT ITEMS.

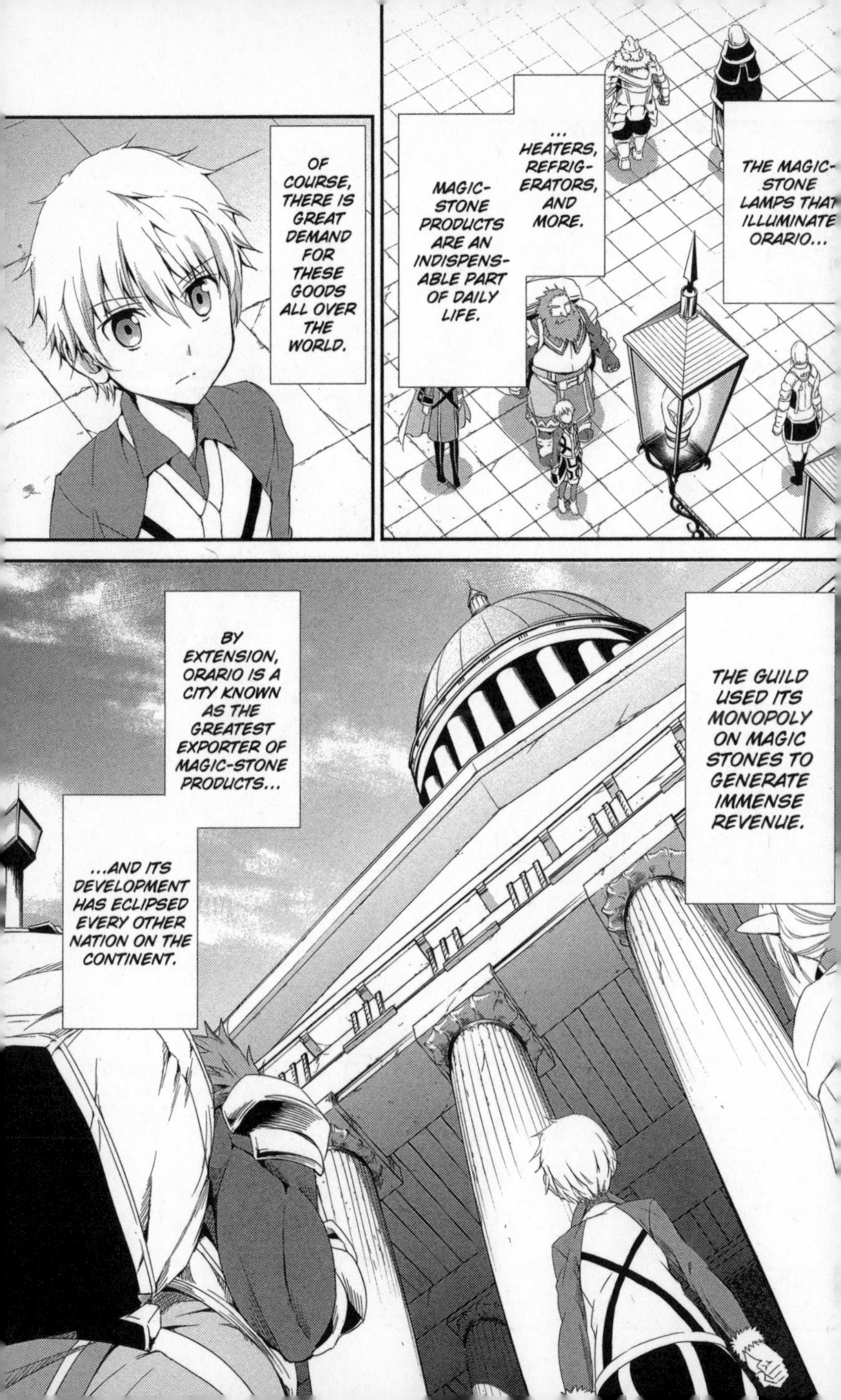
THE MAGIC-STONE LAMPS THAT ILLUMINATE ORARIO...
...HEATERS, REFRIG-ERATORS, AND MORE.
MAGIC-STONE PRODUCTS ARE AN INDISPENS-ABLE PART OF DAILY LIFE.
OF COURSE, THERE IS GREAT DEMAND FOR THESE GOODS ALL OVER THE WORLD.
THE GUILD USED ITS MONOPOLY ON MAGIC STONES TO GENERATE IMMENSE REVENUE.
BY EXTENSION, ORARIO IS A CITY KNOWN AS THE GREATEST EXPORTER OF MAGIC-STONE PRODUCTS...
...AND ITS DEVELOPMENT HAS ECLIPSED EVERY OTHER NATION ON THE CONTINENT.

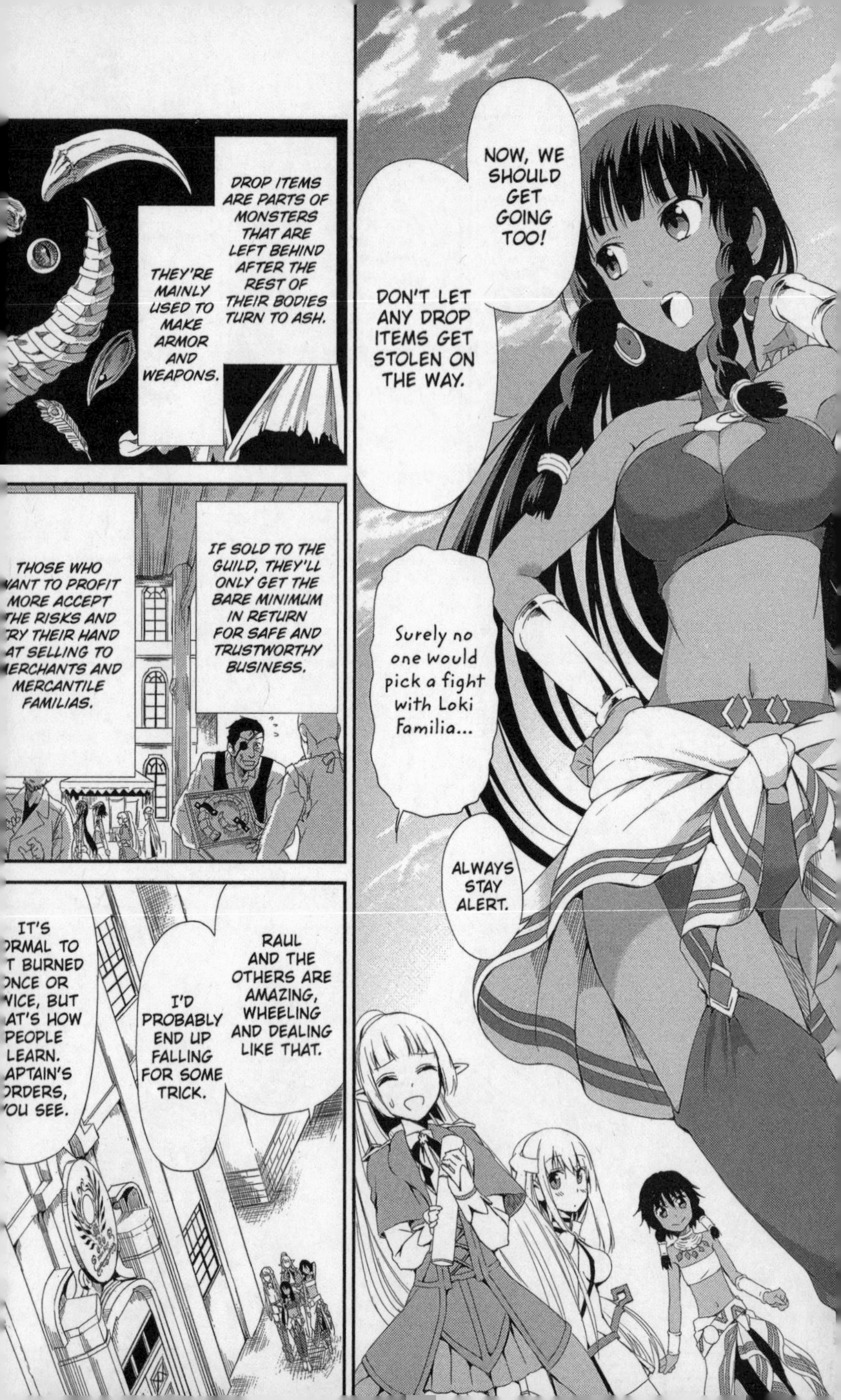

NOW, WE SHOULD GET GOING TOO!
DON'T LET ANY DROP ITEMS GET STOLEN ON THE WAY.
Surely no one would pick a fight with Loki Familia...
ALWAYS STAY ALERT.
DROP ITEMS ARE PARTS OF MONSTERS THAT ARE LEFT BEHIND AFTER THE REST OF THEIR BODIES TURN TO ASH.
THEY'RE MAINLY USED TO MAKE ARMOR AND WEAPONS.
IF SOLD TO THE GUILD, THEY'LL ONLY GET THE BARE MINIMUM IN RETURN FOR SAFE AND TRUSTWORTHY BUSINESS.
THOSE WHO VANT TO PROFIT MORE ACCEPT THE RISKS AND TRY THEIR HAND AT SELLING TO ERCHANTS AND MERCANTILE FAMILIAS.
RAUL AND THE OTHERS ARE AMAZING, WHEELING AND DEALING LIKE THAT.
I'D PROBABLY END UP FALLING FOR SOME TRICK.
IT'S ORMAL TO T BURNED ONCE OR VICE, BUT AT'S HOW PEOPLE LEARN. APTAIN'S ORDERS, YOU SEE.

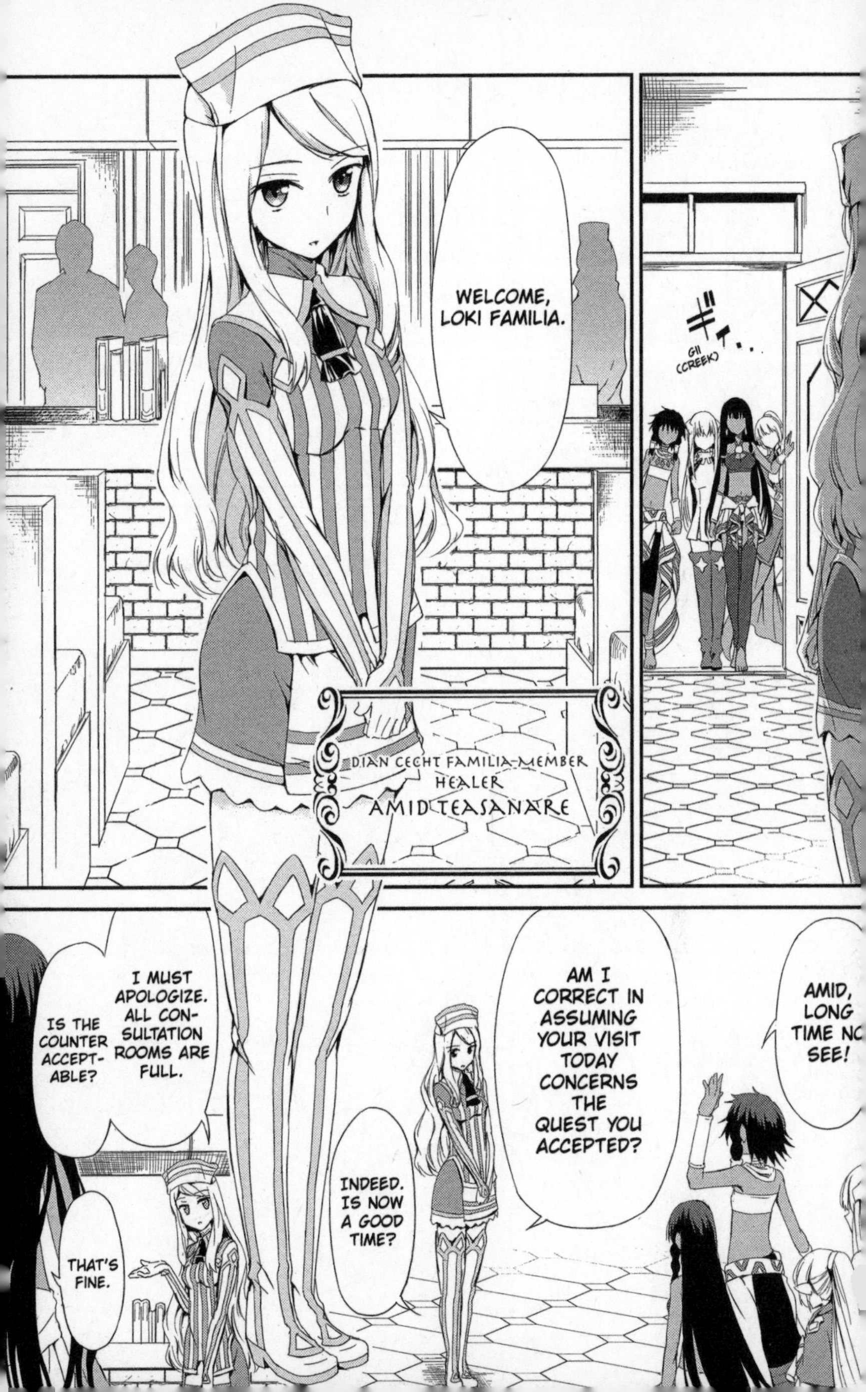

ギィ...
GII (CREEK)
WELCOME, LOKI FAMILIA.
DIAN CECHT FAMILIA MEMBER
HEALER
AMID TEASANARE
AMID, LONG TIME NO SEE!
AM I CORRECT IN ASSUMING YOUR VISIT TODAY CONCERNS THE QUEST YOU ACCEPTED?
INDEED. IS NOW A GOOD TIME?
I MUST APOLOGIZE. ALL CON-SULTATION ROOMS ARE FULL.
IS THE COUNTER ACCEPT-ABLE?
THAT'S FINE.

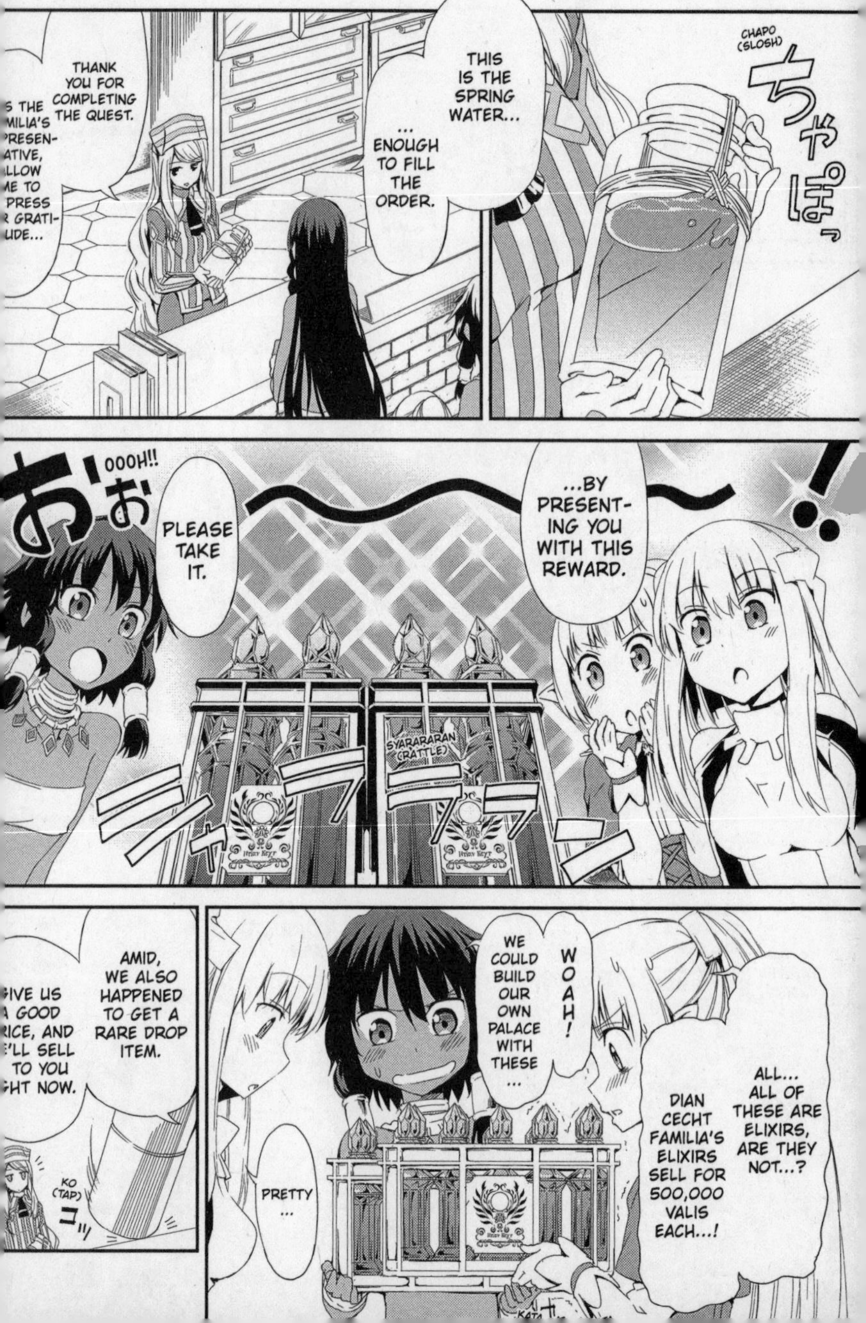
CHAPO (SLOSH)
ちゃぽっ
THIS IS THE SPRING WATER...
... ENOUGH TO FILL THE ORDER.
THANK YOU FOR COMPLETING THE QUEST.
S THE MILIA'S PRESEN- ATIVE, ALLOW ME TO PRESS R GRATI- UDE...
...BY PRESENTING YOU WITH THIS REWARD.
PLEASE TAKE IT.
OOOH!!
おおお〜〜!!
SYARARARAN (RATTLE)
シャラララン
ALL... ALL OF THESE ARE ELIXIRS, ARE THEY NOT...?
DIAN CECHT FAMILIA'S ELIXIRS SELL FOR 500,000 VALIS EACH...!
WOAH!
WE COULD BUILD OUR OWN PALACE WITH THESE...
PRETTY...
AMID, WE ALSO HAPPENED TO GET A RARE DROP ITEM.
IVE US A GOOD RICE, AND 'LL SELL TO YOU GHT NOW.
KO (TAP)
コッ

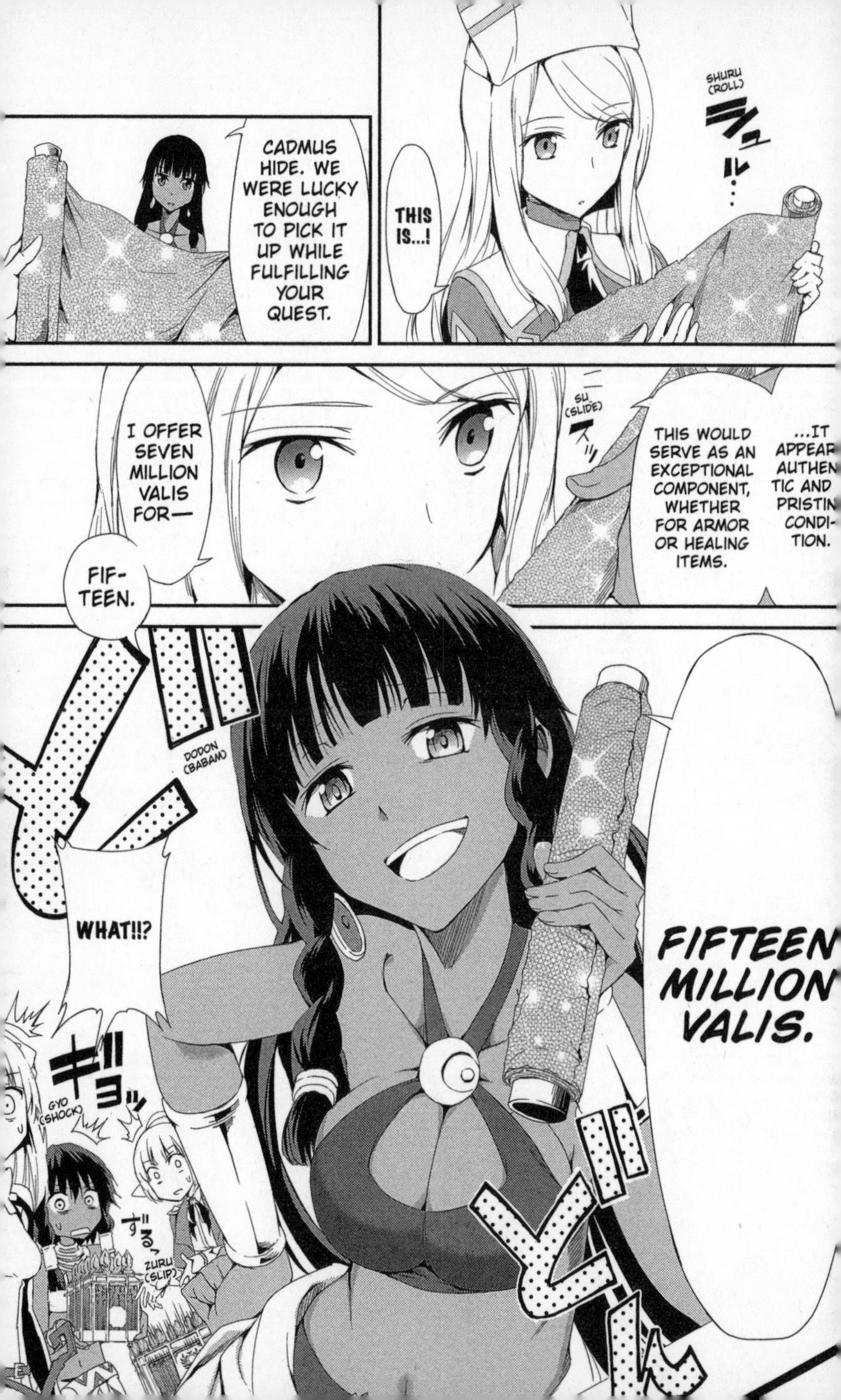
SHURU (ROLL)
THIS IS...!
CADMUS HIDE. WE WERE LUCKY ENOUGH TO PICK IT UP WHILE FULFILLING YOUR QUEST.
...IT APPEAR AUTHEN TIC AND PRISTIN CONDI- TION.
THIS WOULD SERVE AS AN EXCEPTIONAL COMPONENT, WHETHER FOR ARMOR OR HEALING ITEMS.
SU (SLIDE)
I OFFER SEVEN MILLION VALIS FOR—
FIF- TEEN.
FIFTEEN MILLION VALIS.
DODON (BABAM)
WHAT!!?
GYO (SHOCK)
ZURU (SLIP)

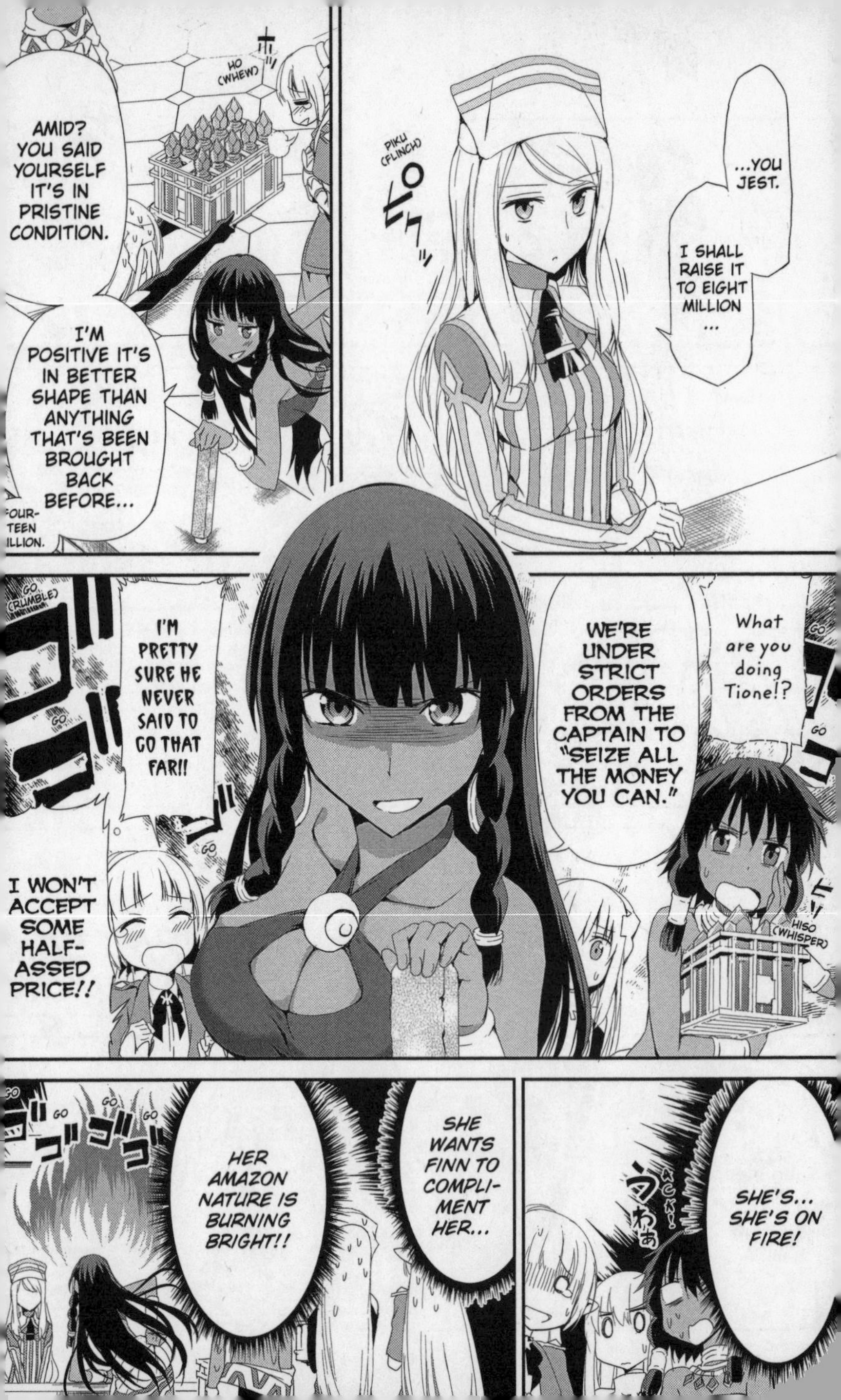
PIKU (FLINCH)
...YOU JEST.
I SHALL RAISE IT TO EIGHT MILLION ...
HO (WHEW)
AMID? YOU SAID YOURSELF IT'S IN PRISTINE CONDITION.
I'M POSITIVE IT'S IN BETTER SHAPE THAN ANYTHING THAT'S BEEN BROUGHT BACK BEFORE...
FOUR-TEEN MILLION.
What are you doing Tione!?
HISO (WHISPER)
WE'RE UNDER STRICT ORDERS FROM THE CAPTAIN TO "SEIZE ALL THE MONEY YOU CAN."
I'M PRETTY SURE HE NEVER SAID TO GO THAT FAR!!
GO (RUMBLE)
I WON'T ACCEPT SOME HALF-ASSED PRICE!!
ACK!
SHE'S... SHE'S ON FIRE!
SHE WANTS FINN TO COMPLIMENT HER...
HER AMAZON NATURE IS BURNING BRIGHT!!
GO GO GO

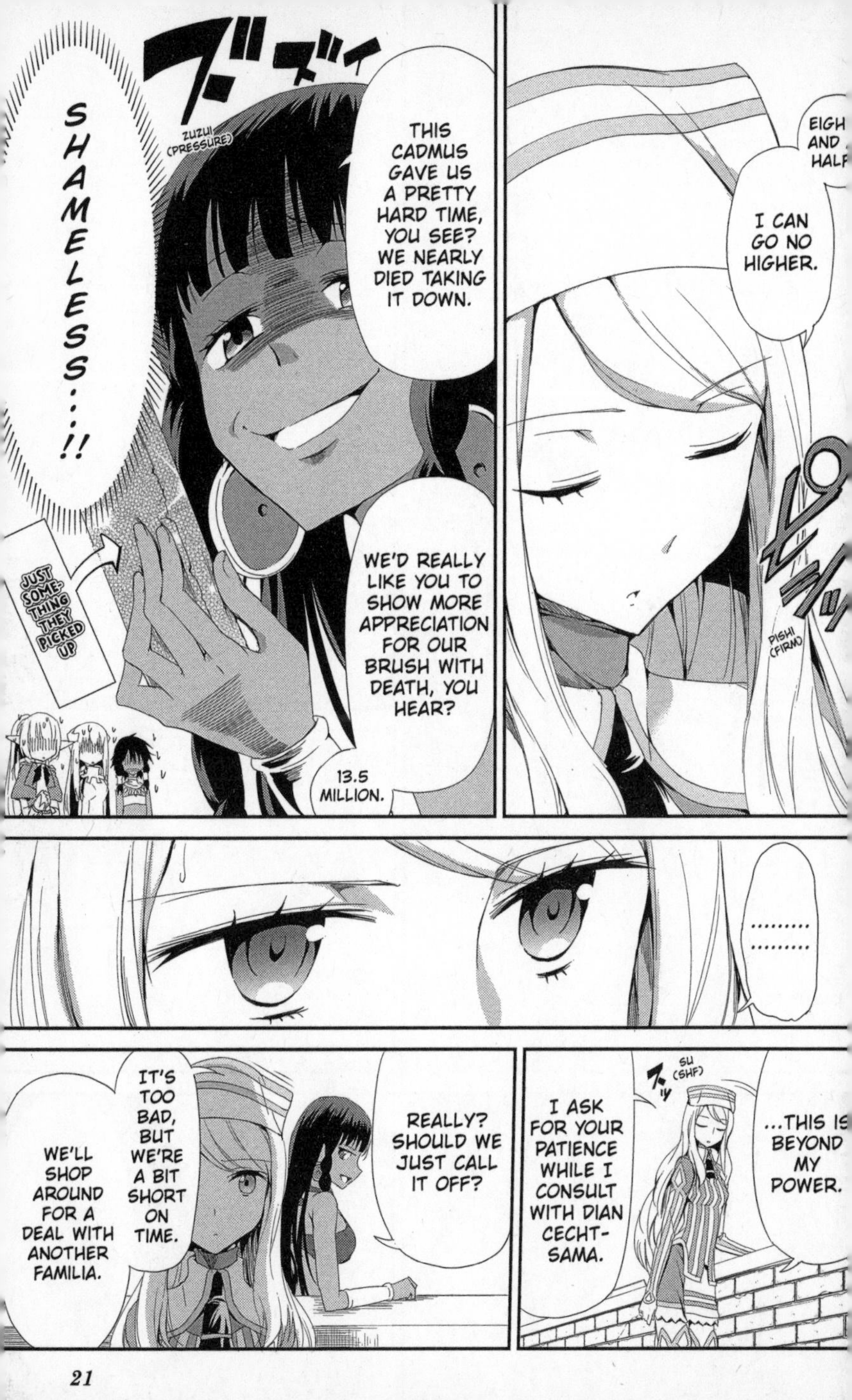
EIGH
AND
HALF
I CAN GO NO HIGHER.
PISHI (FIRM)
ZUZUI (PRESSURE)
THIS CADMUS GAVE US A PRETTY HARD TIME, YOU SEE? WE NEARLY DIED TAKING IT DOWN.
SHAMELESS...!!
WE'D REALLY LIKE YOU TO SHOW MORE APPRECIATION FOR OUR BRUSH WITH DEATH, YOU HEAR?
JUST SOMETHING THEY PICKED UP
13.5 MILLION.
....
....
...THIS IS
BEYOND MY POWER.
SU (SHF)
I ASK FOR YOUR PATIENCE WHILE I CONSULT WITH DIAN CECHT-SAMA.
REALLY? SHOULD WE JUST CALL IT OFF?
IT'S TOO BAD, BUT WE'RE A BIT SHORT ON TIME.
WE'LL SHOP AROUND FOR A DEAL WITH ANOTHER FAMILIA.

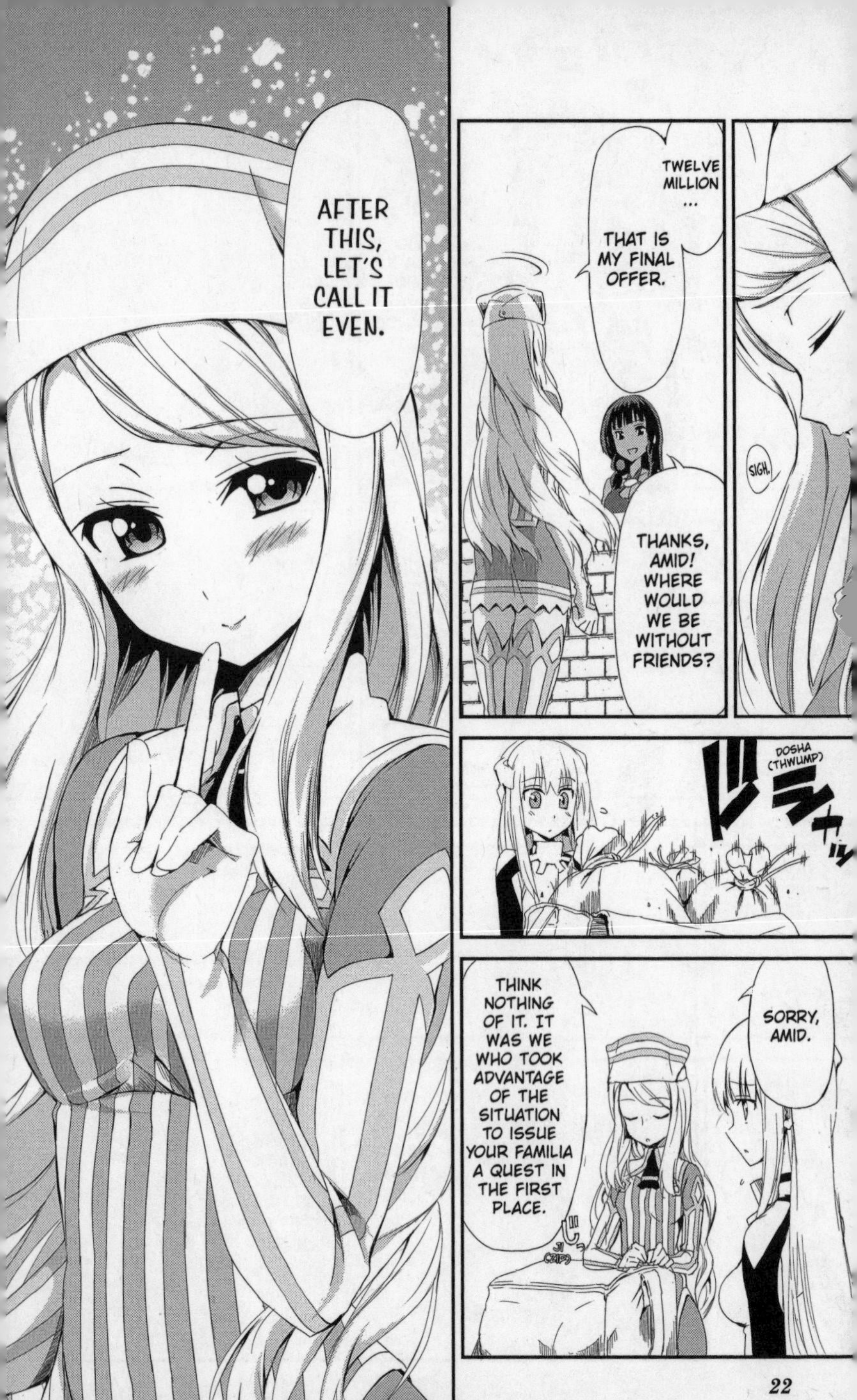
SIGH.
TWELVE MILLION ...
THAT IS MY FINAL OFFER.
THANKS, AMID! WHERE WOULD WE BE WITHOUT FRIENDS?
DOSHA (THWUMP)
SORRY, AMID.
THINK NOTHING OF IT. IT WAS WE WHO TOOK ADVANTAGE OF THE SITUATION TO ISSUE YOUR FAMILIA A QUEST IN THE FIRST PLACE.
JI (ZIP)
AFTER THIS, LET'S CALL IT EVEN.

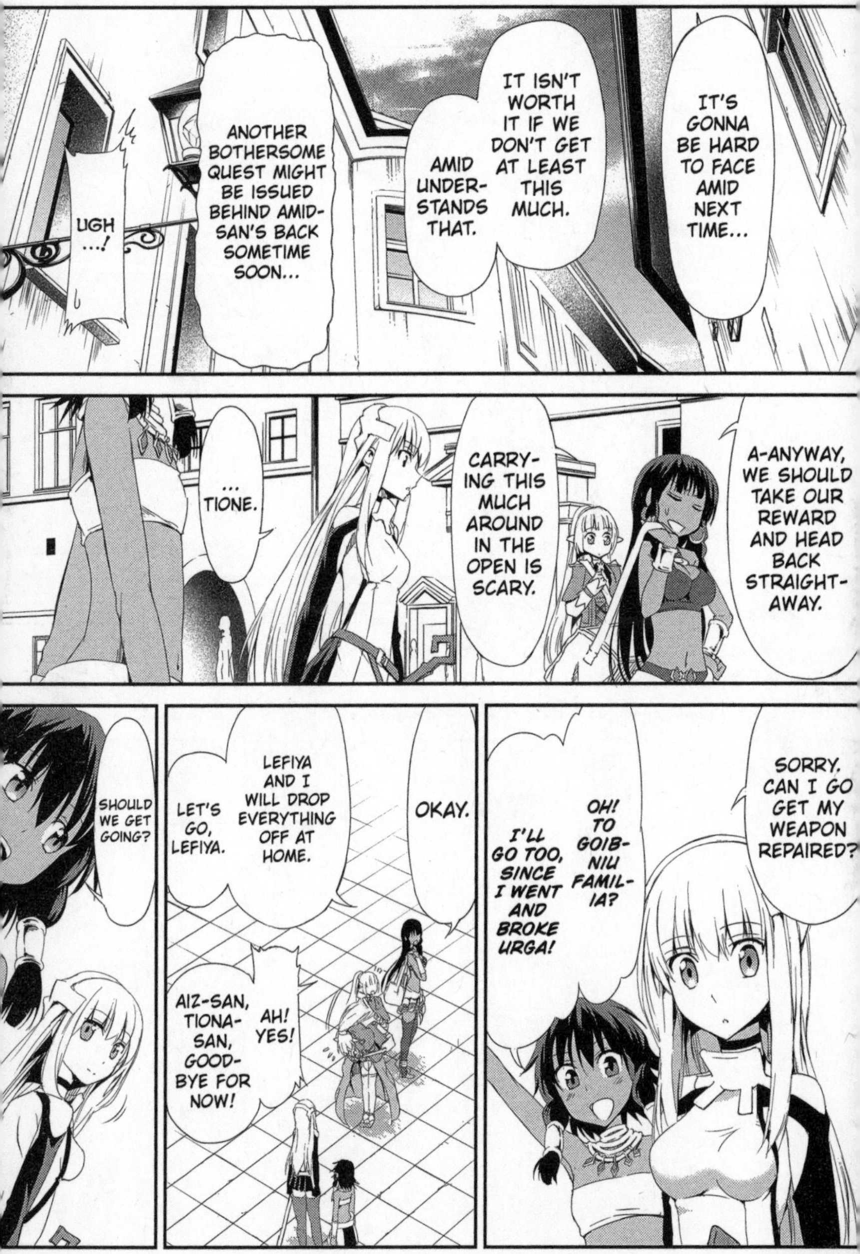
IT'S GONNA BE HARD TO FACE AMID NEXT TIME...
IT ISN'T WORTH IT IF WE DON'T GET AT LEAST THIS MUCH.
AMID UNDER-STANDS THAT.
ANOTHER BOTHERSOME QUEST MIGHT BE ISSUED BEHIND AMID-SAN'S BACK SOMETIME SOON...
UGH ...!
A-ANYWAY, WE SHOULD TAKE OUR REWARD AND HEAD BACK STRAIGHT-AWAY.
CARRY-ING THIS MUCH AROUND IN THE OPEN IS SCARY.
... TIONE.
SORRY. CAN I GO GET MY WEAPON REPAIRED?
OH! TO GOIB-NIU FAMIL-IA?
I'LL GO TOO, SINCE I WENT AND BROKE URGA!
OKAY.
LEFIYA AND I WILL DROP EVERYTHING OFF AT HOME.
LET'S GO, LEFIYA.
AH! YES!
AIZ-SAN, TIONA-SAN, GOOD-BYE FOR NOW!
SHOULD WE GET GOING?

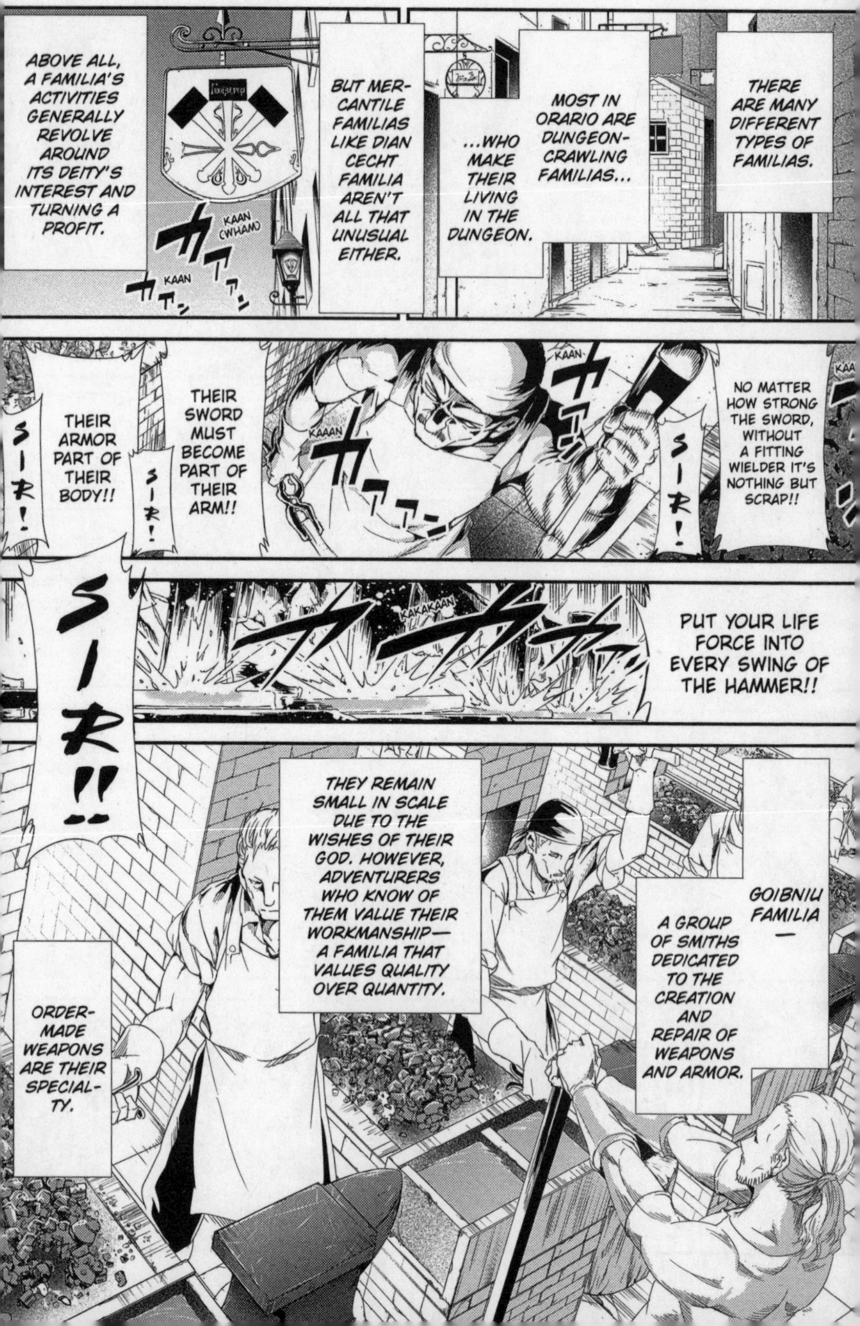

THERE ARE MANY DIFFERENT TYPES OF FAMILIAS.
MOST IN ORARIO ARE DUNGEON-CRAWLING FAMILIAS...
...WHO MAKE THEIR LIVING IN THE DUNGEON.
BUT MERCANTILE FAMILIAS LIKE DIAN CECHT FAMILIA AREN'T ALL THAT UNUSUAL EITHER.
KAAN (WHAM)
KAAN
ABOVE ALL, A FAMILIA'S ACTIVITIES GENERALLY REVOLVE AROUND ITS DEITY'S INTEREST AND TURNING A PROFIT.
KAA
NO MATTER HOW STRONG THE SWORD, WITHOUT A FITTING WIELDER IT'S NOTHING BUT SCRAP!!
S-I-R!
KAAN
KAAAN
THEIR SWORD MUST BECOME PART OF THEIR ARM!!
S-I-R!
THEIR ARMOR PART OF THEIR BODY!!
S-I-R!
PUT YOUR LIFE FORCE INTO EVERY SWING OF THE HAMMER!!
KAKAKAAN
S-I-R!!
GOIBNIU FAMILIA—
A GROUP OF SMITHS DEDICATED TO THE CREATION AND REPAIR OF WEAPONS AND ARMOR.
THEY REMAIN SMALL IN SCALE DUE TO THE WISHES OF THEIR GOD. HOWEVER, ADVENTURERS WHO KNOW OF THEM VALUE THEIR WORKMANSHIP—A FAMILIA THAT VALUES QUALITY OVER QUANTITY.
ORDER-MADE WEAPONS ARE THEIR SPECIALTY.

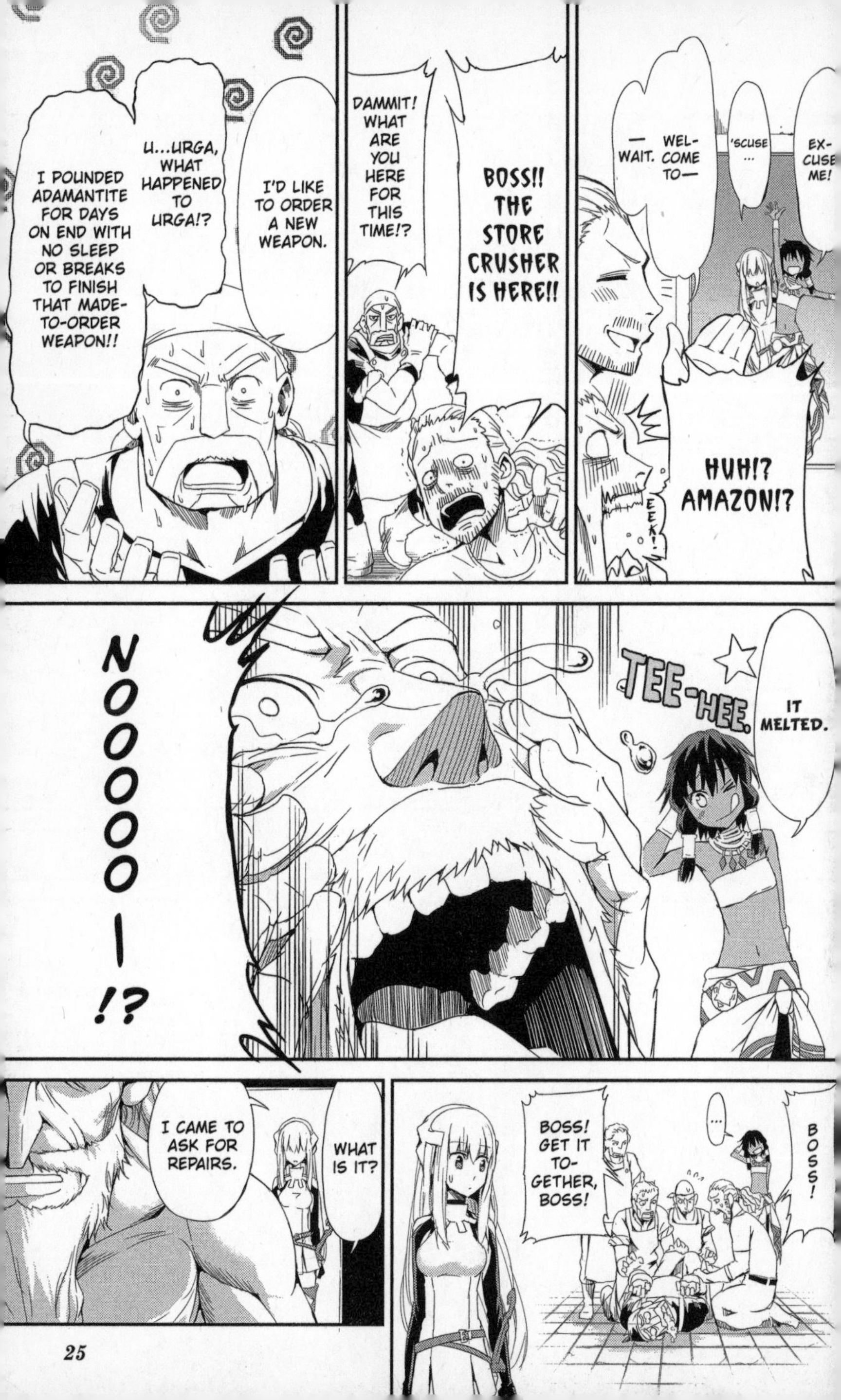
EXCUSE ME!
'SCUSE ...
WELCOME TO—
— WAIT.
HUH!? AMAZON!?
EEK!
BOSS!! THE STORE CRUSHER IS HERE!!
DAMMIT! WHAT ARE YOU HERE FOR THIS TIME!?
I'D LIKE TO ORDER A NEW WEAPON.
U...URGA, WHAT HAPPENED TO URGA!?
I POUNDED ADAMANTITE FOR DAYS ON END WITH NO SLEEP OR BREAKS TO FINISH THAT MADE-TO-ORDER WEAPON!!
IT MELTED.
TEE-HEE.
NOOOOOO—!?
BOSS!
...
BOSS! GET IT TOGETHER, BOSS!
WHAT IS IT?
I CAME TO ASK FOR REPAIRS.

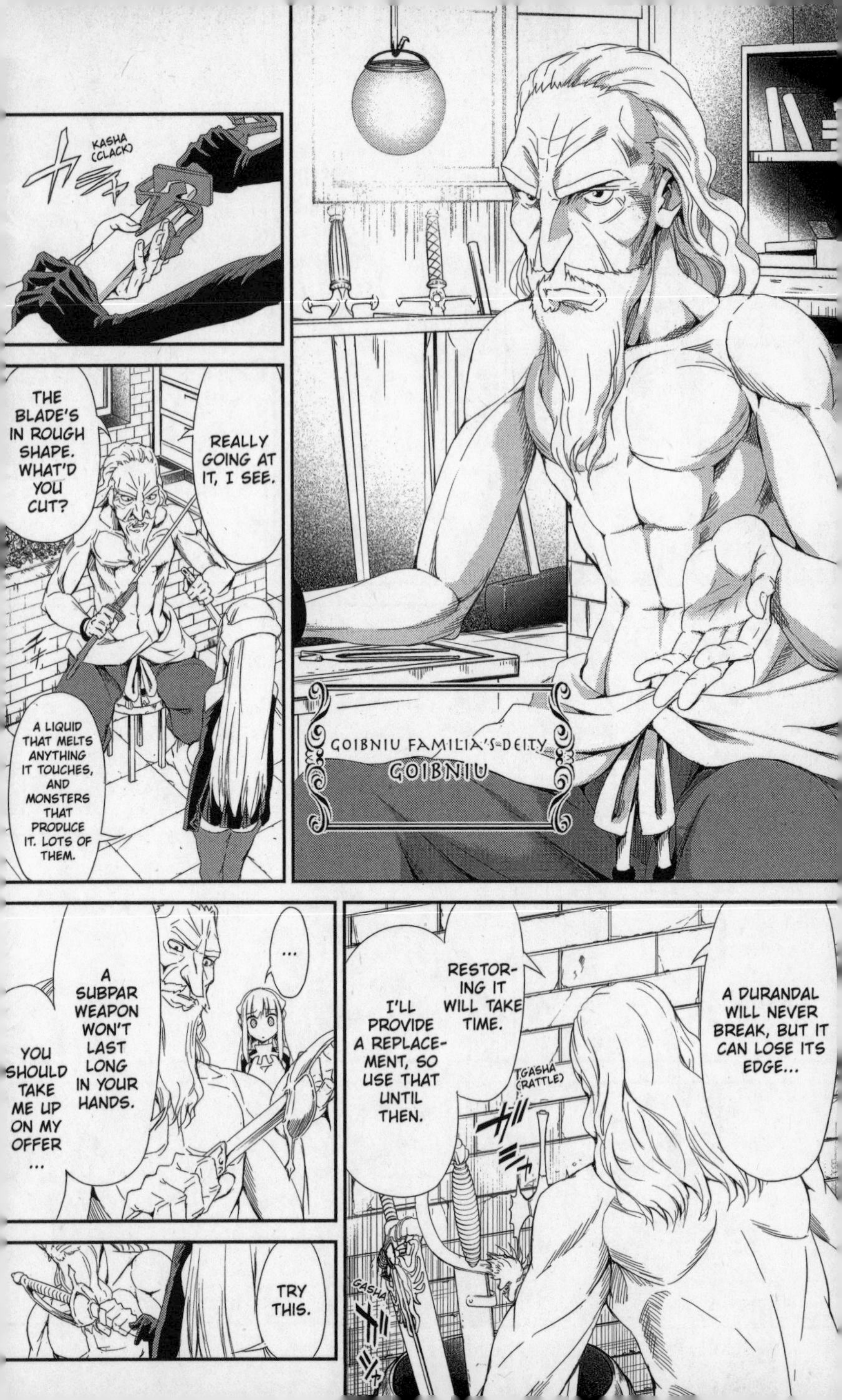
GOIBNIU FAMILIA'S DEITY
GOIBNIU
KASHA (CLACK)
REALLY GOING AT IT, I SEE.
THE BLADE'S IN ROUGH SHAPE. WHAT'D YOU CUT?
A LIQUID THAT MELTS ANYTHING IT TOUCHES, AND MONSTERS THAT PRODUCE IT. LOTS OF THEM.
A DURANDAL WILL NEVER BREAK, BUT IT CAN LOSE ITS EDGE...
RESTORING IT WILL TAKE TIME.
I'LL PROVIDE A REPLACEMENT, SO USE THAT UNTIL THEN.
GASHA (RATTLE)
GASHA
...
A SUBPAR WEAPON WON'T LAST LONG IN YOUR HANDS.
YOU SHOULD TAKE ME UP ON MY OFFER...
TRY THIS.

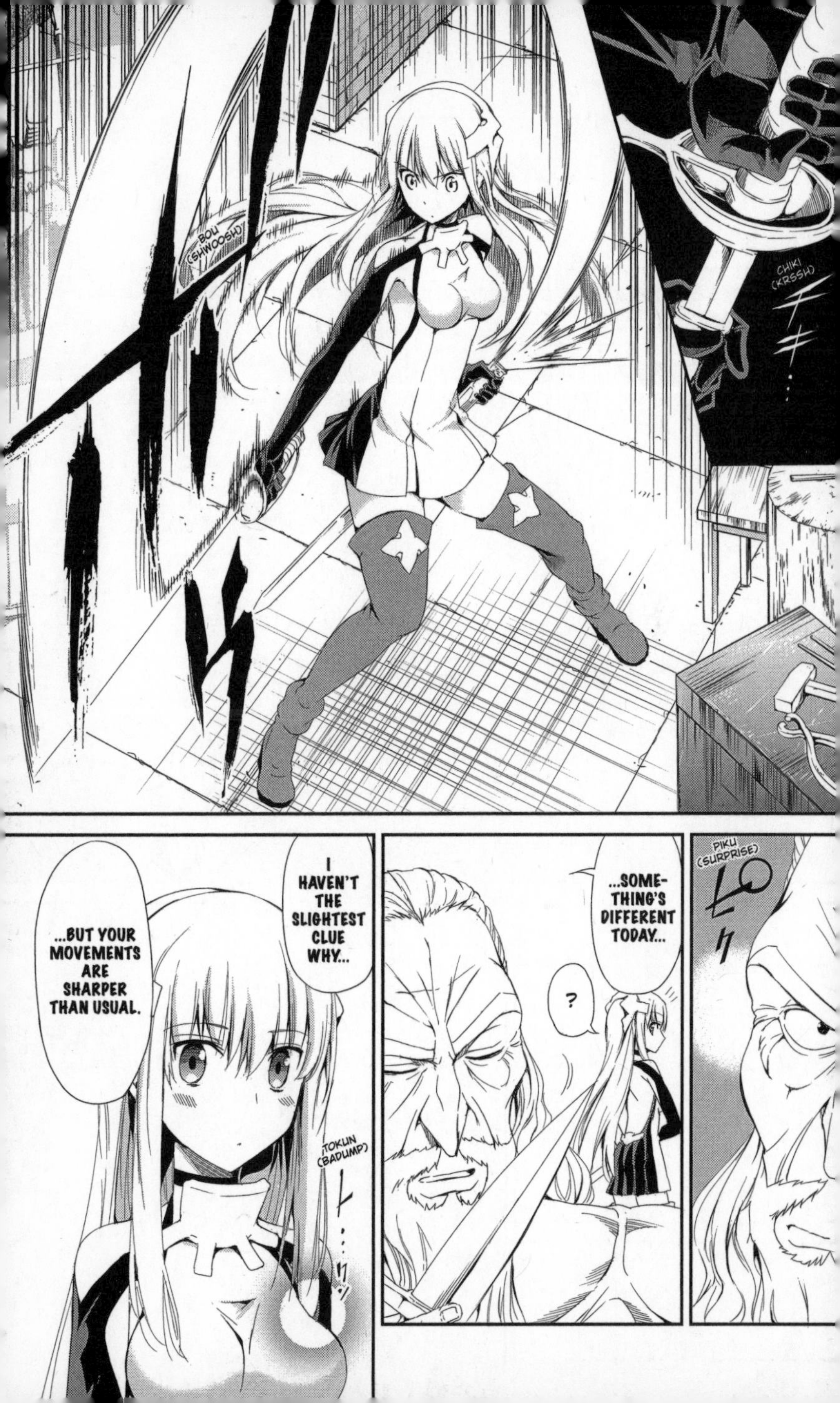
CHIKI (KRSSH)
BOU (SHWOOSH)
PIKU (SURPRISE)
...SOME-THING'S DIFFERENT TODAY...
?
I HAVEN'T THE SLIGHTEST CLUE WHY...
...BUT YOUR MOVEMENTS ARE SHARPER THAN USUAL.
TOKUN (BADUMP)

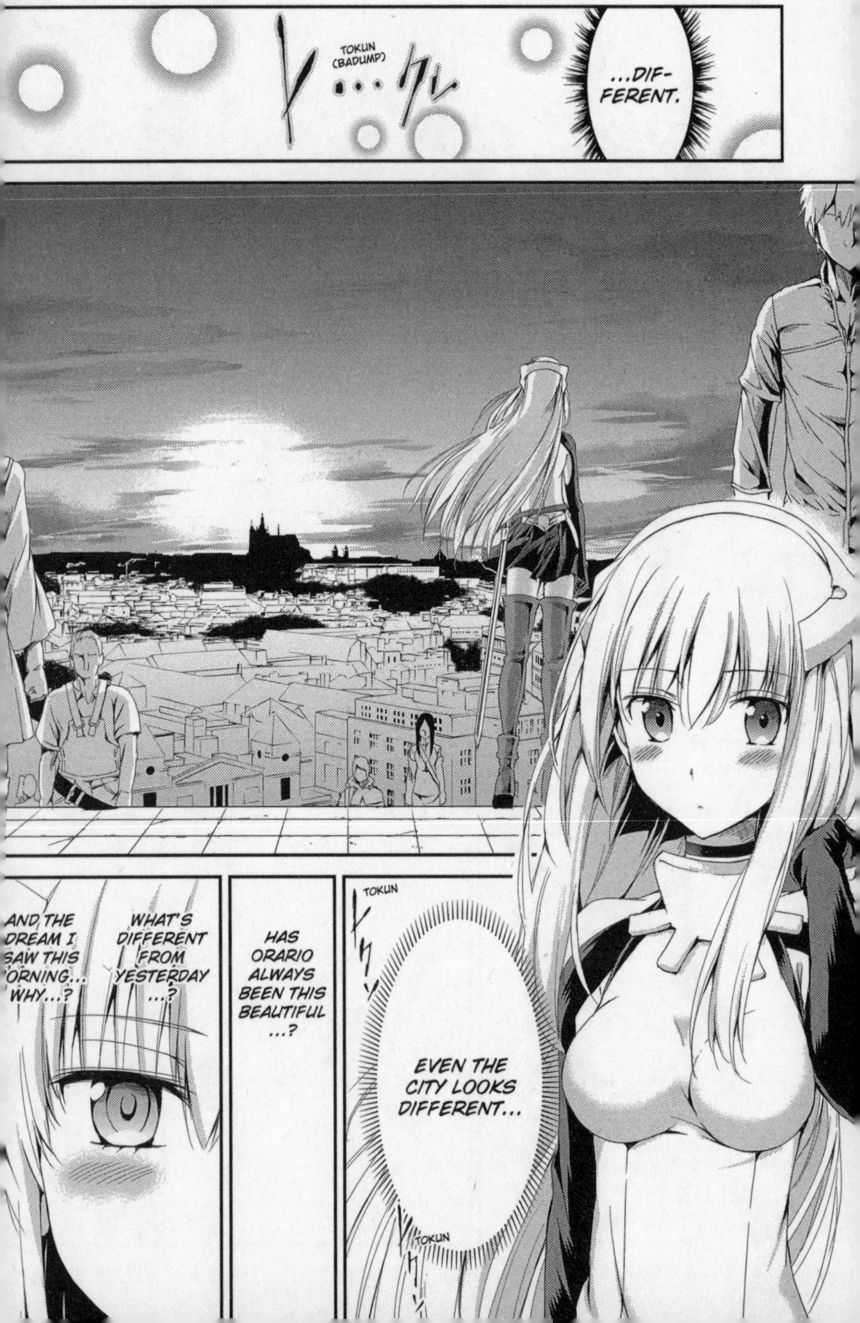
...DIF-
FERENT.
TOKUN
(BADUMP)
TOKUN
EVEN THE CITY LOOKS DIFFERENT...
TOKUN
HAS ORARIO ALWAYS BEEN THIS BEAUTIFUL...?
WHAT'S DIFFERENT FROM YESTERDAY...?
AND THE DREAM I SAW THIS ORNING... WHY...?

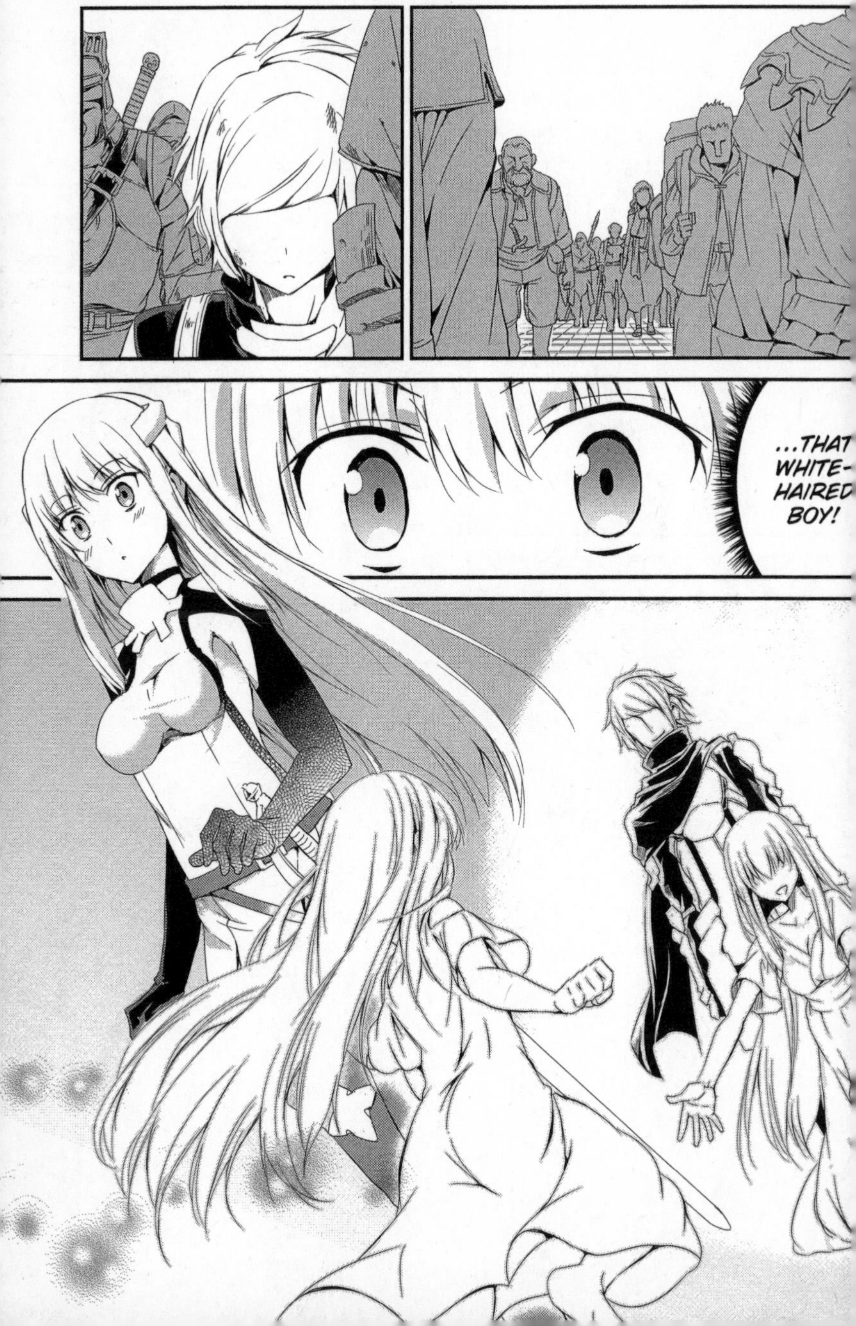
...THAT WHITE-HAIRED BOY!

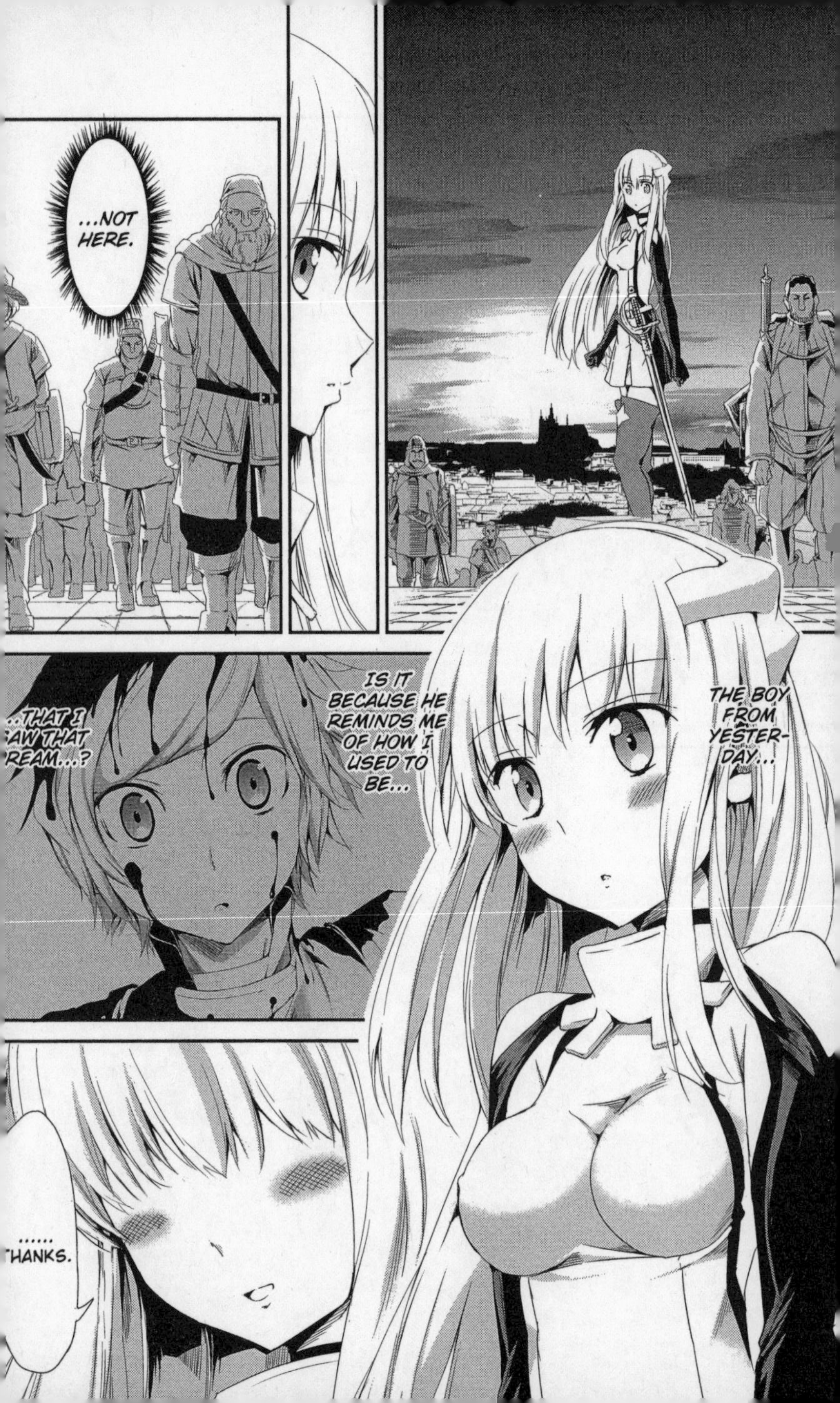

...NOT HERE.
THE BOY FROM YESTER-DAY...
IS IT BECAUSE HE REMINDS ME OF HOW I USED TO BE...
..THAT I SAW THAT REAM...?
...... THANKS.

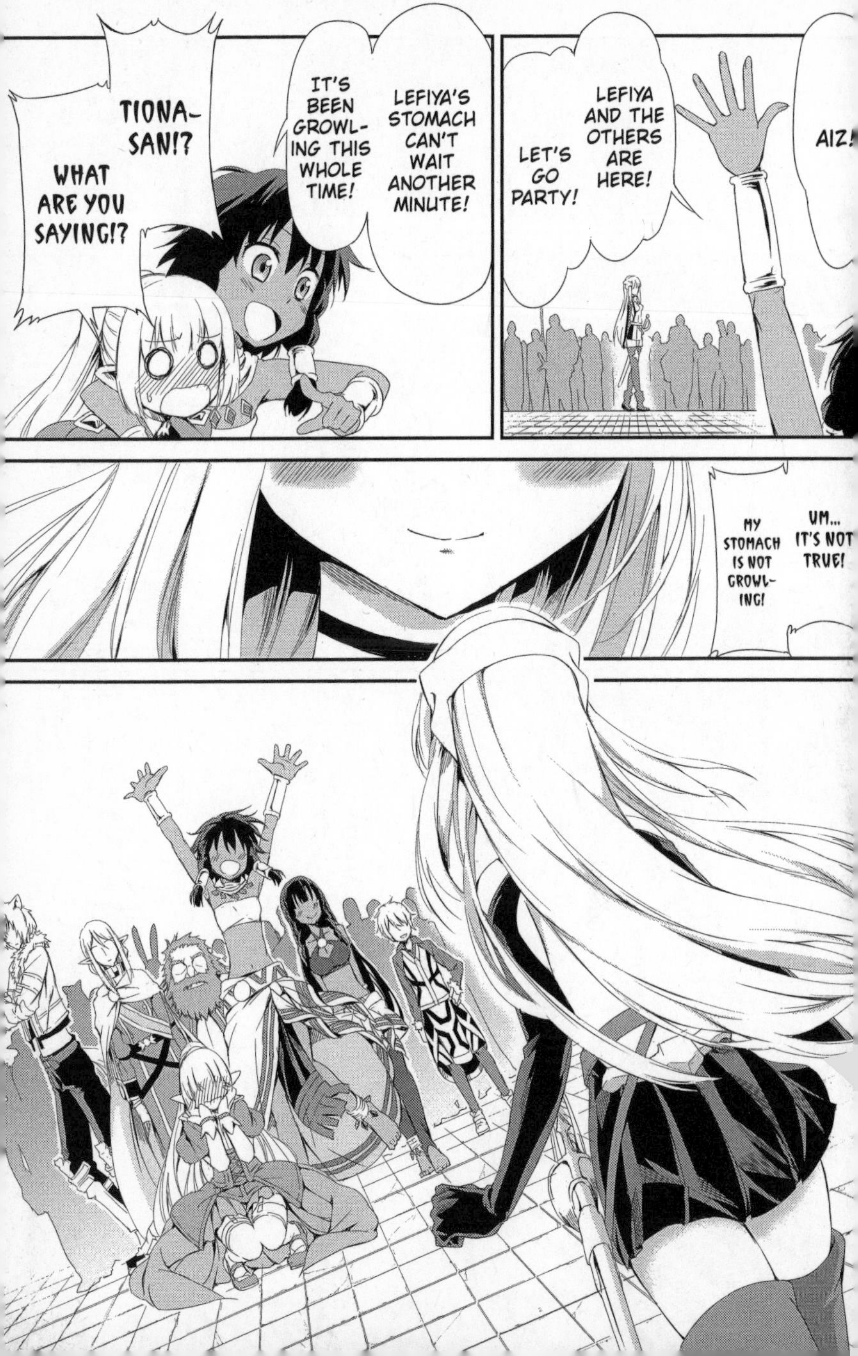
AIZ!
LEFIYA AND THE OTHERS ARE HERE!
LET'S GO PARTY!
LEFIYA'S STOMACH CAN'T WAIT ANOTHER MINUTE!
IT'S BEEN GROWLING THIS WHOLE TIME!
TIONA-SAN!?
WHAT ARE YOU SAYING!?
UM... IT'S NOT TRUE!
MY STOMACH IS NOT GROWLING!

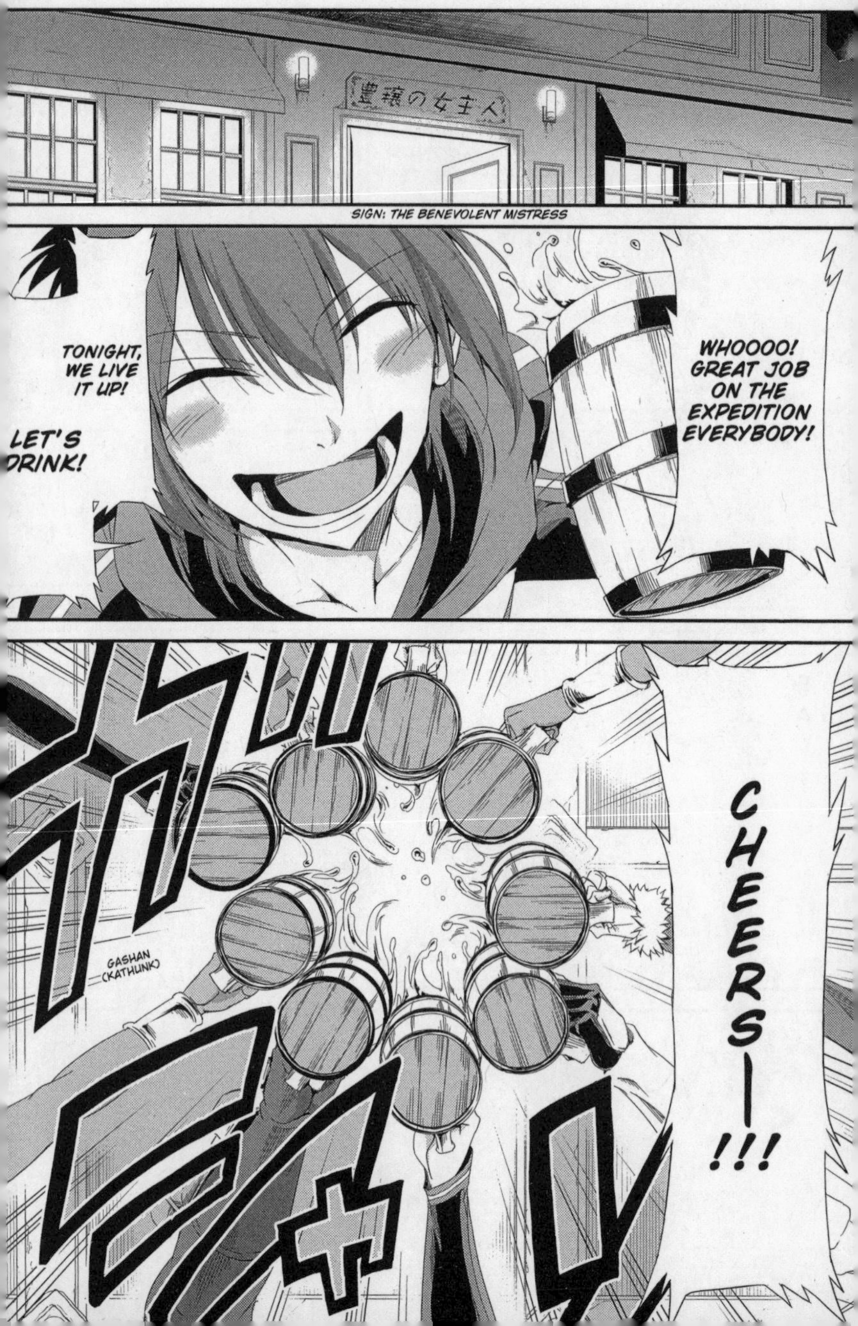
豊穣の女主人
SIGN: THE BENEVOLENT MISTRESS
WHOOOO! GREAT JOB ON THE EXPEDITION EVERYBODY!
TONIGHT, WE LIVE IT UP!
LET'S DRINK!
CHEERS—!!!
GASHAN (KATHUNK)

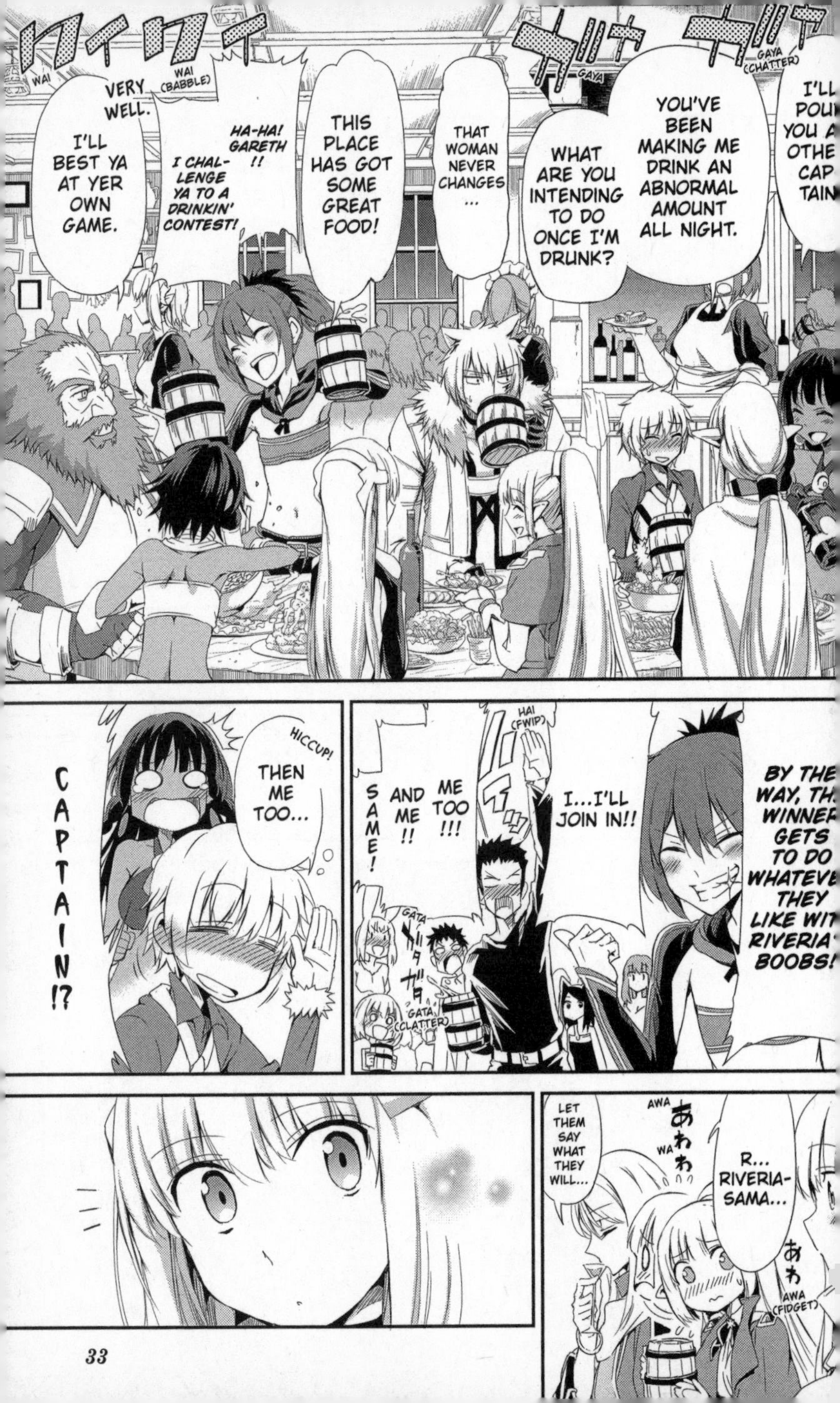
I'LL POU YOU A OTHE CAP TAIN
GAYA (CHATTER)
YOU'VE BEEN MAKING ME DRINK AN ABNORMAL AMOUNT ALL NIGHT.
GAYA
WHAT ARE YOU INTENDING TO DO ONCE I'M DRUNK?
THAT WOMAN NEVER CHANGES...
THIS PLACE HAS GOT SOME GREAT FOOD!
HA-HA! GARETH!!
I CHAL-LENGE YA TO A DRINKIN' CONTEST!
WAI (BABBLE)
VERY WELL.
I'LL BEST YA AT YER OWN GAME.
WAI
BY THE WAY, TH WINNER GETS TO DO WHATEVE THEY LIKE WIT RIVERIA' BOOBS!
I...I'LL JOIN IN!!
HAI (FWIP)
ME TOO!!!
AND ME!!
SAME!
GATA
GATA (CLATTER)
HICCUP!
THEN ME TOO...
CAPTAIN!?
R... RIVERIA-SAMA...
AWA (FIDGET)
AWA WA
LET THEM SAY WHAT THEY WILL...

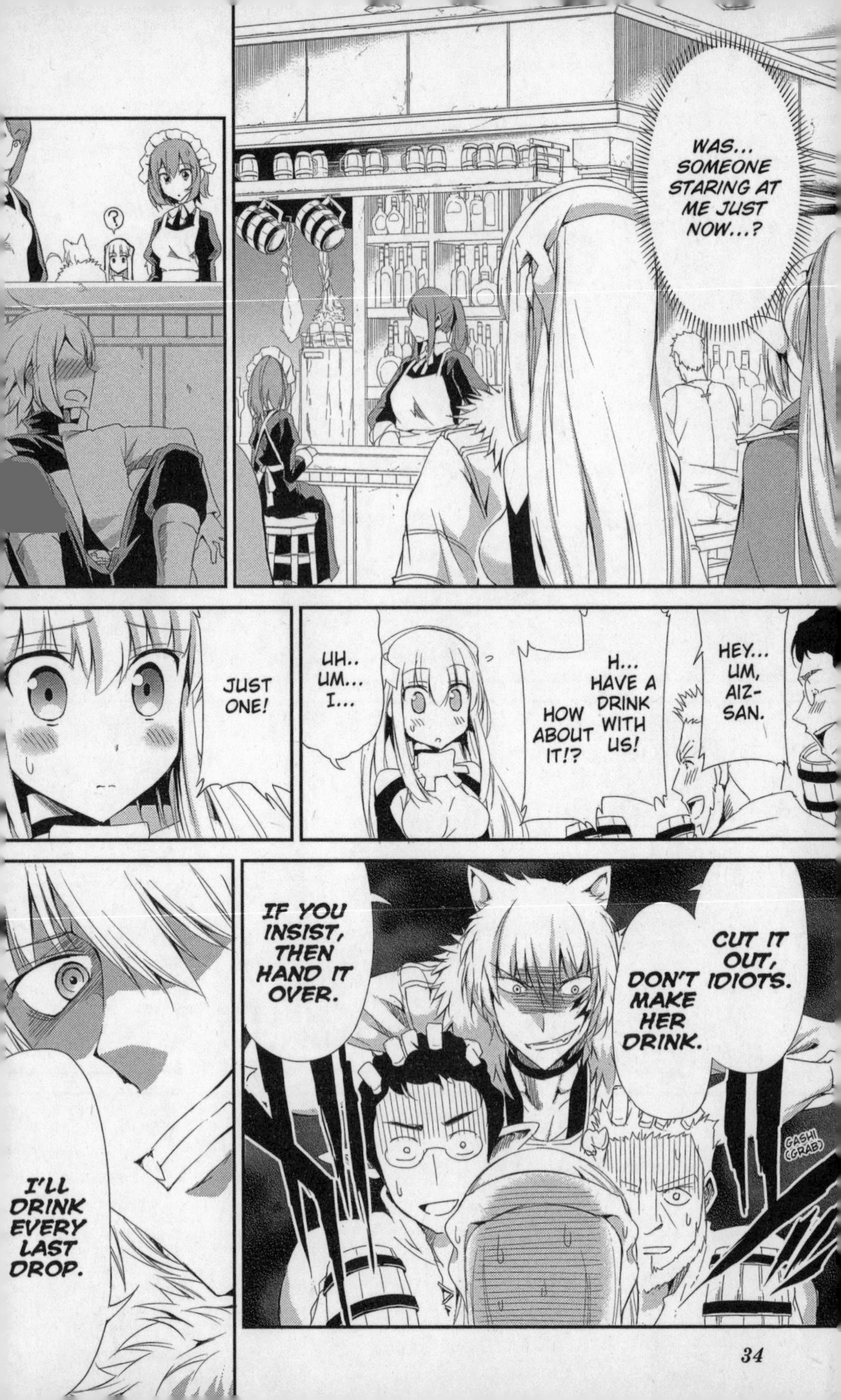
WAS... SOMEONE STARING AT ME JUST NOW...?
?
HEY... UM, AIZ-SAN.
H... HAVE A DRINK WITH US!
HOW ABOUT IT!?
UH.. UM... I...
JUST ONE!
CUT IT OUT, IDIOTS.
DON'T MAKE HER DRINK.
GASHI (GRAB)
IF YOU INSIST, THEN HAND IT OVER.
I'LL DRINK EVERY LAST DROP.

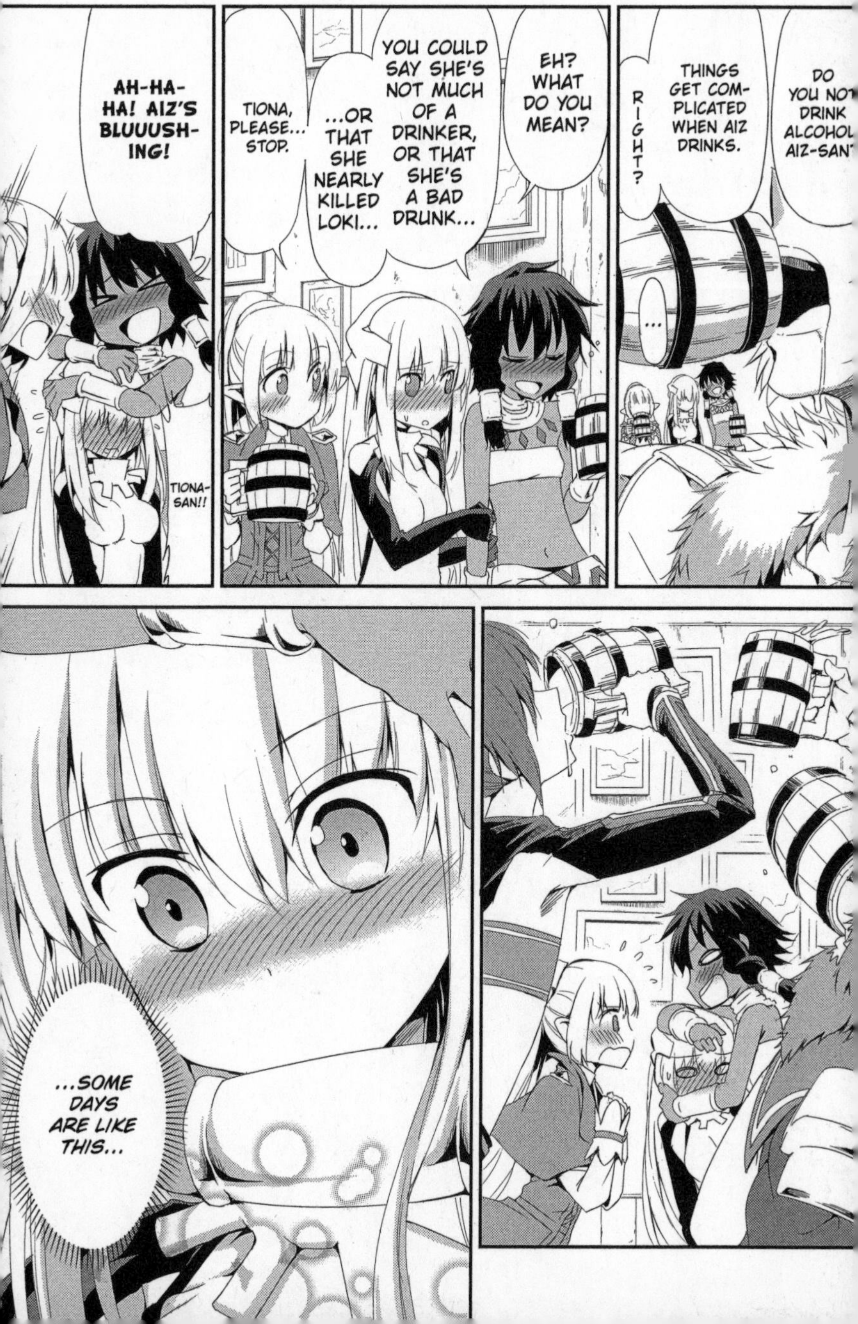
DO YOU NOT DRINK ALCOHOL AIZ-SAN
THINGS GET COMPLICATED WHEN AIZ DRINKS.
RIGHT?
...
EH? WHAT DO YOU MEAN?
YOU COULD SAY SHE'S NOT MUCH OF A DRINKER, OR THAT SHE'S A BAD DRUNK...
...OR THAT SHE NEARLY KILLED LOKI...
TIONA, PLEASE... STOP.
AH-HA-HA! AIZ'S BLUUUSH-ING!
TIONA-SAN!!
...SOME DAYS ARE LIKE THIS...

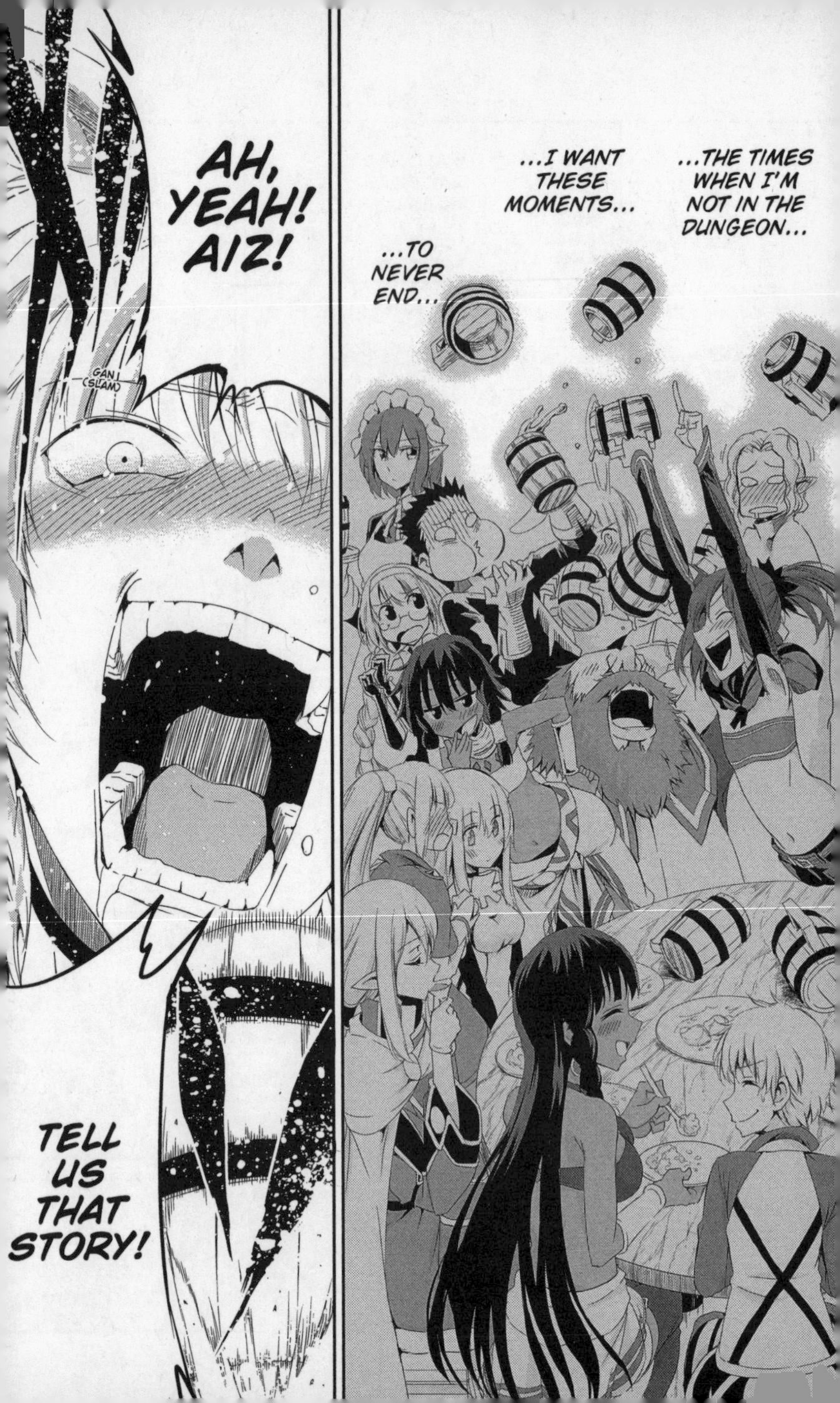
...THE TIMES WHEN I'M NOT IN THE DUNGEON...
...I WANT THESE MOMENTS...
...TO NEVER END...
AH, YEAH! AIZ!
GAN! (SLAM)
TELL US THAT STORY!

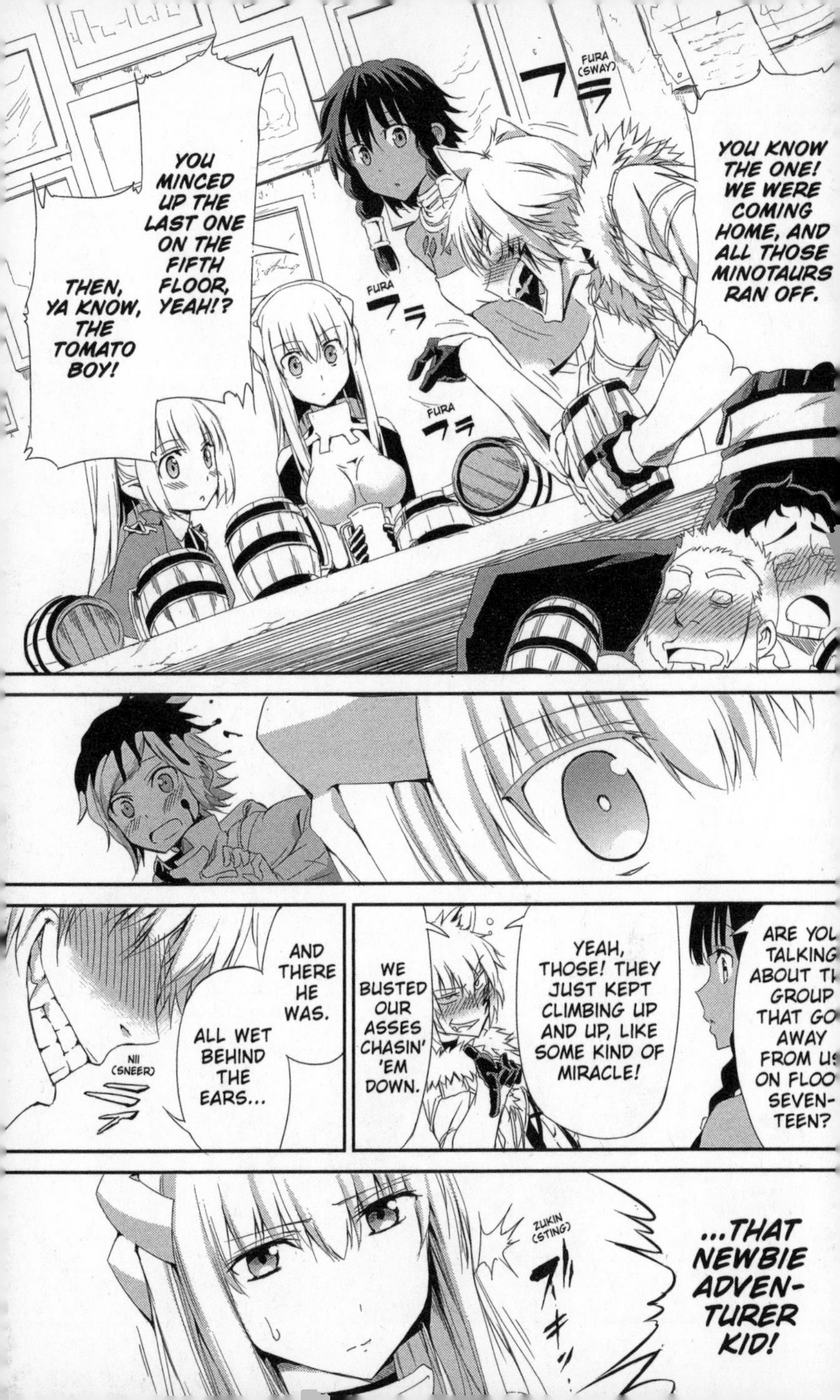
FURA (SWAY)
YOU KNOW THE ONE! WE WERE COMING HOME, AND ALL THOSE MINOTAURS RAN OFF.
YOU MINCED UP THE LAST ONE ON THE FIFTH FLOOR, YEAH!?
THEN, YA KNOW, THE TOMATO BOY!
FURA
FURA
ARE YOU TALKING ABOUT T GROUP THAT GO AWAY FROM US ON FLOO SEVEN-TEEN?
YEAH, THOSE! THEY JUST KEPT CLIMBING UP AND UP, LIKE SOME KIND OF MIRACLE!
WE BUSTED OUR ASSES CHASIN' 'EM DOWN.
AND THERE HE WAS.
ALL WET BEHIND THE EARS...
NII (SNEER)
ZUKIN (STING)
...THAT NEWBIE ADVEN-TURER KID!

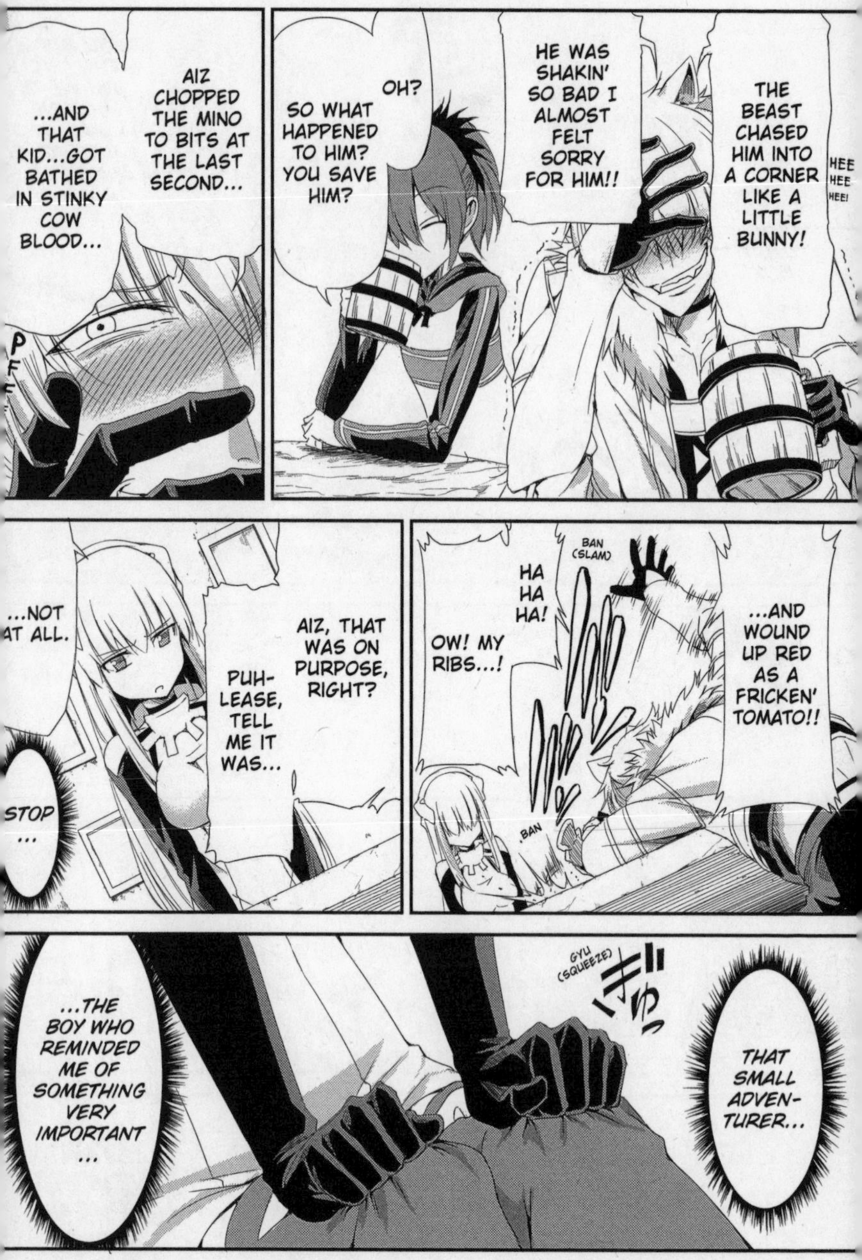
THE BEAST CHASED HIM INTO A CORNER LIKE A LITTLE BUNNY!
HEE HEE HEE!
HE WAS SHAKIN' SO BAD I ALMOST FELT SORRY FOR HIM!!
OH?
SO WHAT HAPPENED TO HIM? YOU SAVE HIM?
AIZ CHOPPED THE MINO TO BITS AT THE LAST SECOND...
...AND THAT KID...GOT BATHED IN STINKY COW BLOOD...
PFF
...AND WOUND UP RED AS A FRICKEN' TOMATO!!
BAN (SLAM)
HA HA HA!
OW! MY RIBS...!
BAN
AIZ, THAT WAS ON PURPOSE, RIGHT?
PUH-LEASE, TELL ME IT WAS...
...NOT AT ALL.
STOP ...
THAT SMALL ADVEN-TURER...
GYU (SQUEEZE)
...THE BOY WHO REMINDED ME OF SOMETHING VERY IMPORTANT ...

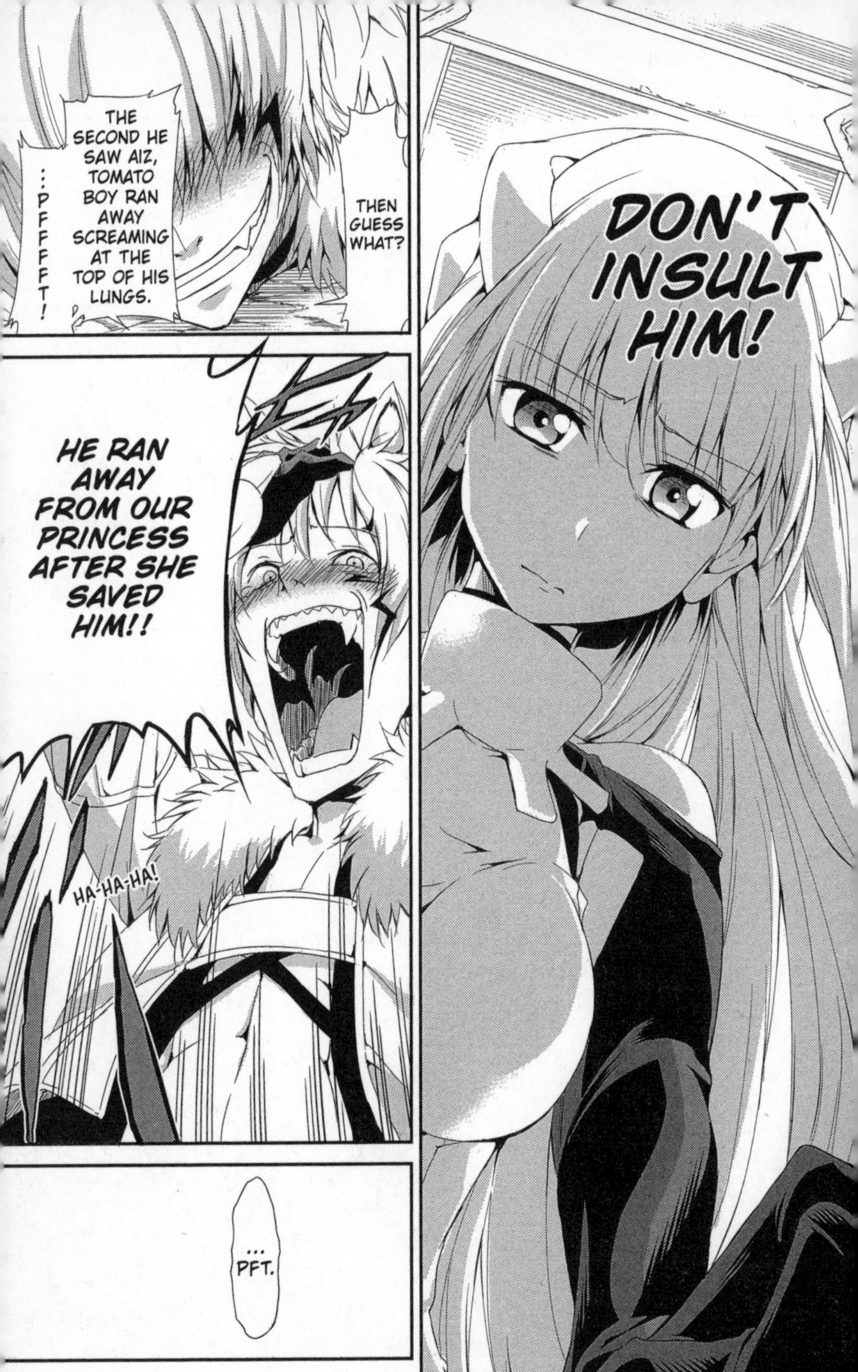
DON'T INSULT HIM!
THEN GUESS WHAT?
THE SECOND HE SAW AIZ, TOMATO BOY RAN AWAY SCREAMING AT THE TOP OF HIS LUNGS.
...PFFFFT!
HE RAN AWAY FROM OUR PRINCESS AFTER SHE SAVED HIM!!
HA-HA-HA!
... PFT.

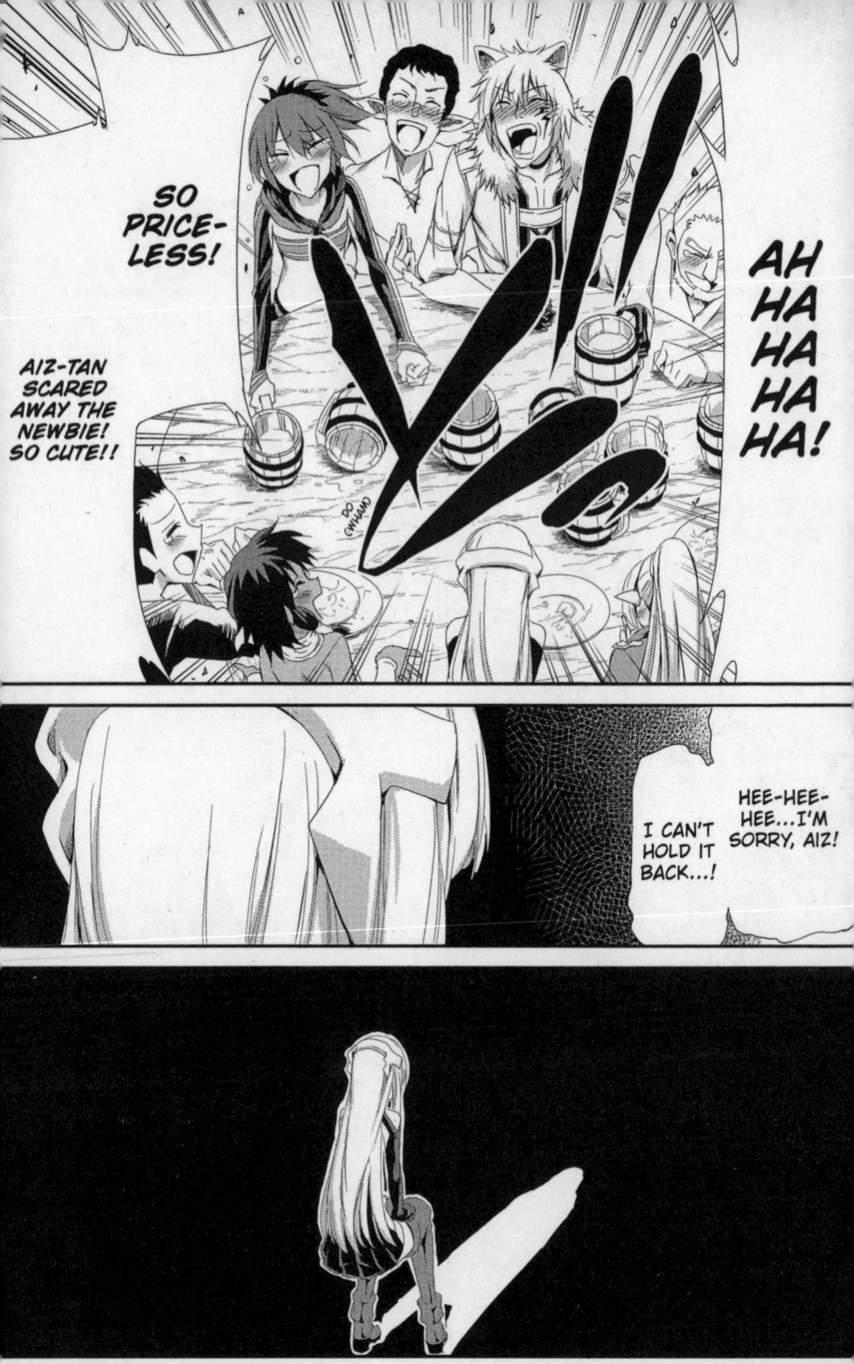
AH HA HA HA HA!
SO PRICE-LESS!
AIZ-TAN SCARED AWAY THE NEWBIE! SO CUTE!!
DO (WHAM)
HEE-HEE-HEE...I'M SORRY, AIZ!
I CAN'T HOLD IT BACK...!

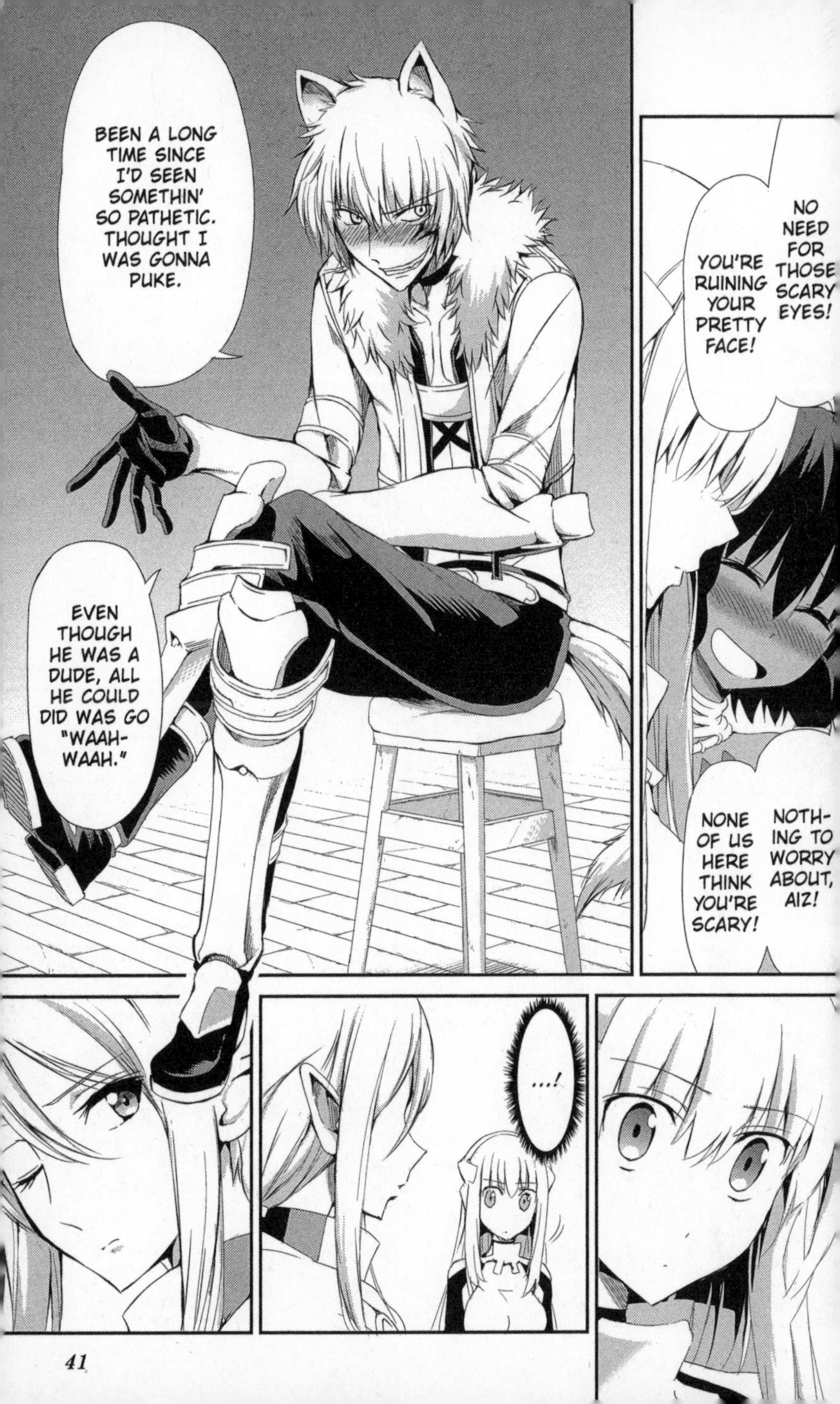
NO NEED FOR THOSE SCARY EYES! YOU'RE RUINING YOUR PRETTY FACE!
NOTH-ING TO WORRY ABOUT, AIZ! NONE OF US HERE THINK YOU'RE SCARY!
BEEN A LONG TIME SINCE I'D SEEN SOMETHIN' SO PATHETIC. THOUGHT I WAS GONNA PUKE.
EVEN THOUGH HE WAS A DUDE, ALL HE COULD DID WAS GO "WAAH-WAAH."
...!

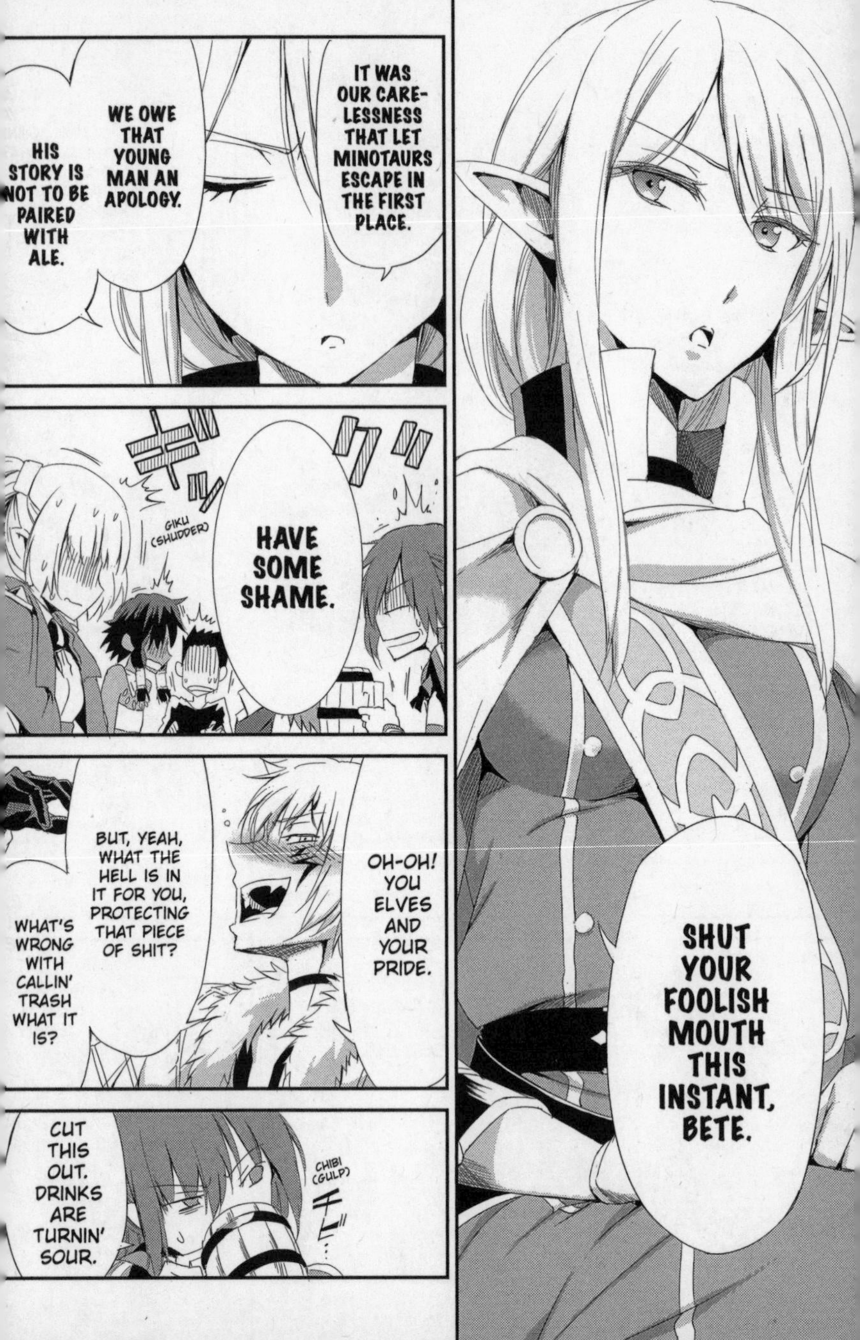
SHUT YOUR FOOLISH MOUTH THIS INSTANT, BETE.
IT WAS OUR CARELESSNESS THAT LET MINOTAURS ESCAPE IN THE FIRST PLACE.
WE OWE THAT YOUNG MAN AN APOLOGY.
HIS STORY IS NOT TO BE PAIRED WITH ALE.
HAVE SOME SHAME.
GIKU (SHUDDER)
OH-OH! YOU ELVES AND YOUR PRIDE.
BUT, YEAH, WHAT THE HELL IS IN IT FOR YOU, PROTECTING THAT PIECE OF SHIT?
WHAT'S WRONG WITH CALLIN' TRASH WHAT IT IS?
CHIBI (GULP)
CUT THIS OUT. DRINKS ARE TURNIN' SOUR.

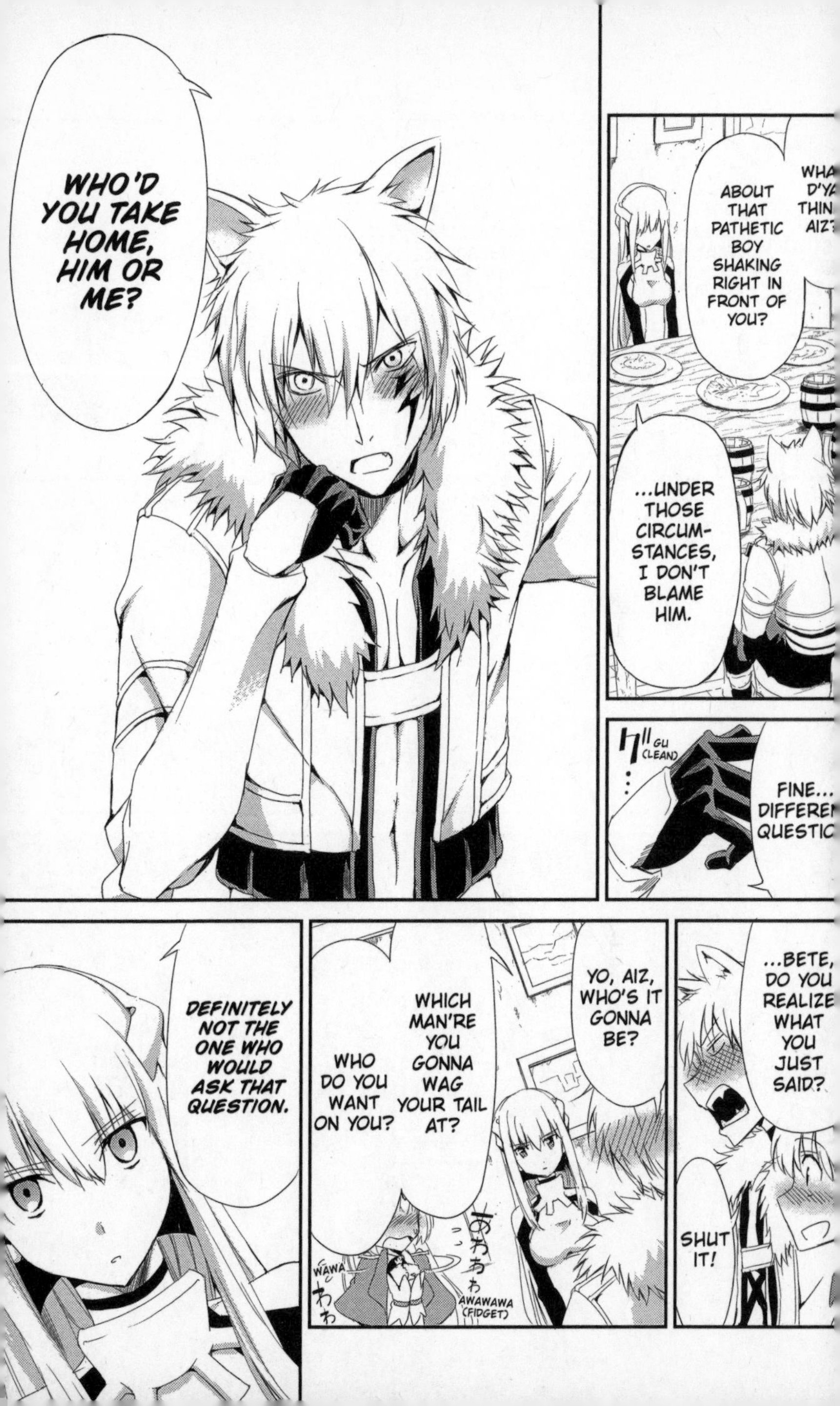
WHA D'YA THIN AIZ?
ABOUT THAT PATHETIC BOY SHAKING RIGHT IN FRONT OF YOU?
...UNDER THOSE CIRCUM-STANCES, I DON'T BLAME HIM.
GU (LEAN)
...
FINE... DIFFEREN QUESTIC
WHO'D YOU TAKE HOME, HIM OR ME?
...BETE, DO YOU REALIZE WHAT YOU JUST SAID?
SHUT IT!
YO, AIZ, WHO'S IT GONNA BE?
WHICH MAN'RE YOU GONNA WAG YOUR TAIL AT?
WHO DO YOU WANT ON YOU?
AWAWAWA (FIDGET)
WAWA
DEFINITELY NOT THE ONE WHO WOULD ASK THAT QUESTION.

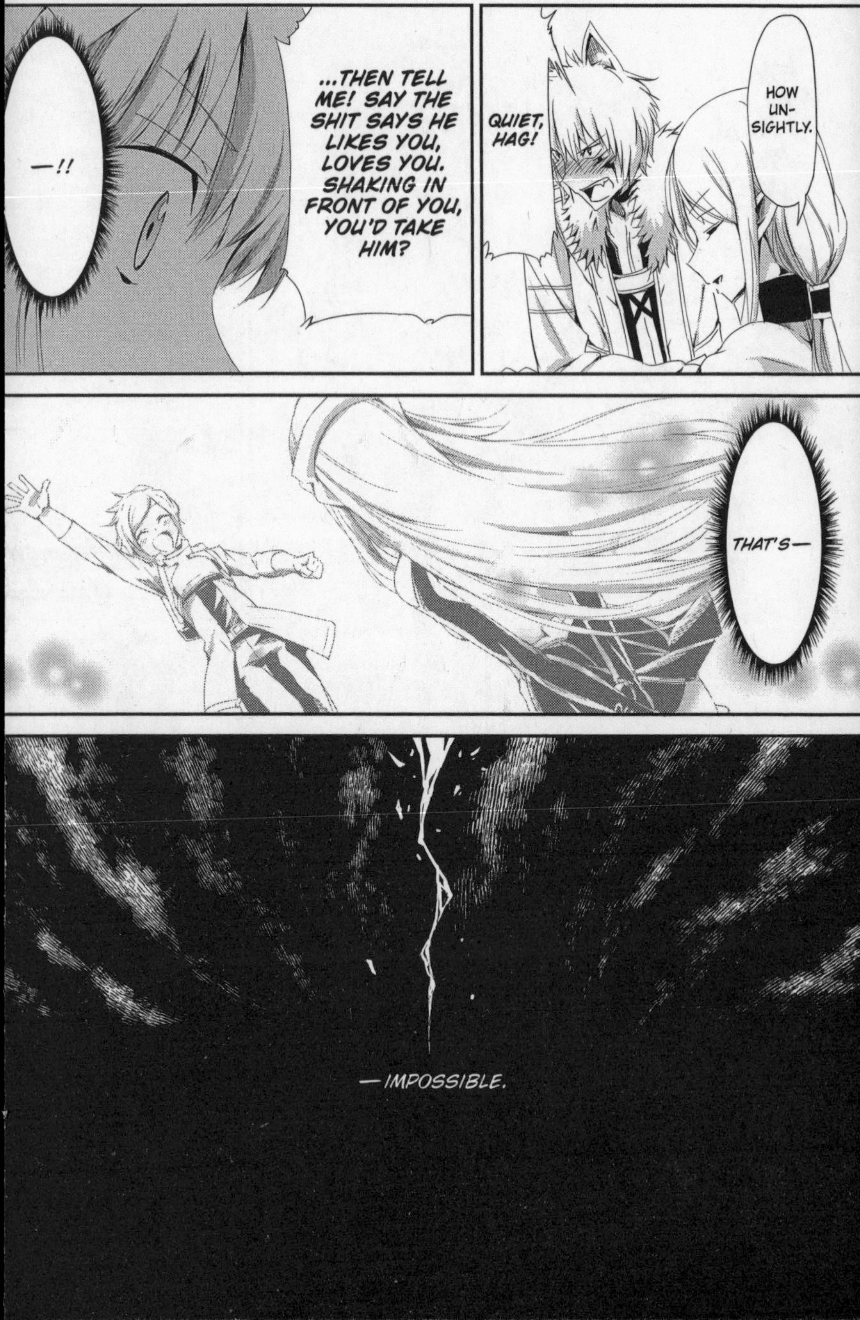
HOW UN-SIGHTLY.
QUIET, HAG!
...THEN TELL ME! SAY THE SHIT SAYS HE LIKES YOU, LOVES YOU. SHAKING IN FRONT OF YOU, YOU'D TAKE HIM?
—!!
THAT'S—
—IMPOSSIBLE.

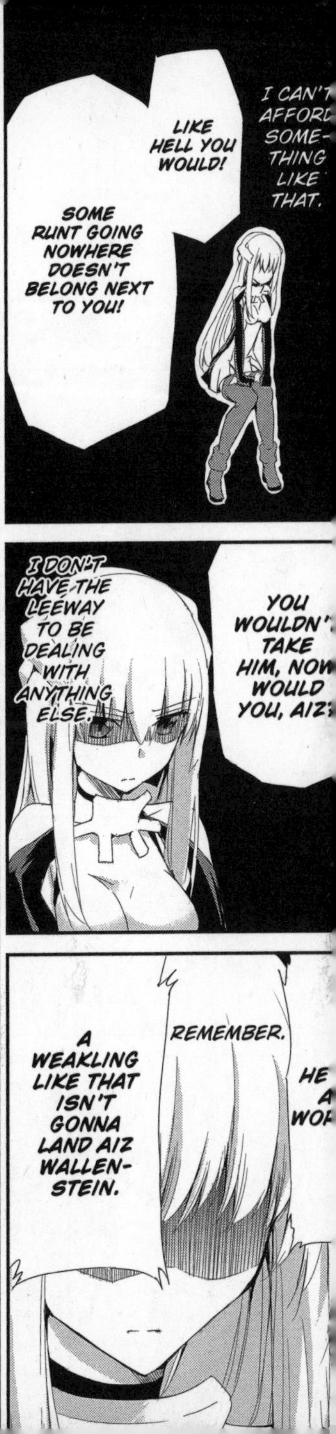
I CAN'T AFFORD SOMETHING LIKE THAT.
LIKE HELL YOU WOULD!
SOME RUNT GOING NOWHERE DOESN'T BELONG NEXT TO YOU!
YOU WOULDN'T TAKE HIM, NOW WOULD YOU, AIZ
I DON'T HAVE THE LEEWAY TO BE DEALING WITH ANYTHING ELSE.
HE A WOR
REMEMBER.
A WEAKLING LIKE THAT ISN'T GONNA LAND AIZ WALLENSTEIN.

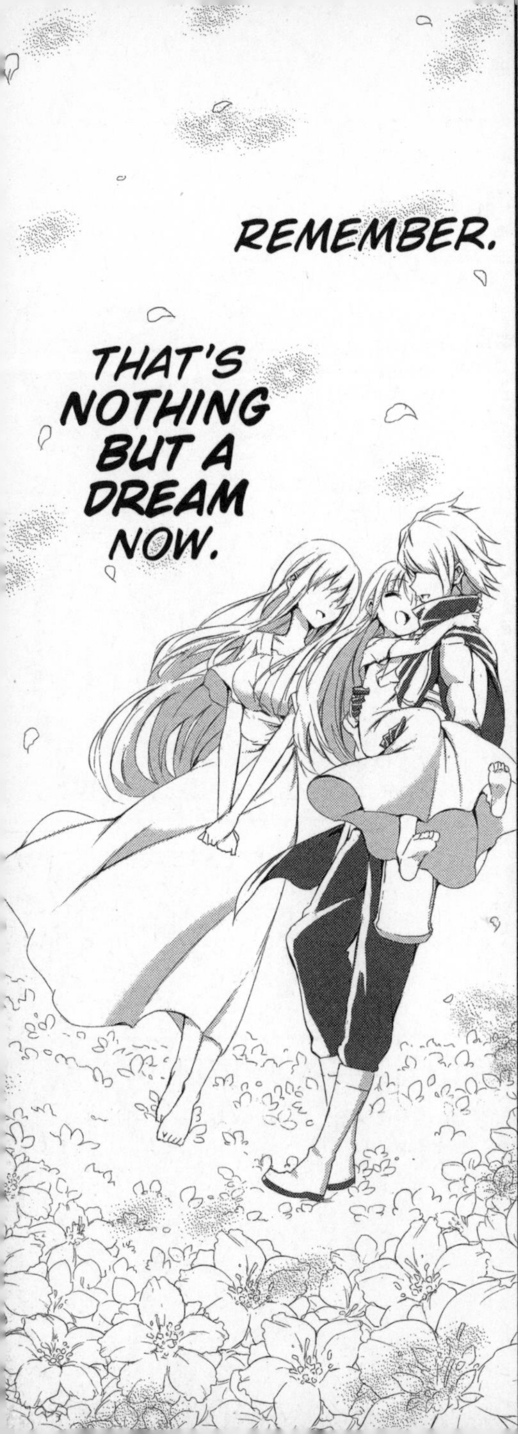
REMEMBER.
THAT'S NOTHING BUT A DREAM NOW.

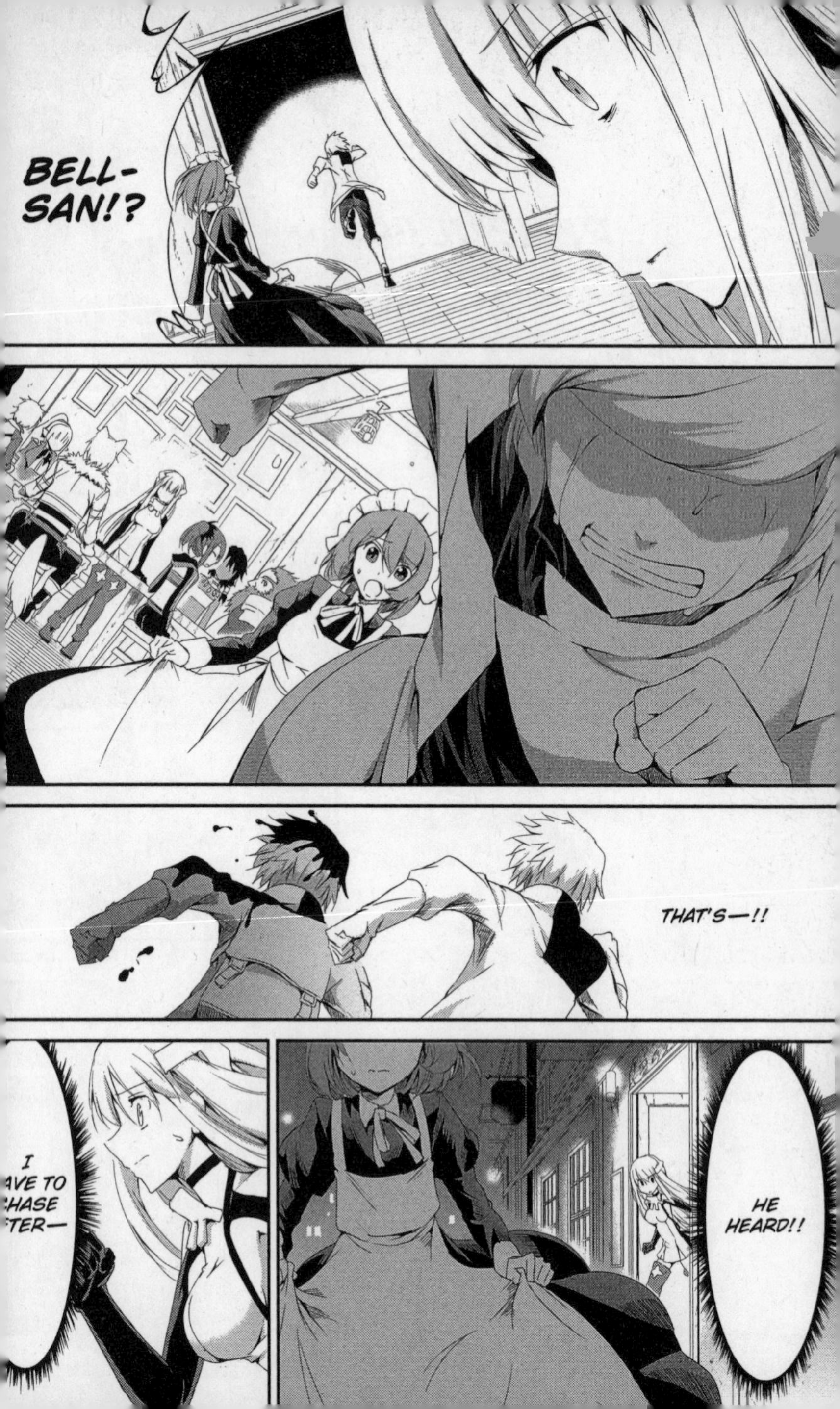
BELL-SAN!?
THAT'S—!!
HE HEARD!!
I AVE TO CHASE FTER—

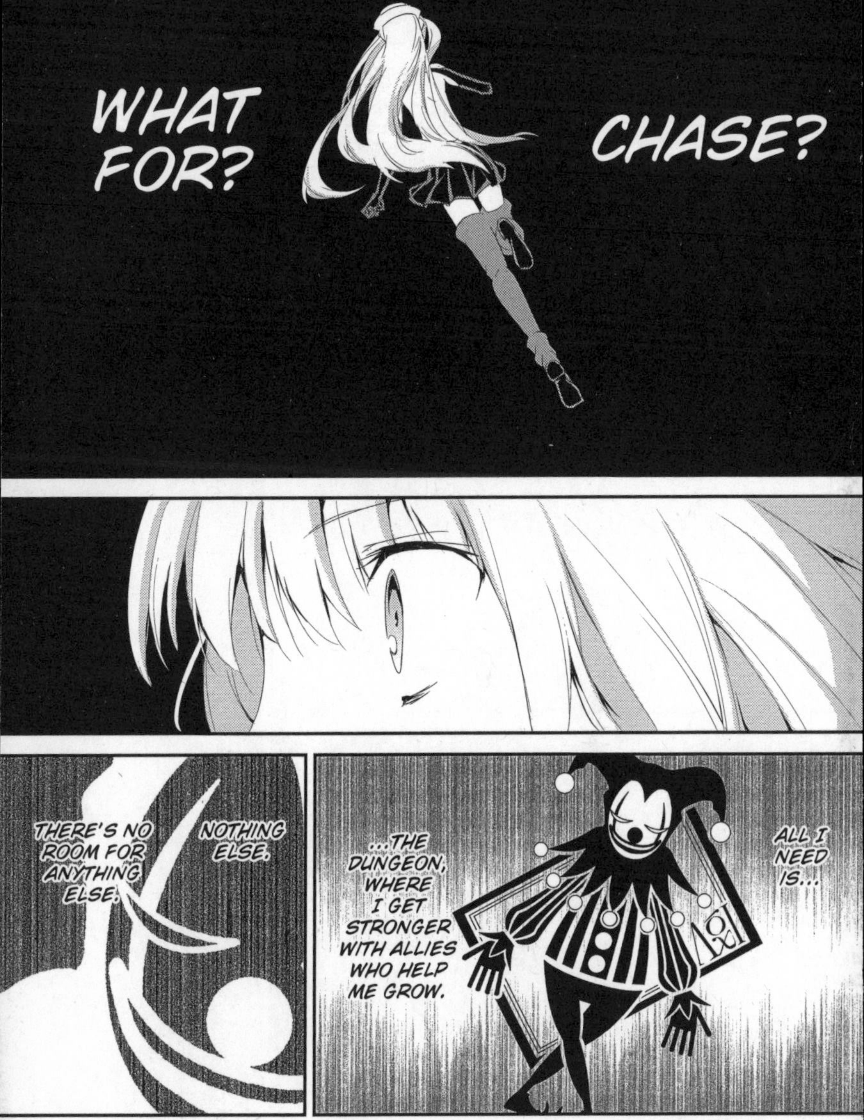
CHASE?
WHAT FOR?
ALL I NEED IS...
...THE DUNGEON, WHERE I GET STRONGER WITH ALLIES WHO HELP ME GROW.
NOTHING ELSE.
THERE'S NO ROOM FOR ANYTHING ELSE.

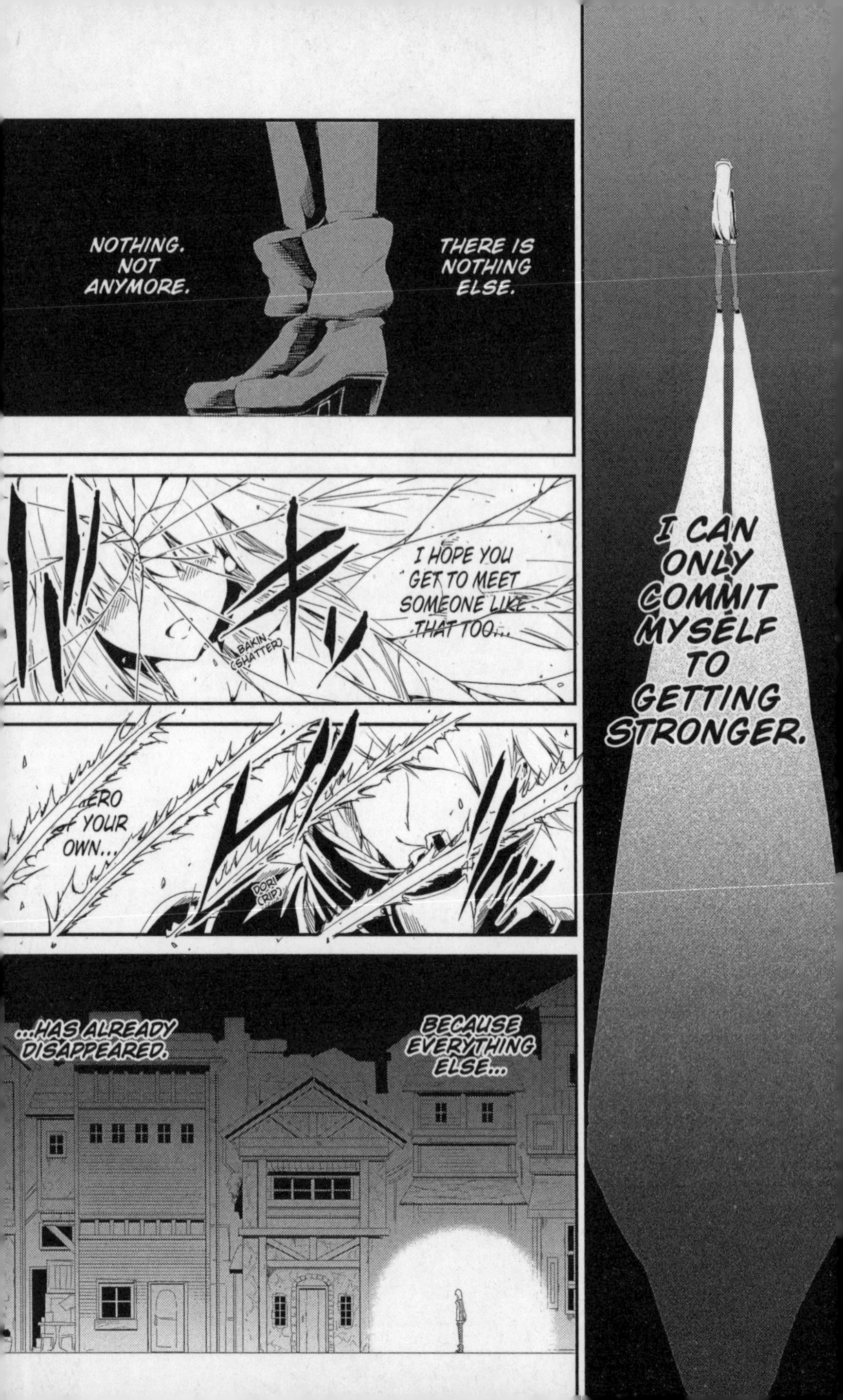
I CAN ONLY COMMIT MYSELF TO GETTING STRONGER.
THERE IS NOTHING ELSE.
NOTHING. NOT ANYMORE.
I HOPE YOU GET TO MEET SOMEONE LIKE THAT TOO...
BAKIN (SHATTER)
DORI (RIP)
...ERO OF YOUR OWN...
BECAUSE EVERYTHING ELSE...
...HAS ALREADY DISAPPEARED.

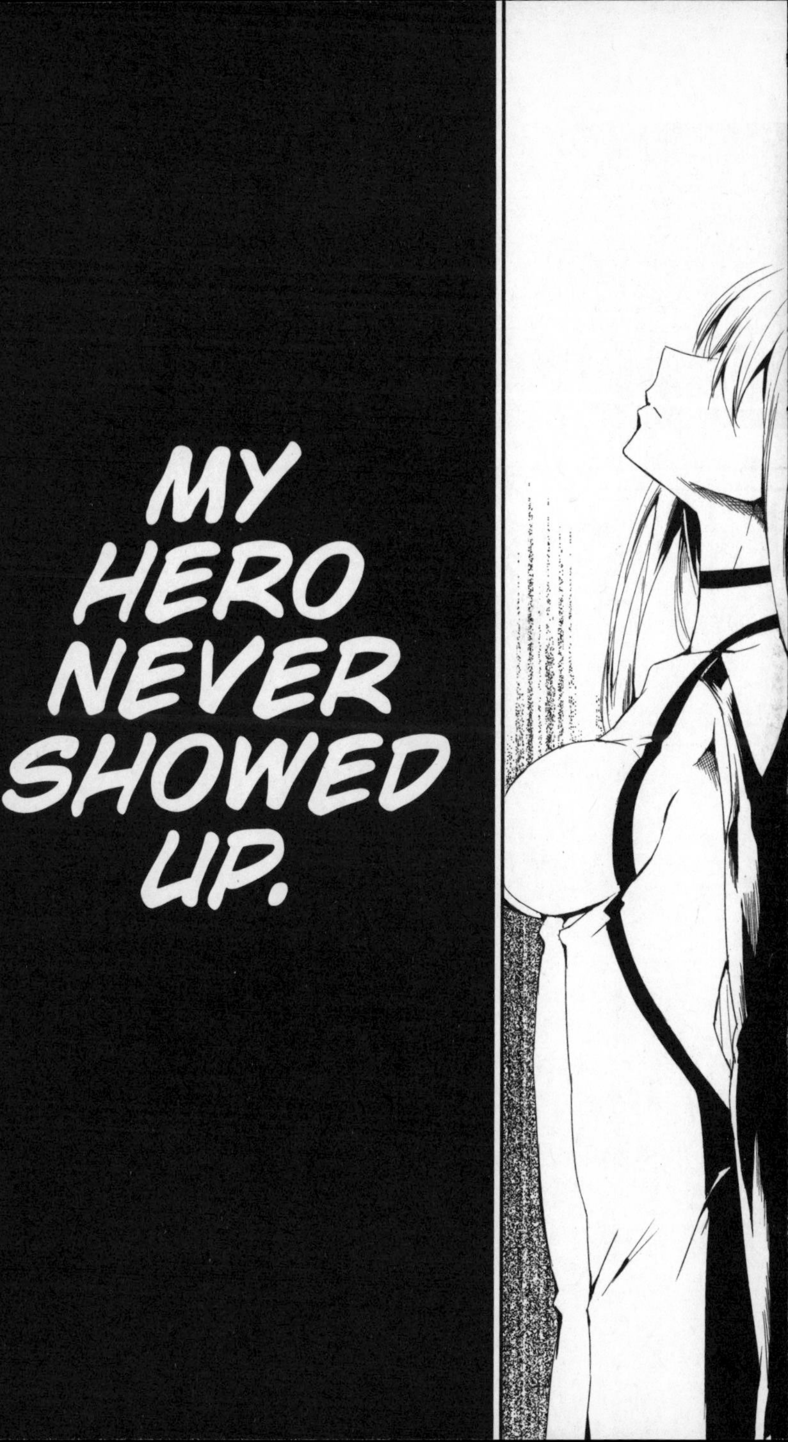
MY HERO NEVER SHOWED UP.

Is it Wrong to Try to Pick Up Girls in a Dungeon? On the Side

Sword Oratoria

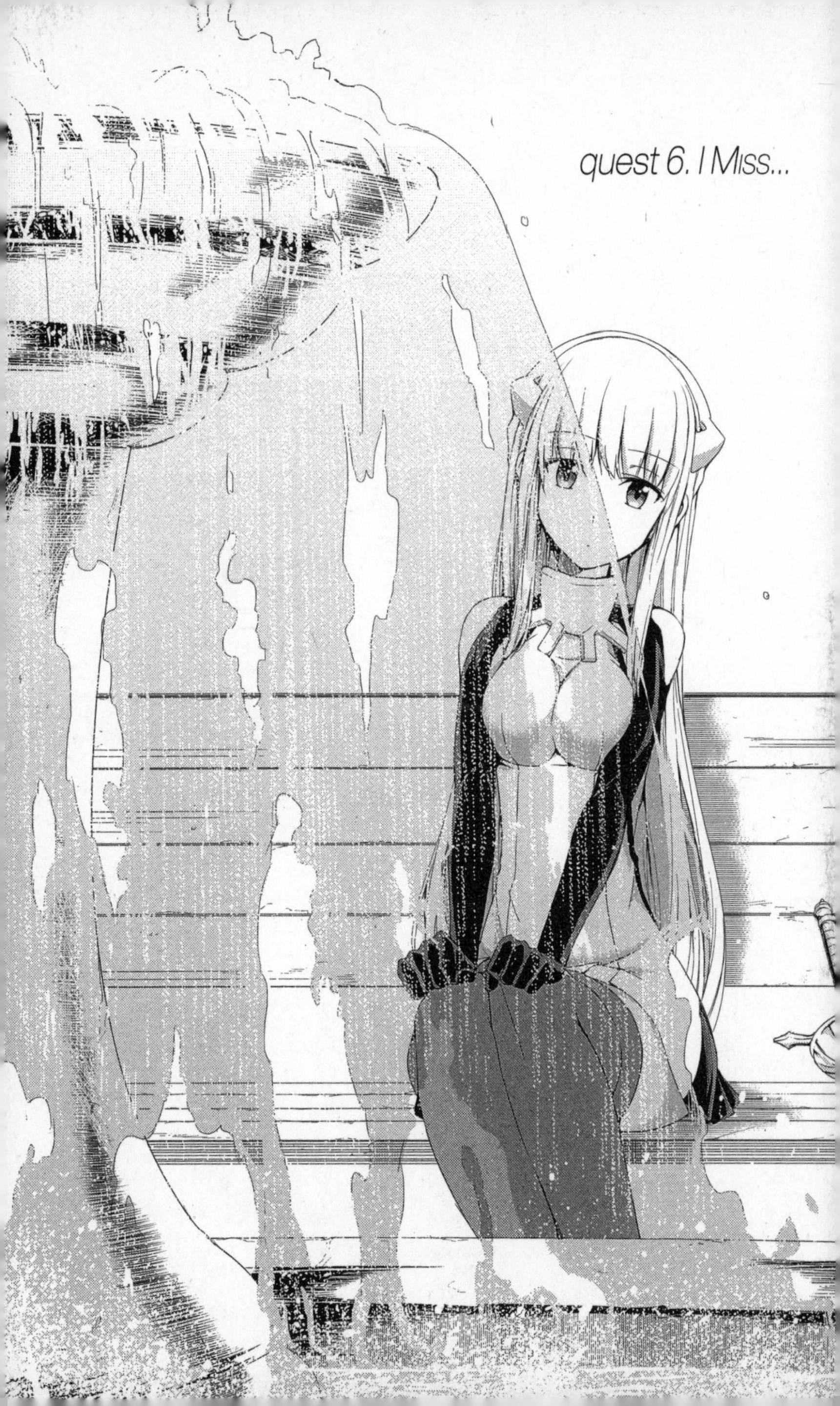
quest 6. I Miss...

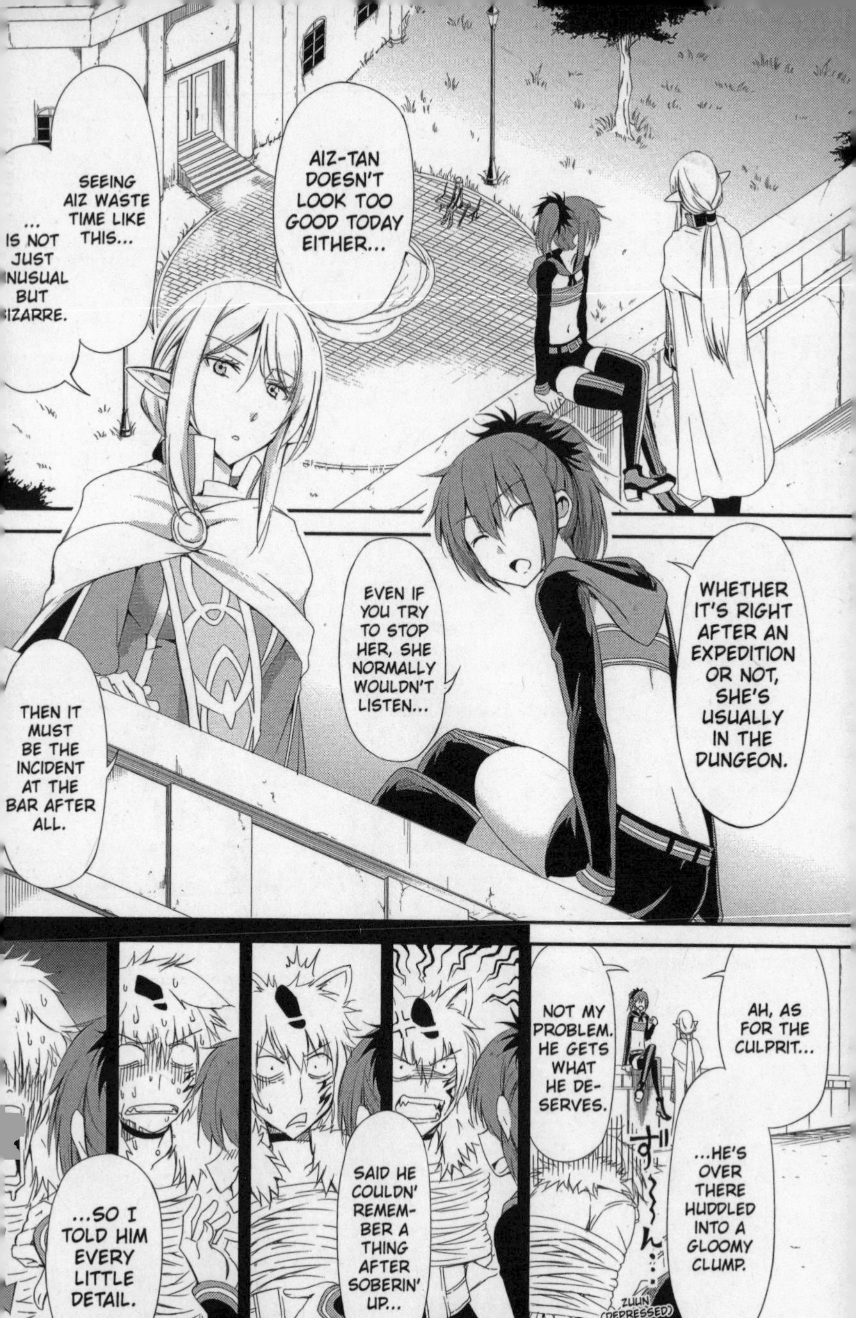
AIZ-TAN DOESN'T LOOK TOO GOOD TODAY EITHER...
SEEING AIZ WASTE TIME LIKE THIS...
... IS NOT JUST NUSUAL BUT IZARRE.
WHETHER IT'S RIGHT AFTER AN EXPEDITION OR NOT, SHE'S USUALLY IN THE DUNGEON.
EVEN IF YOU TRY TO STOP HER, SHE NORMALLY WOULDN'T LISTEN...
THEN IT MUST BE THE INCIDENT AT THE BAR AFTER ALL.
AH, AS FOR THE CULPRIT...
NOT MY PROBLEM. HE GETS WHAT HE DE-SERVES.
...HE'S OVER THERE HUDDLED INTO A GLOOMY CLUMP.
ZUUN (DEPRESSED)
SAID HE COULDN' REMEM-BER A THING AFTER SOBERIN' UP...
...SO I TOLD HIM EVERY LITTLE DETAIL.

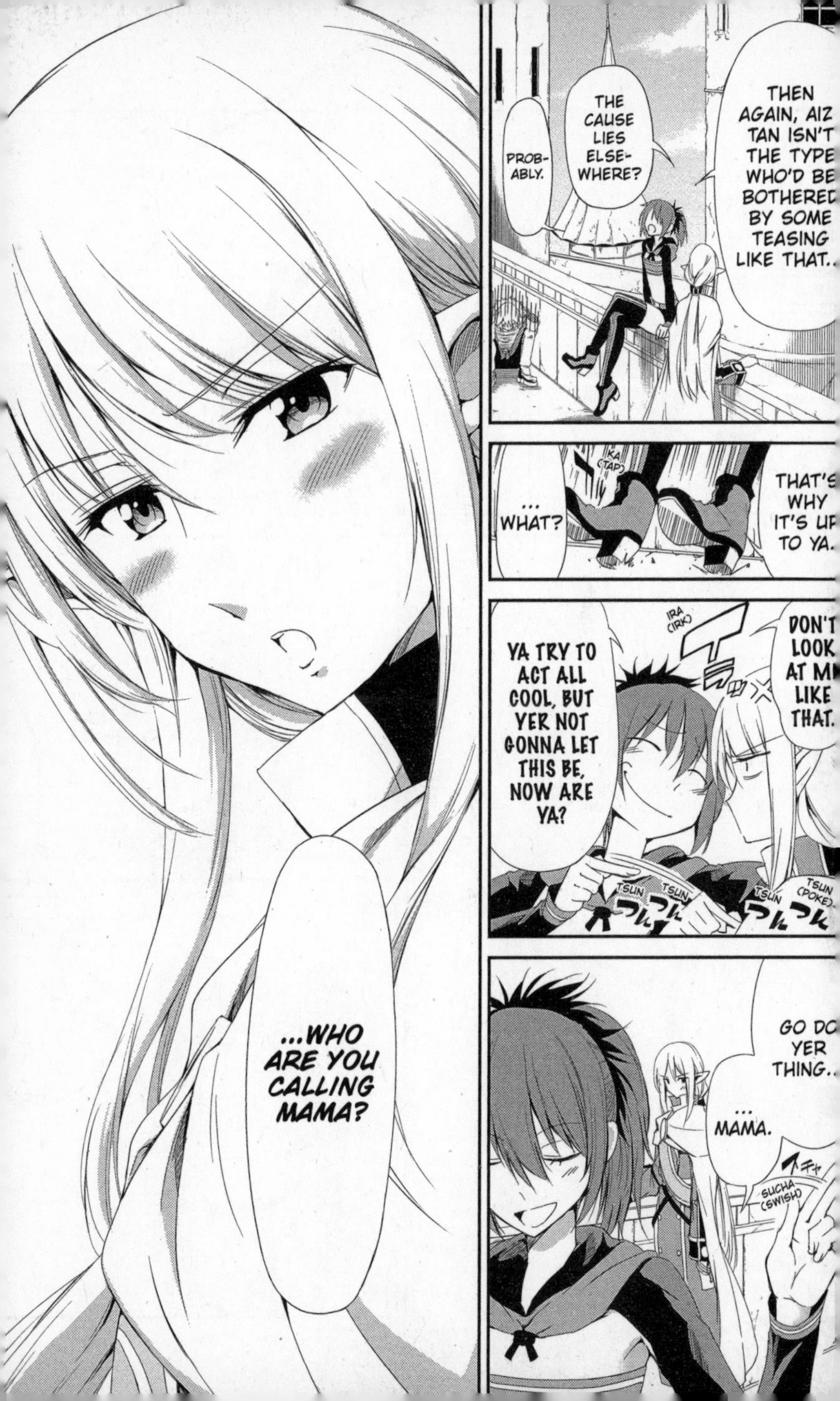
THEN AGAIN, AIZ TAN ISN'T THE TYPE WHO'D BE BOTHERED BY SOME TEASING LIKE THAT...
THE CAUSE LIES ELSE- WHERE?
PROB- ABLY.
THAT'S WHY IT'S UP TO YA.
KA (TAP)
... WHAT?
DON'T LOOK AT M LIKE THAT.
IRA (IRK)
YA TRY TO ACT ALL COOL, BUT YER NOT GONNA LET THIS BE, NOW ARE YA?
TSUN (POKE)
TSUN
TSUN
TSUN
GO DO YER THING...
... MAMA.
SUCHA (SWISH)
...WHO ARE YOU CALLING MAMA?

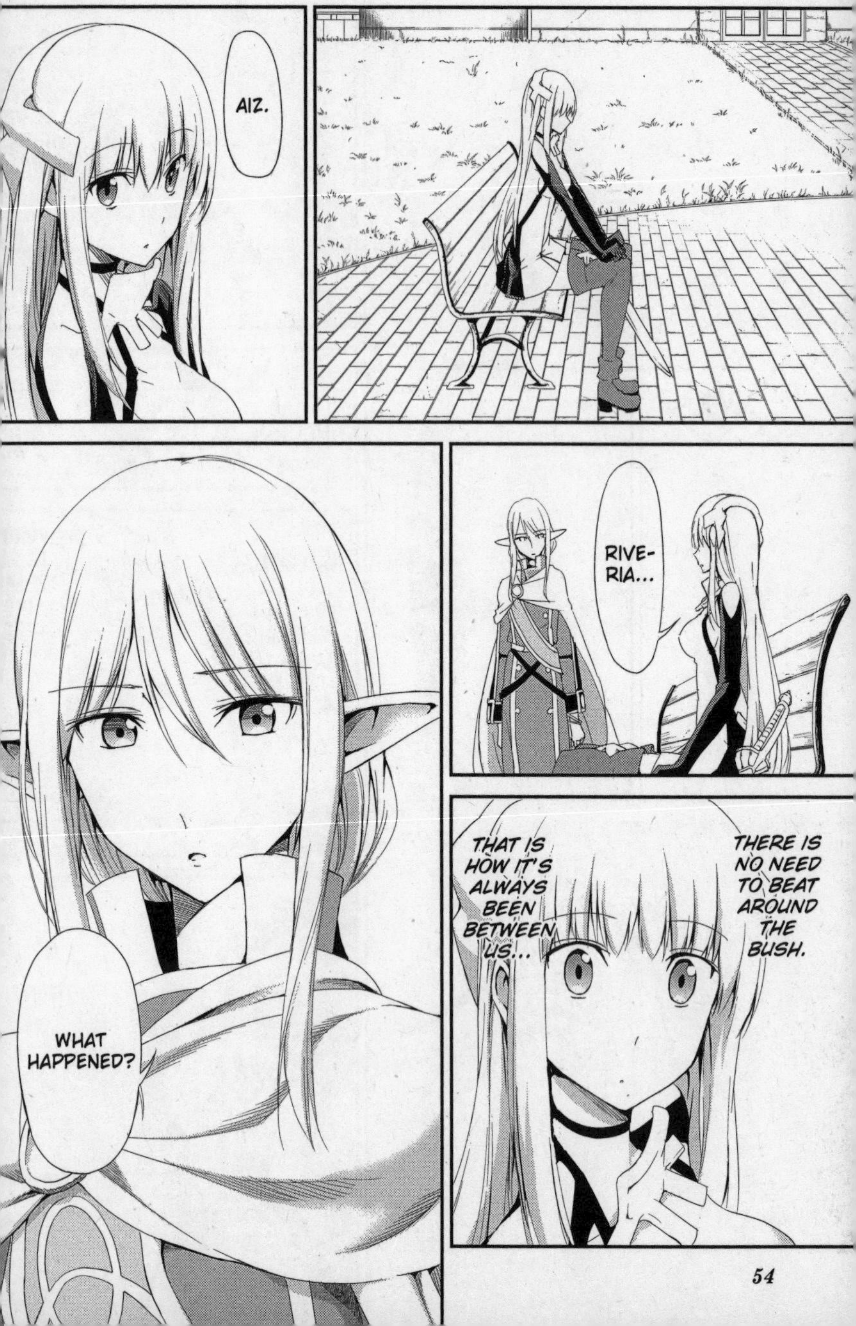
AIZ.
RIVE-RIA...
THERE IS NO NEED TO BEAT AROUND THE BUSH.
THAT IS HOW IT'S ALWAYS BEEN BETWEEN US...
WHAT HAPPENED?

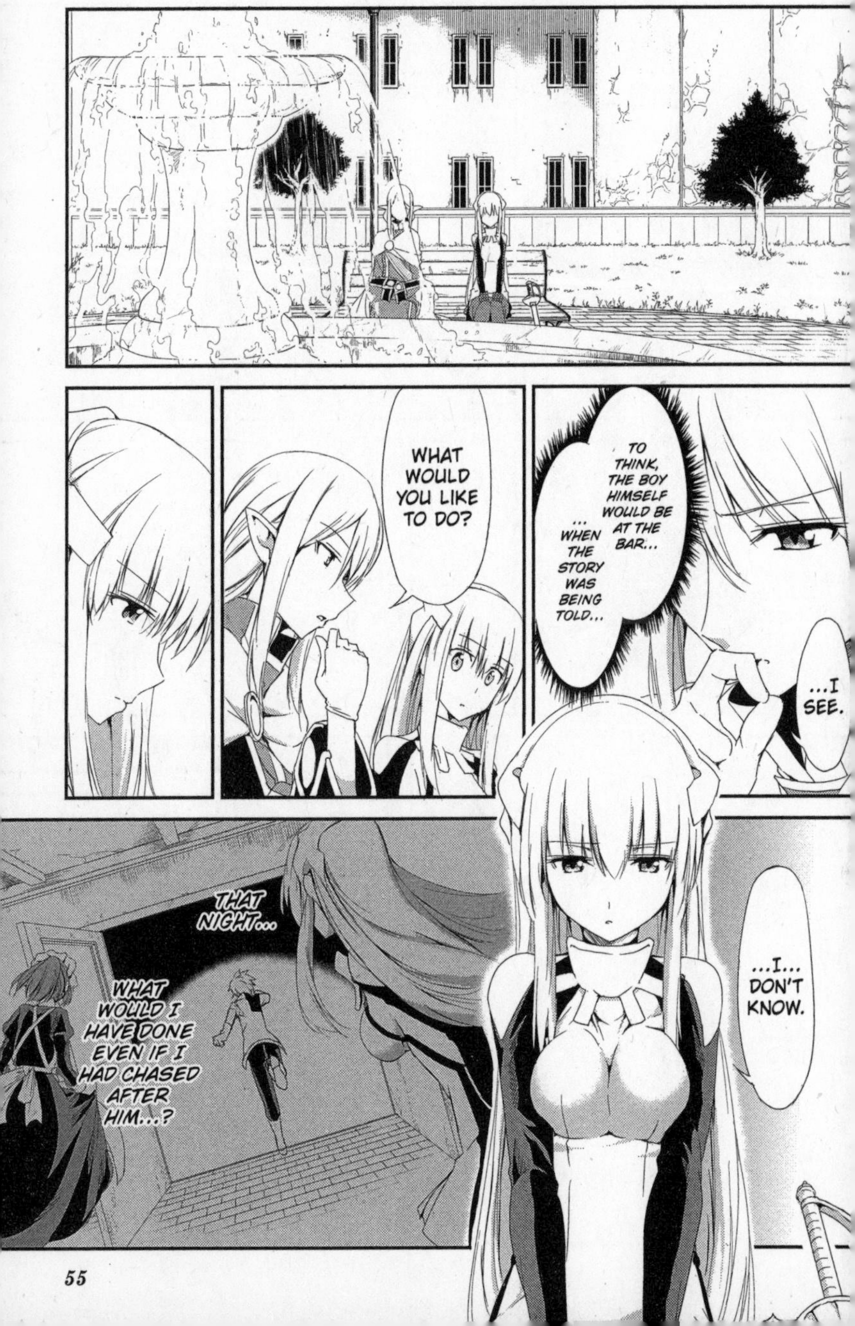
TO THINK, THE BOY HIMSELF WOULD BE AT THE BAR...
...WHEN THE STORY WAS BEING TOLD...
...I SEE.
WHAT WOULD YOU LIKE TO DO?
...I... DON'T KNOW.
THAT NIGHT...
WHAT WOULD I HAVE DONE EVEN IF I HAD CHASED AFTER HIM...?

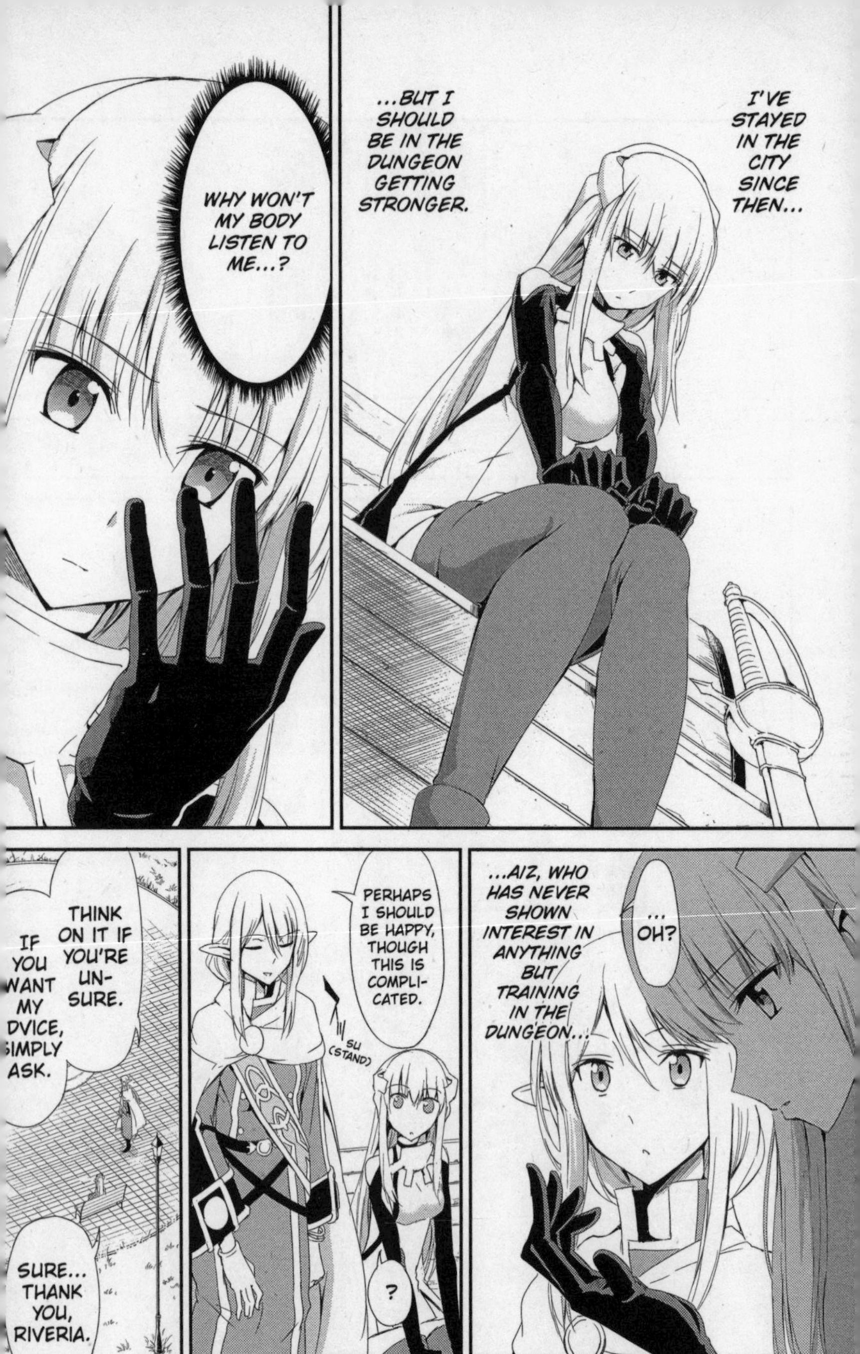
I'VE STAYED IN THE CITY SINCE THEN...
...BUT I SHOULD BE IN THE DUNGEON GETTING STRONGER.
WHY WON'T MY BODY LISTEN TO ME...?
... OH?
...AIZ, WHO HAS NEVER SHOWN INTEREST IN ANYTHING BUT TRAINING IN THE DUNGEON...
PERHAPS I SHOULD BE HAPPY, THOUGH THIS IS COMPLI-CATED.
SU (STAND)
?
THINK ON IT IF YOU'RE UN-SURE.
IF YOU WANT MY DVICE, SIMPLY ASK.
SURE... THANK YOU, RIVERIA.

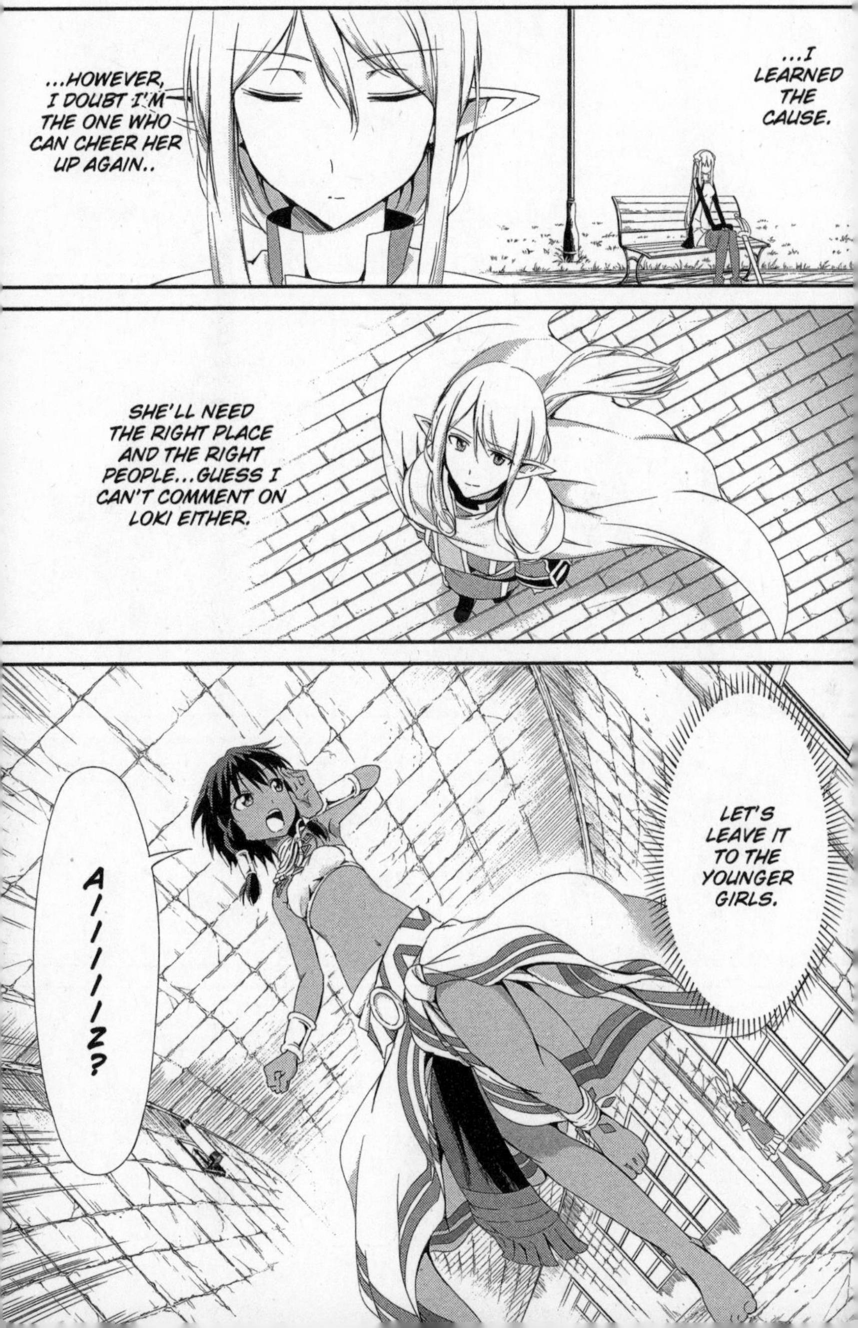
...I LEARNED THE CAUSE.
...HOWEVER, I DOUBT I'M THE ONE WHO CAN CHEER HER UP AGAIN..
SHE'LL NEED THE RIGHT PLACE AND THE RIGHT PEOPLE...GUESS I CAN'T COMMENT ON LOKI EITHER.
LET'S LEAVE IT TO THE YOUNGER GIRLS.
AIIIIIZ?

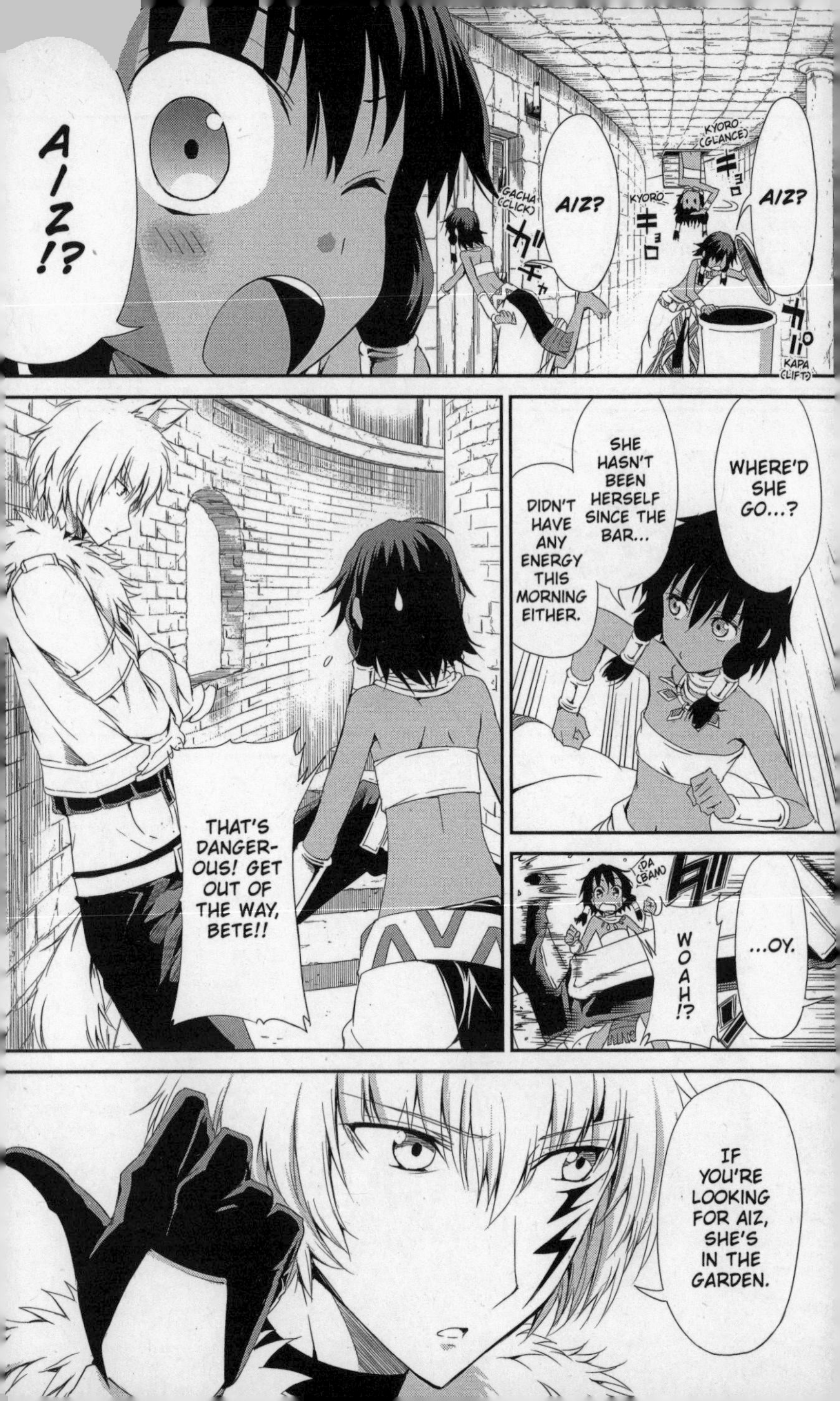

AIZ?
KYORO (GLANCE)
KAPA (LIFT)
KYORO
AIZ?
GACHA (CLICK)
AIZ!?
WHERE'D SHE GO...?
SHE HASN'T BEEN HERSELF SINCE THE BAR...
DIDN'T HAVE ANY ENERGY THIS MORNING EITHER.
...OY.
DA (BAM)
WOAH!?
THAT'S DANGER-OUS! GET OUT OF THE WAY, BETE!!
IF YOU'RE LOOKING FOR AIZ, SHE'S IN THE GARDEN.

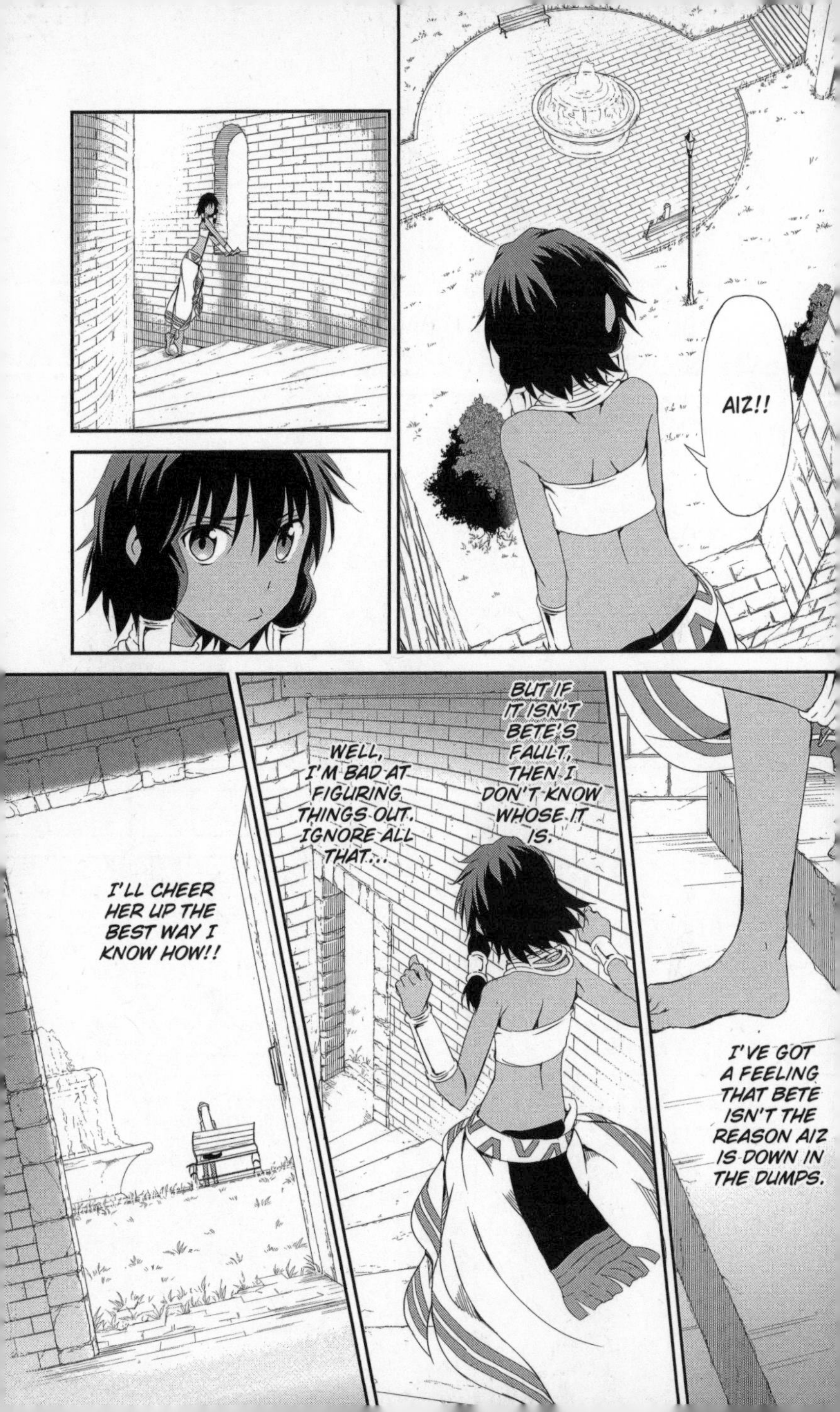
AIZ!!
I'VE GOT A FEELING THAT BETE ISN'T THE REASON AIZ IS DOWN IN THE DUMPS.
BUT IF IT ISN'T BETE'S FAULT, THEN I DON'T KNOW WHOSE IT IS.
WELL, I'M BAD AT FIGURING THINGS OUT. IGNORE ALL THAT...
I'LL CHEER HER UP THE BEST WAY I KNOW HOW!!

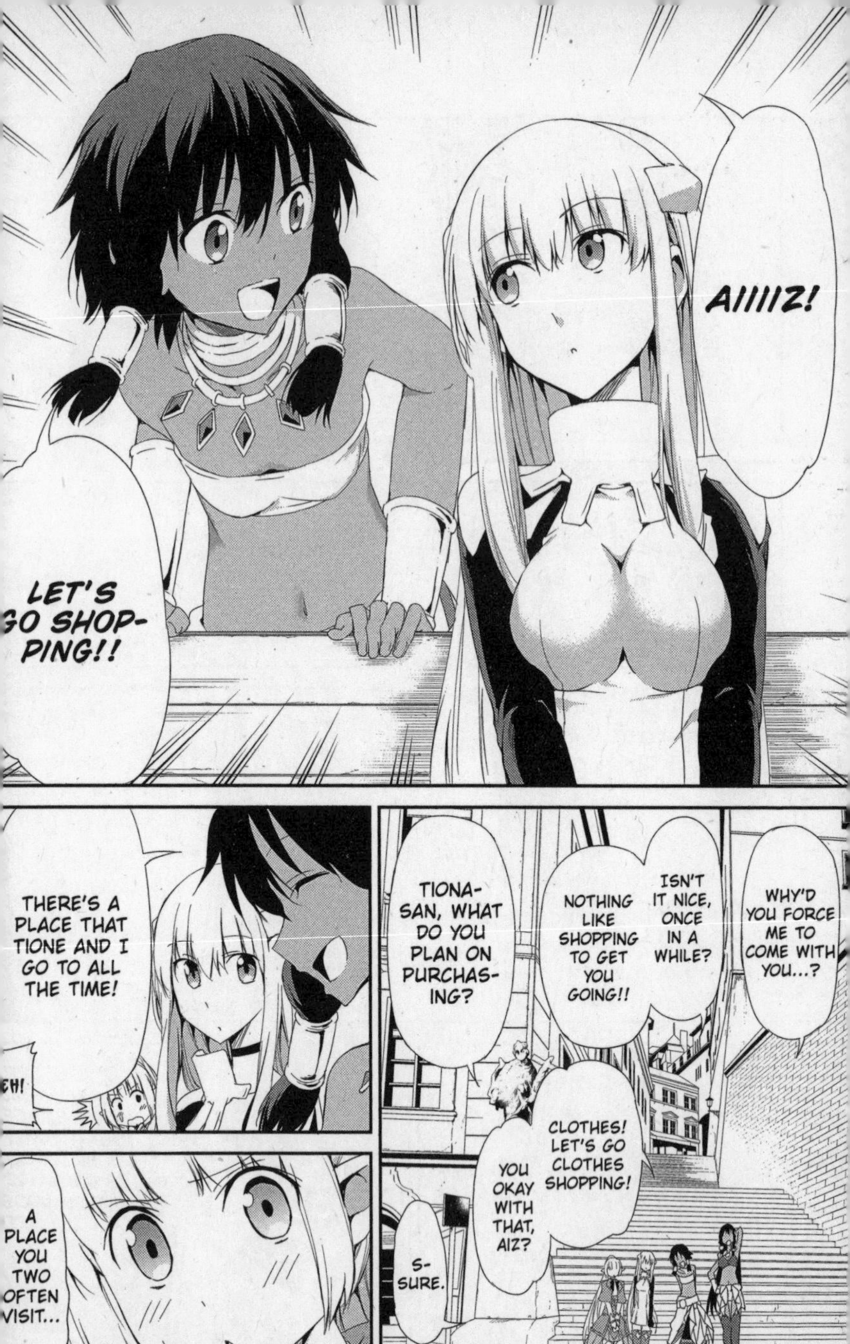
AIIIIZ!
LET'S GO SHOP-PING!!
WHY'D YOU FORCE ME TO COME WITH YOU...?
ISN'T IT NICE, ONCE IN A WHILE?
NOTHING LIKE SHOPPING TO GET YOU GOING!!
TIONA-SAN, WHAT DO YOU PLAN ON PURCHAS-ING?
CLOTHES! LET'S GO CLOTHES SHOPPING!
YOU OKAY WITH THAT, AIZ?
S-SURE.
THERE'S A PLACE THAT TIONE AND I GO TO ALL THE TIME!
EH!
A PLACE YOU TWO OFTEN VISIT...

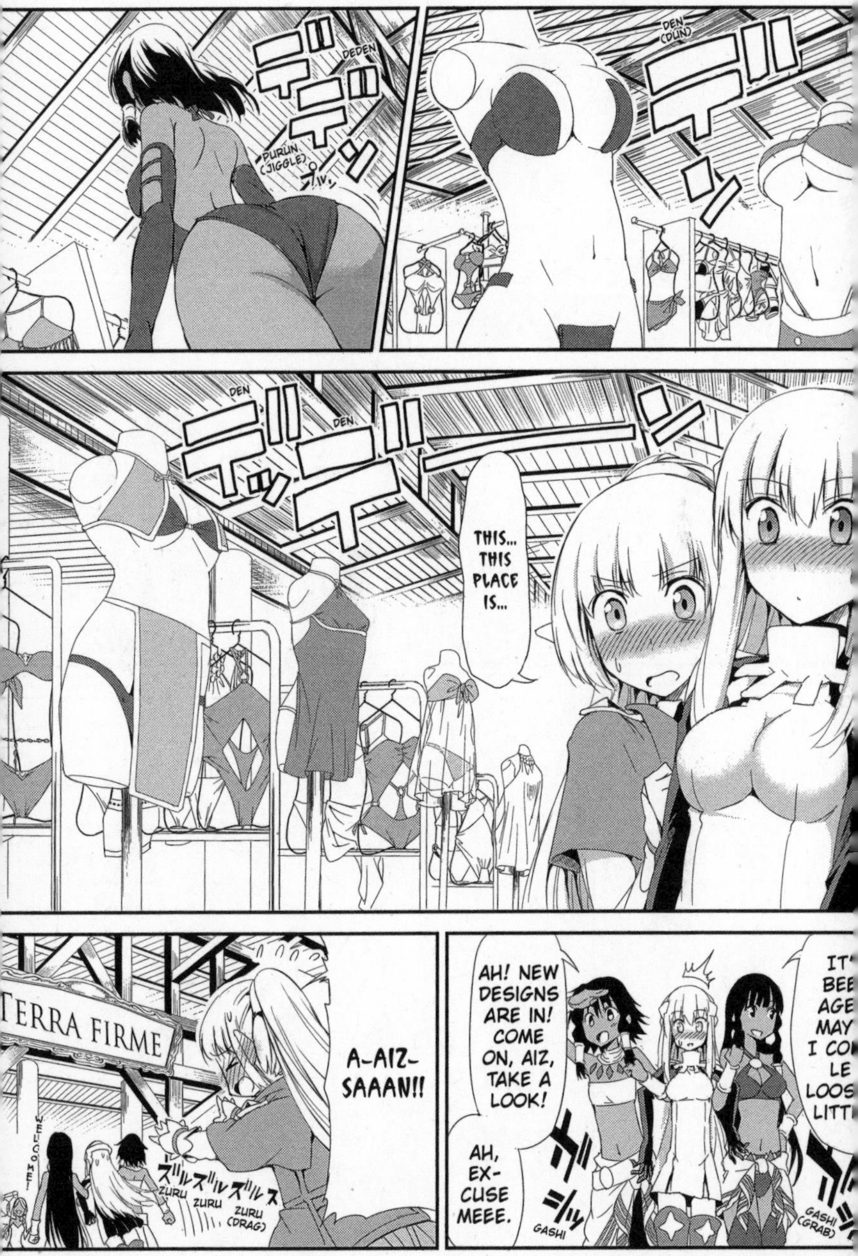
DEN (DUN)
DEDEN
PURUN (JIGGLE)
DEN
DEN
THIS... THIS PLACE IS...
IT' BEE AGE MAY I CO LE LOOS LITT
AH! NEW DESIGNS ARE IN! COME ON, AIZ, TAKE A LOOK!
AH, EX-CUSE MEEE.
GASHI (GRAB)
GASHI
A-AIZ-SAAAN!!
TERRA FIRME
WELCOME!
ZURU ZURU ZURU (DRAG)

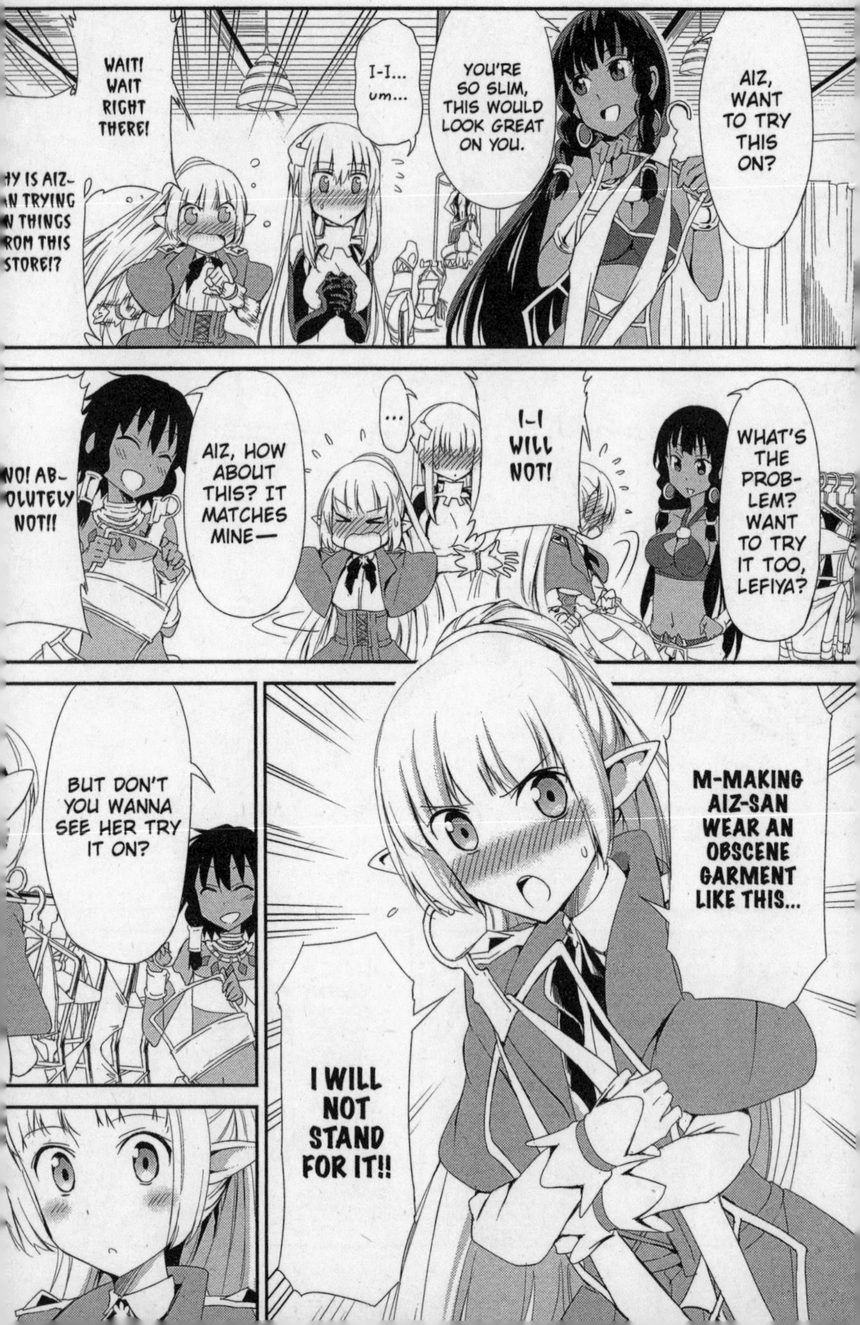
AIZ, WANT TO TRY THIS ON?
YOU'RE SO SLIM, THIS WOULD LOOK GREAT ON YOU.
I-I... um...
WAIT! WAIT RIGHT THERE!
HY IS AIZ-AN TRYING N THINGS ROM THIS STORE!?
WHAT'S THE PROB-LEM? WANT TO TRY IT TOO, LEFIYA?
I-I WILL NOT!
...
AIZ, HOW ABOUT THIS? IT MATCHES MINE—
NO! AB-OLUTELY NOT!!
M-MAKING AIZ-SAN WEAR AN OBSCENE GARMENT LIKE THIS...
I WILL NOT STAND FOR IT!!
BUT DON'T YOU WANNA SEE HER TRY IT ON?

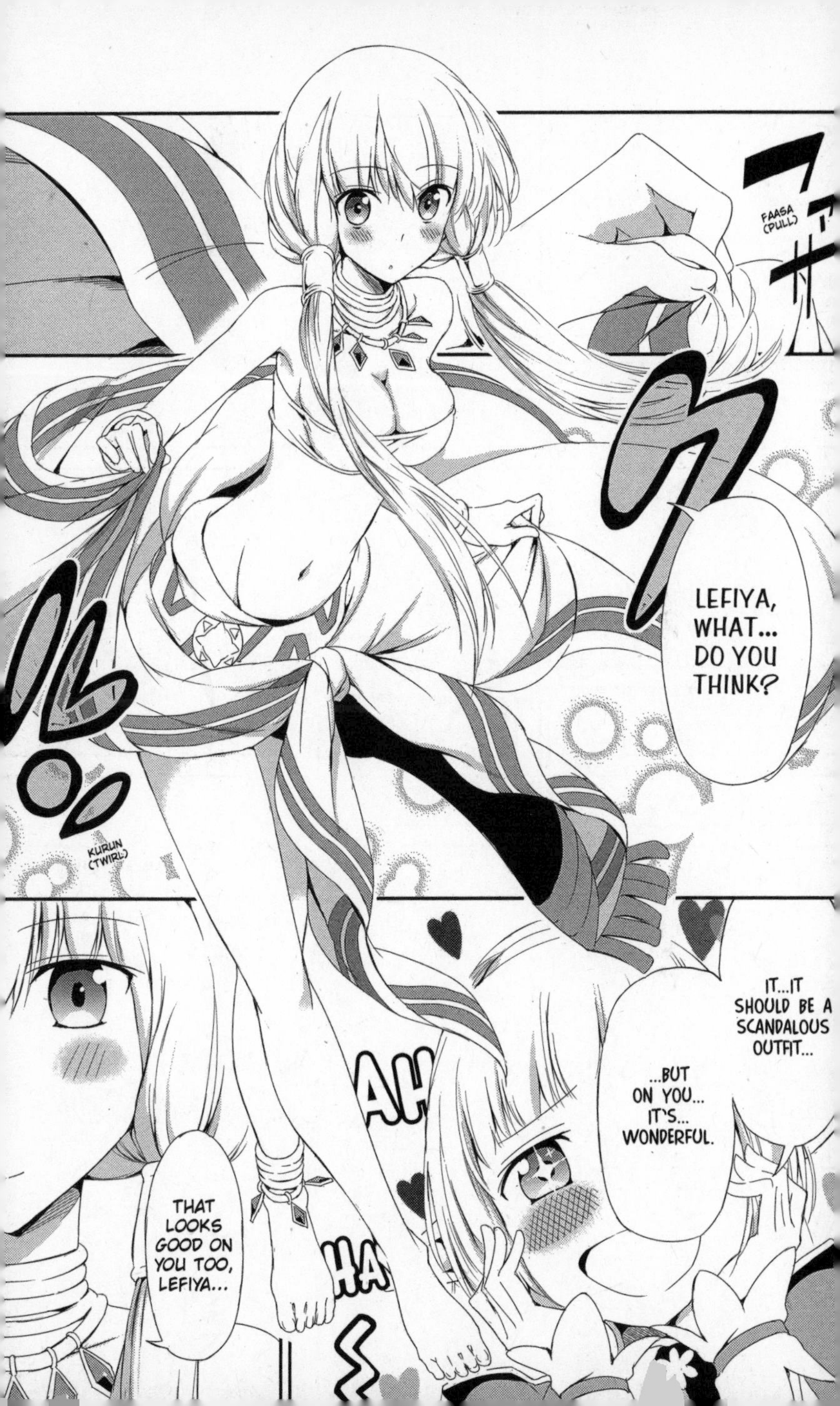
FAASA (PULL)
LEFIYA, WHAT... DO YOU THINK?
KURUN (TWIRL)
IT...IT SHOULD BE A SCANDALOUS OUTFIT...
...BUT ON YOU... IT'S... WONDERFUL.
AH
HA
THAT LOOKS GOOD ON YOU TOO, LEFIYA...

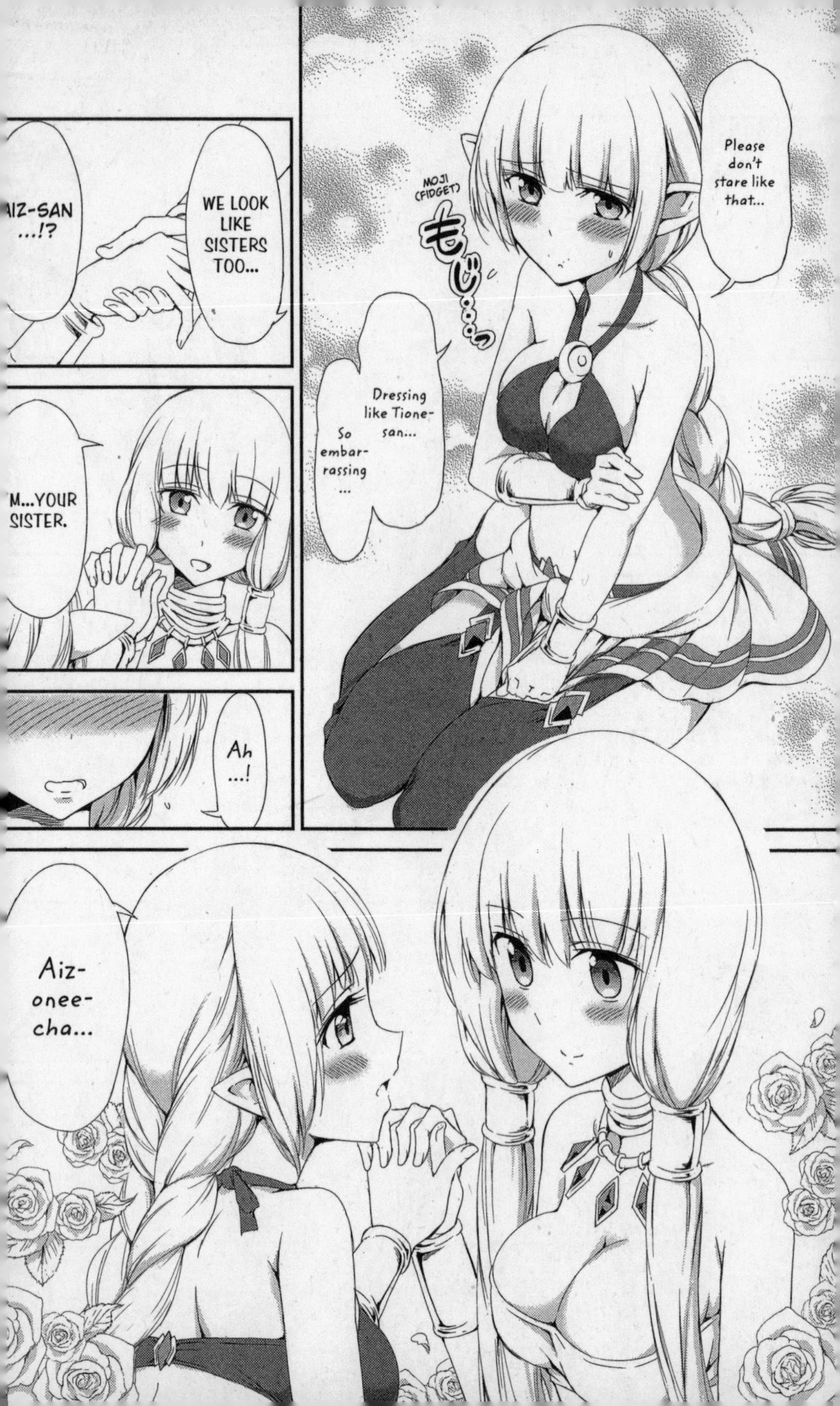
Please don't stare like that...
MOJI (FIDGET)
もじ…
Dressing like Tione-san... So embarrassing...
WE LOOK LIKE SISTERS TOO...
AIZ-SAN ...!?
'M...YOUR SISTER.
Ah ...!
Aiz-onee-cha...

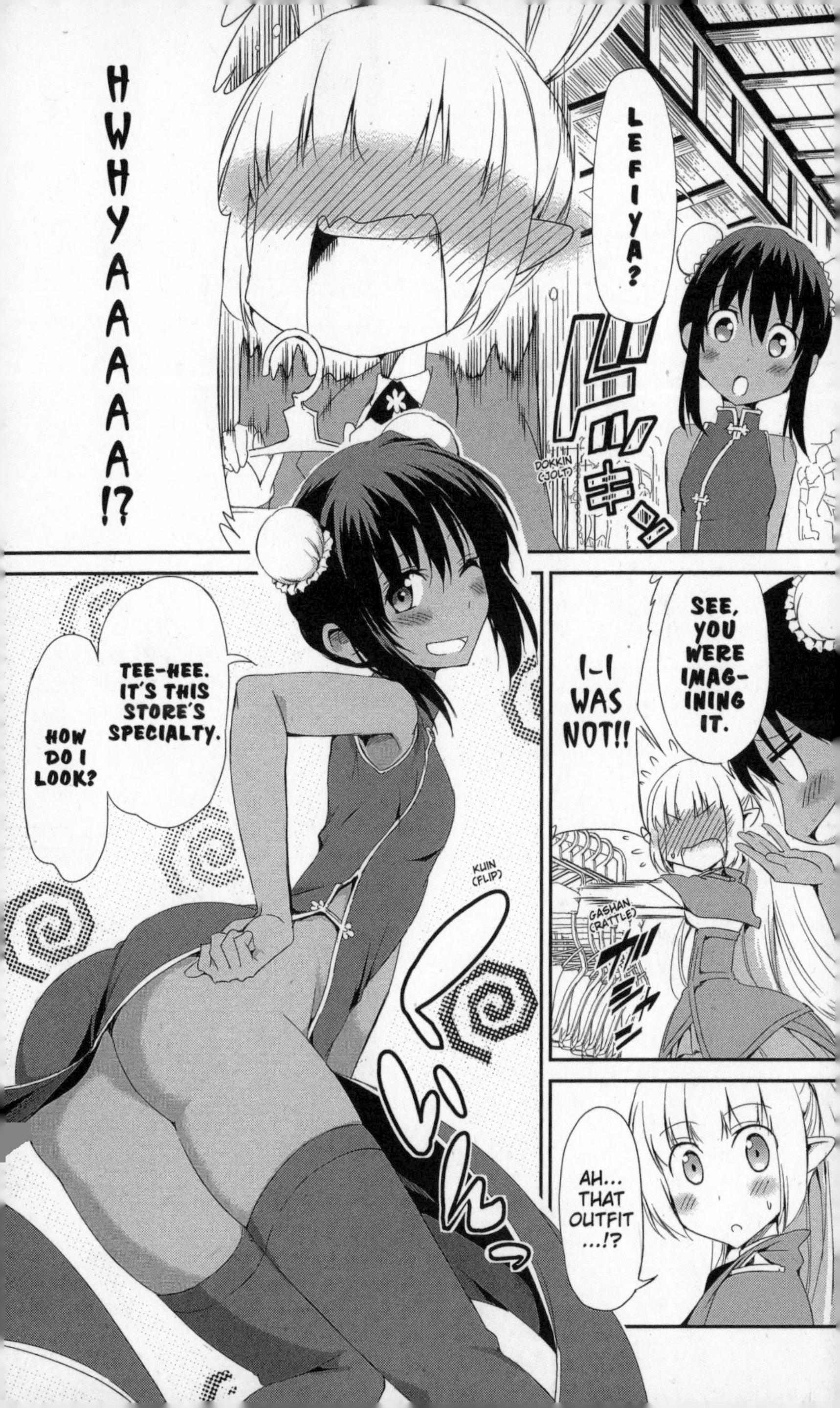
LEFIYA?
DOKKIN (JOLT)
HWHYAAAAAAA!?
SEE, YOU WERE IMAGINING IT.
I-I WAS NOT!!
GASHAN (RATTLE)
AH... THAT OUTFIT ...!?
TEE-HEE. IT'S THIS STORE'S SPECIALTY.
HOW DO I LOOK?
KUIN (FLIP)

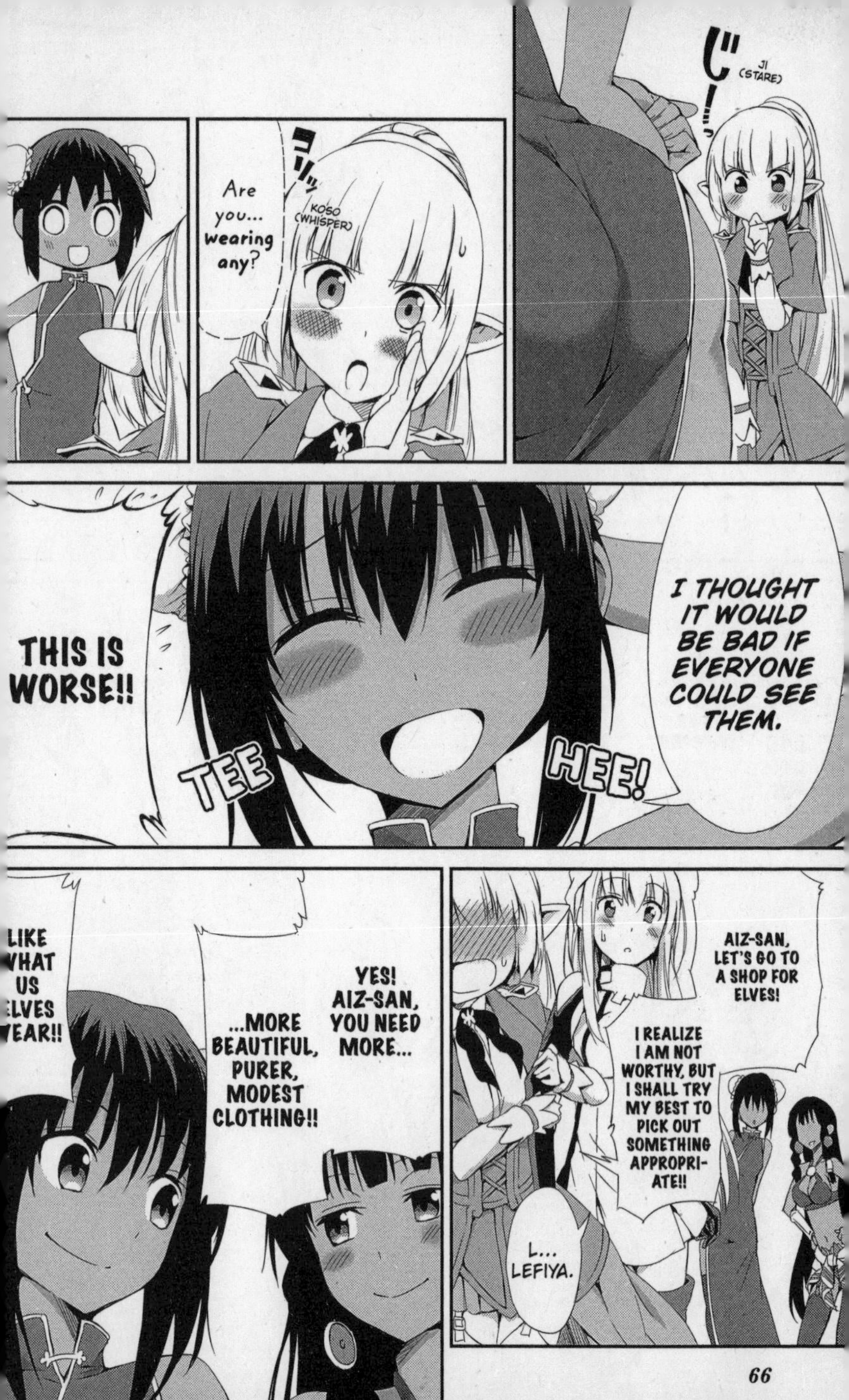
JI (STARE)
KOSO (WHISPER)
Are you... wearing any?
I THOUGHT IT WOULD BE BAD IF EVERYONE COULD SEE THEM.
TEE HEE!
THIS IS WORSE!!
AIZ-SAN, LET'S GO TO A SHOP FOR ELVES!
I REALIZE I AM NOT WORTHY, BUT I SHALL TRY MY BEST TO PICK OUT SOMETHING APPROPRI-ATE!!
L... LEFIYA.
YES! AIZ-SAN, YOU NEED MORE...
...MORE BEAUTIFUL, PURER, MODEST CLOTHING!!
LIKE VHAT US LVES VEAR!!

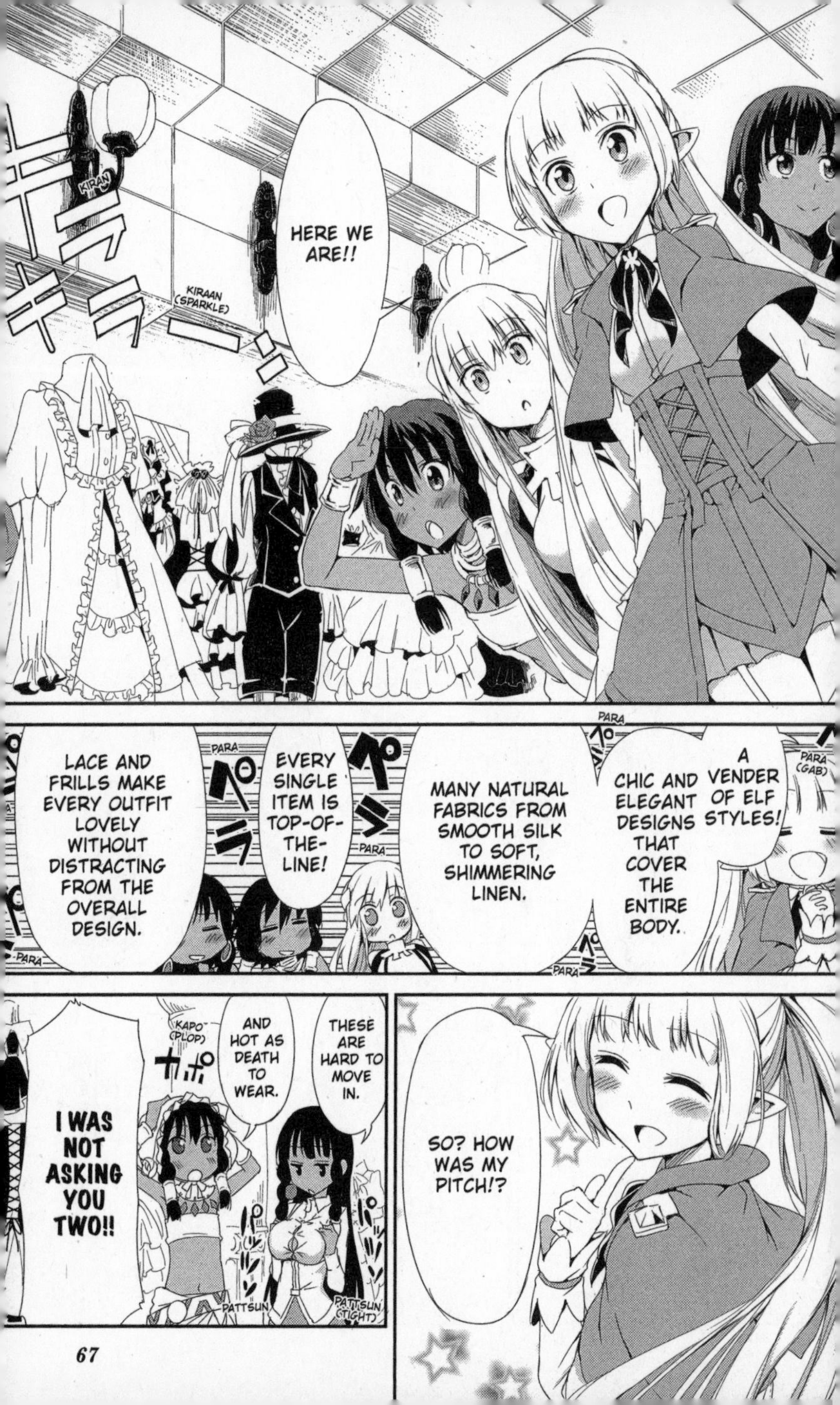
HERE WE ARE!!
KIRAN
KIRAAN (SPARKLE)
PARA (GAB)
A VENDER OF ELF STYLES!
CHIC AND ELEGANT DESIGNS THAT COVER THE ENTIRE BODY.
PARA
PARA
MANY NATURAL FABRICS FROM SMOOTH SILK TO SOFT, SHIMMERING LINEN.
PARA
EVERY SINGLE ITEM IS TOP-OF-THE-LINE!
PARA
LACE AND FRILLS MAKE EVERY OUTFIT LOVELY WITHOUT DISTRACTING FROM THE OVERALL DESIGN.
PARA
SO? HOW WAS MY PITCH!?
THESE ARE HARD TO MOVE IN.
AND HOT AS DEATH TO WEAR.
KAPO (PLOP)
PATTSUN (TIGHT)
PATTSUN
I WAS NOT ASKING YOU TWO!!

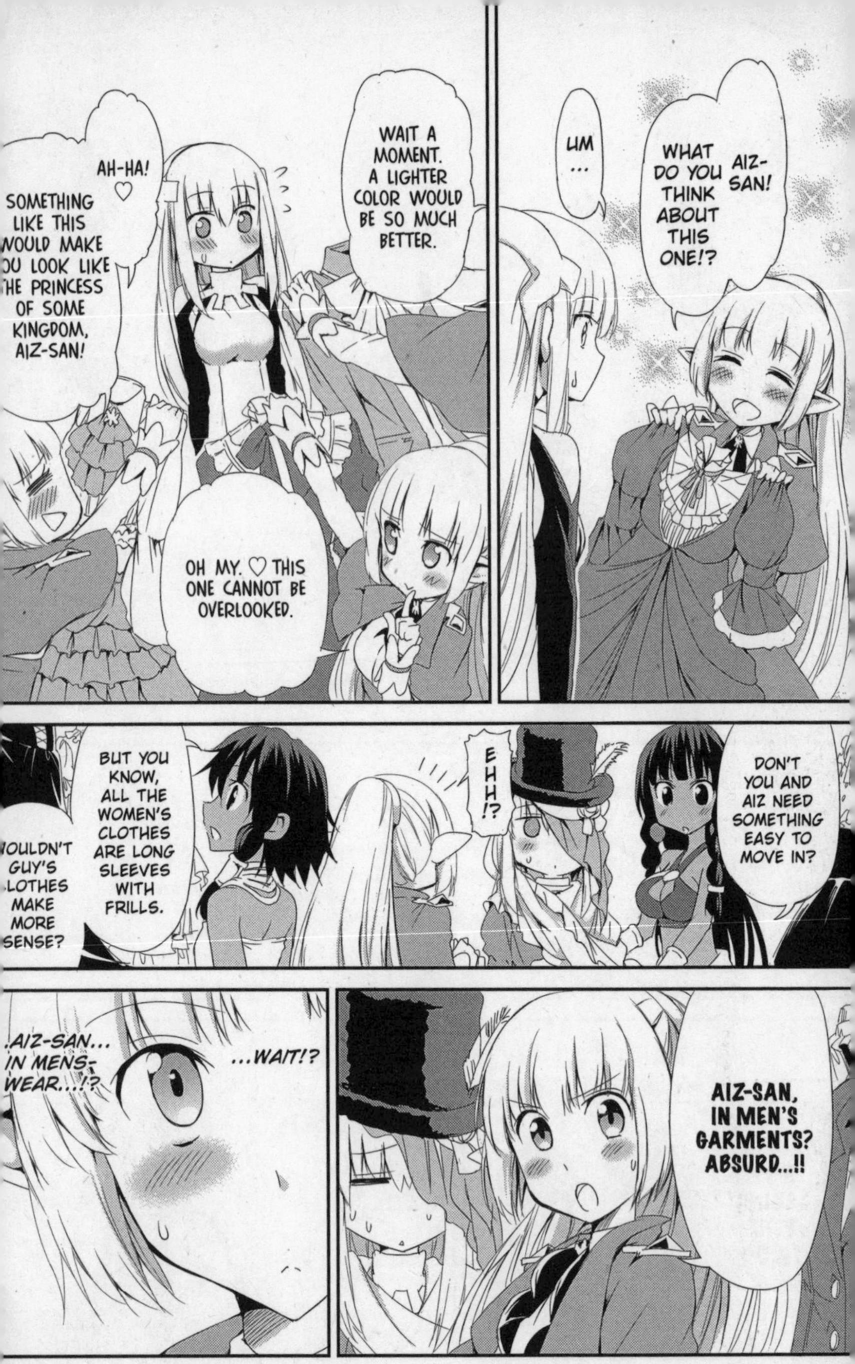
AIZ-SAN! WHAT DO YOU THINK ABOUT THIS ONE!?
UM ...
WAIT A MOMENT. A LIGHTER COLOR WOULD BE SO MUCH BETTER.
AH-HA! ♡
SOMETHING LIKE THIS OULD MAKE OU LOOK LIKE HE PRINCESS OF SOME KINGDOM, AIZ-SAN!
OH MY. ♡ THIS ONE CANNOT BE OVERLOOKED.
DON'T YOU AND AIZ NEED SOMETHING EASY TO MOVE IN?
EHH!?
BUT YOU KNOW, ALL THE WOMEN'S CLOTHES ARE LONG SLEEVES WITH FRILLS.
OULDN'T GUY'S LOTHES MAKE MORE SENSE?
AIZ-SAN, IN MEN'S GARMENTS? ABSURD...!!
...WAIT!?
.AIZ-SAN... IN MENS-WEAR...!?

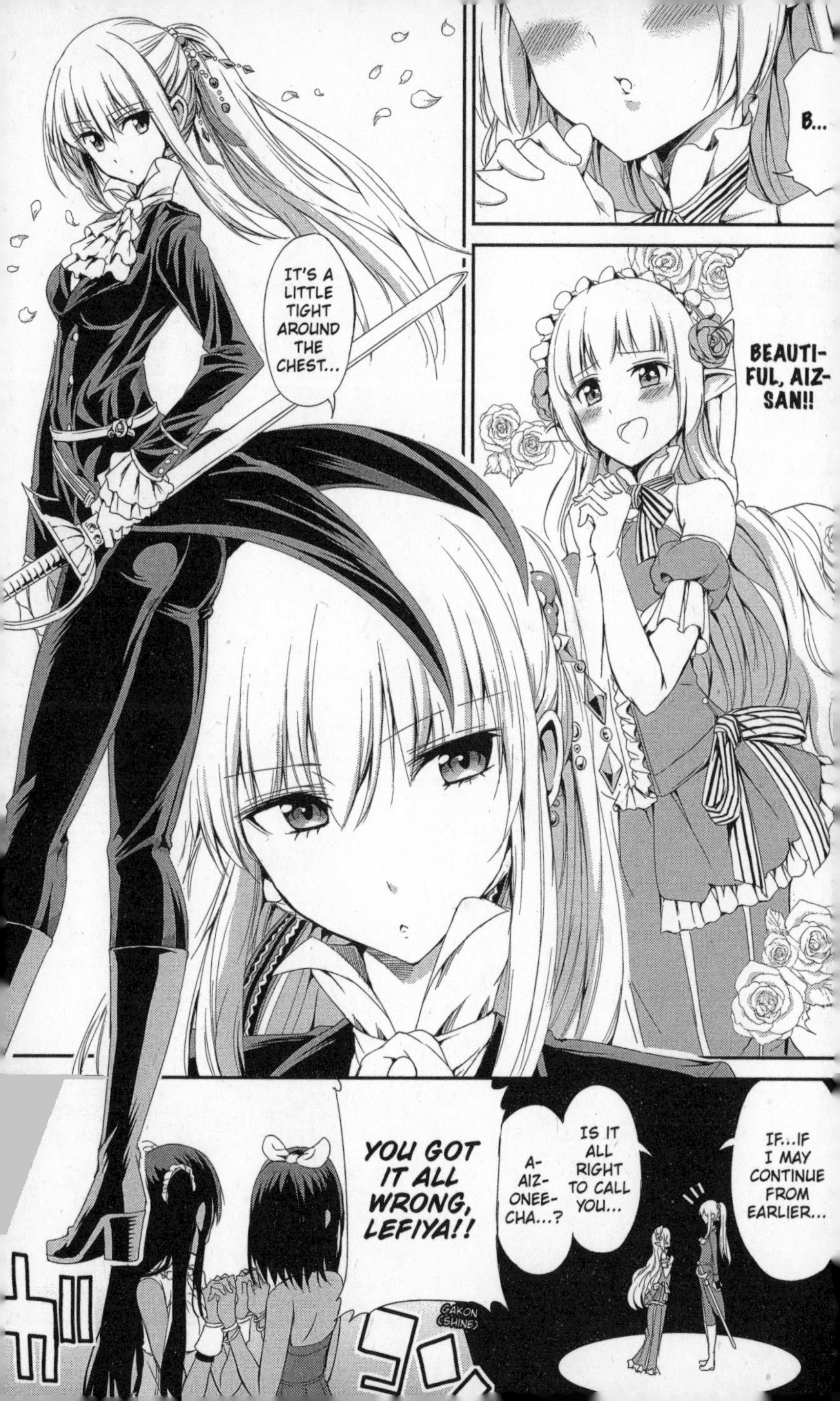
B...
BEAUTI-FUL, AIZ-SAN!!
IT'S A LITTLE TIGHT AROUND THE CHEST...
IF...IF I MAY CONTINUE FROM EARLIER...
IS IT ALL RIGHT TO CALL YOU...
A-AIZ-ONEE-CHA...?
YOU GOT IT ALL WRONG, LEFIYA!!
GAKON (SHINE)

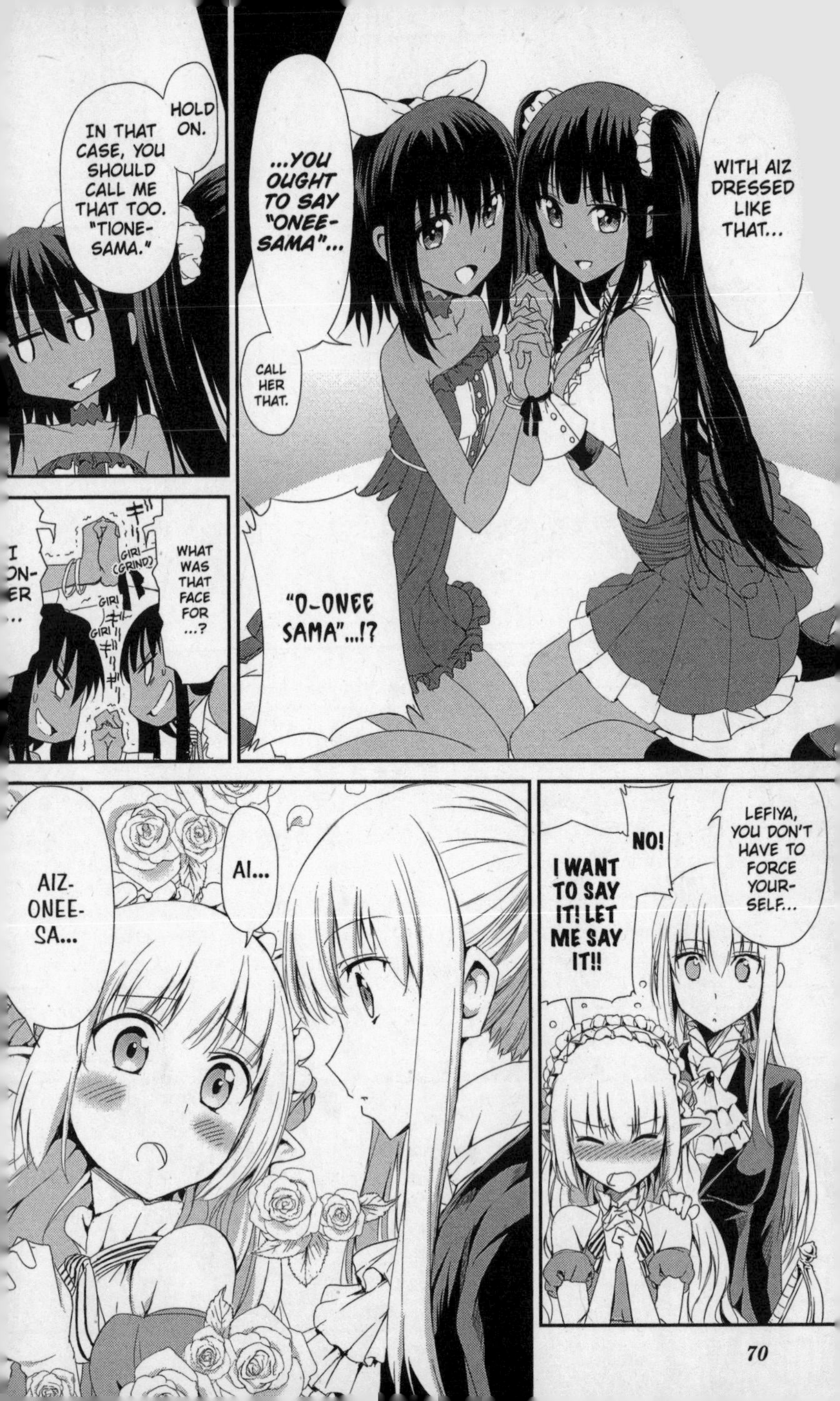

WITH AIZ DRESSED LIKE THAT...
...YOU OUGHT TO SAY "ONEE-SAMA"...
CALL HER THAT.
"O-ONEE SAMA"...!?
HOLD ON.
IN THAT CASE, YOU SHOULD CALL ME THAT TOO. "TIONE-SAMA."
WHAT WAS THAT FACE FOR ...?
GIRI (GRIND)
GIRI
GIRI
LEFIYA, YOU DON'T HAVE TO FORCE YOUR-SELF...
NO!
I WANT TO SAY IT! LET ME SAY IT!!
AI...
AIZ-ONEE-SA...

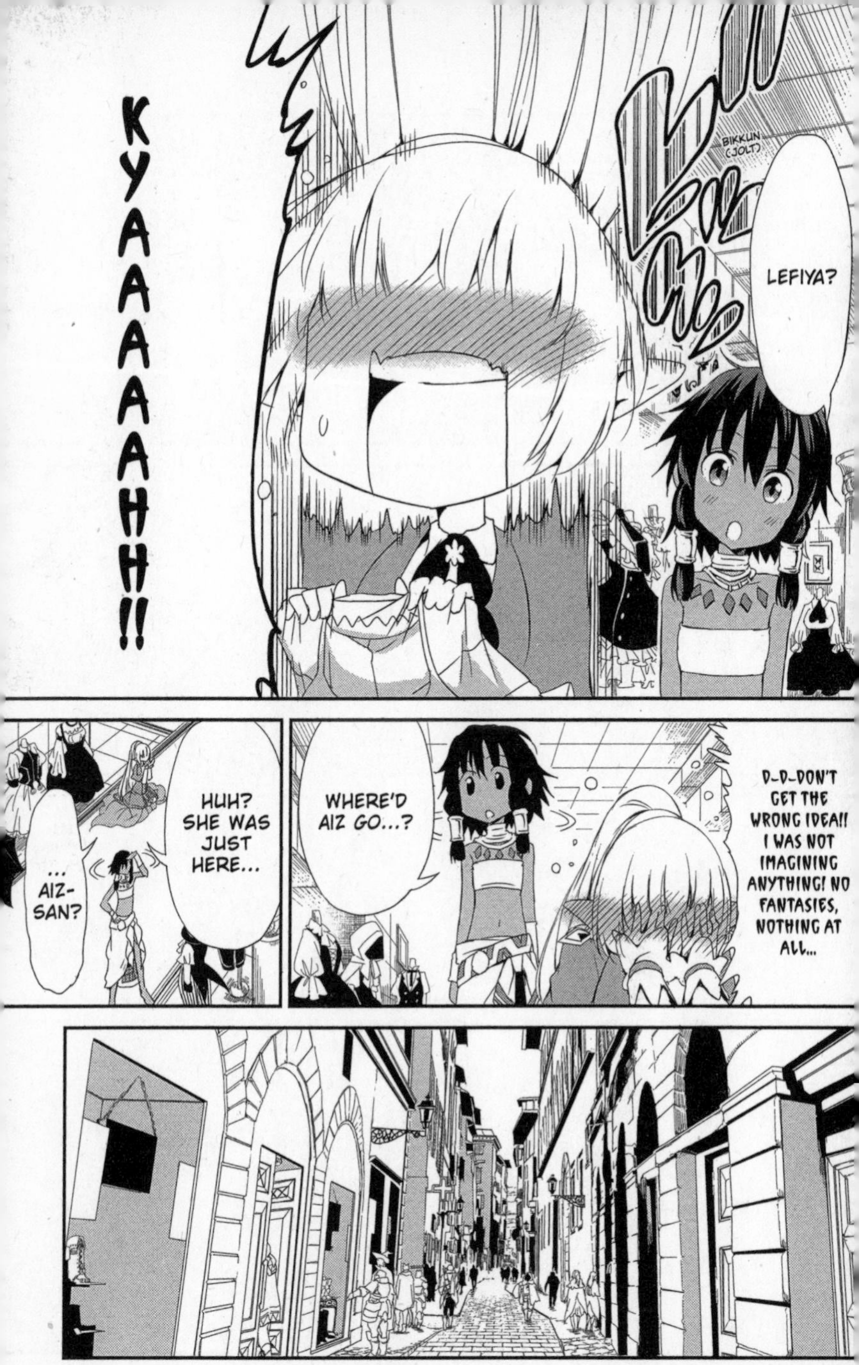
BIKKUN (JOLT)
LEFIYA?
KYAAAAAHH!!
D-D-DON'T GET THE WRONG IDEA!! I WAS NOT IMAGINING ANYTHING! NO FANTASIES, NOTHING AT ALL...
WHERE'D AIZ GO...?
HUH? SHE WAS JUST HERE...
... AIZ-SAN?

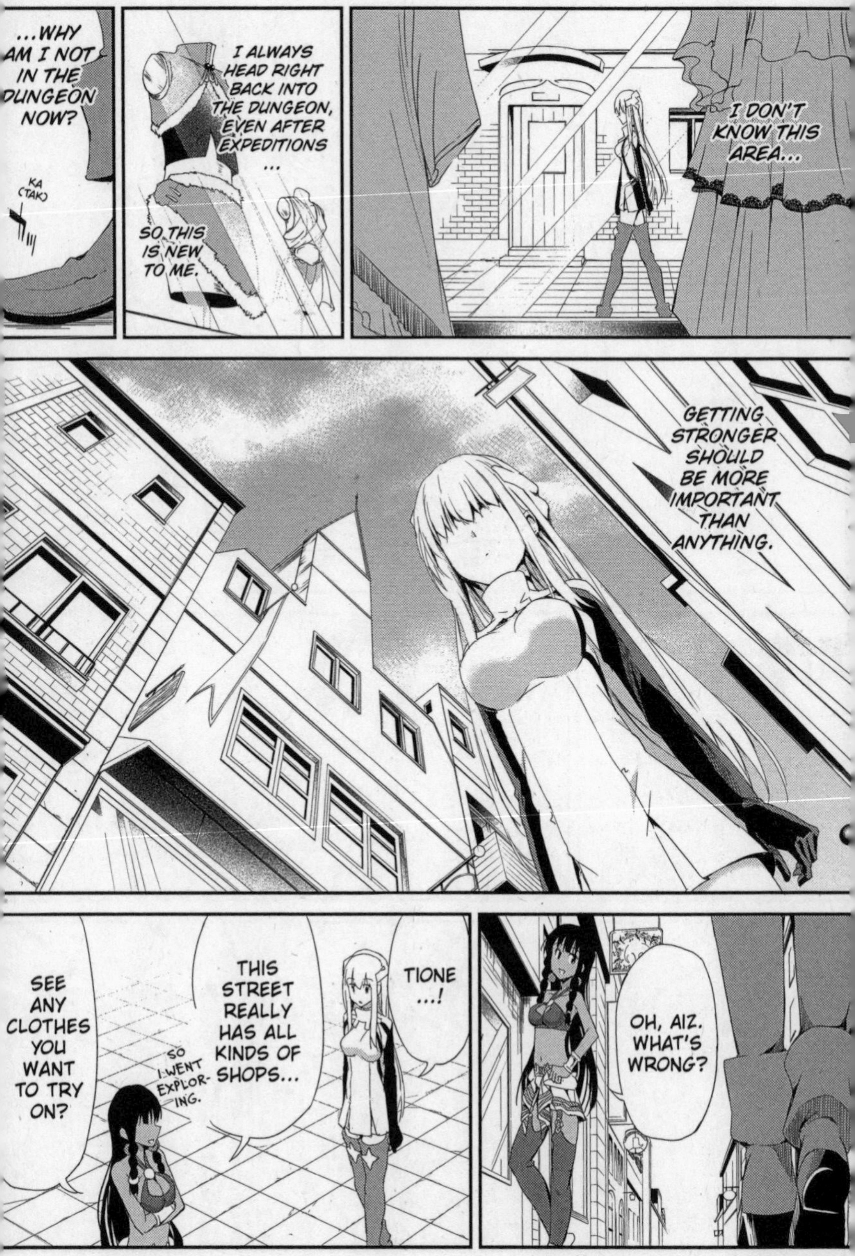
I DON'T KNOW THIS AREA...
I ALWAYS HEAD RIGHT BACK INTO THE DUNGEON, EVEN AFTER EXPEDITIONS...
SO THIS IS NEW TO ME.
...WHY AM I NOT IN THE DUNGEON NOW?
KA (TAK)
GETTING STRONGER SHOULD BE MORE IMPORTANT THAN ANYTHING.
OH, AIZ. WHAT'S WRONG?
TIONE ...!
THIS STREET REALLY HAS ALL KINDS OF SHOPS...
SO I WENT EXPLOR-ING.
SEE ANY CLOTHES YOU WANT TO TRY ON?

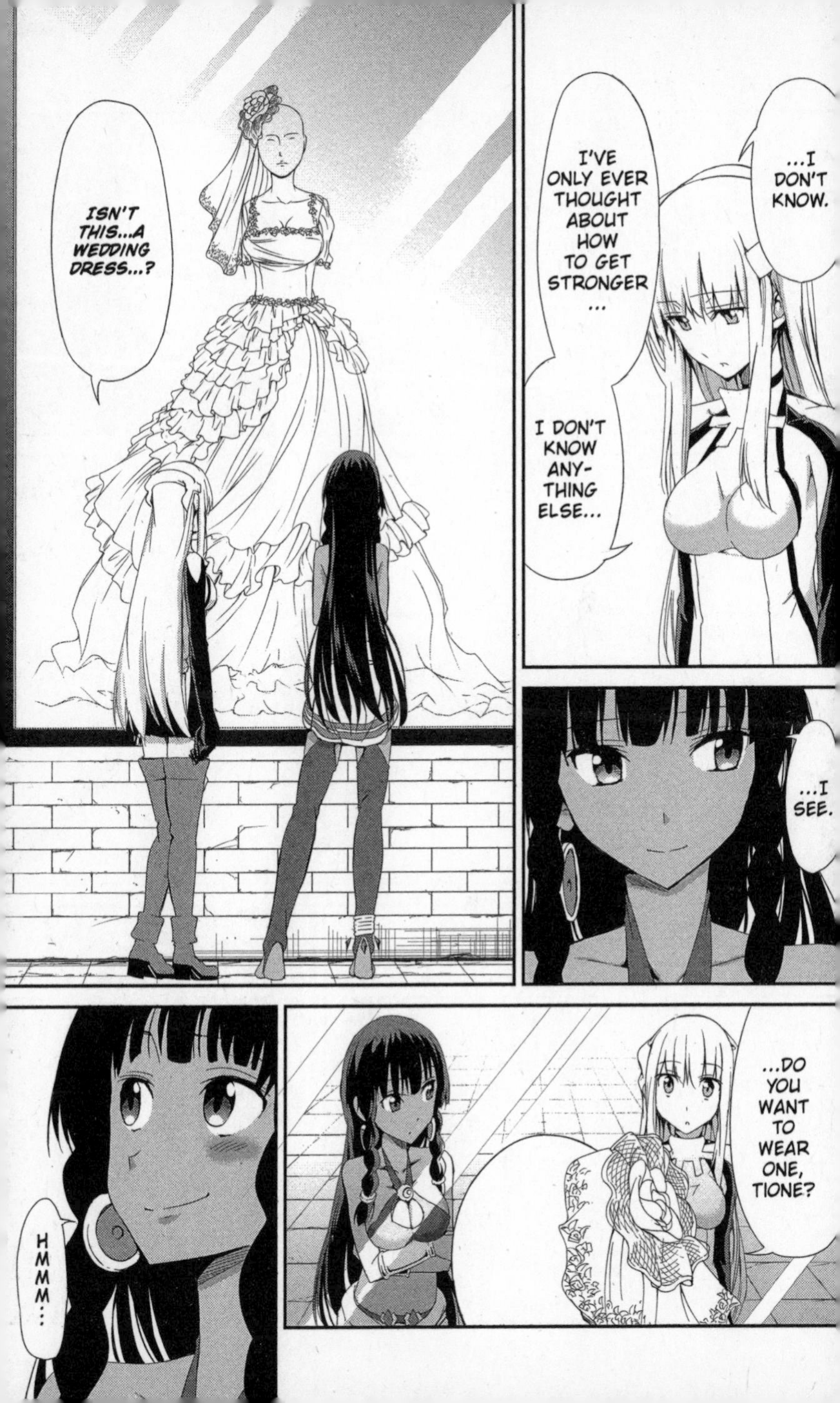
...I DON'T KNOW.
I'VE ONLY EVER THOUGHT ABOUT HOW TO GET STRONGER...
I DON'T KNOW ANY-THING ELSE...
...I SEE.
ISN'T THIS...A WEDDING DRESS...?
...DO YOU WANT TO WEAR ONE, TIONE?
HMMM...

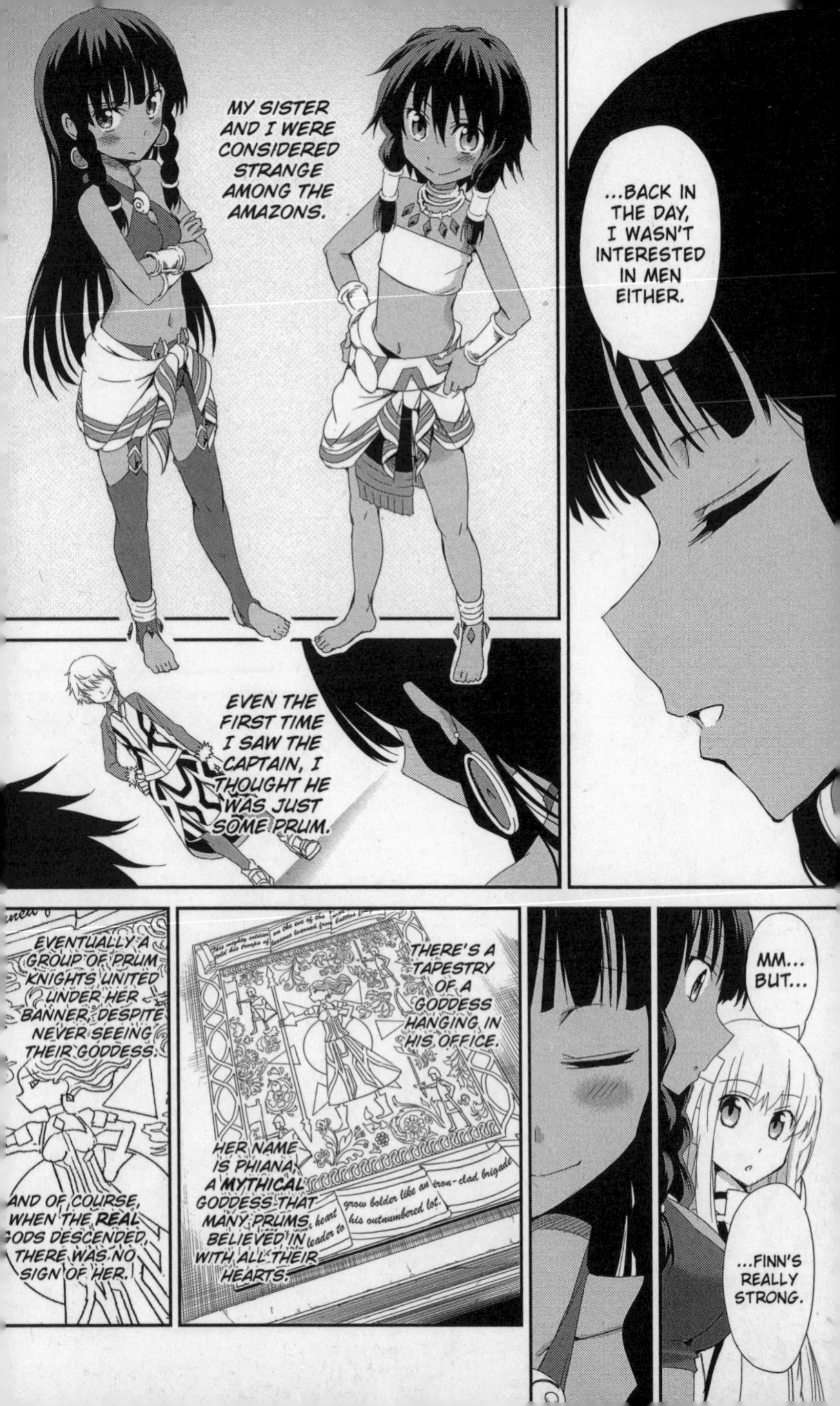
...BACK IN THE DAY, I WASN'T INTERESTED IN MEN EITHER.
MY SISTER AND I WERE CONSIDERED STRANGE AMONG THE AMAZONS.
EVEN THE FIRST TIME I SAW THE CAPTAIN, I THOUGHT HE WAS JUST SOME PRUM.
MM... BUT...
...FINN'S REALLY STRONG.
THERE'S A TAPESTRY OF A GODDESS HANGING IN HIS OFFICE.
grow bolder like an iron-clad brigade
his outnumbered lot.
HER NAME IS PHIANA, A **MYTHICAL** GODDESS THAT MANY PRUMS BELIEVED IN WITH ALL THEIR HEARTS.
EVENTUALLY A GROUP OF PRUM KNIGHTS UNITED UNDER HER BANNER DESPITE NEVER SEEING THEIR GODDESS.
AND OF COURSE, WHEN THE **REAL** GODS DESCENDED, THERE WAS NO SIGN OF HER.

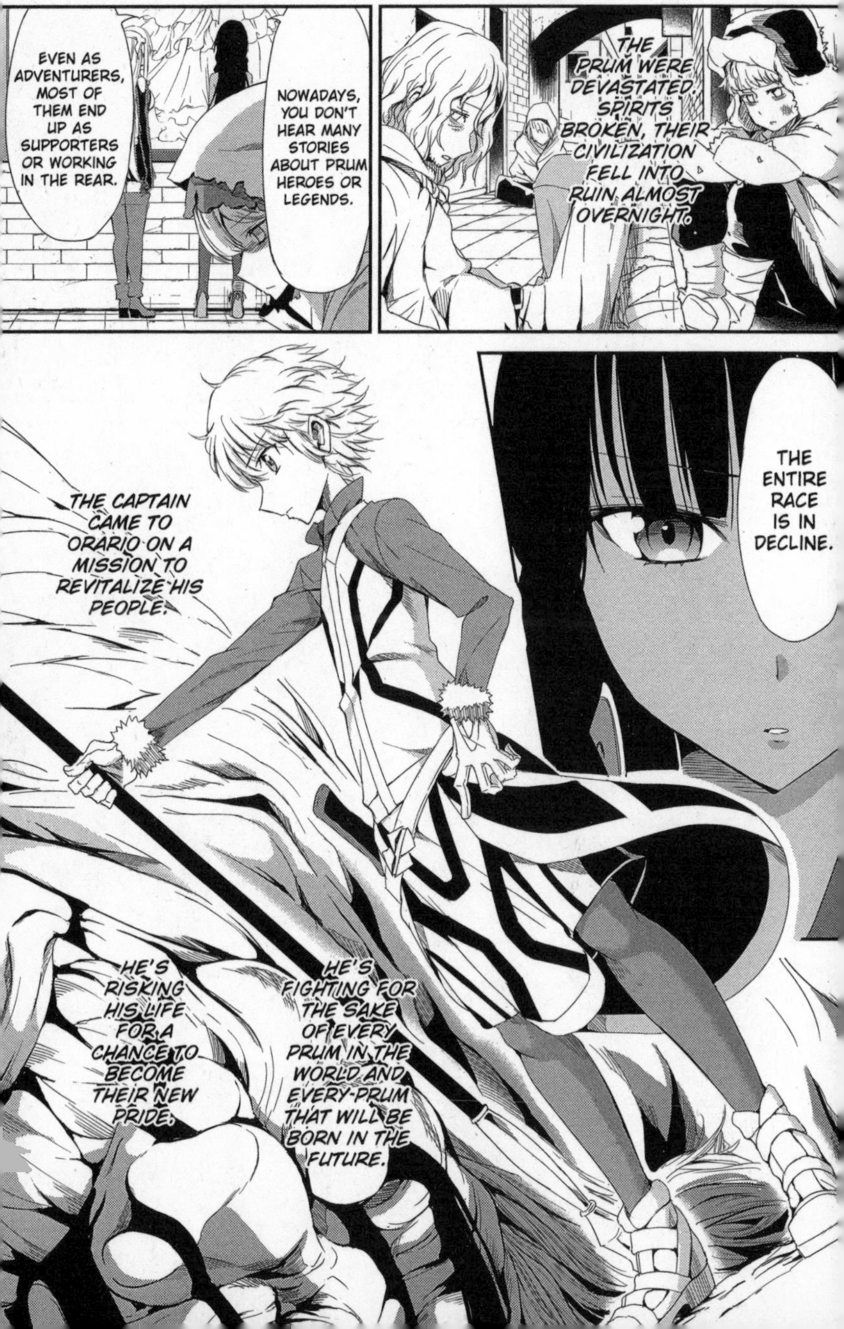
THE PRUM WERE DEVASTATED. SPIRITS BROKEN, THEIR CIVILIZATION FELL INTO RUIN ALMOST OVERNIGHT.
NOWADAYS, YOU DON'T HEAR MANY STORIES ABOUT PRUM HEROES OR LEGENDS.
EVEN AS ADVENTURERS, MOST OF THEM END UP AS SUPPORTERS OR WORKING IN THE REAR.
THE ENTIRE RACE IS IN DECLINE.
THE CAPTAIN CAME TO ORARIO ON A MISSION TO REVITALIZE HIS PEOPLE.
HE'S FIGHTING FOR THE SAKE OF EVERY PRUM IN THE WORLD AND EVERY PRUM THAT WILL BE BORN IN THE FUTURE.
HE'S RISKING HIS LIFE FOR A CHANCE TO BECOME THEIR NEW PRIDE.

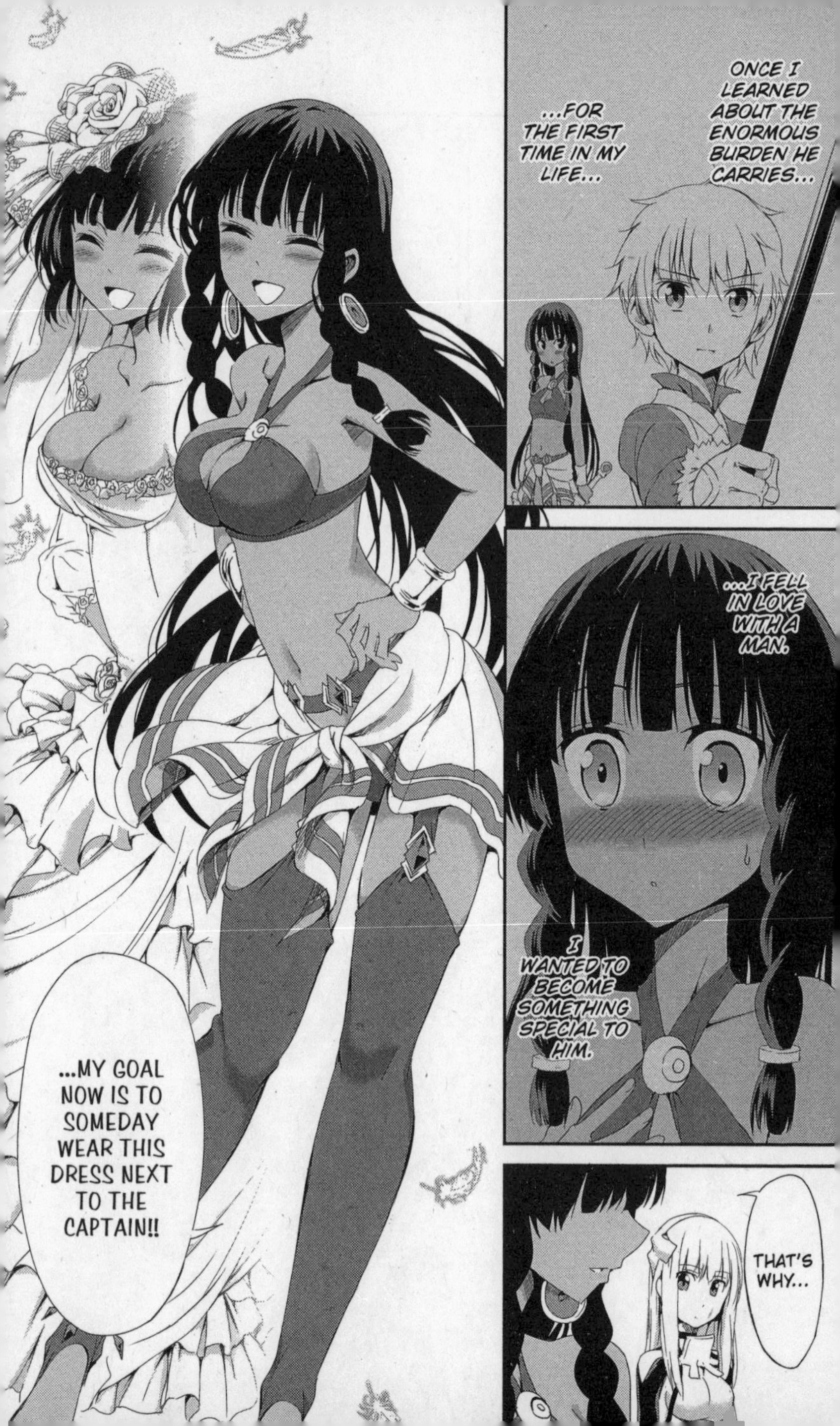
ONCE I LEARNED ABOUT THE ENORMOUS BURDEN HE CARRIES...
...FOR THE FIRST TIME IN MY LIFE...
...I FELL IN LOVE WITH A MAN.
I WANTED TO BECOME SOMETHING SPECIAL TO HIM.
THAT'S WHY...
...MY GOAL NOW IS TO SOMEDAY WEAR THIS DRESS NEXT TO THE CAPTAIN!!

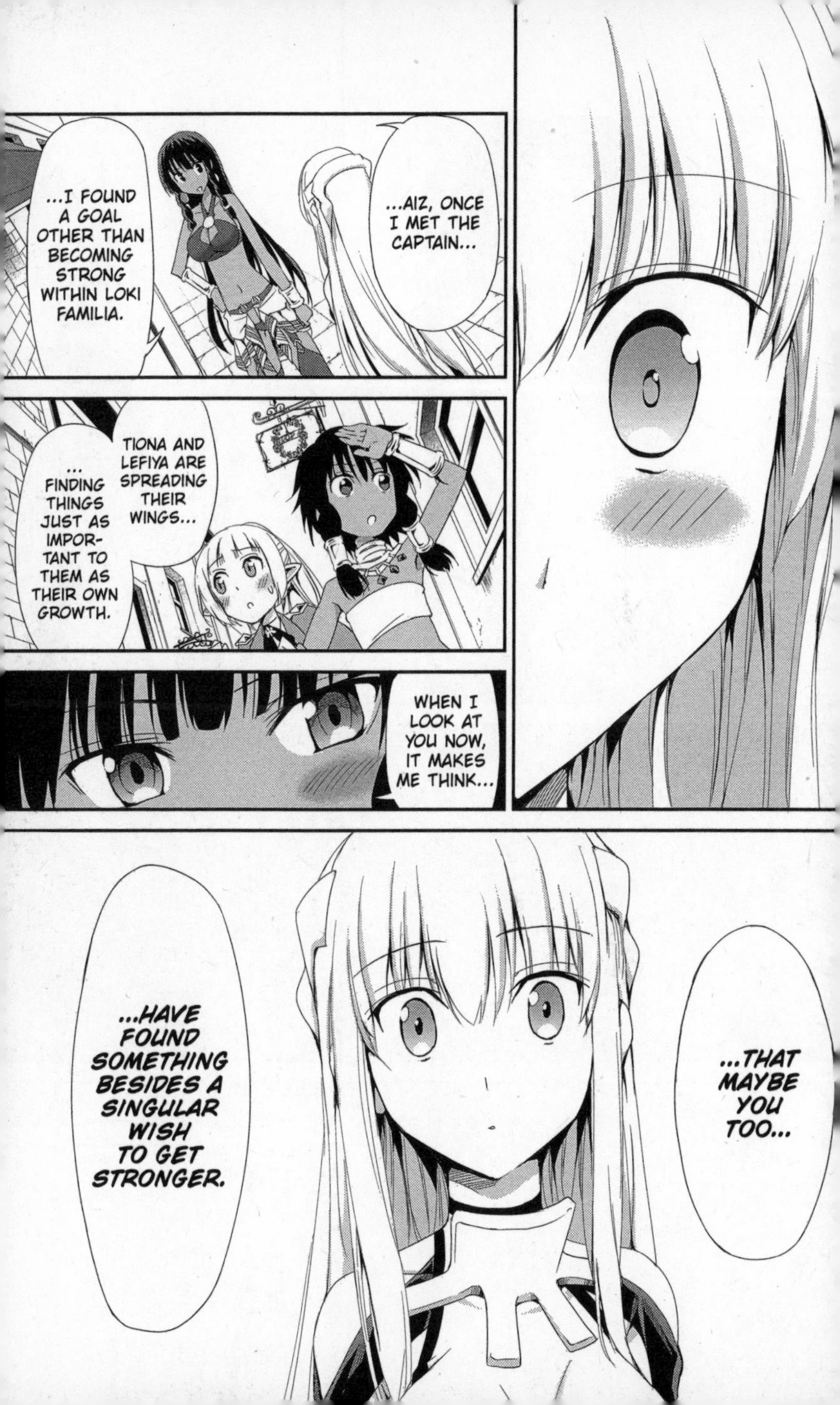
...AIZ, ONCE I MET THE CAPTAIN...
...I FOUND A GOAL OTHER THAN BECOMING STRONG WITHIN LOKI FAMILIA.
TIONA AND LEFIYA ARE SPREADING THEIR WINGS...
...FINDING THINGS JUST AS IMPOR-TANT TO THEM AS THEIR OWN GROWTH.
WHEN I LOOK AT YOU NOW, IT MAKES ME THINK...
...THAT MAYBE YOU TOO...
...HAVE FOUND SOMETHING BESIDES A SINGULAR WISH TO GET STRONGER.

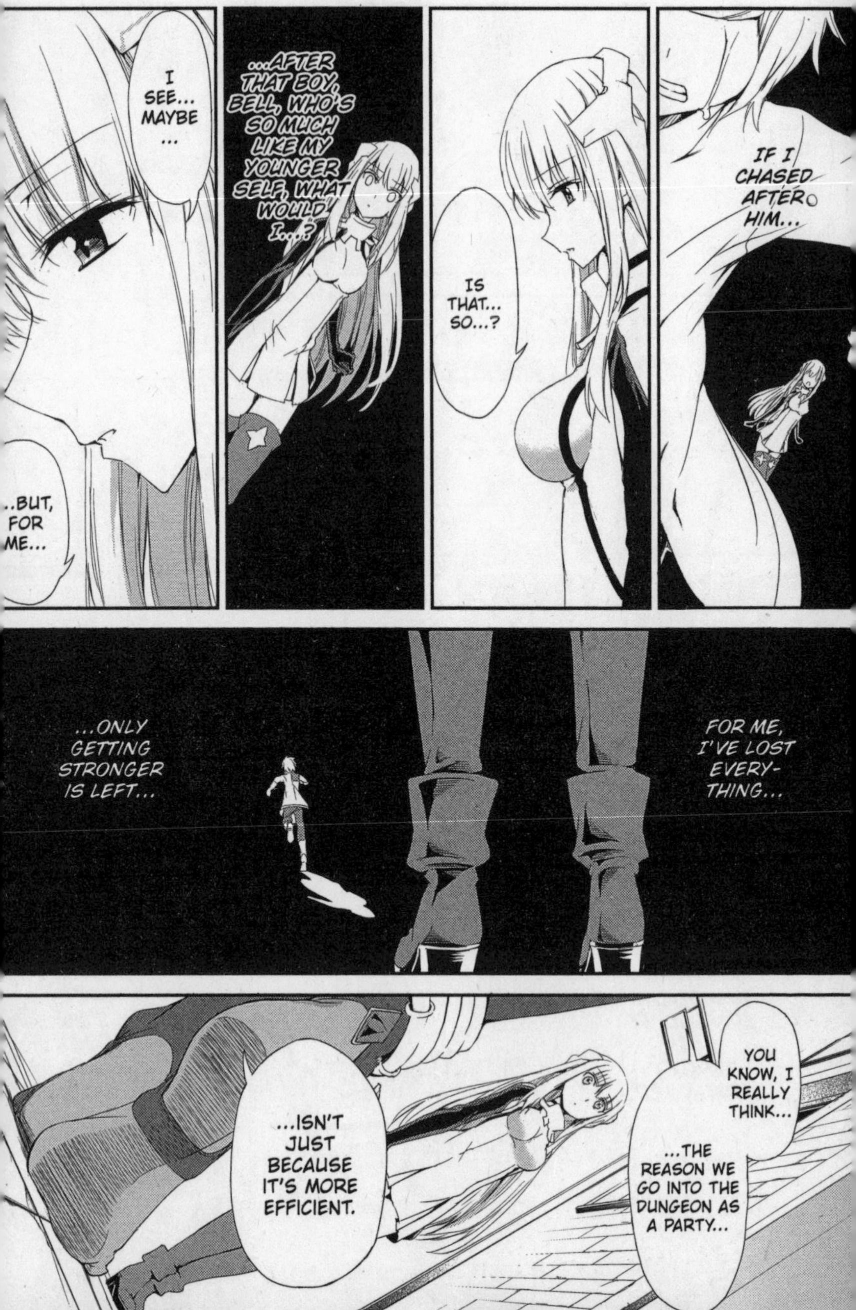
IF I CHASED AFTER HIM...
IS THAT... SO...?
...AFTER THAT BOY, BELL, WHO'S SO MUCH LIKE MY YOUNGER SELF, WHAT WOULD I...?
I SEE... MAYBE...
..BUT, FOR ME...
FOR ME, I'VE LOST EVERYTHING...
...ONLY GETTING STRONGER IS LEFT...
YOU KNOW, I REALLY THINK...
...THE REASON WE GO INTO THE DUNGEON AS A PARTY...
...ISN'T JUST BECAUSE IT'S MORE EFFICIENT.

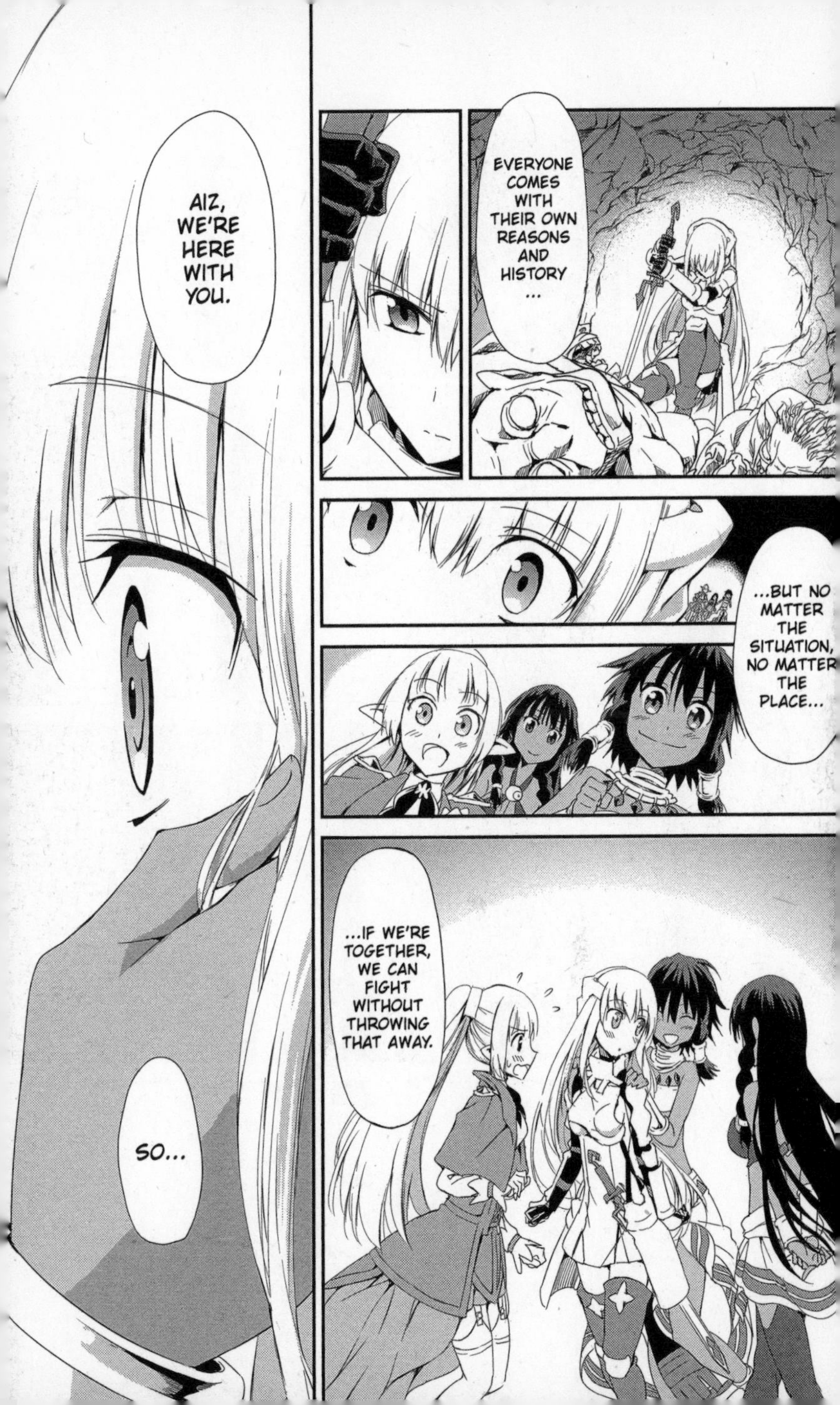
EVERYONE COMES WITH THEIR OWN REASONS AND HISTORY ...
...BUT NO MATTER THE SITUATION, NO MATTER THE PLACE...
...IF WE'RE TOGETHER, WE CAN FIGHT WITHOUT THROWING THAT AWAY.
AIZ, WE'RE HERE WITH YOU.
SO...

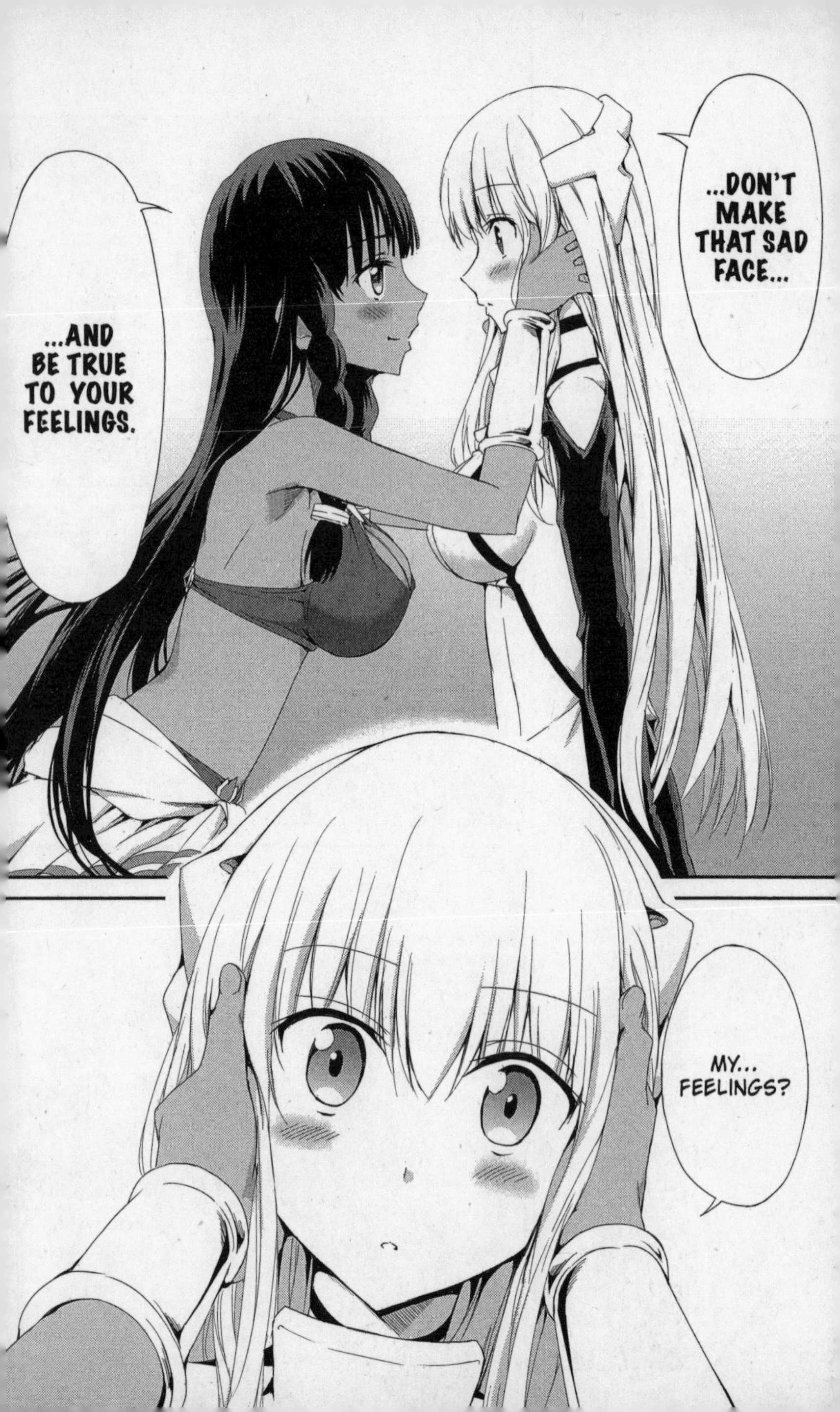
...DON'T MAKE THAT SAD FACE...
...AND BE TRUE TO YOUR FEELINGS.
MY... FEELINGS?

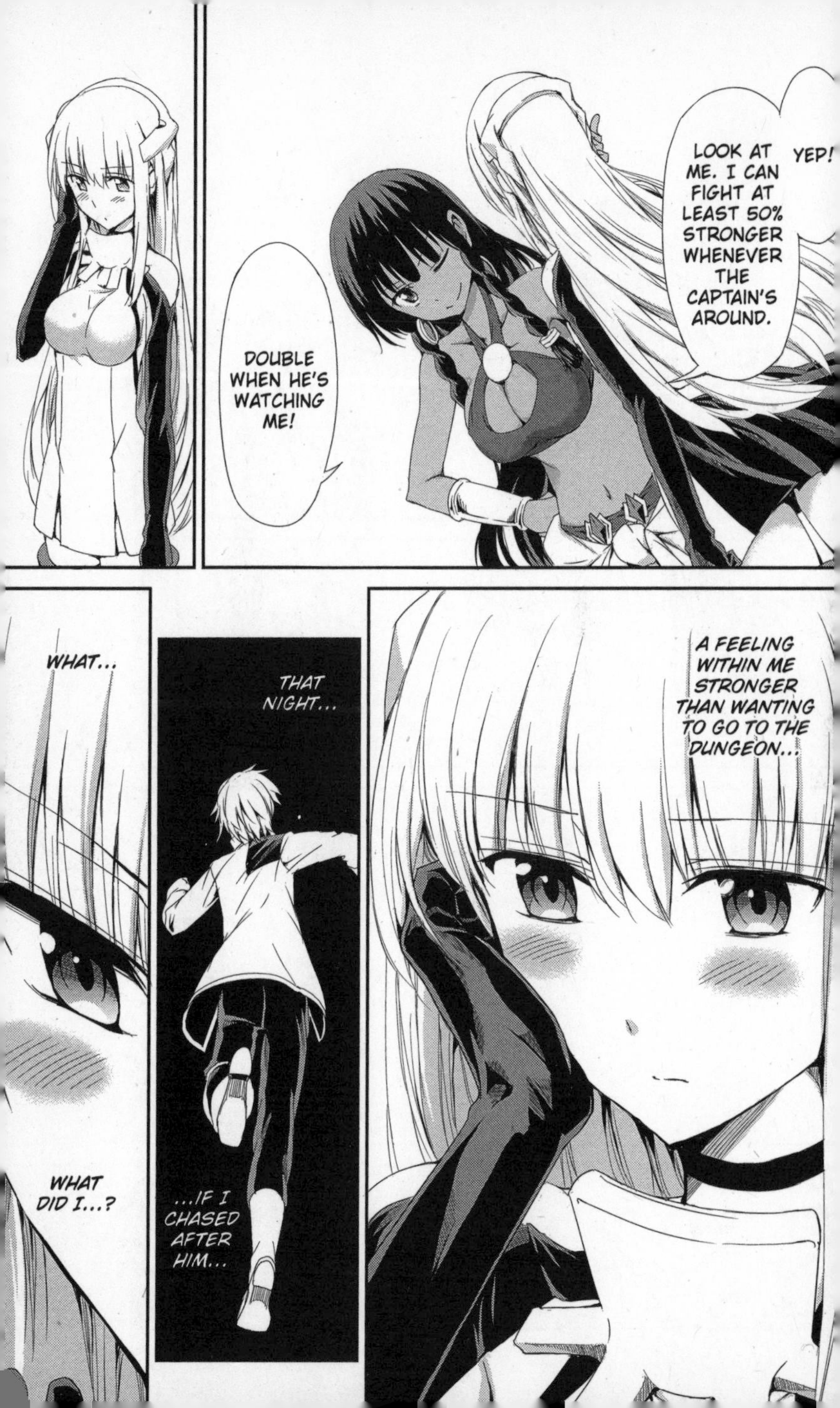
YEP!
LOOK AT ME. I CAN FIGHT AT LEAST 50% STRONGER WHENEVER THE CAPTAIN'S AROUND.
DOUBLE WHEN HE'S WATCHING ME!
A FEELING WITHIN ME STRONGER THAN WANTING TO GO TO THE DUNGEON...
THAT NIGHT...
...IF I CHASED AFTER HIM...
WHAT...
WHAT DID I...?

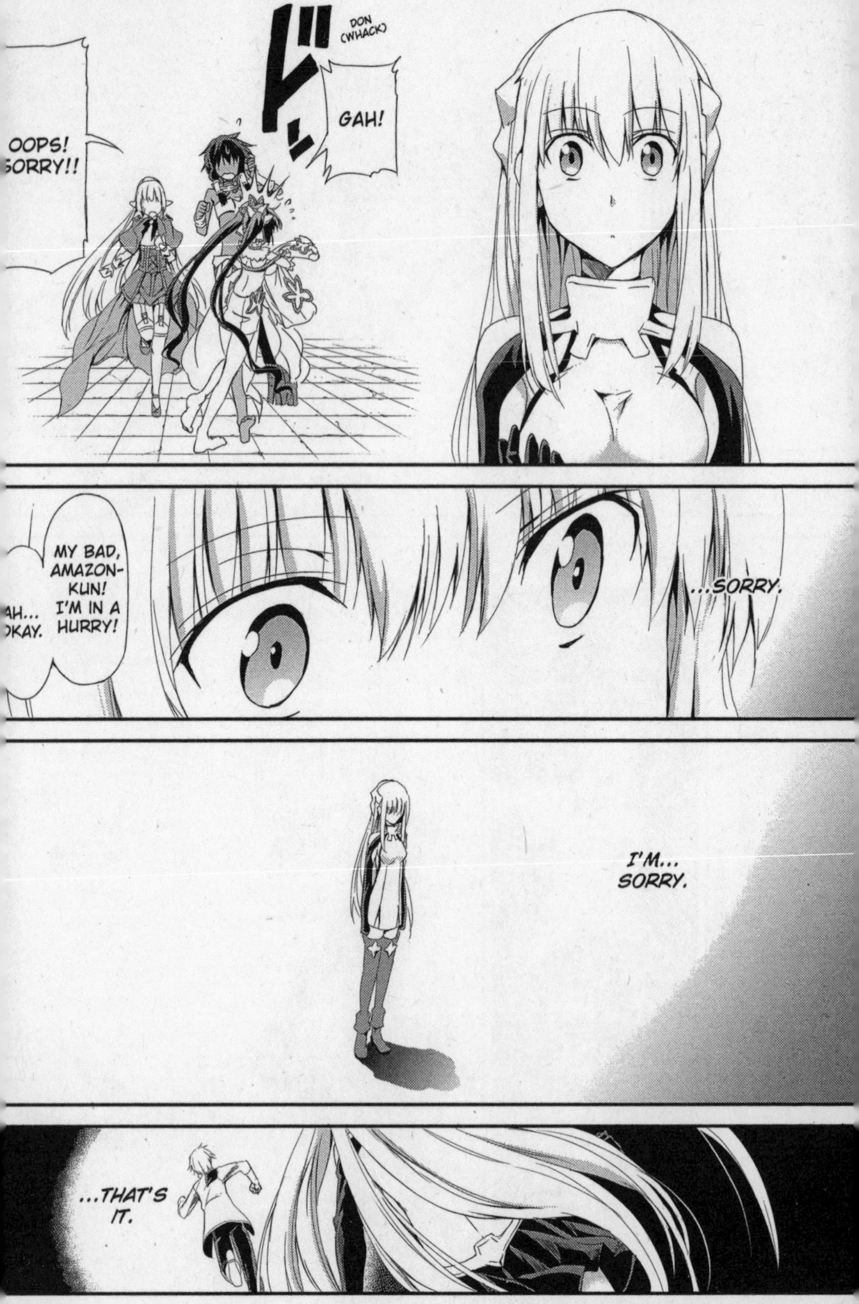
DON (WHACK)
GAH!
OOPS! SORRY!!
...SORRY.
MY BAD, AMAZON-KUN! I'M IN A HURRY!
AH... OKAY.
I'M... SORRY.
...THAT'S IT.

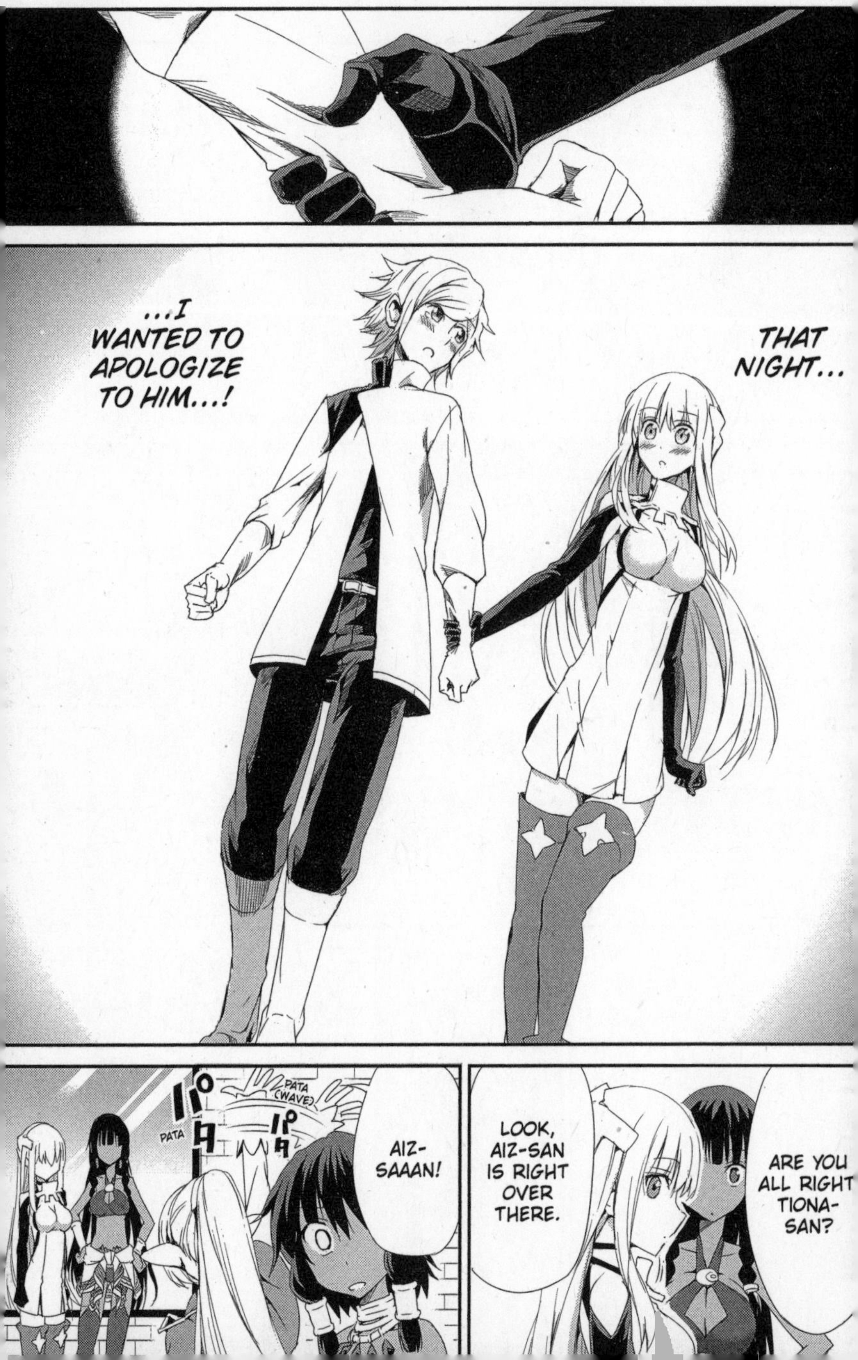
THAT NIGHT...
...I WANTED TO APOLOGIZE TO HIM...!
ARE YOU ALL RIGHT TIONA-SAN?
LOOK, AIZ-SAN IS RIGHT OVER THERE.
AIZ-SAAAN!
PATA (WAVE)
PATA

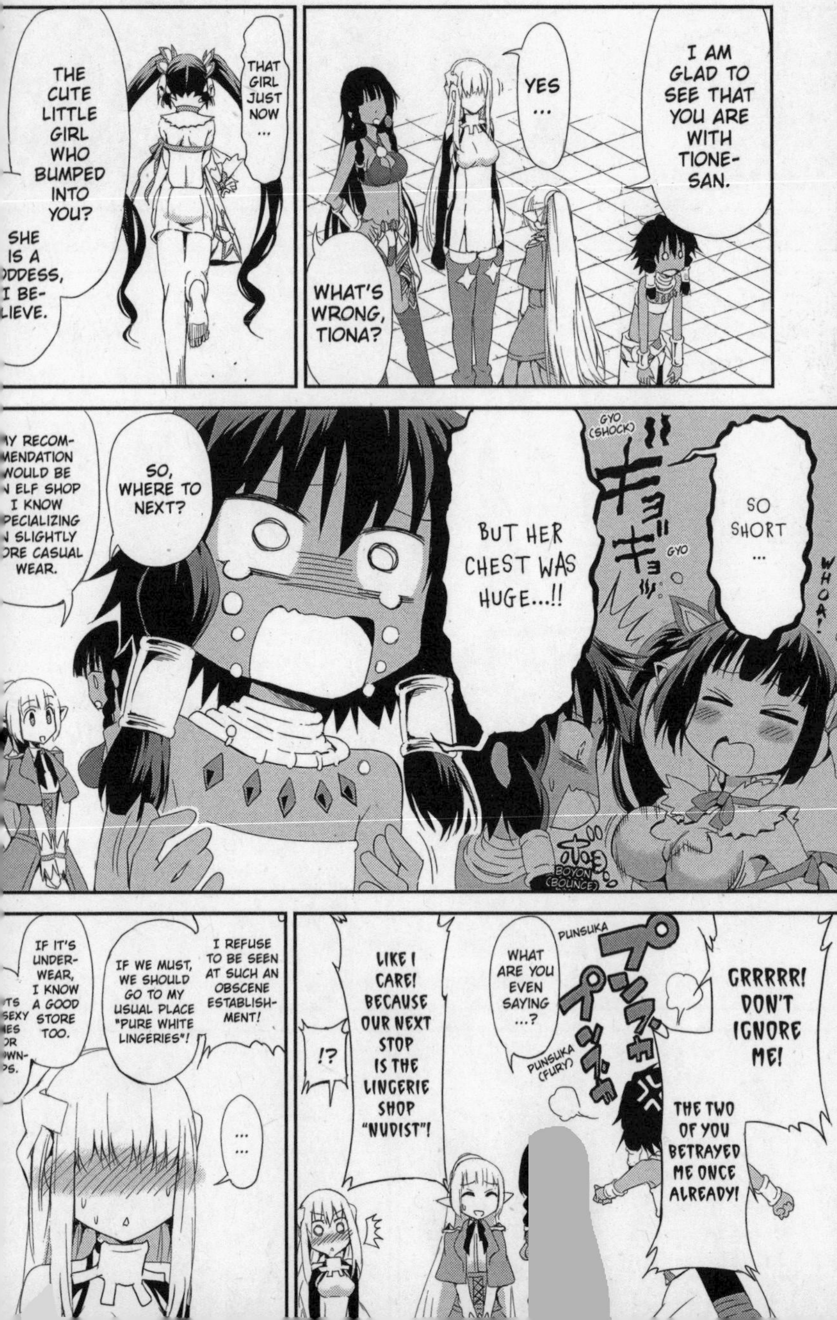
I AM GLAD TO SEE THAT YOU ARE WITH TIONE-SAN.
YES ...
WHAT'S WRONG, TIONA?
THAT GIRL JUST NOW ...
THE CUTE LITTLE GIRL WHO BUMPED INTO YOU?
SHE IS A ODDESS, I BE- LIEVE.
SO SHORT ...
GYO (SHOCK)
GYO
WHOA!
BUT HER CHEST WAS HUGE...!!
BOYON (BOUNCE)
SO, WHERE TO NEXT?
MY RECOM- MENDATION WOULD BE N ELF SHOP I KNOW PECIALIZING N SLIGHTLY ORE CASUAL WEAR.
GRRRRR! DON'T IGNORE ME!
PUNSUKA
WHAT ARE YOU EVEN SAYING ...?
PUNSUKA (FURY)
THE TWO OF YOU BETRAYED ME ONCE ALREADY!
LIKE I CARE! BECAUSE OUR NEXT STOP IS THE LINGERIE SHOP "NUDIST"!
!?
I REFUSE TO BE SEEN AT SUCH AN OBSCENE ESTABLISHMENT!
IF WE MUST, WE SHOULD GO TO MY USUAL PLACE "PURE WHITE LINGERIES"!
IF IT'S UNDER- WEAR, I KNOW A GOOD STORE TOO.
... ...

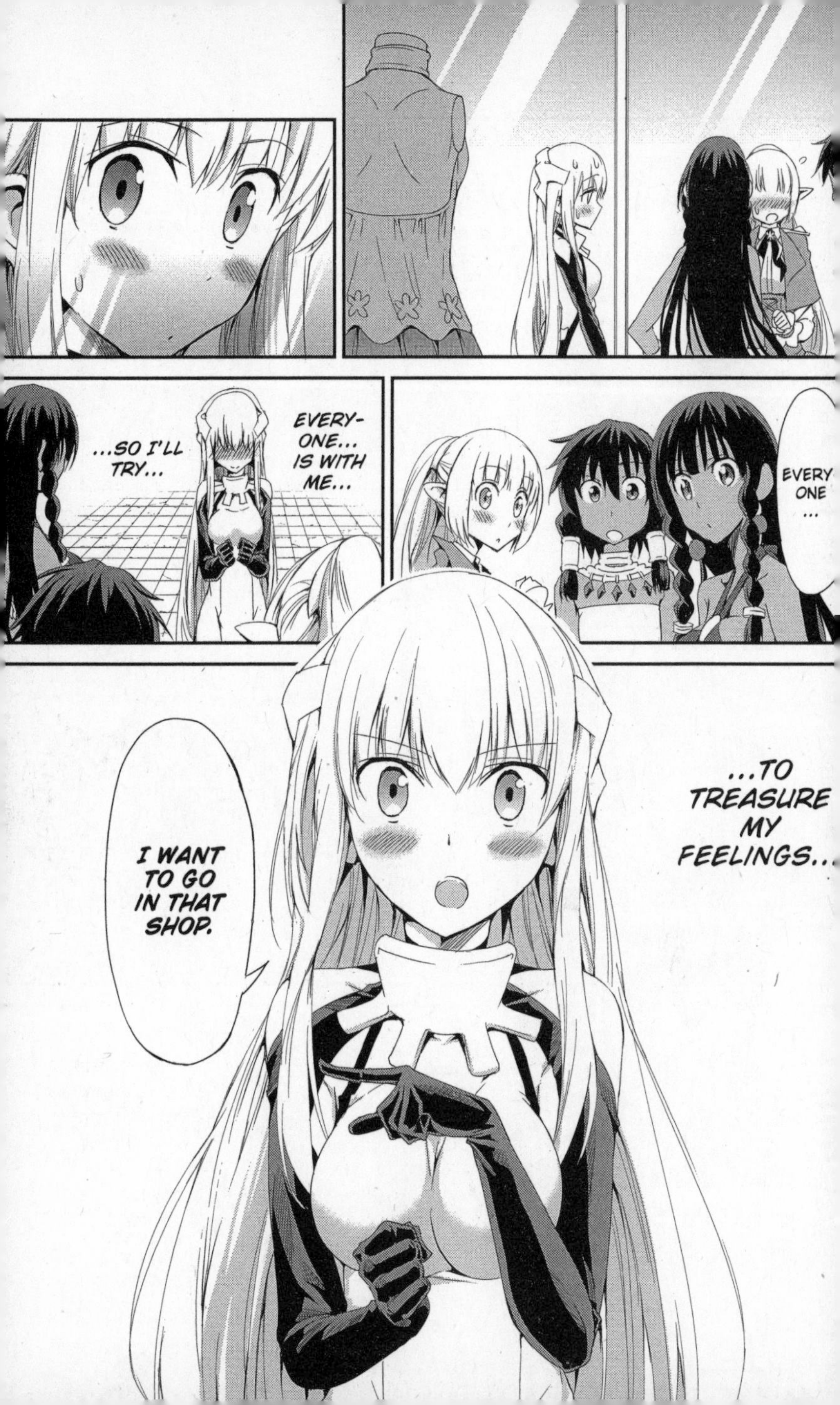
EVERY ONE ...
EVERY-ONE... IS WITH ME...
...SO I'LL TRY...
...TO TREASURE MY FEELINGS...
I WANT TO GO IN THAT SHOP.

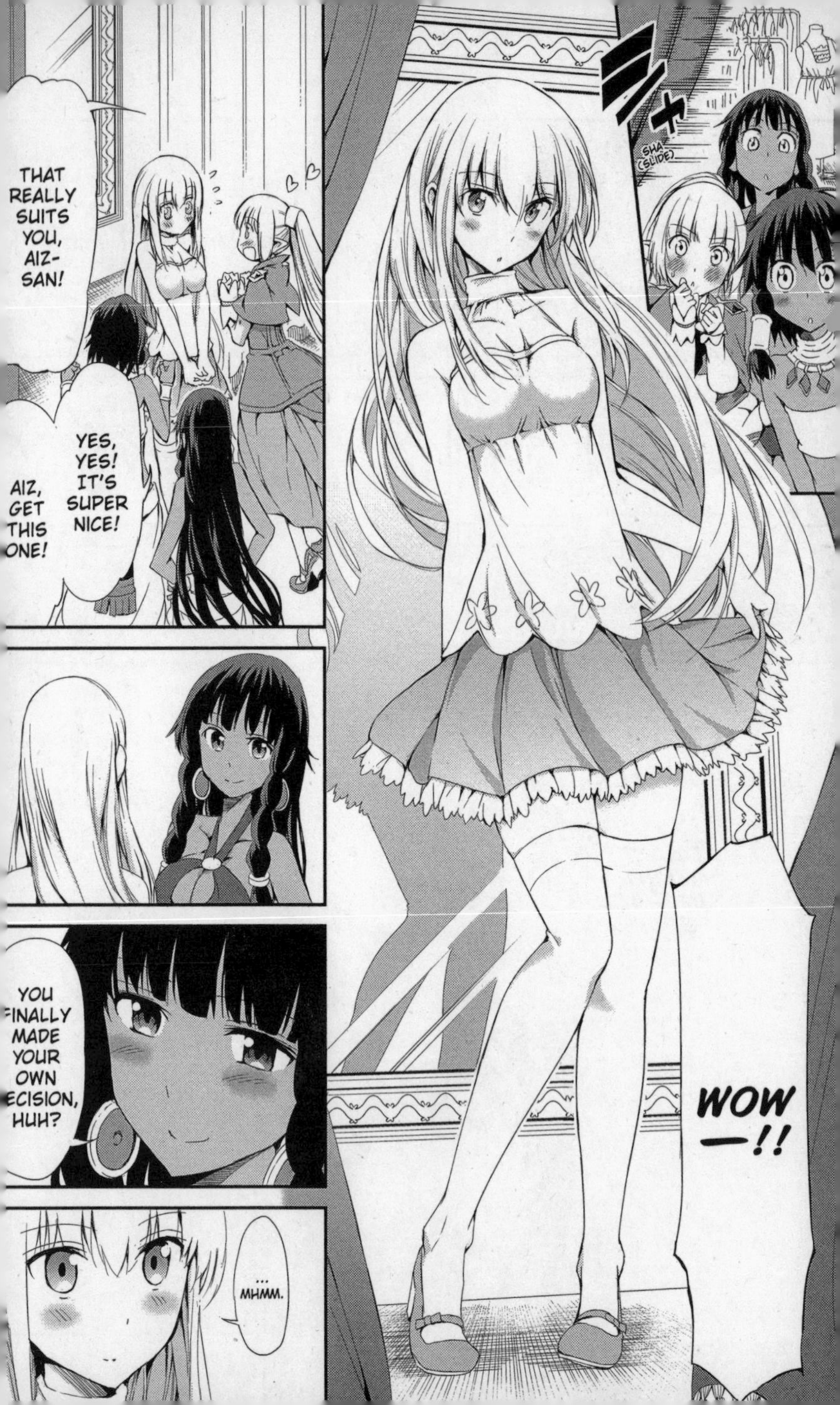

SHA (SLIDE)
WOW—!!
THAT REALLY SUITS YOU, AIZ-SAN!
YES, YES! IT'S SUPER NICE!
AIZ, GET THIS ONE!
YOU FINALLY MADE YOUR OWN ECISION, HUH?
... MHMM.

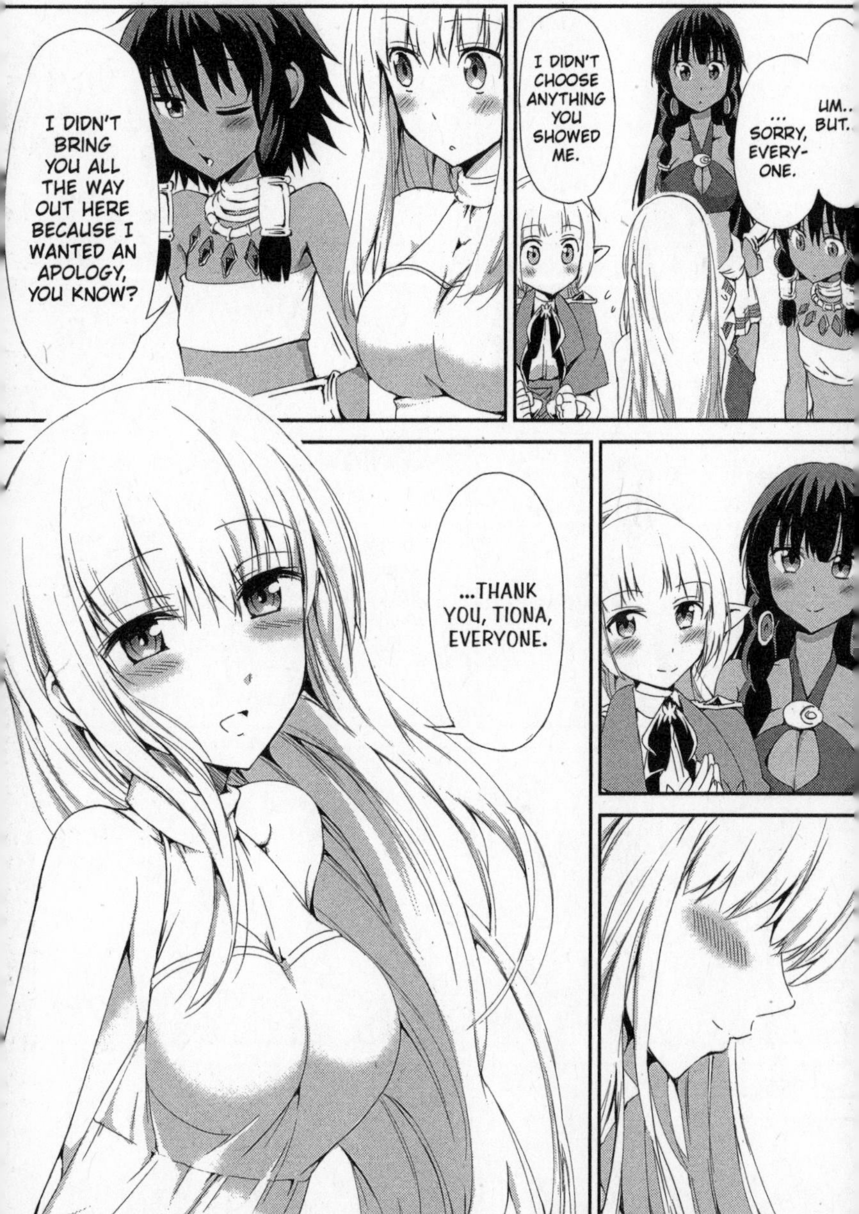
UM.. BUT.
... SORRY, EVERY-ONE.
I DIDN'T CHOOSE ANYTHING YOU SHOWED ME.
I DIDN'T BRING YOU ALL THE WAY OUT HERE BECAUSE I WANTED AN APOLOGY, YOU KNOW?
...THANK YOU, TIONA, EVERYONE.

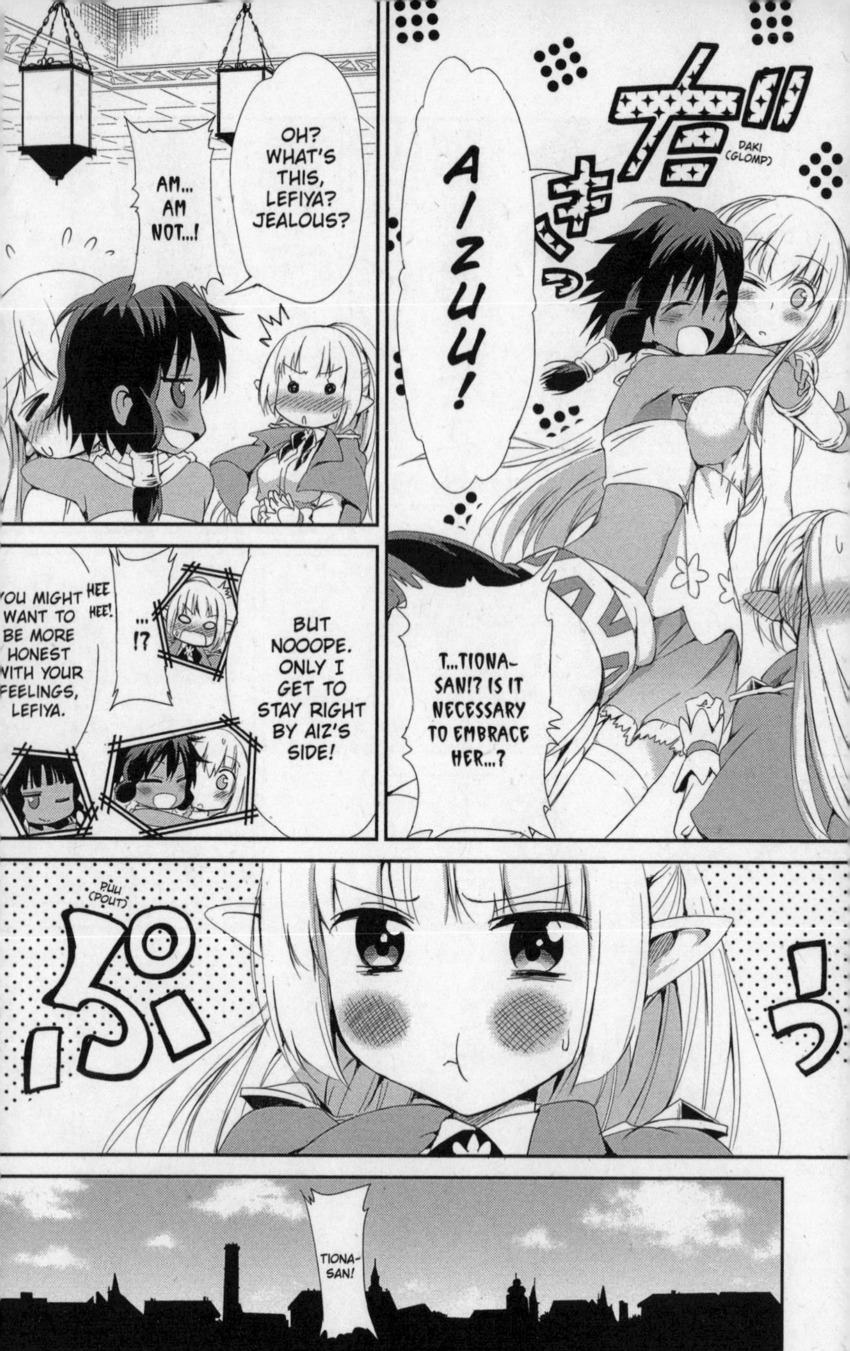

AIZUU!
DAKI (GLOMP)
T...TIONA-SAN!? IS IT NECESSARY TO EMBRACE HER...?
OH? WHAT'S THIS, LEFIYA? JEALOUS?
AM... AM NOT...!
BUT NOOOPE. ONLY I GET TO STAY RIGHT BY AIZ'S SIDE!
...!?
HEE HEE!
YOU MIGHT WANT TO BE MORE HONEST WITH YOUR FEELINGS, LEFIYA.
PUU (POUT)
TIONA-SAN!

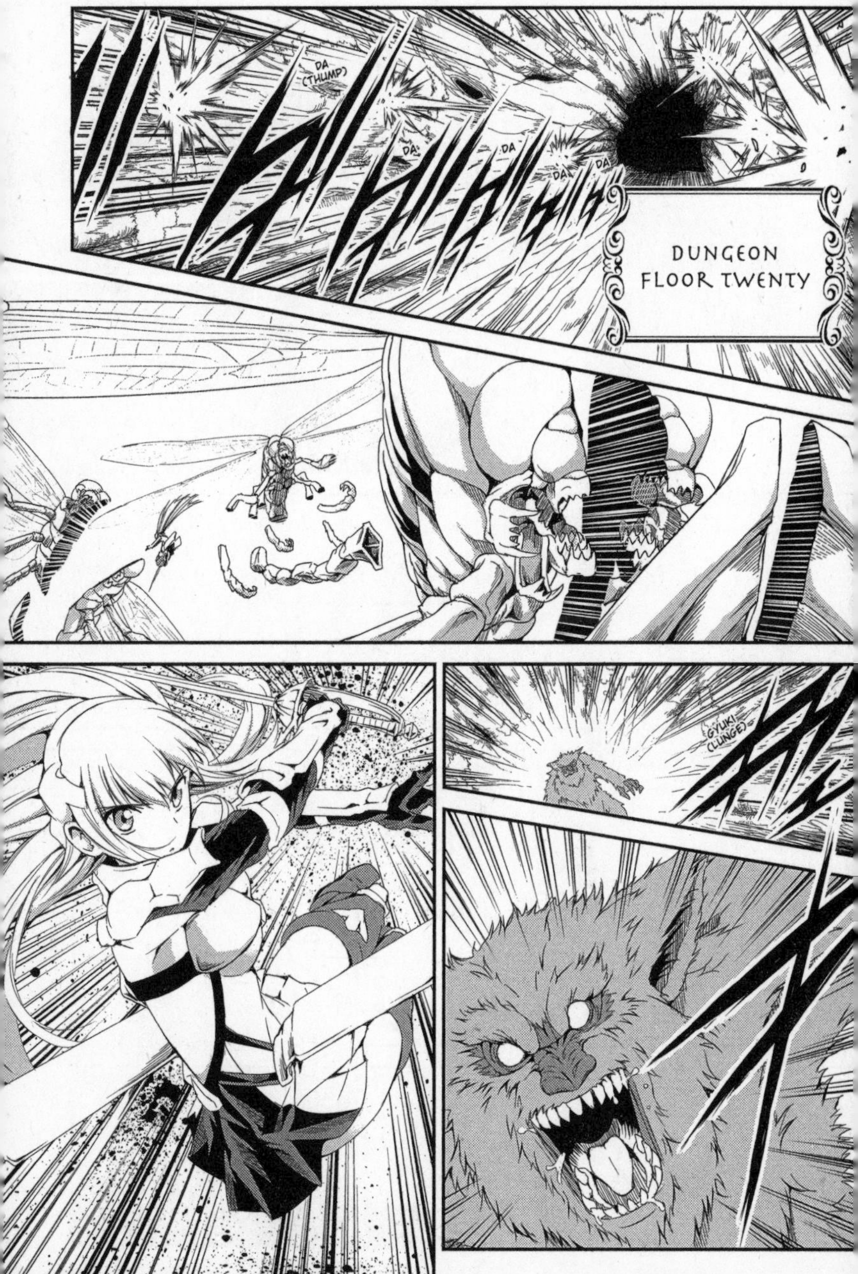
D
D
DA
DA
DA
DA
DA
(THUMP)
DUNGEON FLOOR TWENTY
GYUKI
(LUNGE)

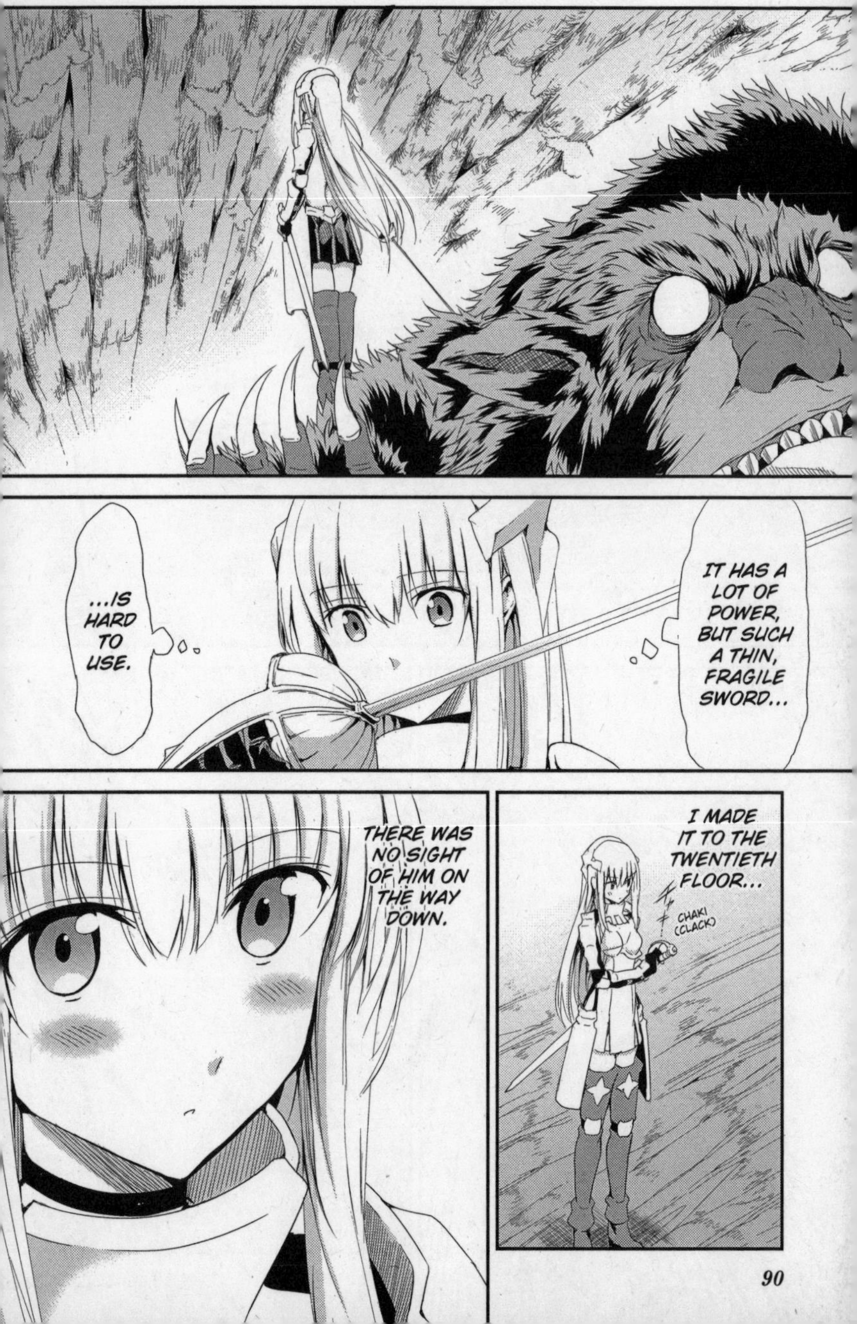
IT HAS A LOT OF POWER, BUT SUCH A THIN, FRAGILE SWORD...
...IS HARD TO USE.
I MADE IT TO THE TWENTIETH FLOOR...
CHAKI (CLACK)
THERE WAS NO SIGHT OF HIM ON THE WAY DOWN.

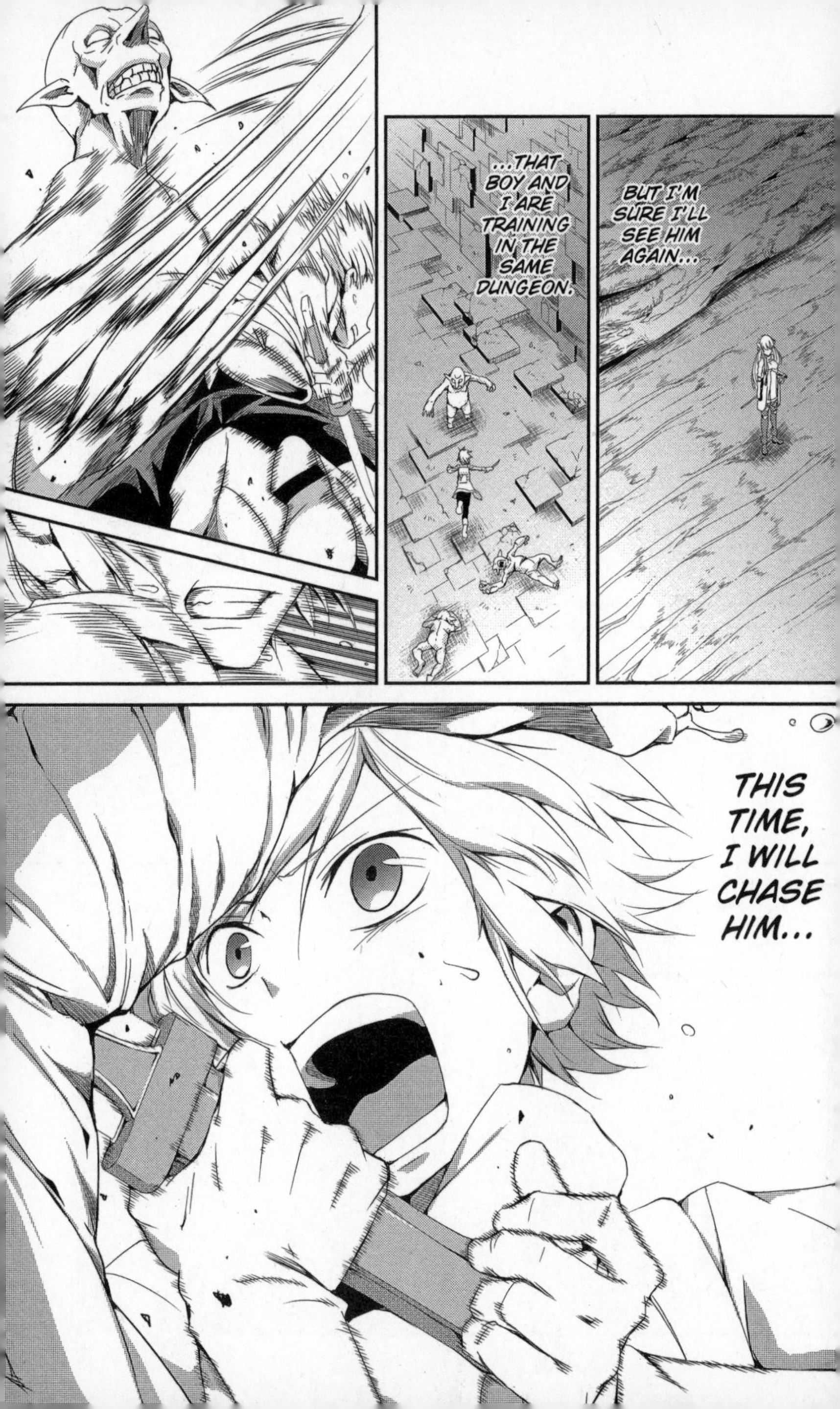
BUT I'M SURE I'LL SEE HIM AGAIN...
...THAT BOY AND I ARE TRAINING IN THE SAME DUNGEON.
THIS TIME, I WILL CHASE HIM...

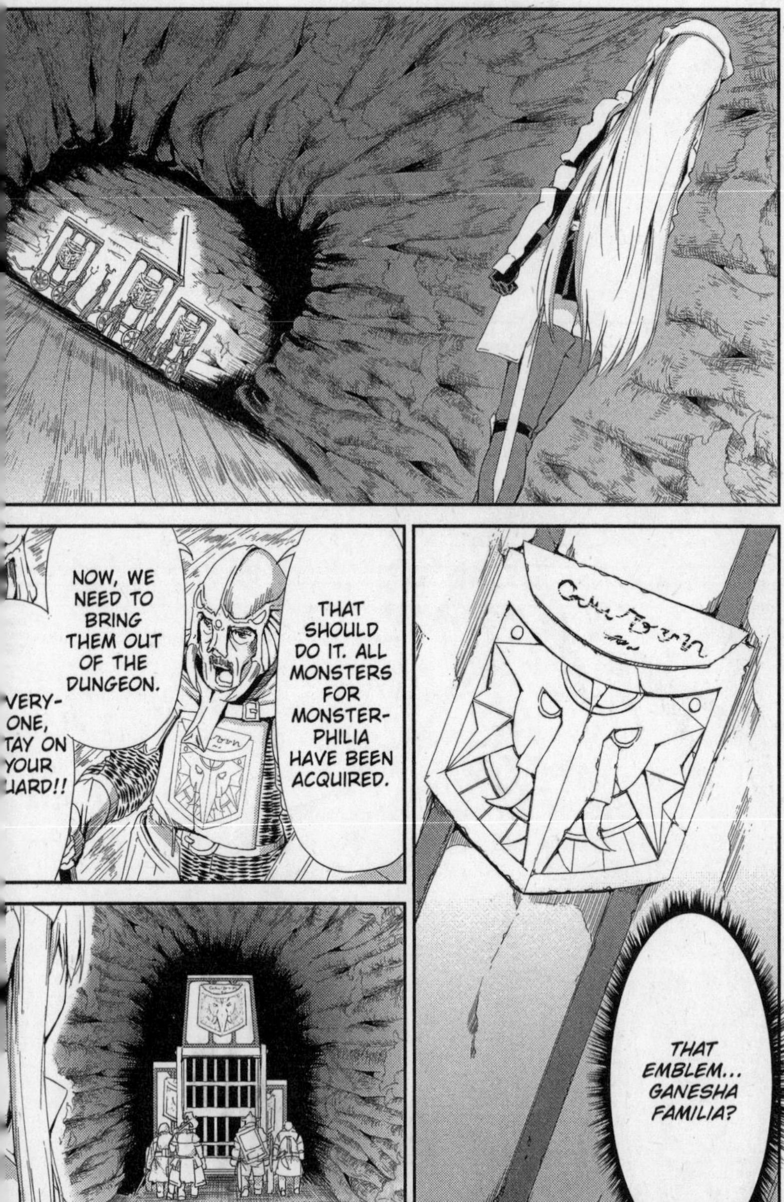
THAT EMBLEM... GANESHA FAMILIA?
THAT SHOULD DO IT. ALL MONSTERS FOR MONSTERPHILIA HAVE BEEN ACQUIRED.
NOW, WE NEED TO BRING THEM OUT OF THE DUNGEON.
VERY-ONE, TAY ON YOUR UARD!!

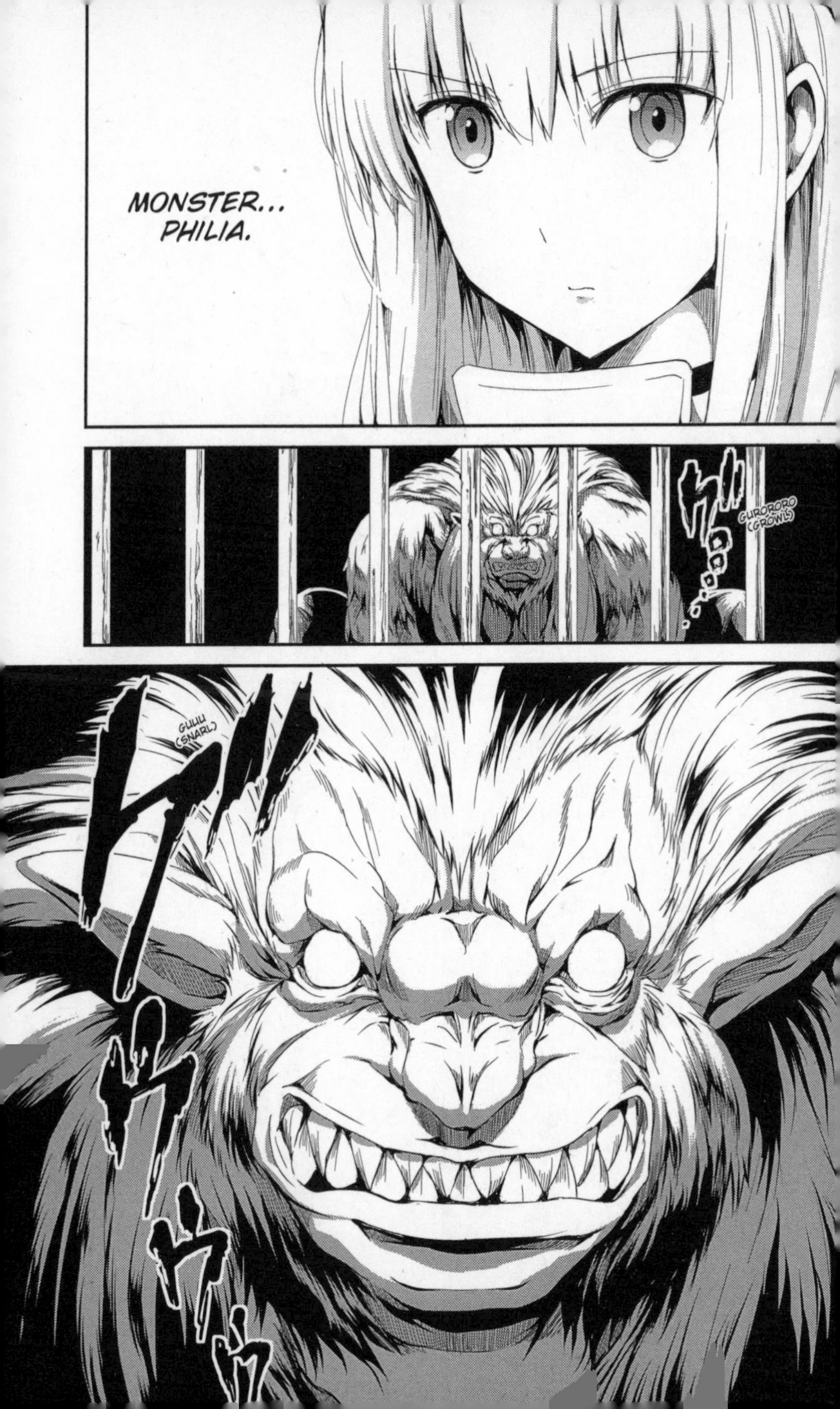
MONSTER... PHILIA.
GURORORO (GROWLS)
GUUU (SNARL)

Is it WRONG to TRY to PICK UP GIRLS IN A DUNGEON? ON THE SIDE

Sword Oratoria

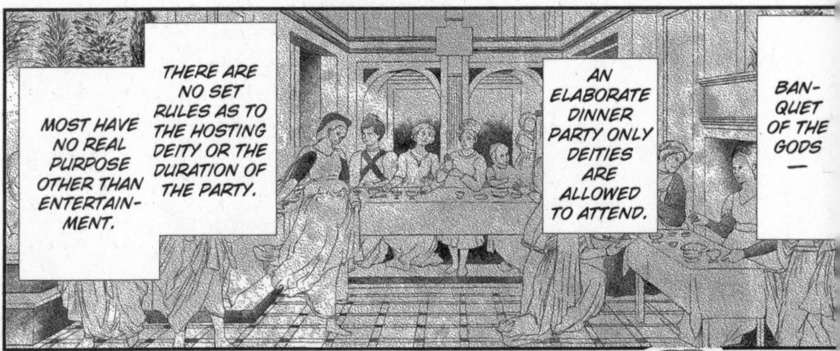
BANQUET OF THE GODS —
AN ELABORATE DINNER PARTY ONLY DEITIES ARE ALLOWED TO ATTEND.
THERE ARE NO SET RULES AS TO THE HOSTING DEITY OR THE DURATION OF THE PARTY.
MOST HAVE NO REAL PURPOSE OTHER THAN ENTERTAINMENT.
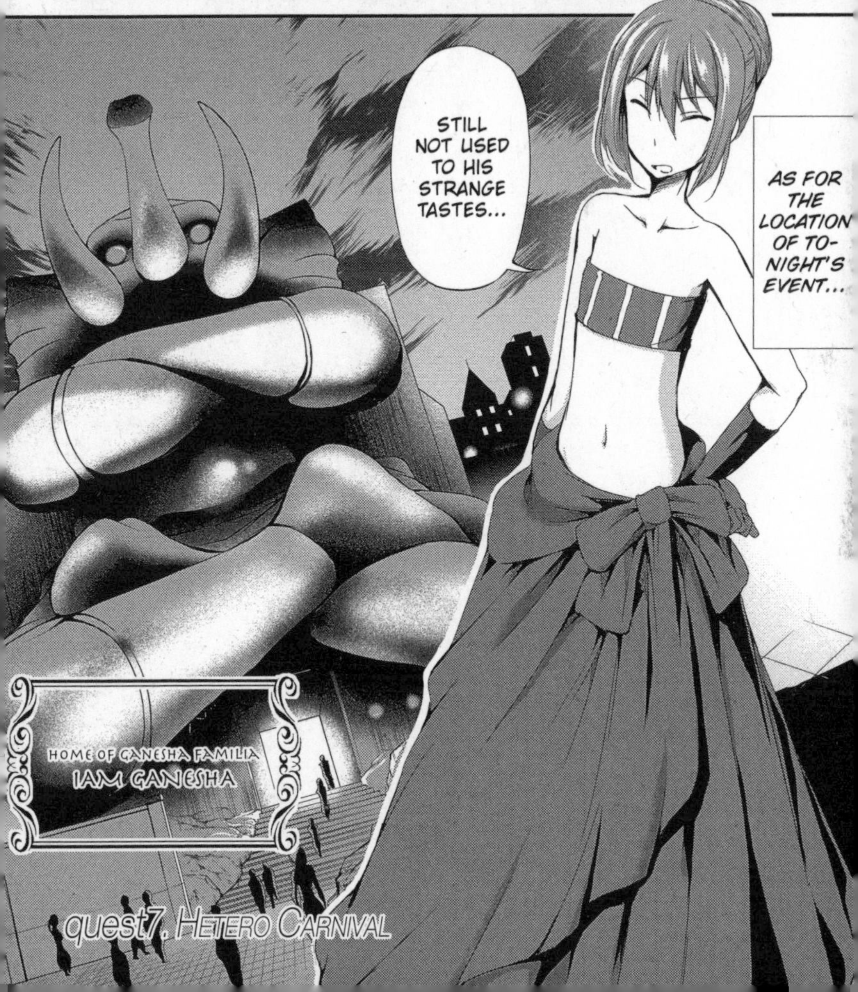
AS FOR THE LOCATION OF TONIGHT'S EVENT...
STILL NOT USED TO HIS STRANGE TASTES...
HOME OF GANESHA FAMILIA
IAM GANESHA
quest7. HETERO CARNIVAL

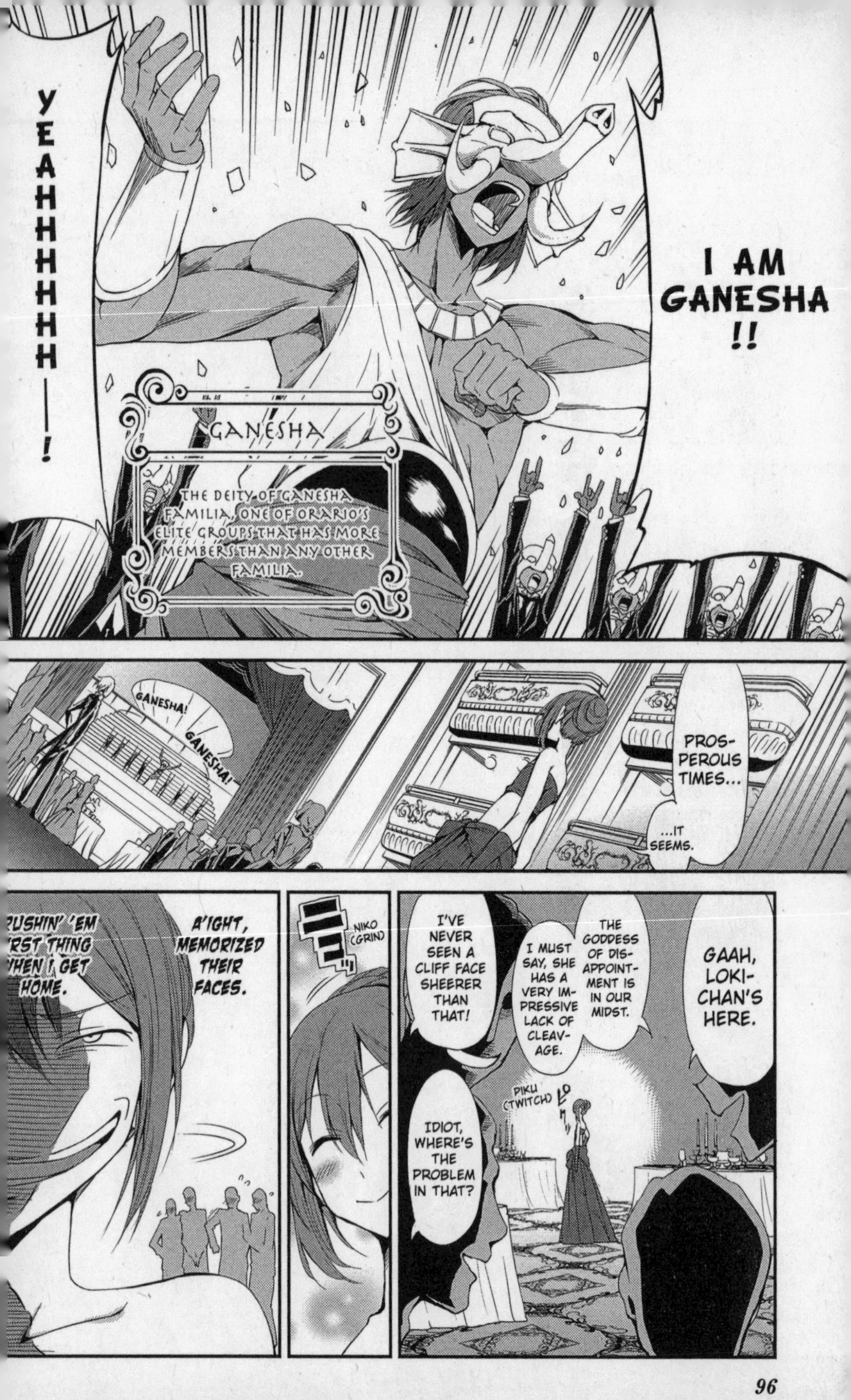
I AM GANESHA!!
YEAHHHHHHHH—!
GANESHA
THE DEITY OF GANESHA FAMILIA, ONE OF ORARIO'S ELITE GROUPS THAT HAS MORE MEMBERS THAN ANY OTHER FAMILIA.
PROS-PEROUS TIMES...
...IT SEEMS.
GANESHA!
GANESHA!
GAAH, LOKI-CHAN'S HERE.
THE GODDESS OF DIS-APPOINT-MENT IS IN OUR MIDST.
I MUST SAY, SHE HAS A VERY IM-PRESSIVE LACK OF CLEAV-AGE.
I'VE NEVER SEEN A CLIFF FACE SHEERER THAN THAT!
PIKU (TWITCH)
IDIOT, WHERE'S THE PROBLEM IN THAT?
NIKO (GRIND)
A'IGHT, MEMORIZED THEIR FACES.
RUSHIN' 'EM RST THING HEN I GET HOME.

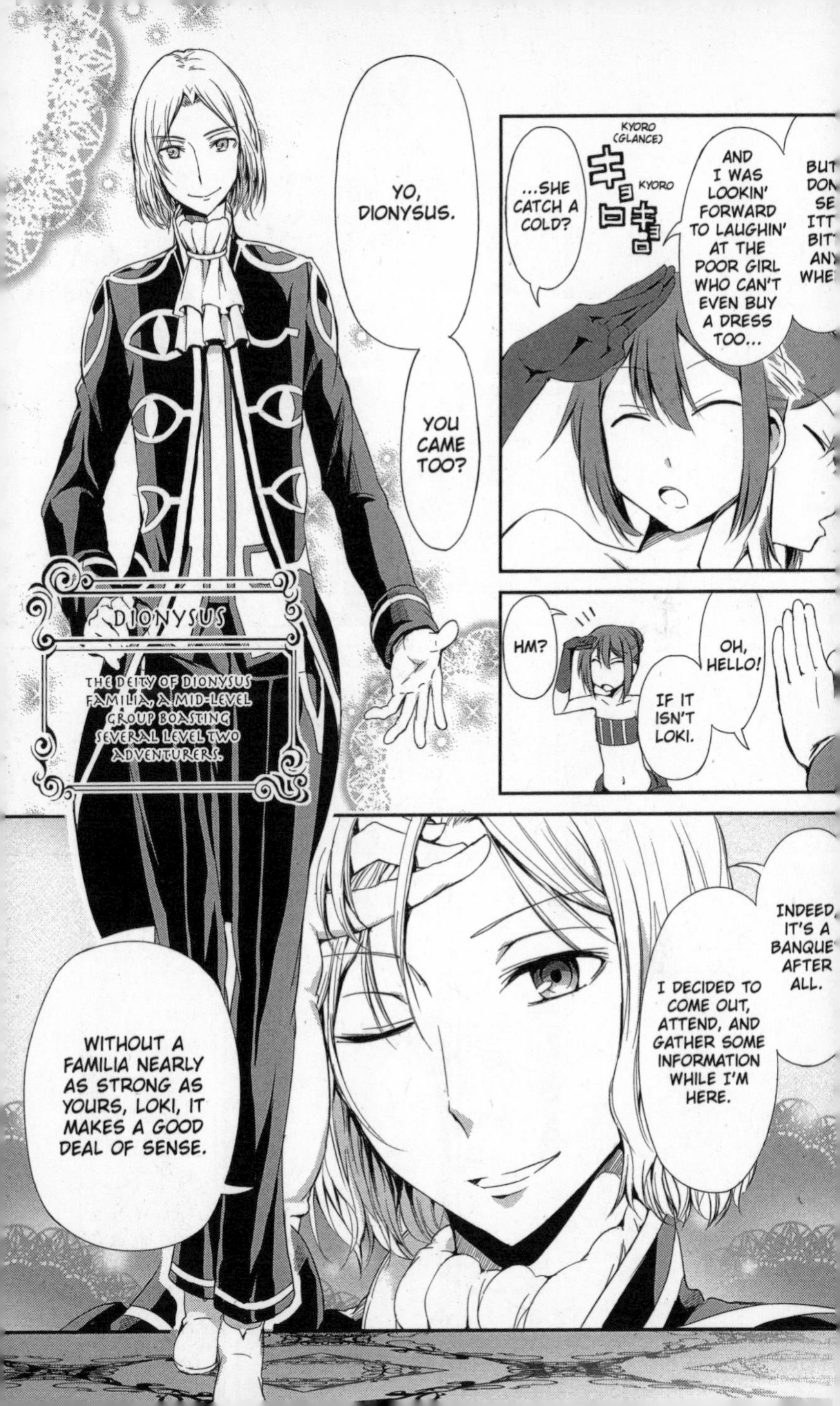
BUT DON SE ITT BIT ANY WHE
AND I WAS LOOKIN' FORWARD TO LAUGHIN' AT THE POOR GIRL WHO CAN'T EVEN BUY A DRESS TOO...
KYORO (GLANCE)
キョロ
KYORO
キョ
...SHE CATCH A COLD?
OH, HELLO!
IF IT ISN'T LOKI.
HM?
YO, DIONYSUS.
YOU CAME TOO?
DIONYSUS
THE DEITY OF DIONYSUS FAMILIA, A MID-LEVEL GROUP BOASTING SEVERAL LEVEL TWO ADVENTURERS.
INDEED, IT'S A BANQUE AFTER ALL.
I DECIDED TO COME OUT, ATTEND, AND GATHER SOME INFORMATION WHILE I'M HERE.
WITHOUT A FAMILIA NEARLY AS STRONG AS YOURS, LOKI, IT MAKES A GOOD DEAL OF SENSE.

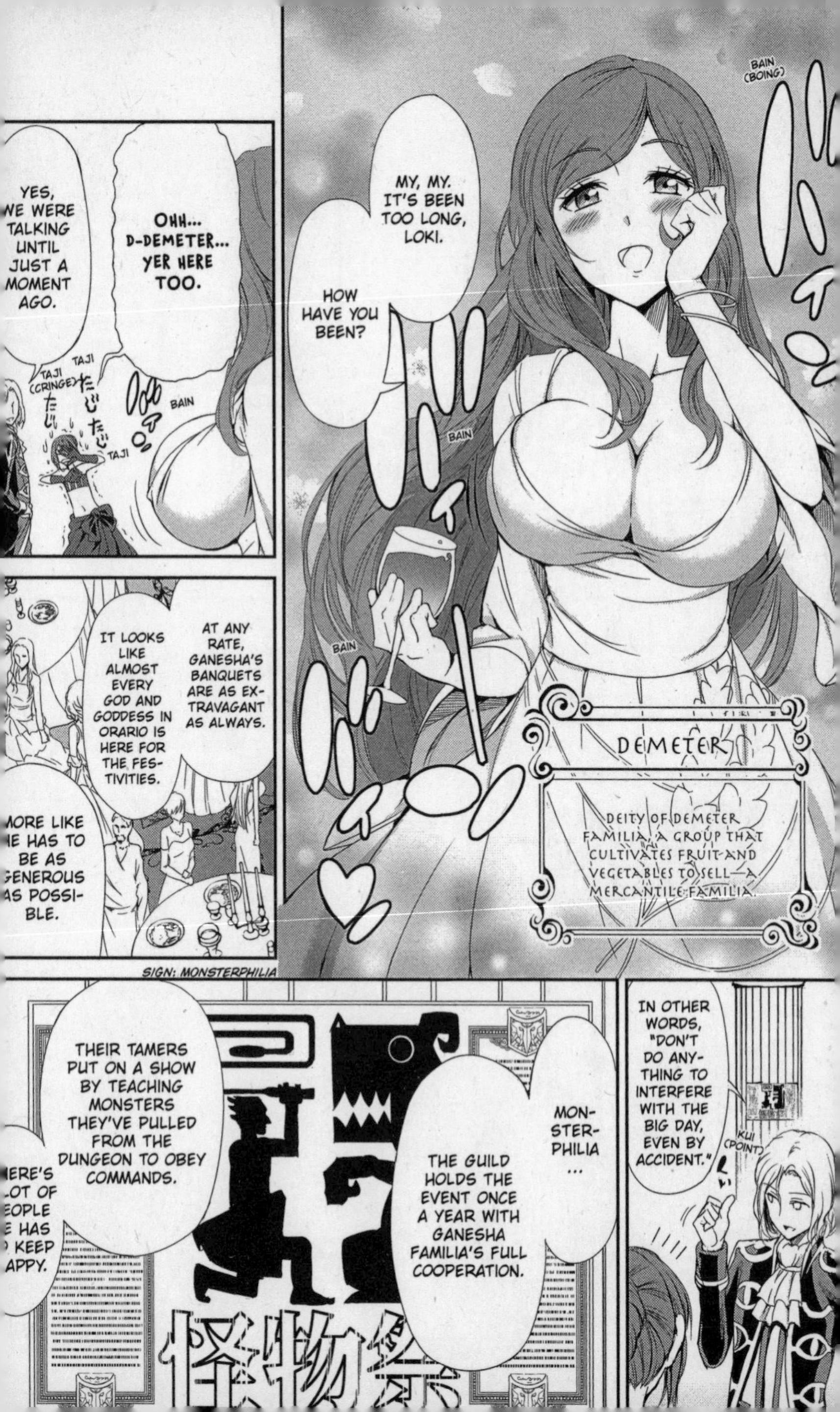
BAIN (BOING)
MY, MY. IT'S BEEN TOO LONG, LOKI.
HOW HAVE YOU BEEN?
BAIN
BAIN
DEMETER
DEITY OF DEMETER FAMILIA, A GROUP THAT CULTIVATES FRUIT AND VEGETABLES TO SELL—A MERCANTILE FAMILIA.
OHH... D-DEMETER... YER HERE TOO.
YES, WE WERE TALKING UNTIL JUST A MOMENT AGO.
BAIN
TAJI
TAJI (CRINGE)
TAJI
AT ANY RATE, GANESHA'S BANQUETS ARE AS EXTRAVAGANT AS ALWAYS.
IT LOOKS LIKE ALMOST EVERY GOD AND GODDESS IN ORARIO IS HERE FOR THE FESTIVITIES.
ORE LIKE E HAS TO BE AS ENEROUS S POSSIBLE.
IN OTHER WORDS, "DON'T DO ANYTHING TO INTERFERE WITH THE BIG DAY, EVEN BY ACCIDENT."
KUI (POINT)
SIGN: MONSTERPHILIA
MONSTERPHILIA...
THE GUILD HOLDS THE EVENT ONCE A YEAR WITH GANESHA FAMILIA'S FULL COOPERATION.
THEIR TAMERS PUT ON A SHOW BY TEACHING MONSTERS THEY'VE PULLED FROM THE DUNGEON TO OBEY COMMANDS.
ERE'S LOT OF EOPLE E HAS KEEP APPY.

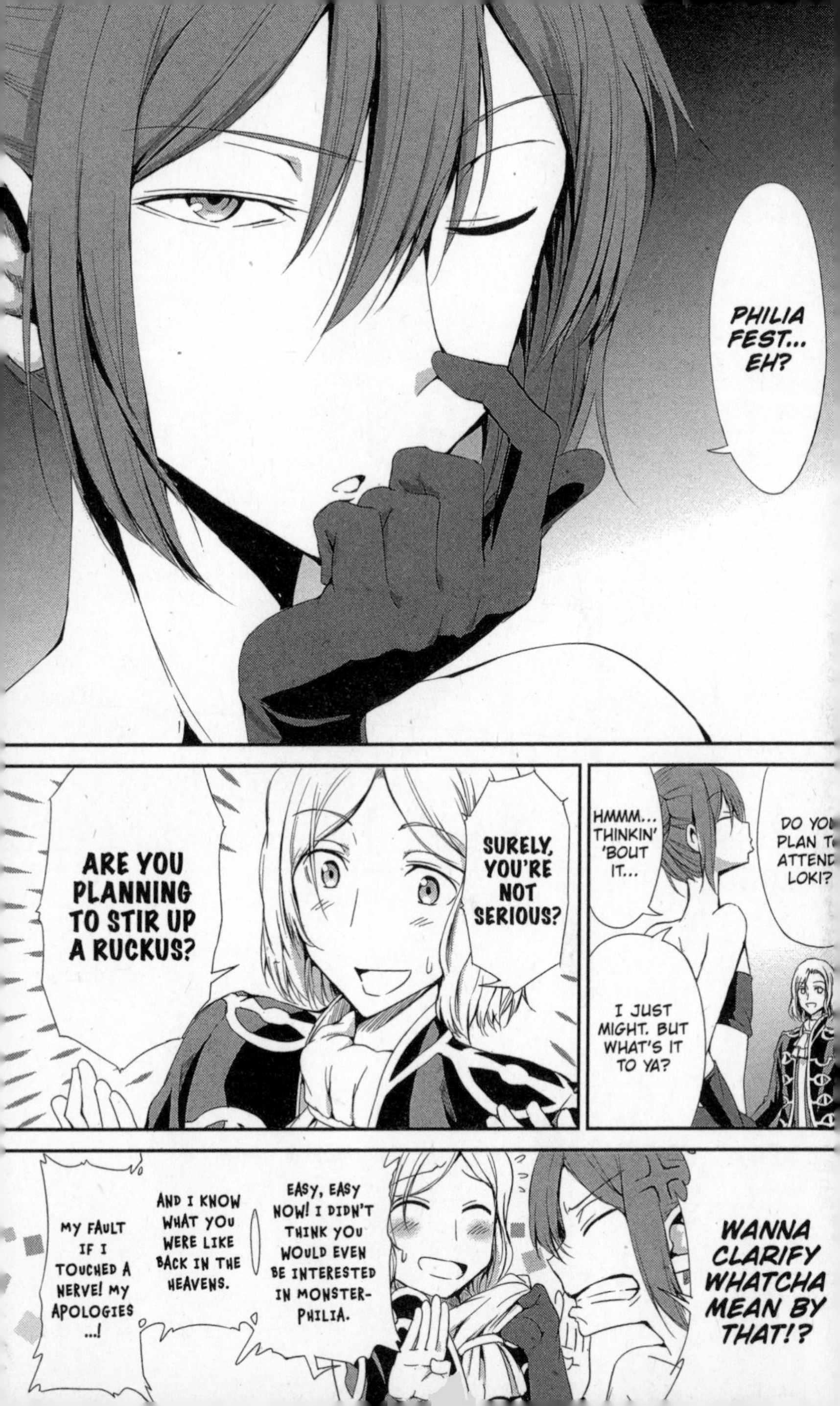
PHILIA FEST... EH?
DO YOU PLAN TO ATTEND LOKI?
HMMM... THINKIN' 'BOUT IT...
I JUST MIGHT. BUT WHAT'S IT TO YA?
SURELY, YOU'RE NOT SERIOUS?
ARE YOU PLANNING TO STIR UP A RUCKUS?
WANNA CLARIFY WHATCHA MEAN BY THAT!?
EASY, EASY NOW! I DIDN'T THINK YOU WOULD EVEN BE INTERESTED IN MONSTER-PHILIA.
AND I KNOW WHAT YOU WERE LIKE BACK IN THE HEAVENS.
MY FAULT IF I TOUCHED A NERVE! MY APOLOGIES ...!

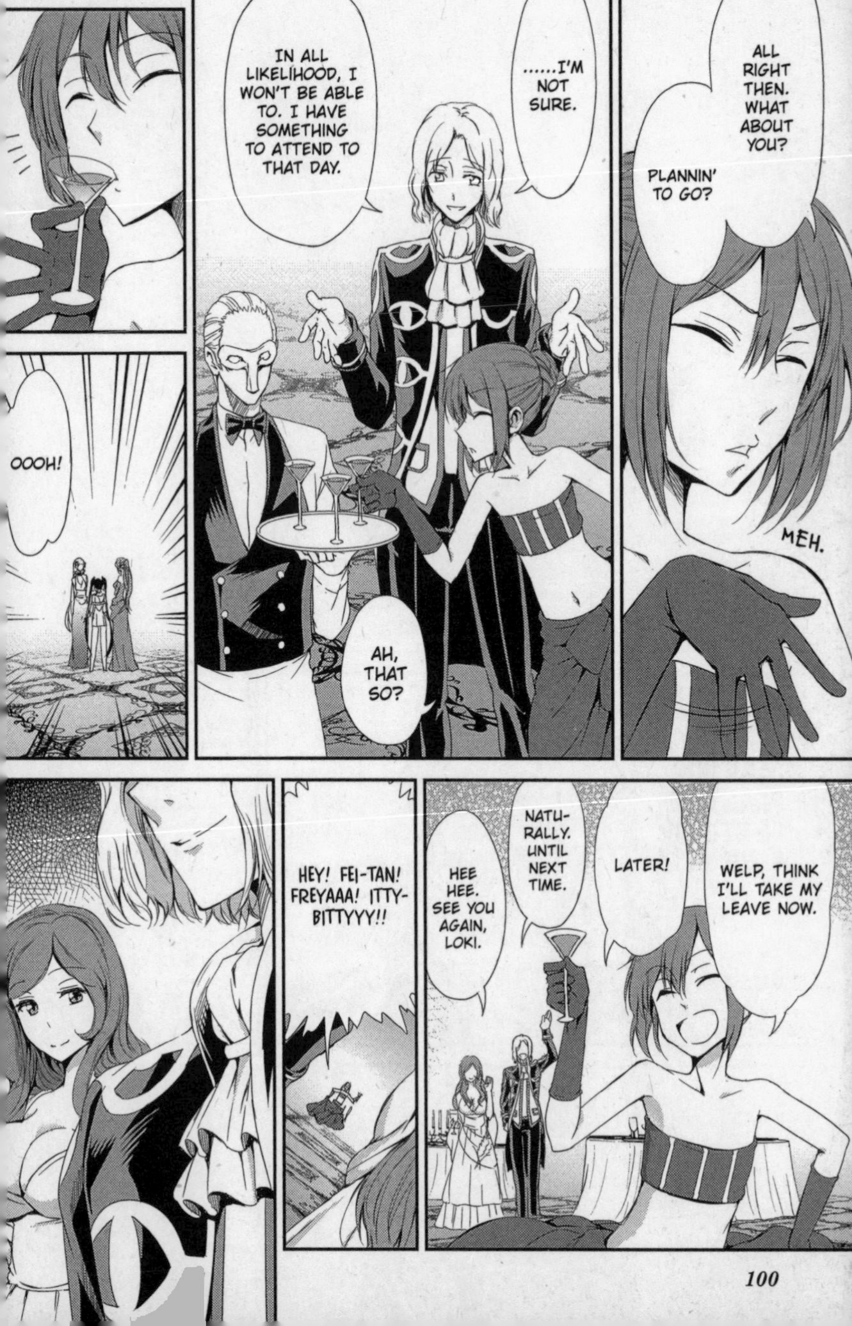
ALL RIGHT THEN. WHAT ABOUT YOU?
PLANNIN' TO GO?
MEH.
......I'M NOT SURE.
IN ALL LIKELIHOOD, I WON'T BE ABLE TO. I HAVE SOMETHING TO ATTEND TO THAT DAY.
AH, THAT SO?
OOOH!
WELP, THINK I'LL TAKE MY LEAVE NOW.
LATER!
NATU-RALLY. UNTIL NEXT TIME.
HEE HEE. SEE YOU AGAIN, LOKI.
HEY! FEI-TAN! FREYAAA! ITTY-BITTYYY!!

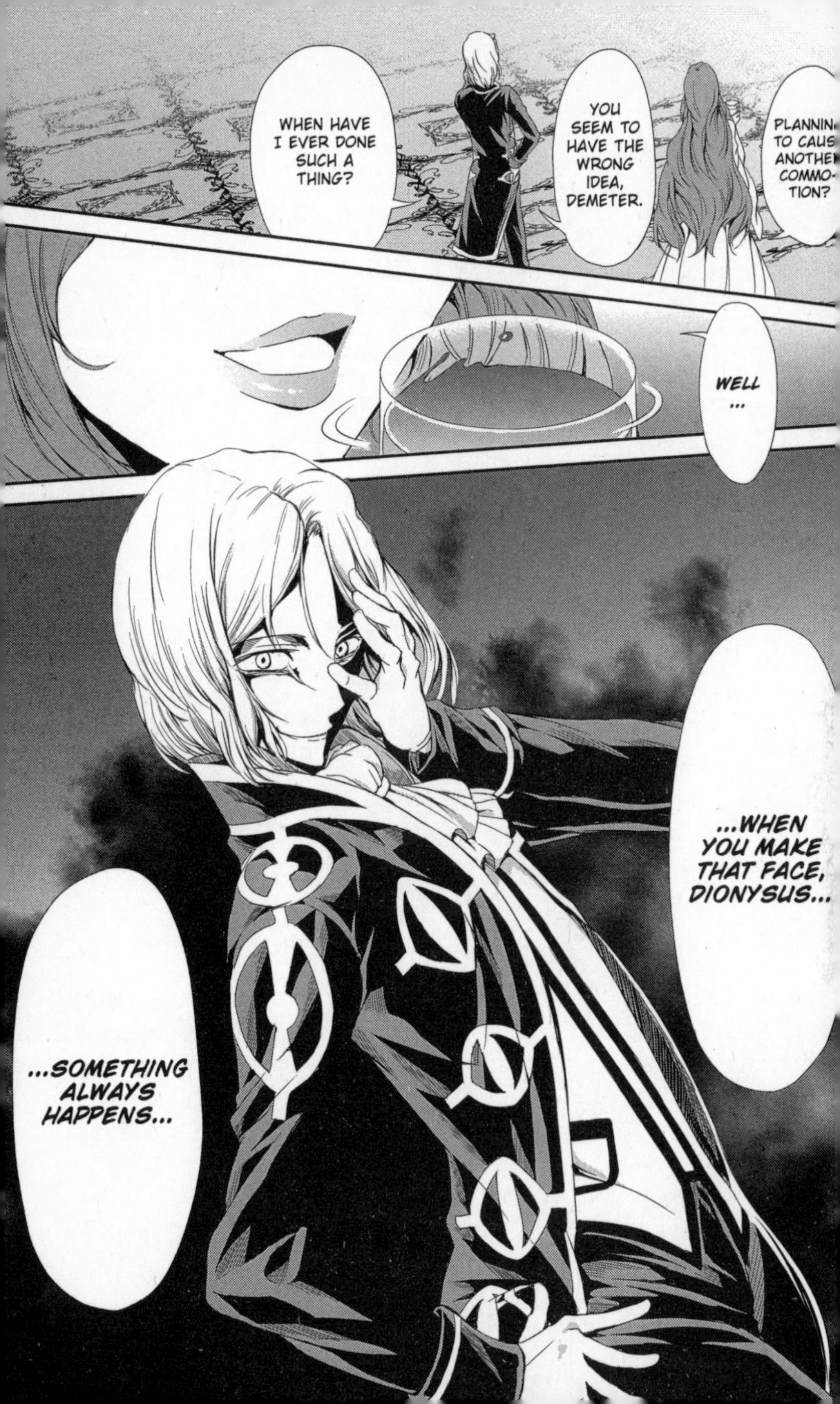
PLANNIN TO CAUS ANOTHE COMMO-TION?
YOU SEEM TO HAVE THE WRONG IDEA, DEMETER.
WHEN HAVE I EVER DONE SUCH A THING?
WELL ...
...WHEN YOU MAKE THAT FACE, DIONYSUS...
...SOMETHING ALWAYS HAPPENS...

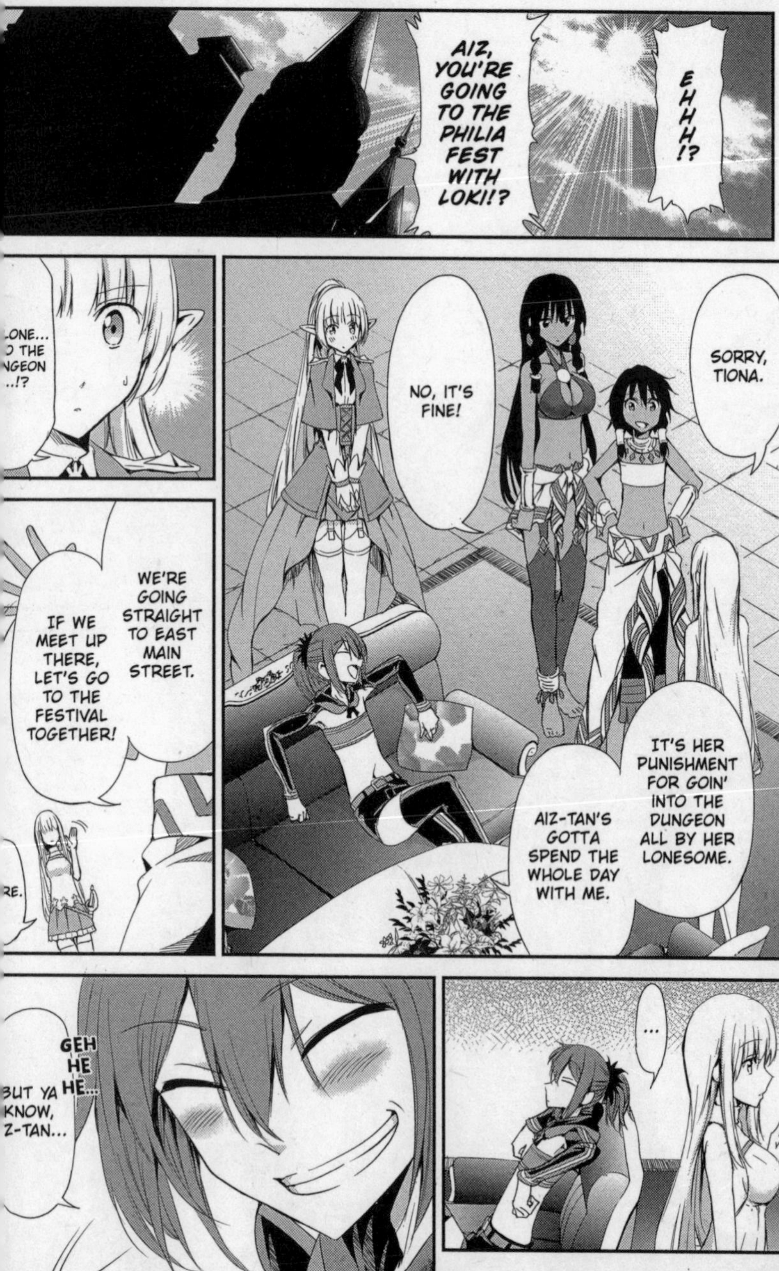
EHHH!?
AIZ, YOU'RE GOING TO THE PHILIA FEST WITH LOKI!?
SORRY, TIONA.
NO, IT'S FINE!
IT'S HER PUNISHMENT FOR GOIN' INTO THE DUNGEON ALL BY HER LONESOME.
AIZ-TAN'S GOTTA SPEND THE WHOLE DAY WITH ME.
ONE... O THE NGEON ..!?
WE'RE GOING STRAIGHT TO EAST MAIN STREET.
IF WE MEET UP THERE, LET'S GO TO THE FESTIVAL TOGETHER!
RE.
...
GEH HE HE...
BUT YA KNOW, Z-TAN...

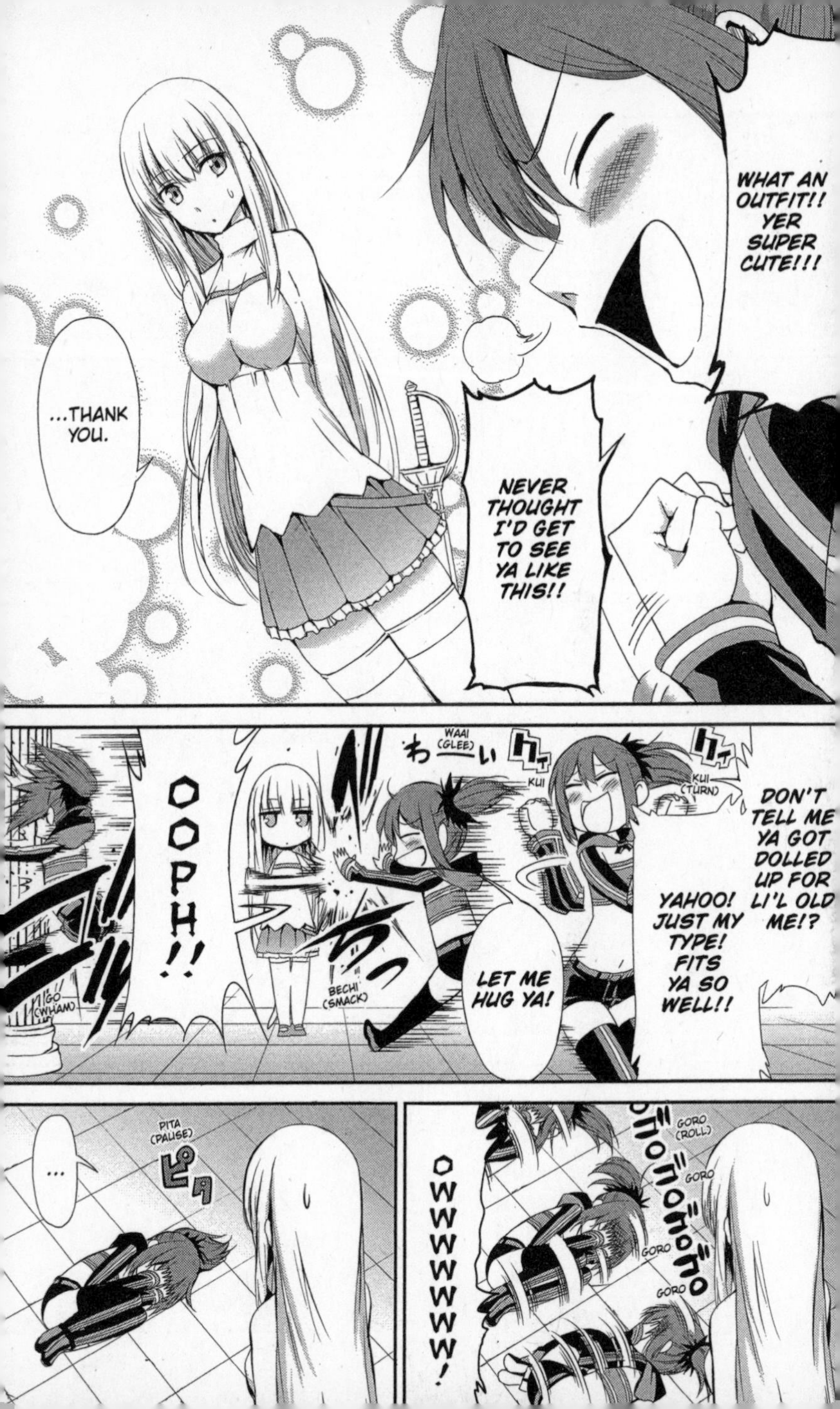
WHAT AN OUTFIT!! YER SUPER CUTE!!!
NEVER THOUGHT I'D GET TO SEE YA LIKE THIS!!
...THANK YOU.
DON'T TELL ME YA GOT DOLLED UP FOR LI'L OLD ME!?
KUI (TURN)
KUI
YAHOO! JUST MY TYPE! FITS YA SO WELL!!
WAAI (GLEE)
LET ME HUG YA!
BECHI (SMACK)
OOPH!!
GO (WHAM)
GORO (ROLL)
GORO
GORO
GORO
OWWWWWWWWW!
PITA (PAUSE)
...

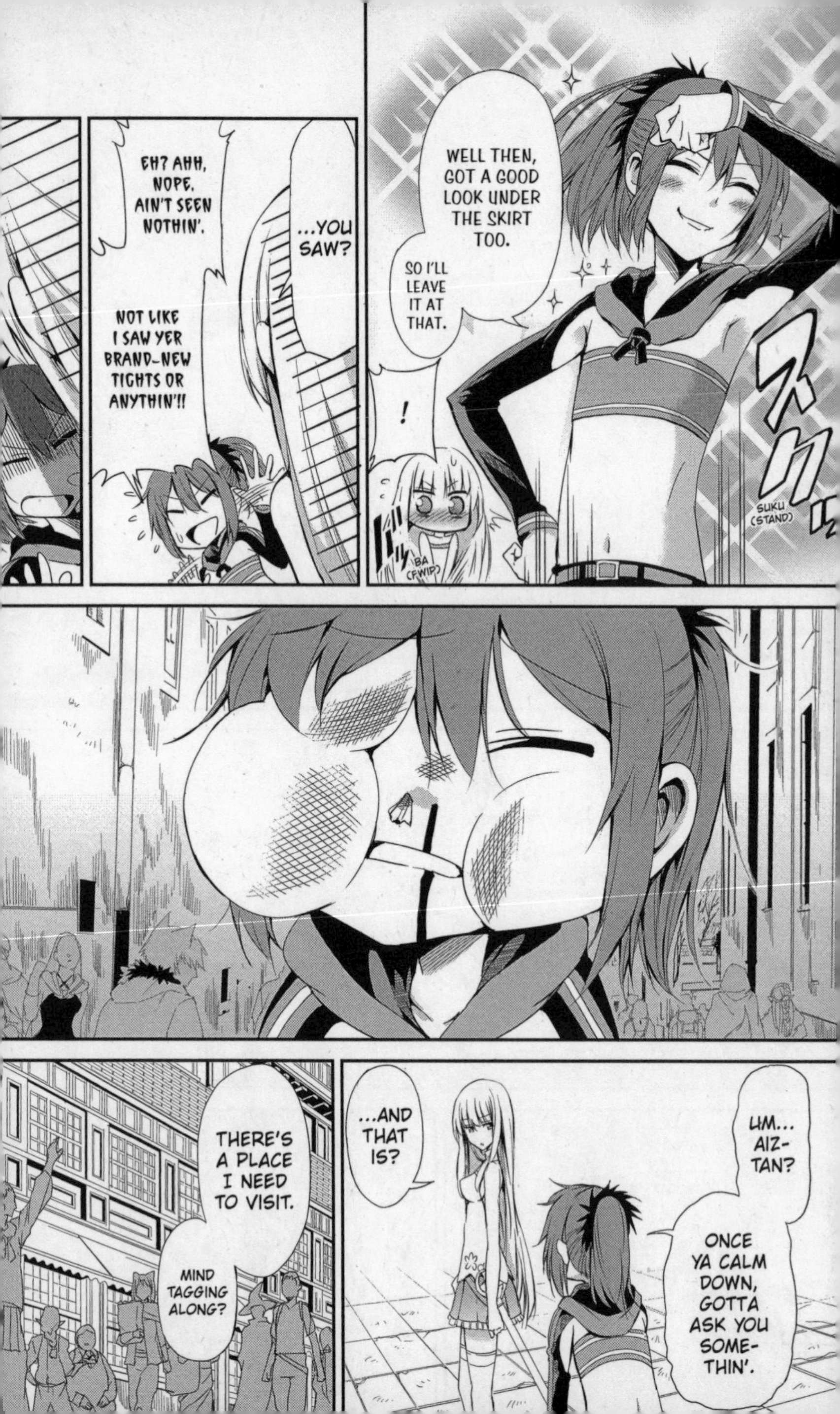
WELL THEN, GOT A GOOD LOOK UNDER THE SKIRT TOO.
SO I'LL LEAVE IT AT THAT.
SUKU (STAND)
!
BA (FWIP)
...YOU SAW?
EH? AHH, NOPE. AIN'T SEEN NOTHIN'.
NOT LIKE I SAW YER BRAND-NEW TIGHTS OR ANYTHIN'!!
UM... AIZ-TAN?
ONCE YA CALM DOWN, GOTTA ASK YOU SOME-THIN'.
...AND THAT IS?
THERE'S A PLACE I NEED TO VISIT.
MIND TAGGING ALONG?

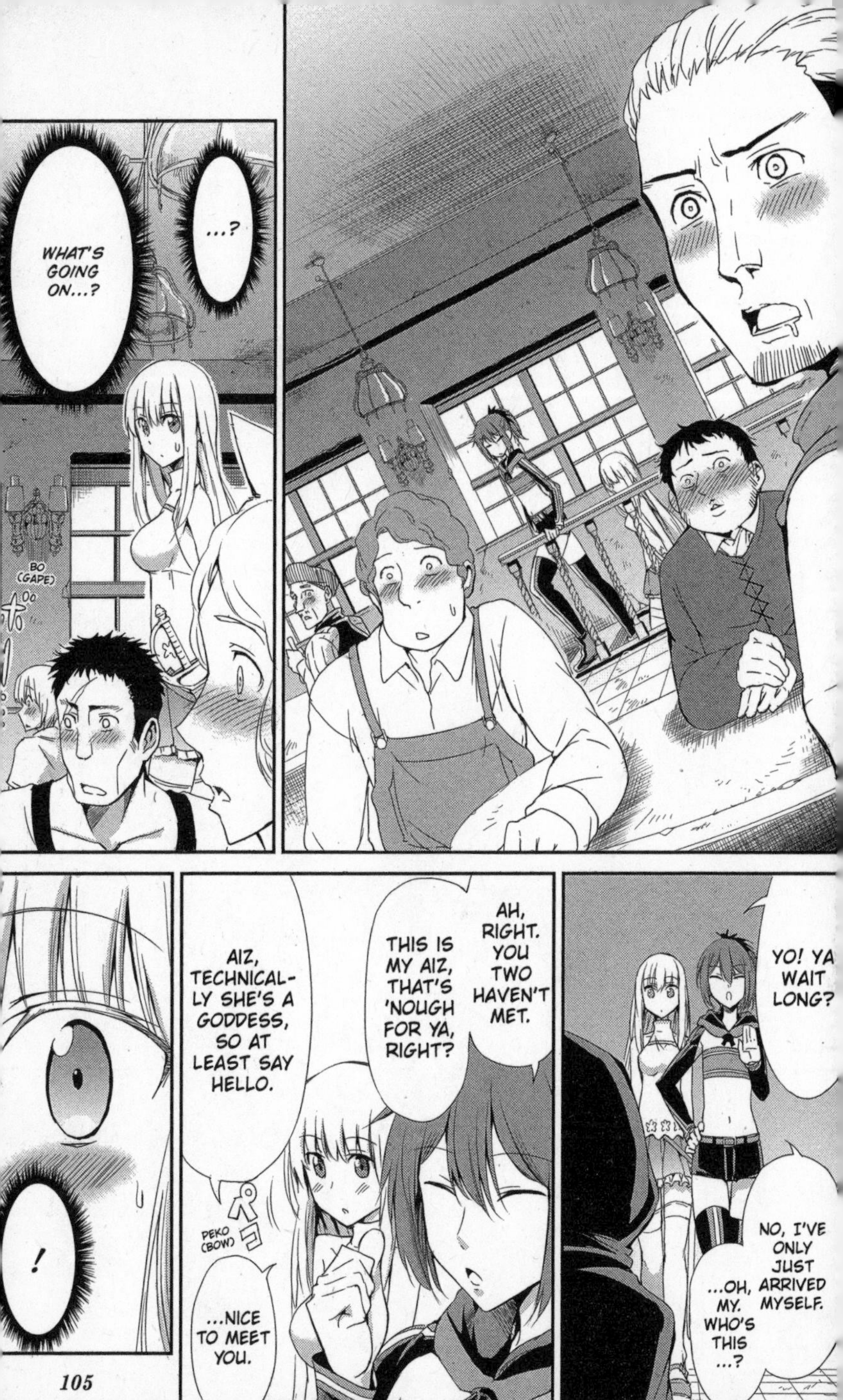
...?
WHAT'S GOING ON...?
BO (GAPE)
YO! YA WAIT LONG?
NO, I'VE ONLY JUST ARRIVED MYSELF.
...OH, MY. WHO'S THIS ...?
AH, RIGHT. YOU TWO HAVEN'T MET.
THIS IS MY AIZ, THAT'S 'NOUGH FOR YA, RIGHT?
AIZ, TECHNICAL-LY SHE'S A GODDESS, SO AT LEAST SAY HELLO.
PEKO (BOW)
...NICE TO MEET YOU.
!

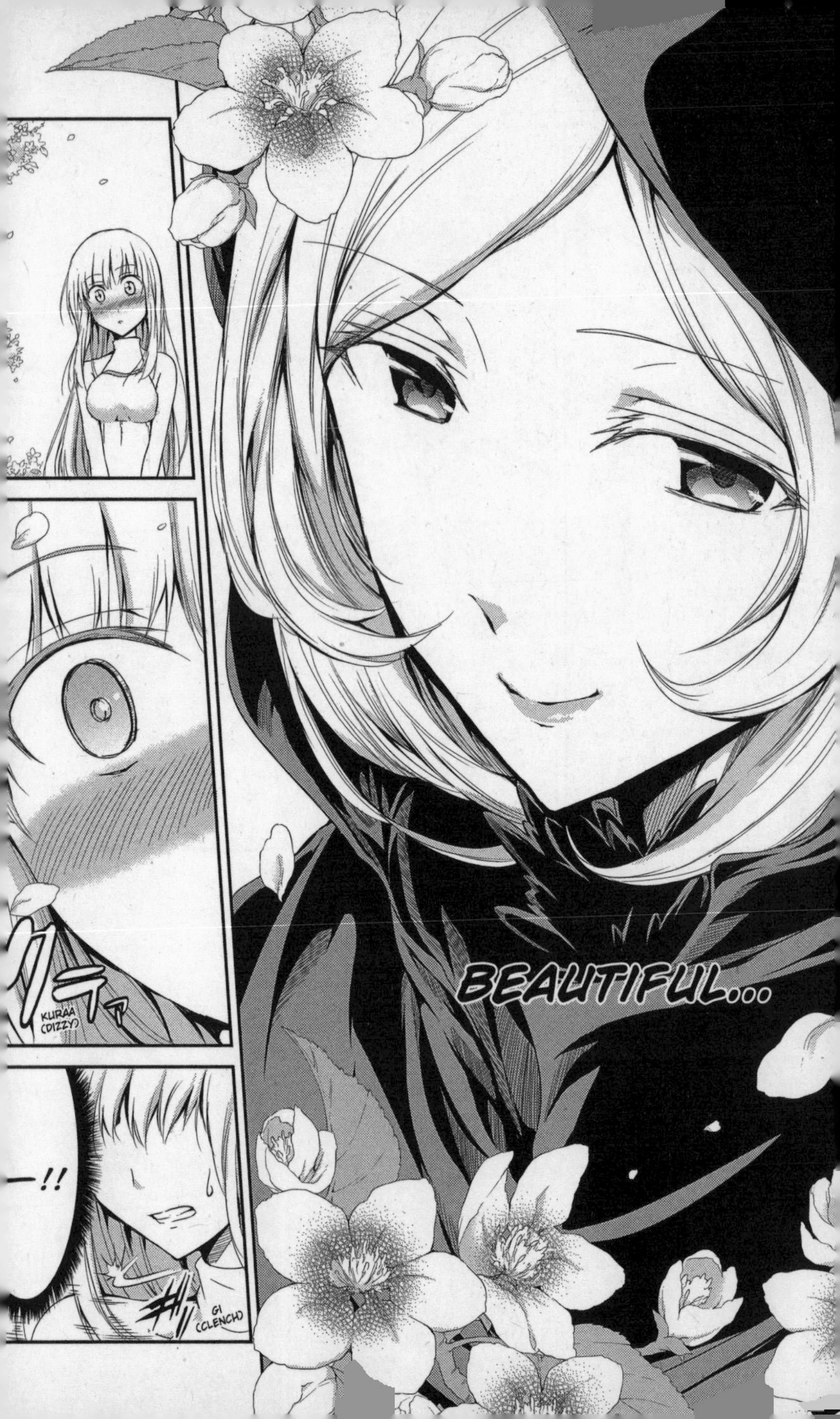
BEAUTIFUL...
KURAA
(DIZZY)
—!!
GI
(CLENCH)

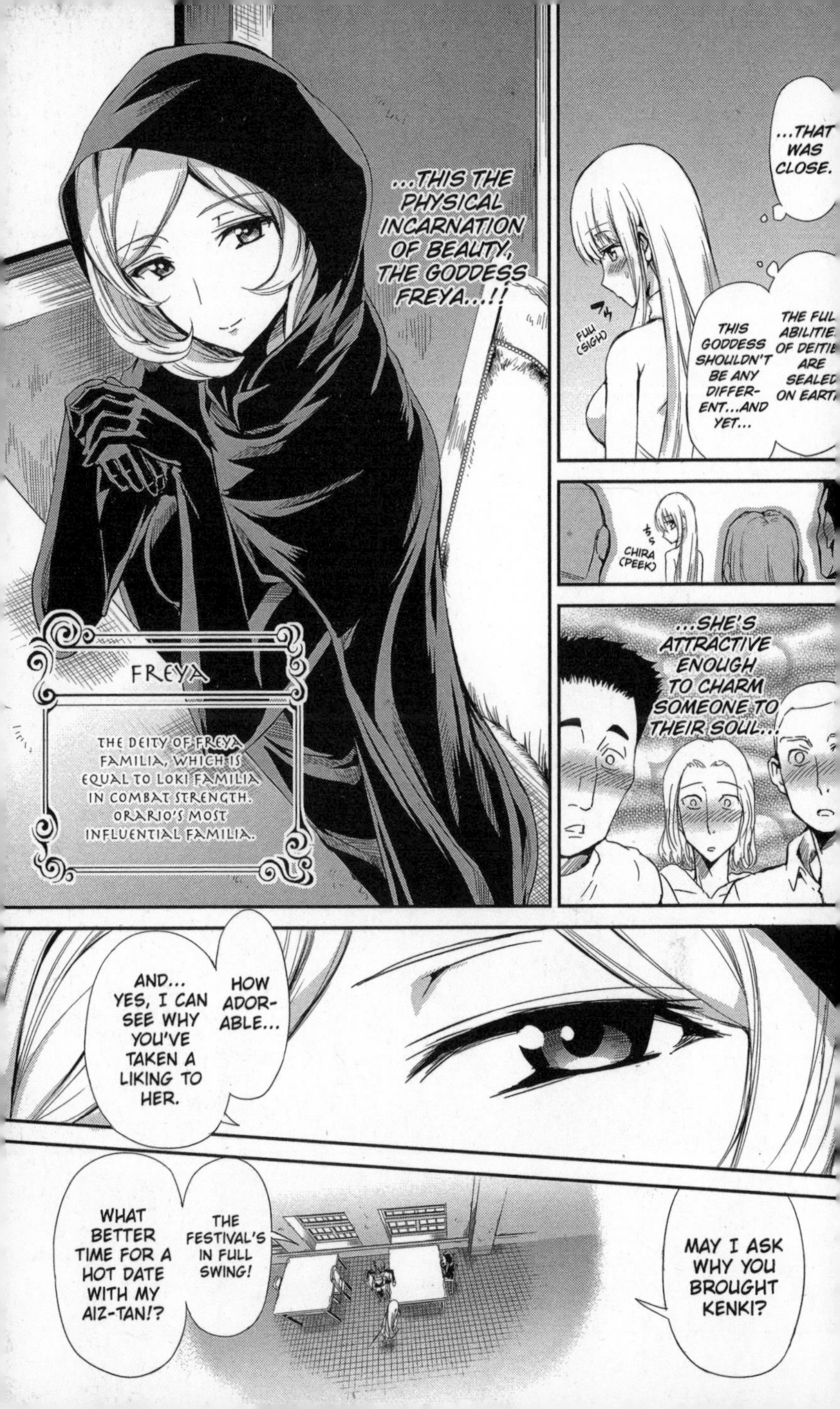

...THAT WAS CLOSE.
THE FUL ABILITIE OF DEITIE ARE SEALED ON EART
THIS GODDESS SHOULDN'T BE ANY DIFFER-ENT...AND YET...
FUU (SIGH)
CHIRA (PEEK)
...SHE'S ATTRACTIVE ENOUGH TO CHARM SOMEONE TO THEIR SOUL...
...THIS THE PHYSICAL INCARNATION OF BEAUTY, THE GODDESS FREYA...!!
FREYA
THE DEITY OF FREYA FAMILIA, WHICH IS EQUAL TO LOKI FAMILIA IN COMBAT STRENGTH. ORARIO'S MOST INFLUENTIAL FAMILIA.
HOW ADOR-ABLE...
AND... YES, I CAN SEE WHY YOU'VE TAKEN A LIKING TO HER.
MAY I ASK WHY YOU BROUGHT KENKI?
THE FESTIVAL'S IN FULL SWING!
WHAT BETTER TIME FOR A HOT DATE WITH MY AIZ-TAN!?

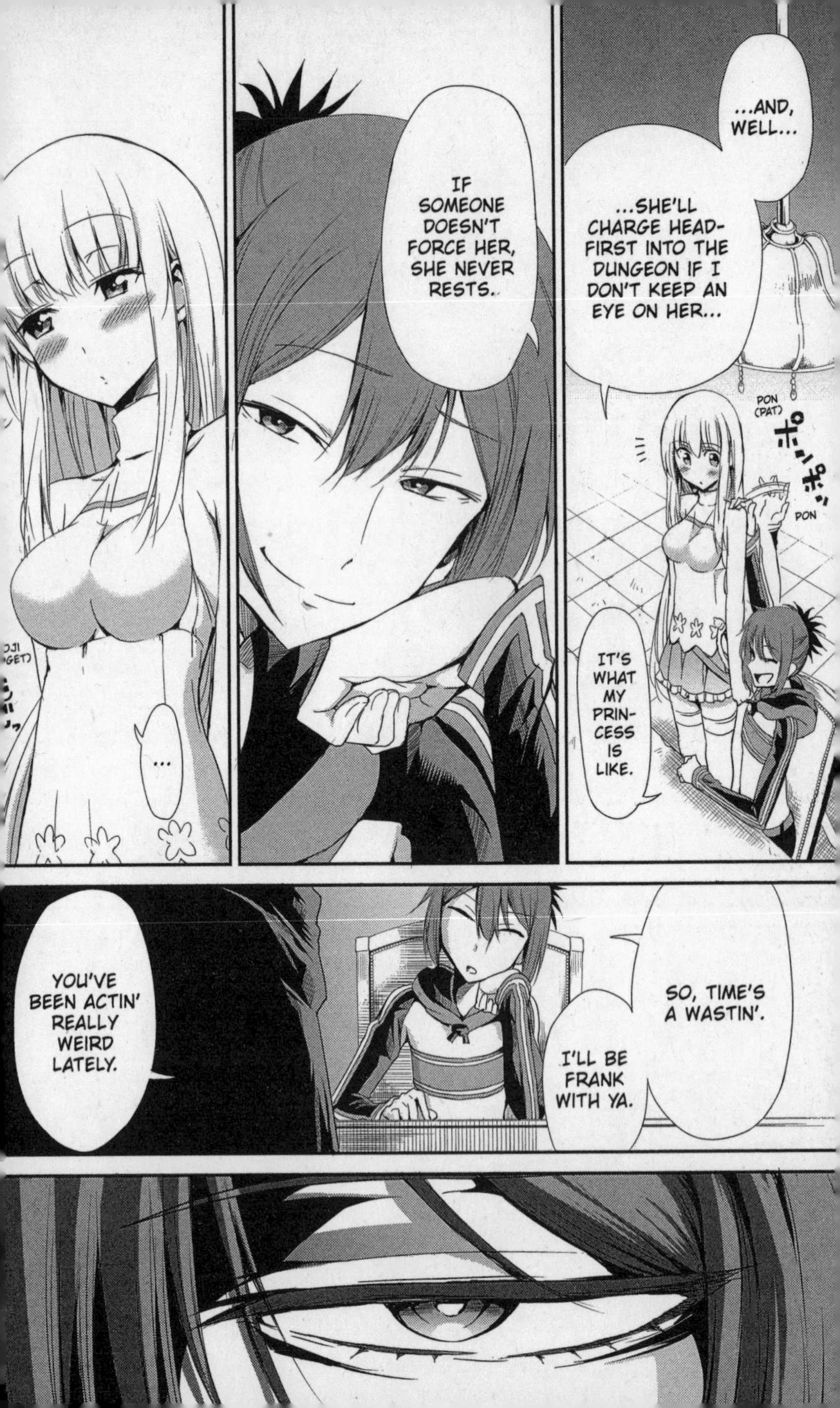
...AND, WELL...
...SHE'LL CHARGE HEAD-FIRST INTO THE DUNGEON IF I DON'T KEEP AN EYE ON HER...
PON (PAT)
PON
IT'S WHAT MY PRIN-CESS IS LIKE.
IF SOMEONE DOESN'T FORCE HER, SHE NEVER RESTS.
...
SO, TIME'S A WASTIN'.
I'LL BE FRANK WITH YA.
YOU'VE BEEN ACTIN' REALLY WEIRD LATELY.

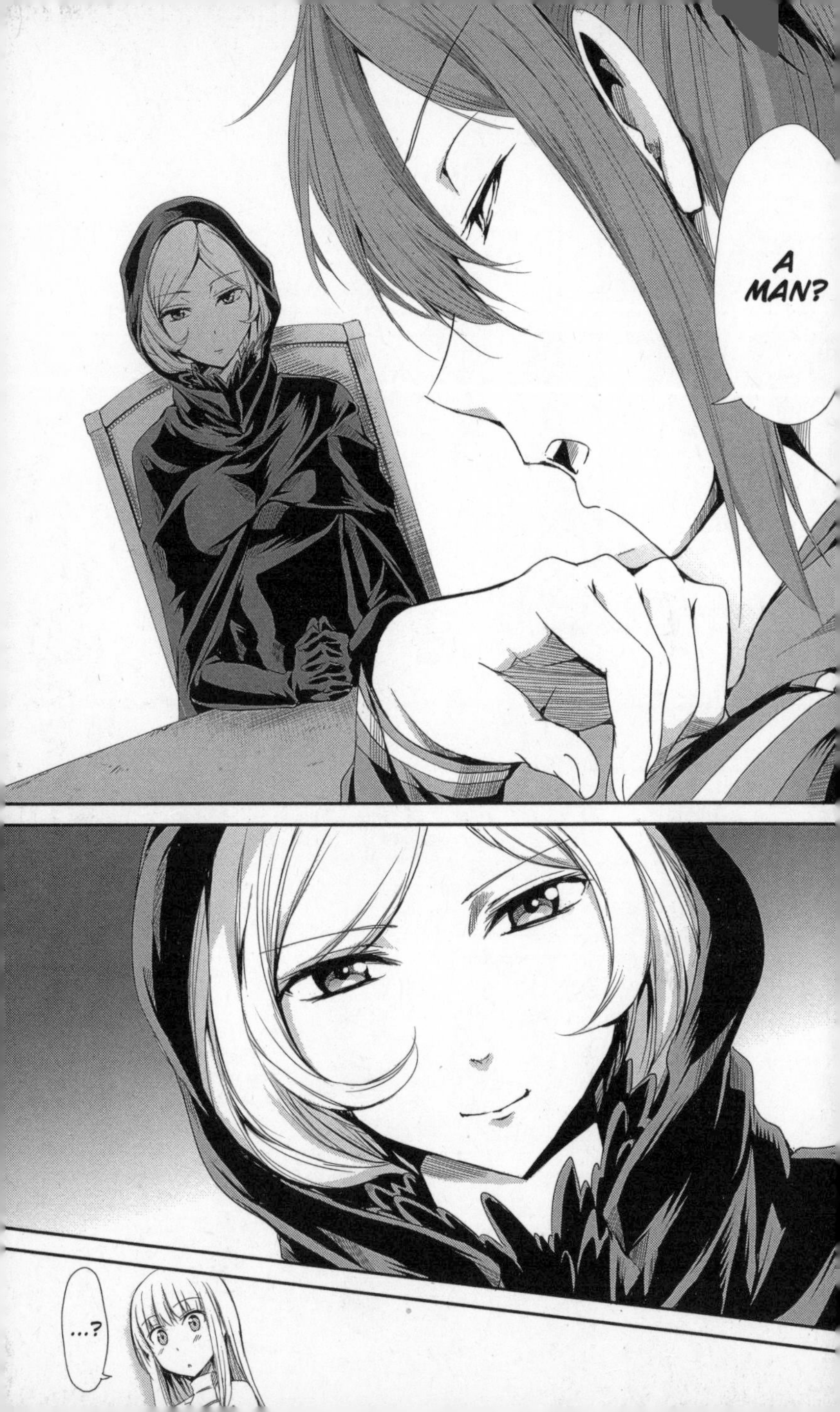
A MAN?
...?

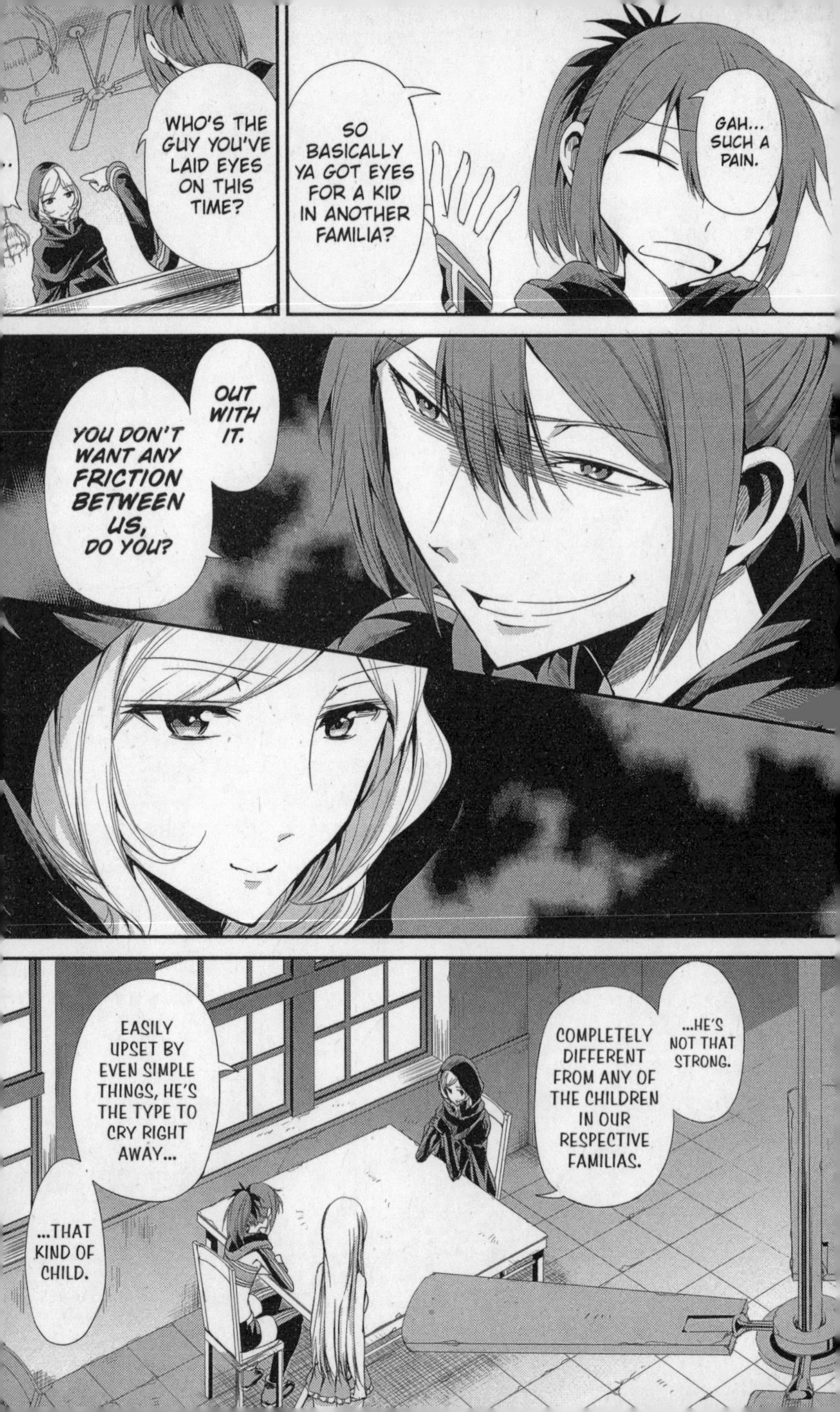
GAH... SUCH A PAIN.
SO BASICALLY YA GOT EYES FOR A KID IN ANOTHER FAMILIA?
WHO'S THE GUY YOU'VE LAID EYES ON THIS TIME?
OUT WITH IT.
YOU DON'T WANT ANY FRICTION BETWEEN US, DO YOU?
...HE'S NOT THAT STRONG.
COMPLETELY DIFFERENT FROM ANY OF THE CHILDREN IN OUR RESPECTIVE FAMILIAS.
EASILY UPSET BY EVEN SIMPLE THINGS, HE'S THE TYPE TO CRY RIGHT AWAY...
...THAT KIND OF CHILD.

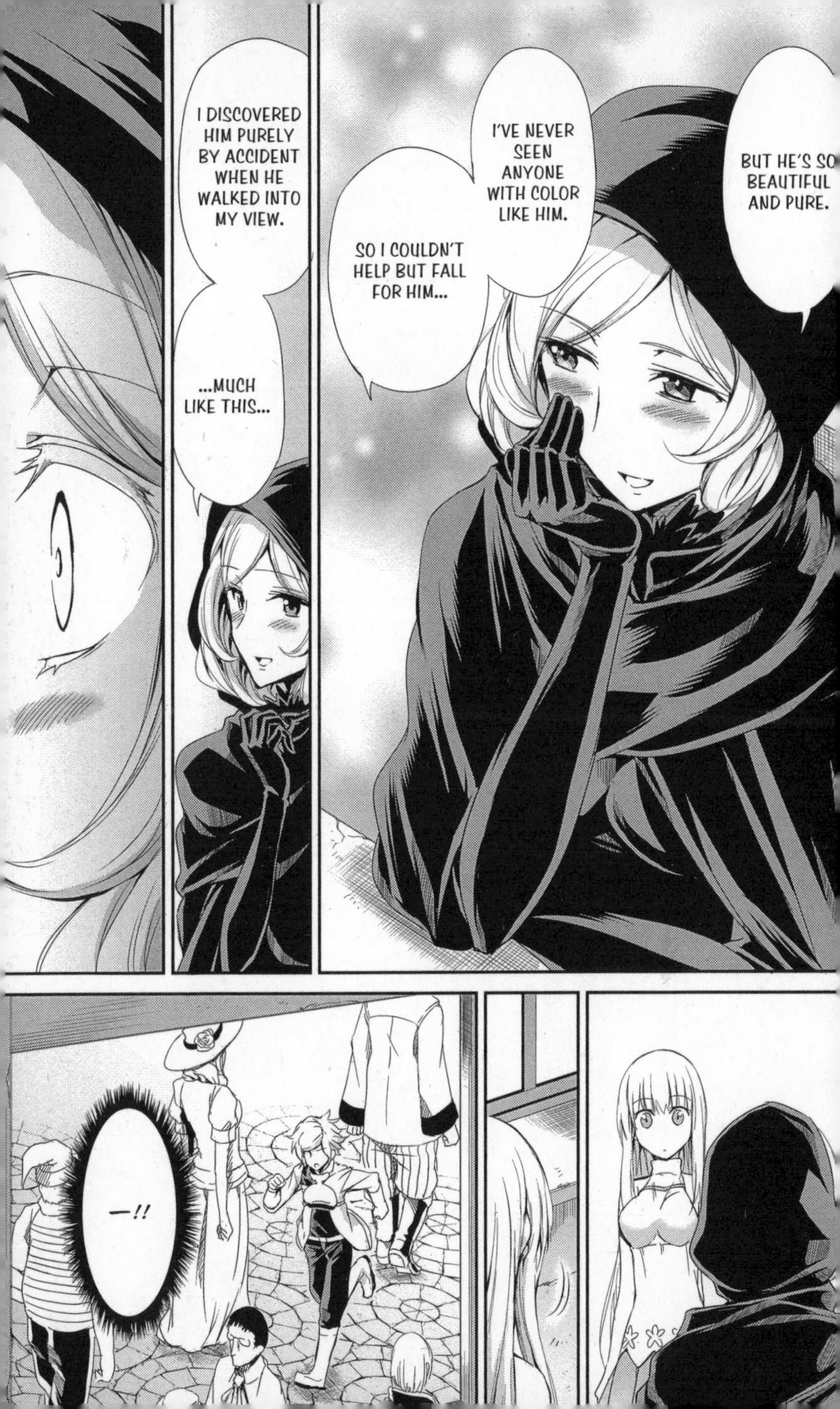
BUT HE'S SO BEAUTIFUL AND PURE.
I'VE NEVER SEEN ANYONE WITH COLOR LIKE HIM.
SO I COULDN'T HELP BUT FALL FOR HIM...
I DISCOVERED HIM PURELY BY ACCIDENT WHEN HE WALKED INTO MY VIEW.
...MUCH LIKE THIS...
—!!

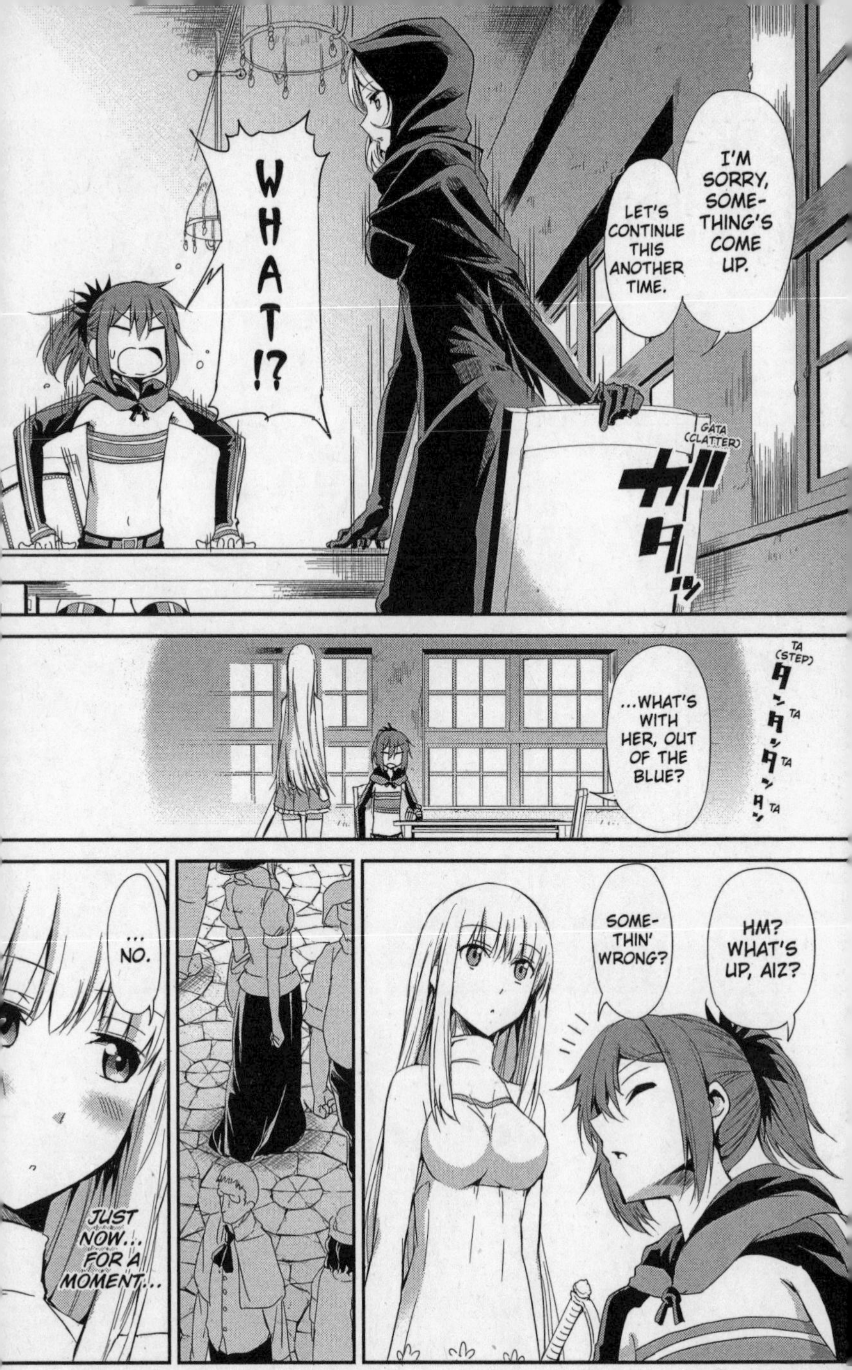
I'M SORRY, SOMETHING'S COME UP.
LET'S CONTINUE THIS ANOTHER TIME.
WHAT!?
GATA (CLATTER)
TA (STEP)
...WHAT'S WITH HER, OUT OF THE BLUE?
TA TA TA
HM? WHAT'S UP, AIZ?
SOMETHIN' WRONG?
...NO.
JUST NOW... FOR A MOMENT...

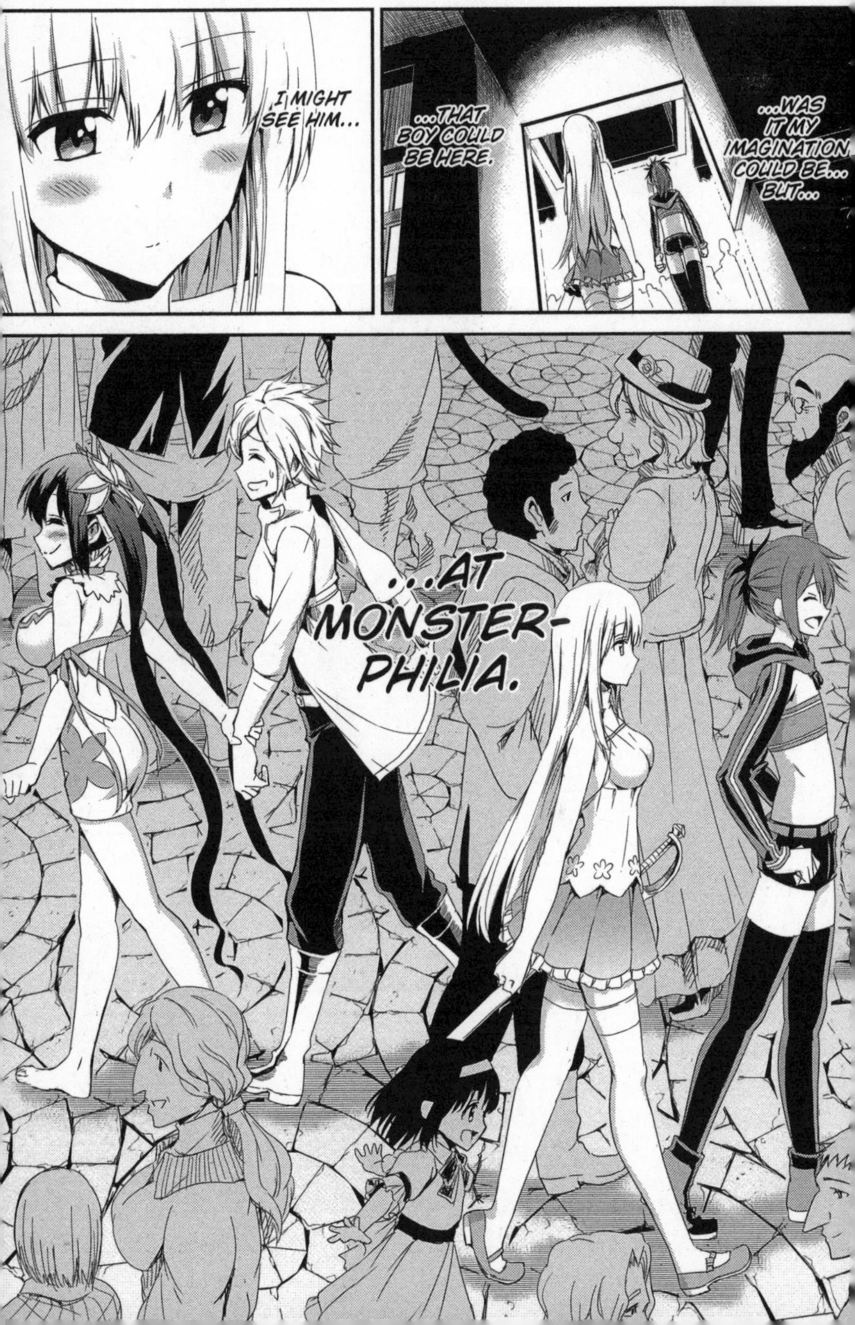
...WAS IT MY IMAGINATION COULD BE... BUT...
...THAT BOY COULD BE HERE.
I MIGHT SEE HIM...
...AT MONSTER-PHILIA.

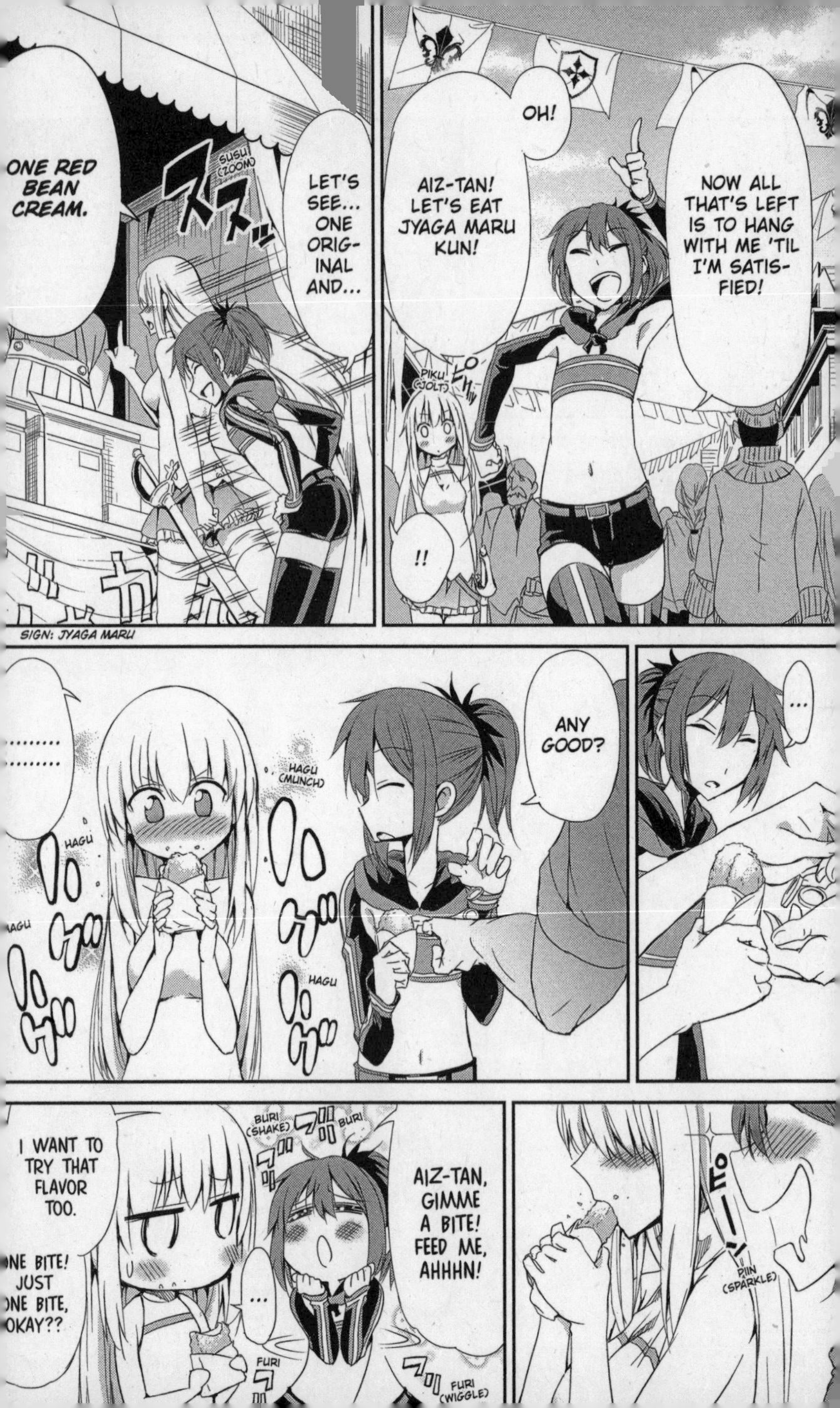
OH!
NOW ALL THAT'S LEFT IS TO HANG WITH ME 'TIL I'M SATIS-FIED!
AIZ-TAN! LET'S EAT JYAGA MARU KUN!
PIKU (JOLT)
!!
LET'S SEE... ONE ORIG-INAL AND...
SUSU (ZOOM)
ONE RED BEAN CREAM.
SIGN: JYAGA MARU
...
ANY GOOD?
HAGU (MUNCH)
HAGU
....
....
HAGU
HAGU
PIIN (SPARKLE)
AIZ-TAN, GIMME A BITE! FEED ME, AHHHN!
BURI (SHAKE)
BURI
...
I WANT TO TRY THAT FLAVOR TOO.
NE BITE! JUST NE BITE, OKAY??
FURI
FURI (WIGGLE)

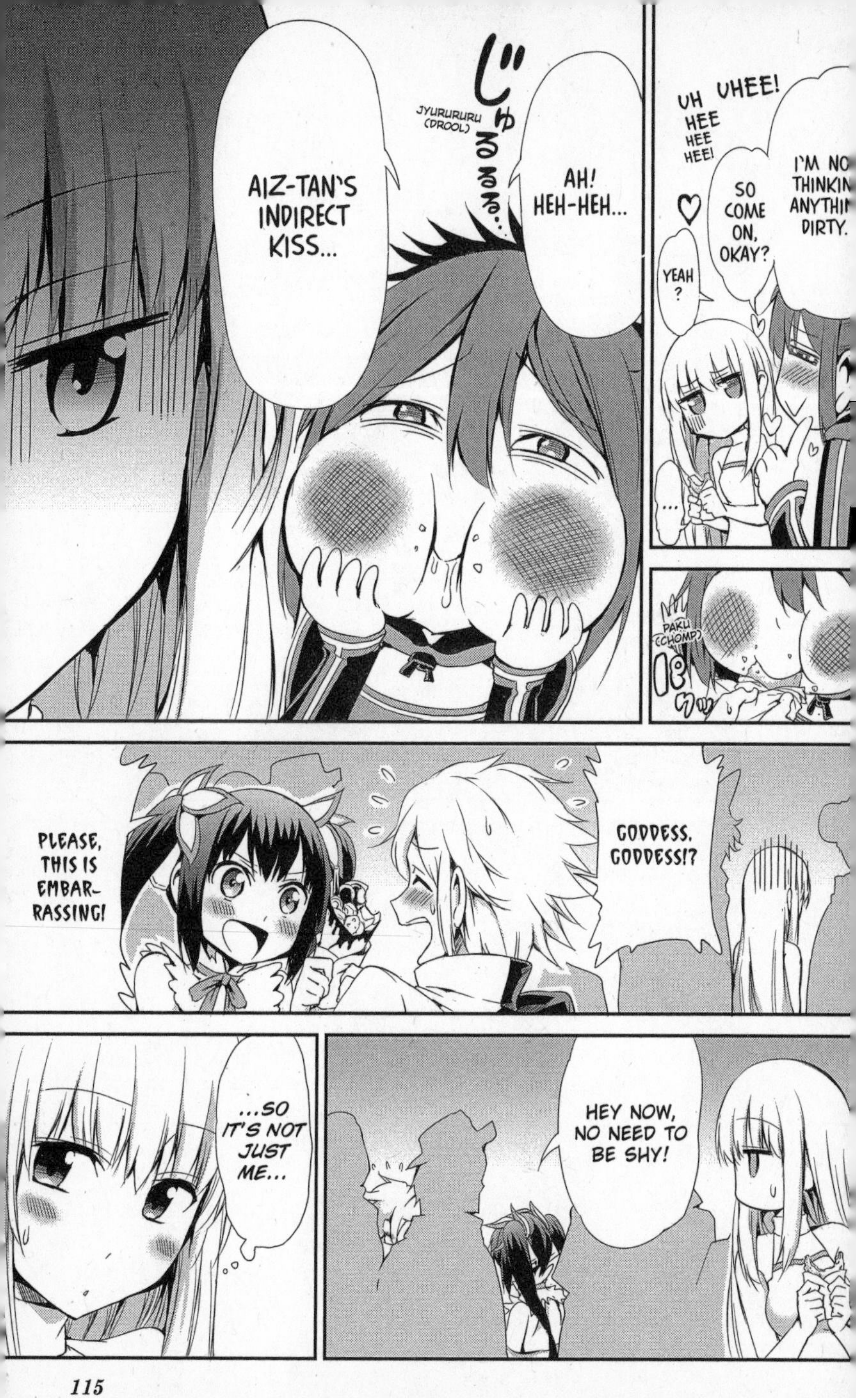
I'M NO
THINKIN
ANYTHI
DIRTY.
UHEE!
UH HEE HEE HEE!
SO COME ON, OKAY?
YEAH?
...
PAKU (CHOMP)
AH! HEH-HEH...
JYURURURU (DROOL)
じゅるるる…
AIZ-TAN'S INDIRECT KISS...
GODDESS, GODDESS!?
PLEASE, THIS IS EMBARRASSING!
HEY NOW, NO NEED TO BE SHY!
...SO IT'S NOT JUST ME...

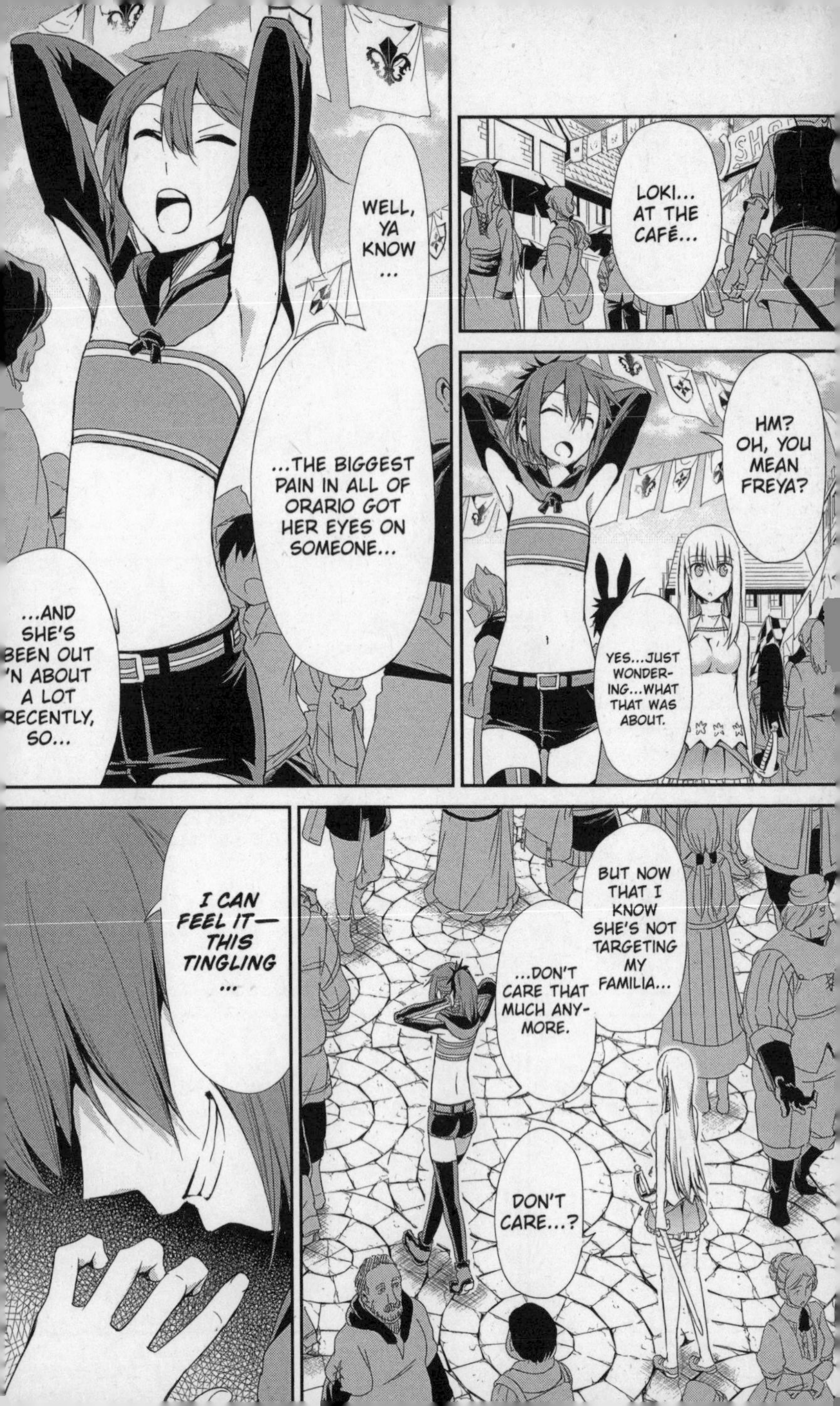
LOKI... AT THE CAFÉ...
HM? OH, YOU MEAN FREYA?
YES...JUST WONDERING...WHAT THAT WAS ABOUT.
WELL, YA KNOW...
...THE BIGGEST PAIN IN ALL OF ORARIO GOT HER EYES ON SOMEONE...
...AND SHE'S BEEN OUT 'N ABOUT A LOT RECENTLY, SO...
BUT NOW THAT I KNOW SHE'S NOT TARGETING MY FAMILIA...
...DON'T CARE THAT MUCH ANYMORE.
DON'T CARE...?
I CAN FEEL IT—THIS TINGLING...

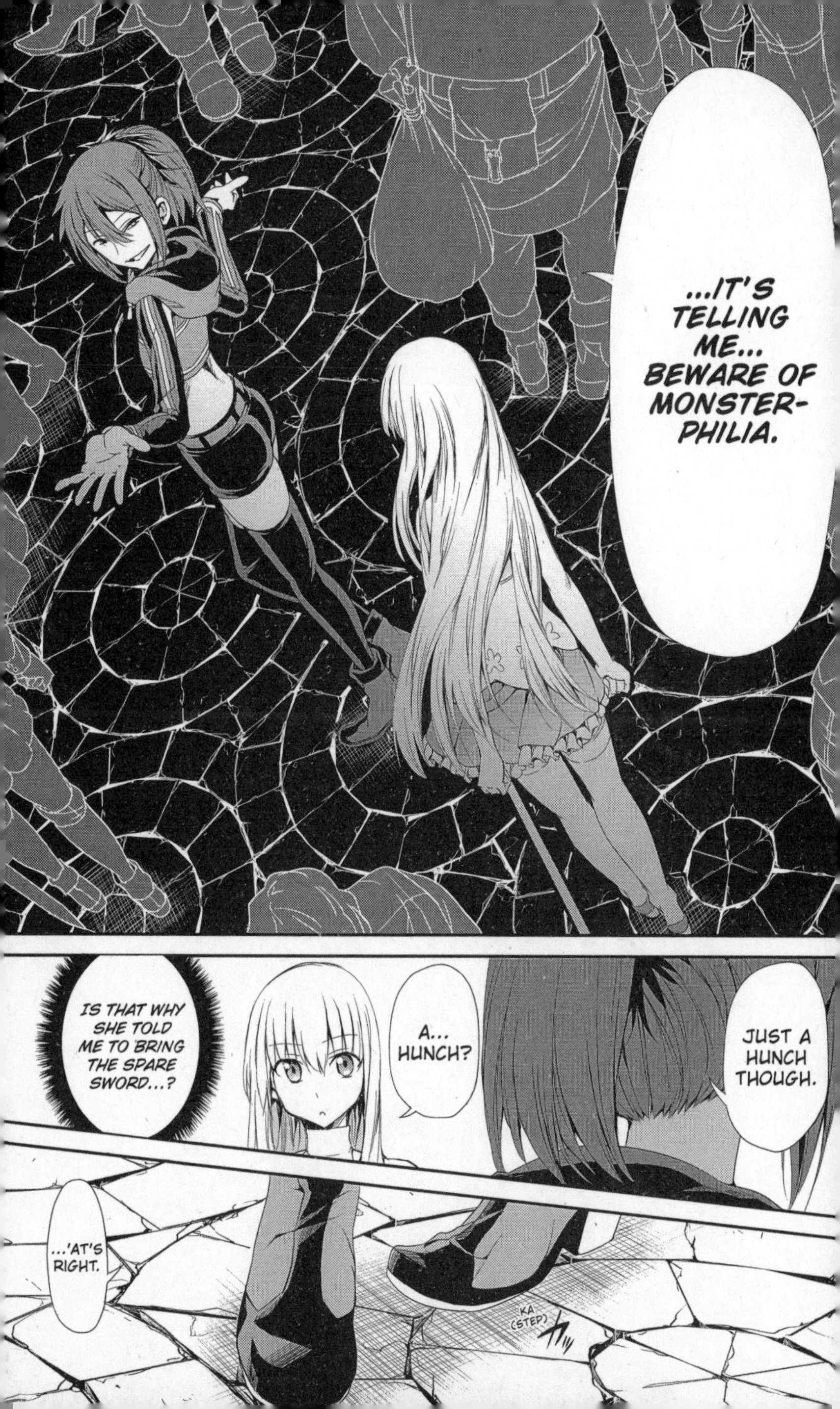
...IT'S TELLING ME... BEWARE OF MONSTER-PHILIA.
JUST A HUNCH THOUGH.
A... HUNCH?
IS THAT WHY SHE TOLD ME TO BRING THE SPARE SWORD...?
...'AT'S RIGHT.
KA (STEP)

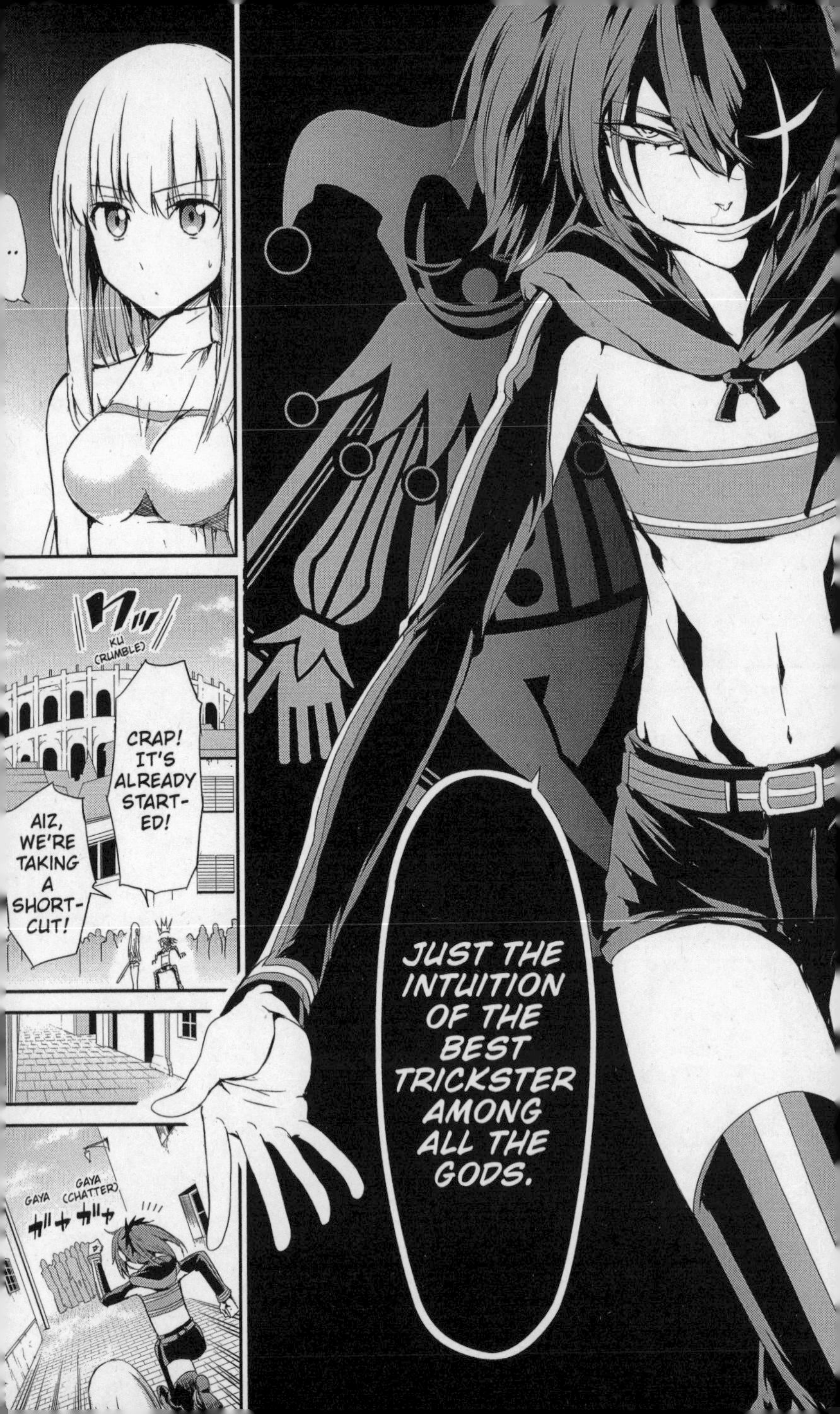
JUST THE INTUITION OF THE BEST TRICKSTER AMONG ALL THE GODS.
...
KU (RUMBLE)
CRAP! IT'S ALREADY START-ED!
AIZ, WE'RE TAKING A SHORT-CUT!
GAYA GAYA (CHATTER)

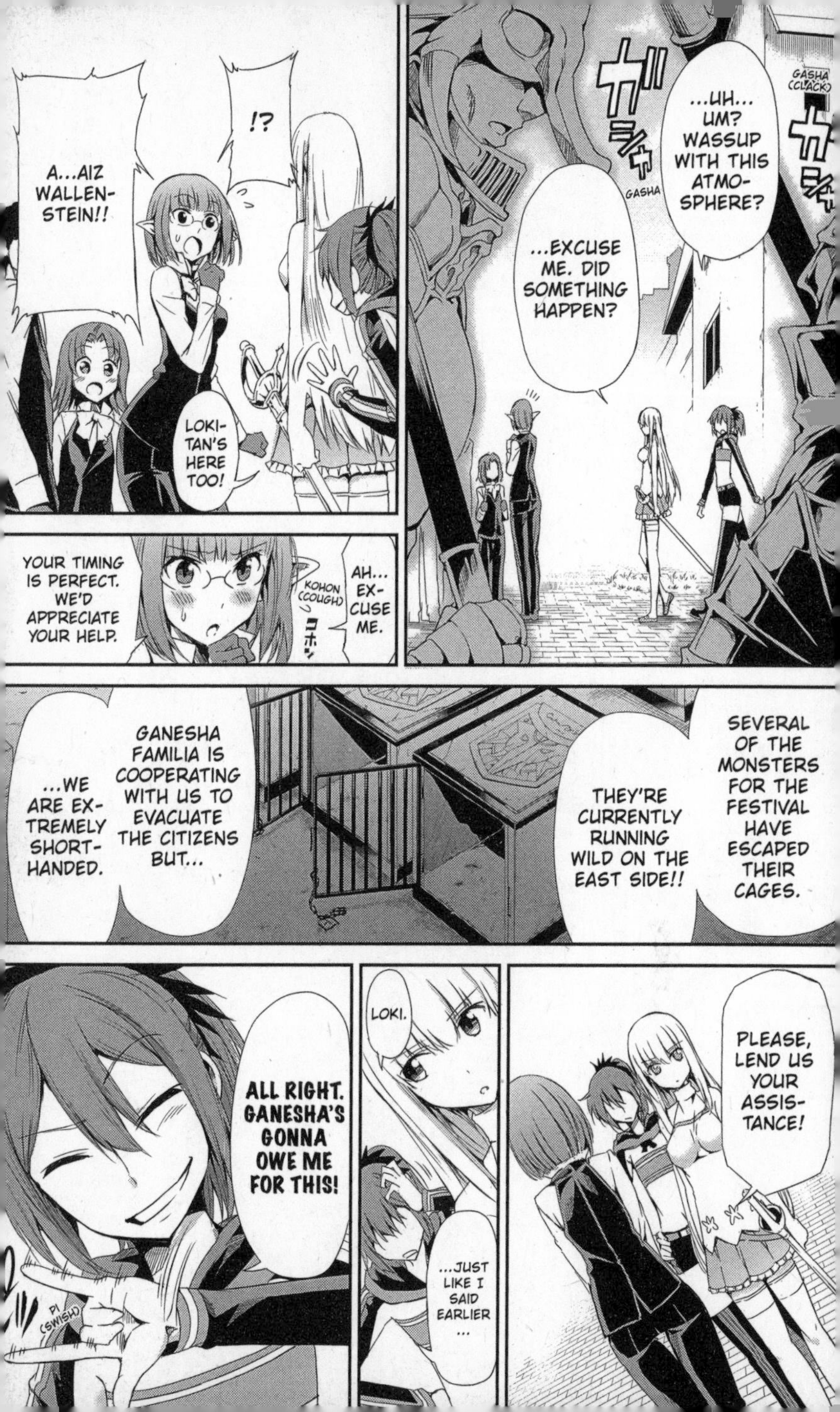
GASHA (CLACK)
...UH... UM? WASSUP WITH THIS ATMOSPHERE?
GASHA
...EXCUSE ME. DID SOMETHING HAPPEN?
A...AIZ WALLENSTEIN!!
!?
LOKI-TAN'S HERE TOO!
AH... EXCUSE ME.
KOHON (COUGH)
YOUR TIMING IS PERFECT. WE'D APPRECIATE YOUR HELP.
SEVERAL OF THE MONSTERS FOR THE FESTIVAL HAVE ESCAPED THEIR CAGES.
THEY'RE CURRENTLY RUNNING WILD ON THE EAST SIDE!!
GANESHA FAMILIA IS COOPERATING WITH US TO EVACUATE THE CITIZENS BUT...
...WE ARE EXTREMELY SHORT-HANDED.
PLEASE, LEND US YOUR ASSISTANCE!
LOKI.
...JUST LIKE I SAID EARLIER ...
ALL RIGHT. GANESHA'S GONNA OWE ME FOR THIS!
PI (SWISH)

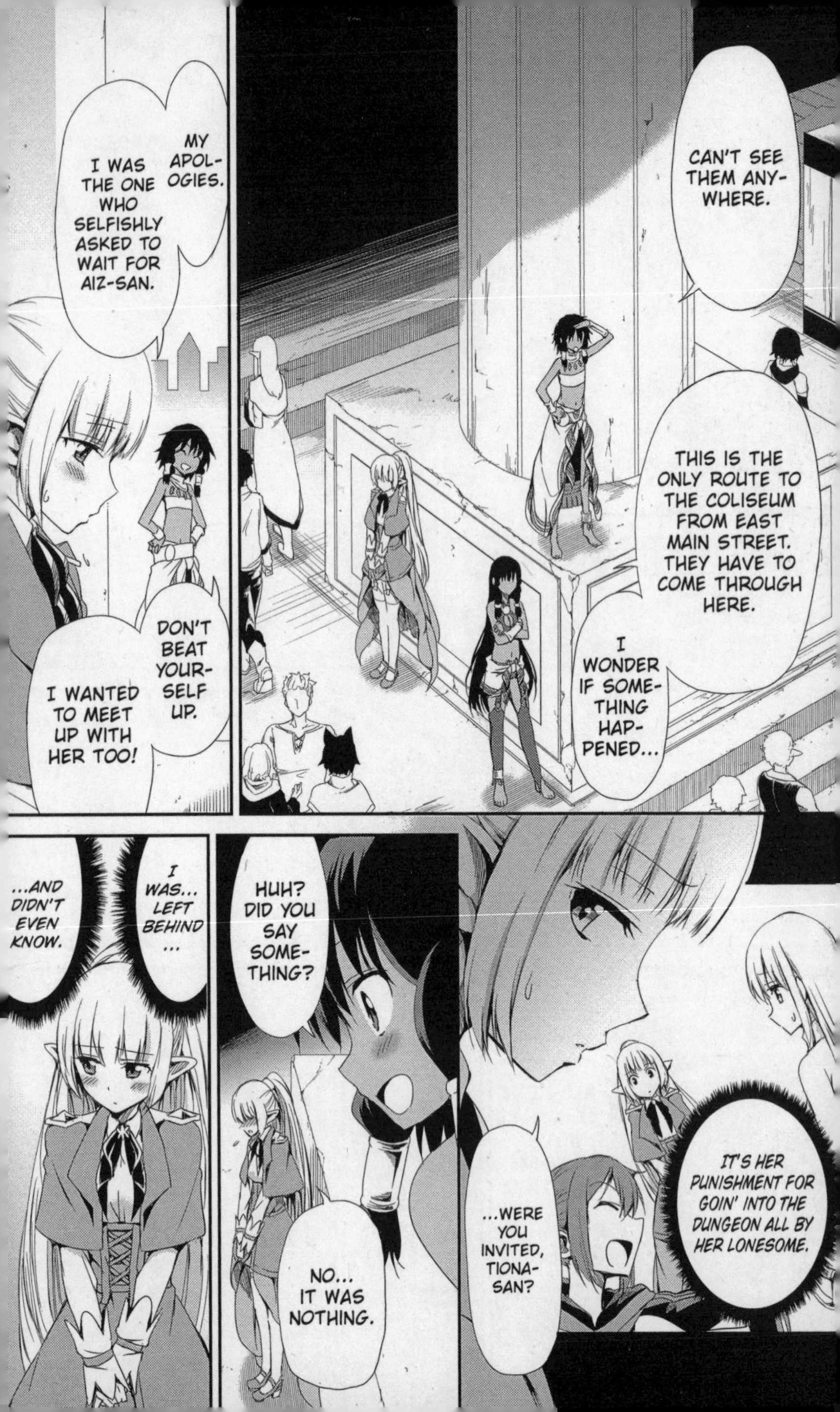
CAN'T SEE THEM ANY-WHERE.
THIS IS THE ONLY ROUTE TO THE COLISEUM FROM EAST MAIN STREET. THEY HAVE TO COME THROUGH HERE.
I WONDER IF SOME-THING HAP-PENED...
MY APOL-OGIES.
I WAS THE ONE WHO SELFISHLY ASKED TO WAIT FOR AIZ-SAN.
DON'T BEAT YOUR-SELF UP.
I WANTED TO MEET UP WITH HER TOO!
IT'S HER PUNISHMENT FOR GOIN' INTO THE DUNGEON ALL BY HER LONESOME.
...WERE YOU INVITED, TIONA-SAN?
HUH? DID YOU SAY SOME-THING?
NO... IT WAS NOTHING.
I WAS... LEFT BEHIND...
...AND DIDN'T EVEN KNOW.

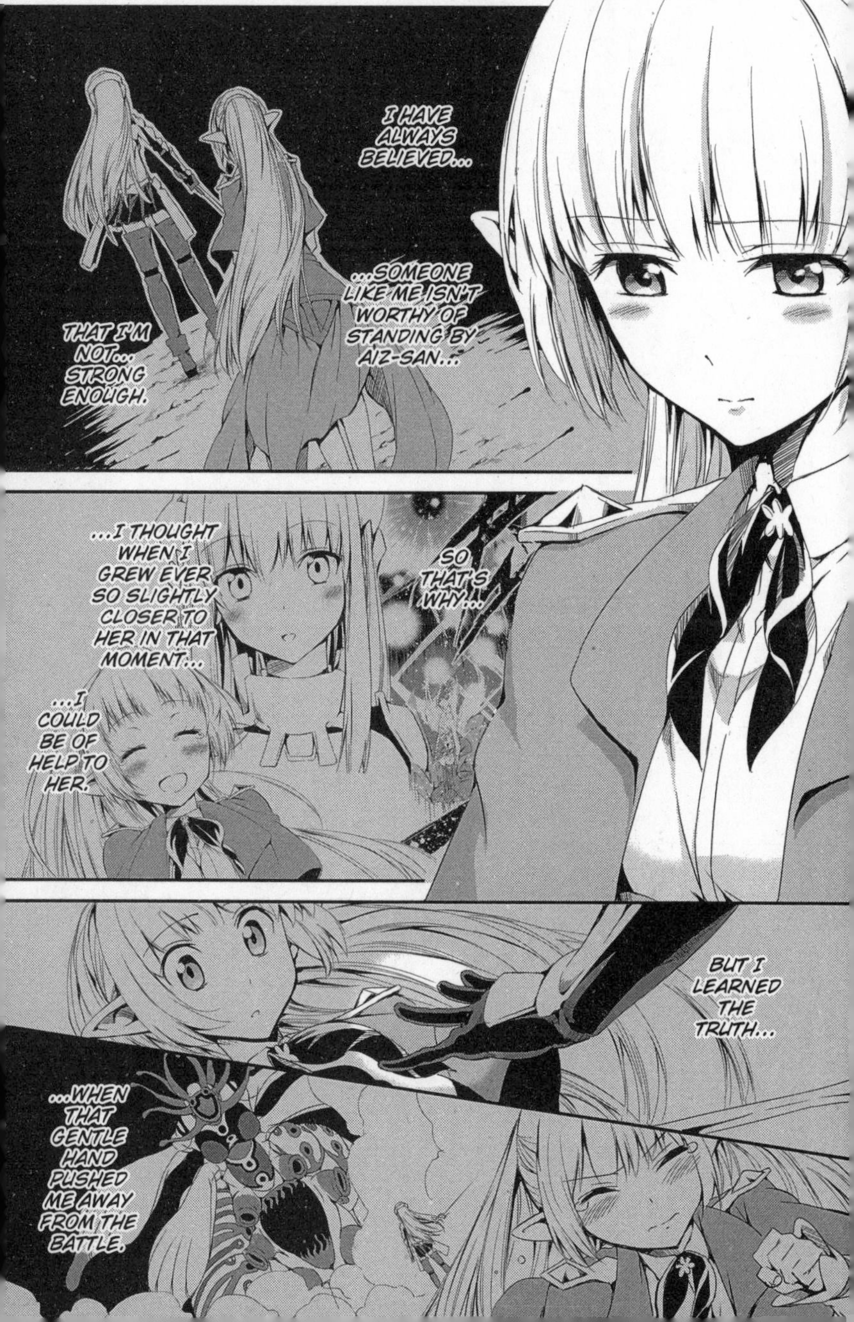
I HAVE ALWAYS BELIEVED...
...SOMEONE LIKE ME ISN'T WORTHY OF STANDING BY AIZ-SAN...
THAT I'M NOT... STRONG ENOUGH.
SO THAT'S WHY...
...I THOUGHT WHEN I GREW EVER SO SLIGHTLY CLOSER TO HER IN THAT MOMENT...
...I COULD BE OF HELP TO HER.
BUT I LEARNED THE TRUTH...
...WHEN THAT GENTLE HAND PUSHED ME AWAY FROM THE BATTLE.

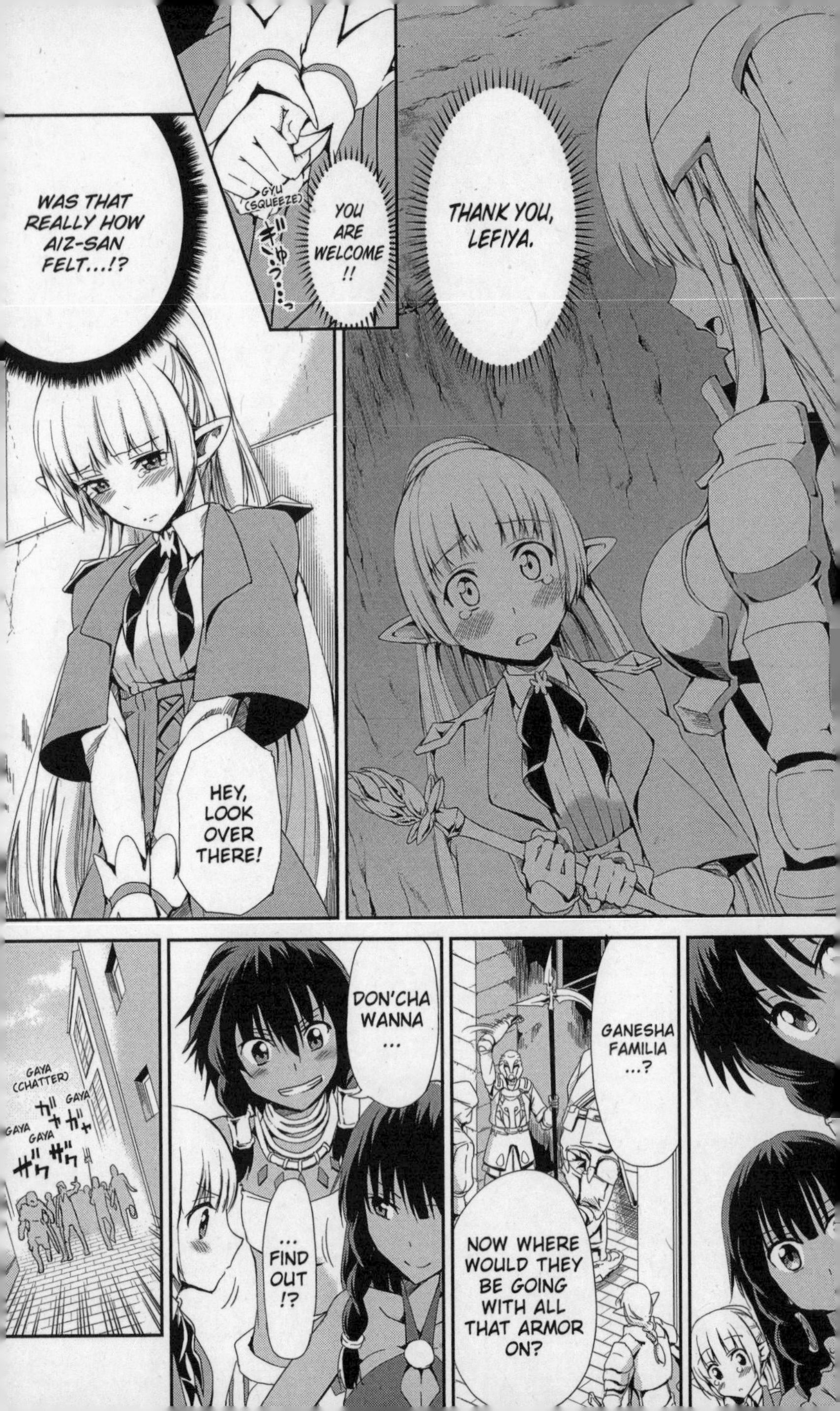
THANK YOU, LEFIYA.
GYU (SQUEEZE)
ギゅっ…っ
YOU ARE WELCOME!!
WAS THAT REALLY HOW AIZ-SAN FELT...!?
HEY, LOOK OVER THERE!
GANESHA FAMILIA ...?
NOW WHERE WOULD THEY BE GOING WITH ALL THAT ARMOR ON?
DON'CHA WANNA ...
... FIND OUT!?
GAYA (CHATTER)
ガヤ GAYA
ガヤ
GAYA
GAYA
ザクザク

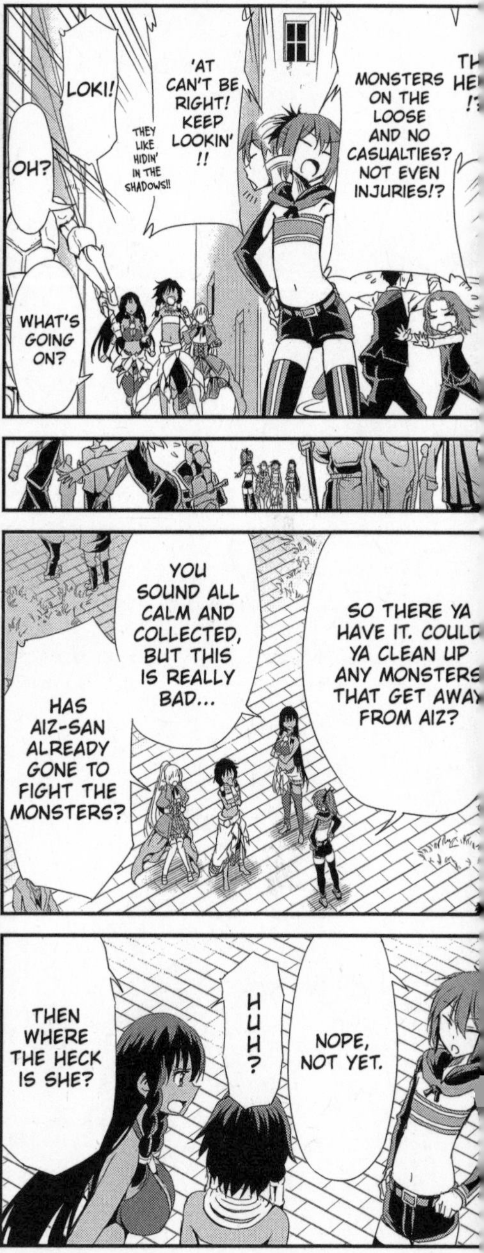
MONSTERS ON THE LOOSE AND NO CASUALTIES? NOT EVEN INJURIES!?
'AT CAN'T BE RIGHT! KEEP LOOKIN' !!
THEY LIKE HIDIN' IN THE SHADOWS!!
LOKI!
OH?
WHAT'S GOING ON?
SO THERE YA HAVE IT. COULD YA CLEAN UP ANY MONSTERS THAT GET AWAY FROM AIZ?
YOU SOUND ALL CALM AND COLLECTED, BUT THIS IS REALLY BAD...
HAS AIZ-SAN ALREADY GONE TO FIGHT THE MONSTERS?
NOPE, NOT YET.
HUH?
THEN WHERE THE HECK IS SHE?
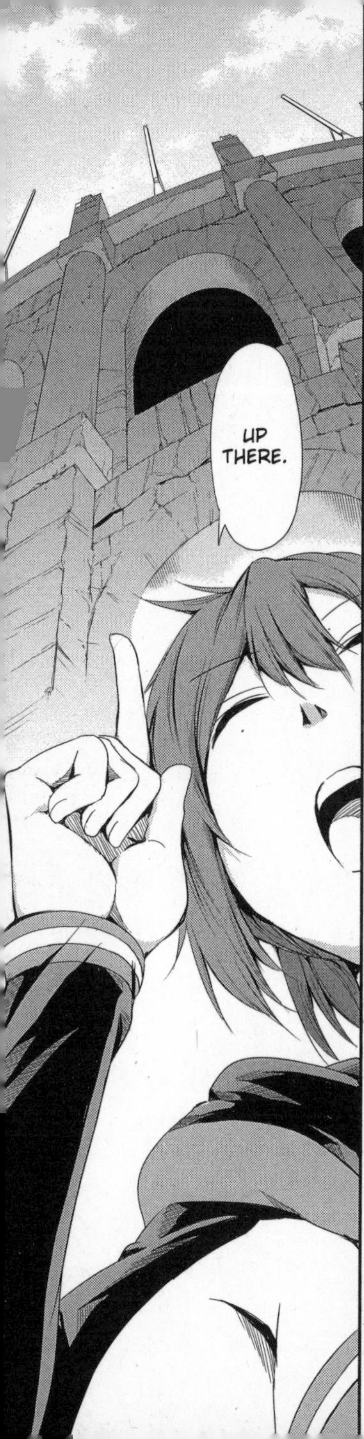
UP THERE.

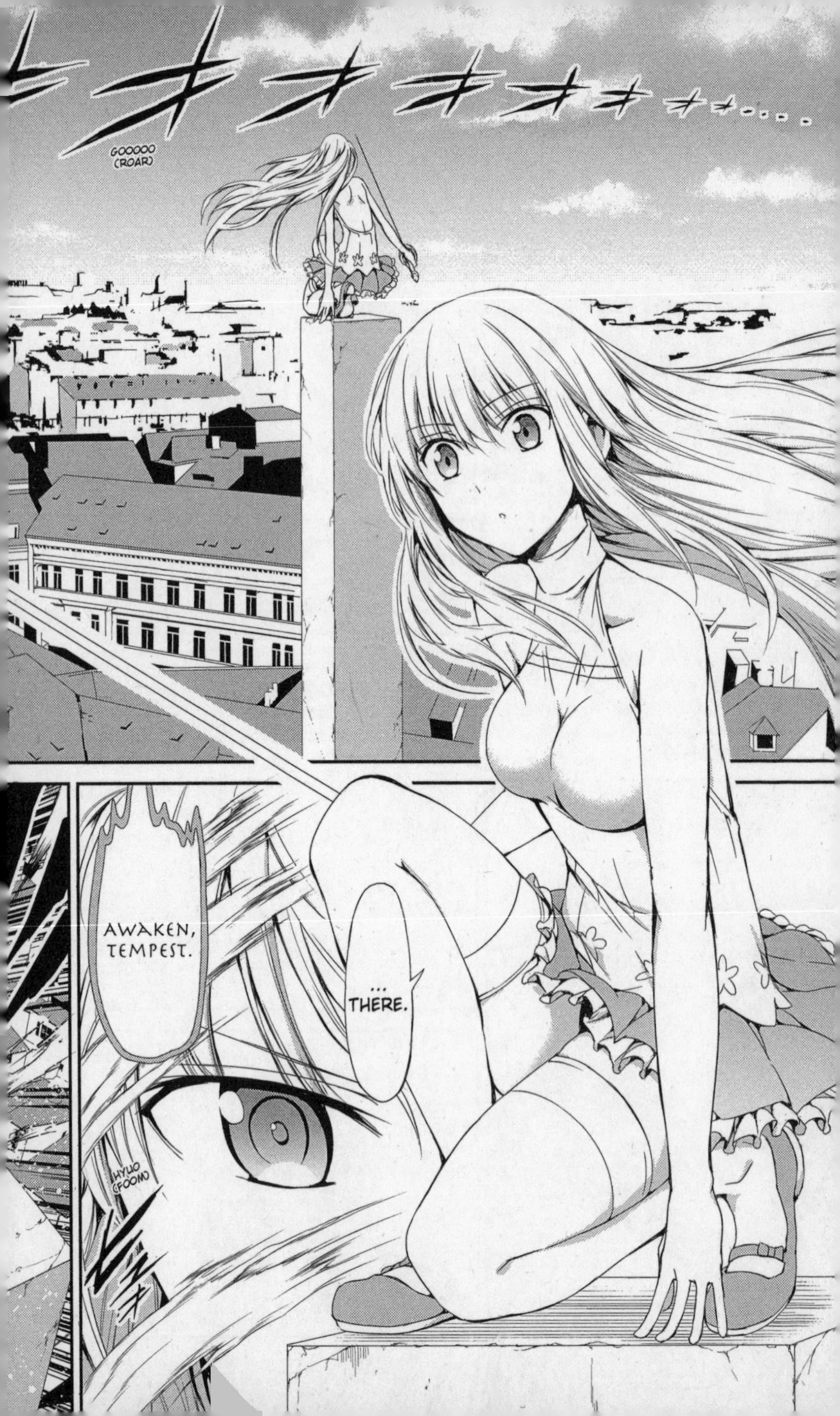
GOOOOO
(ROAR)
...THERE.
AWAKEN, TEMPEST.
HYUO
(FOOM)

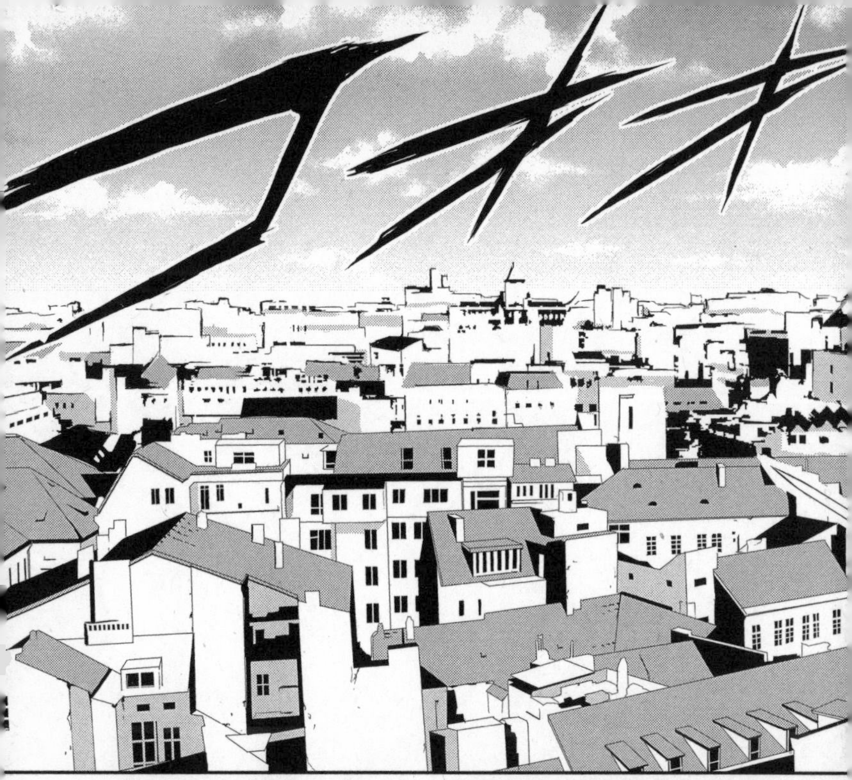

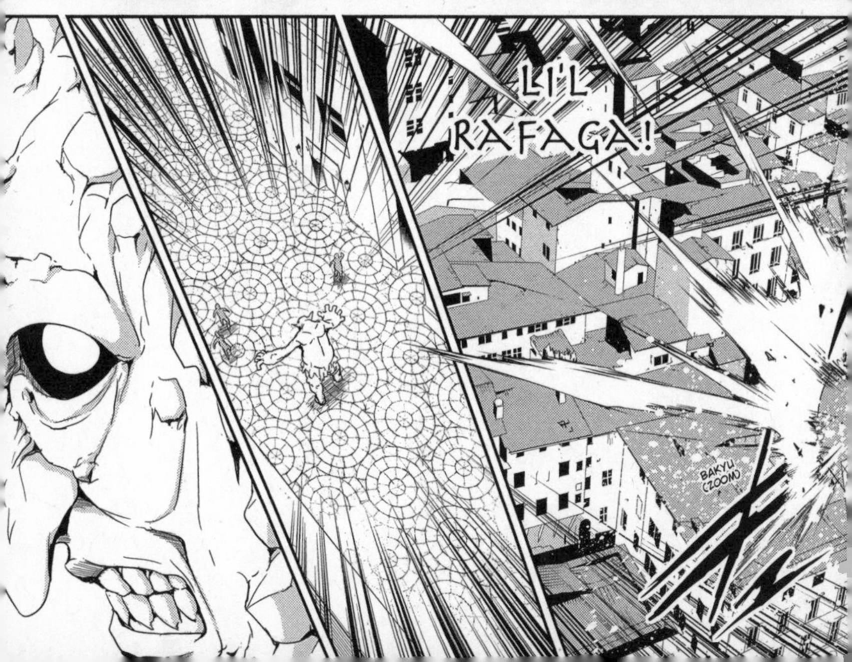
LI'L RAFAGA!
BAKYU (ZOOM)

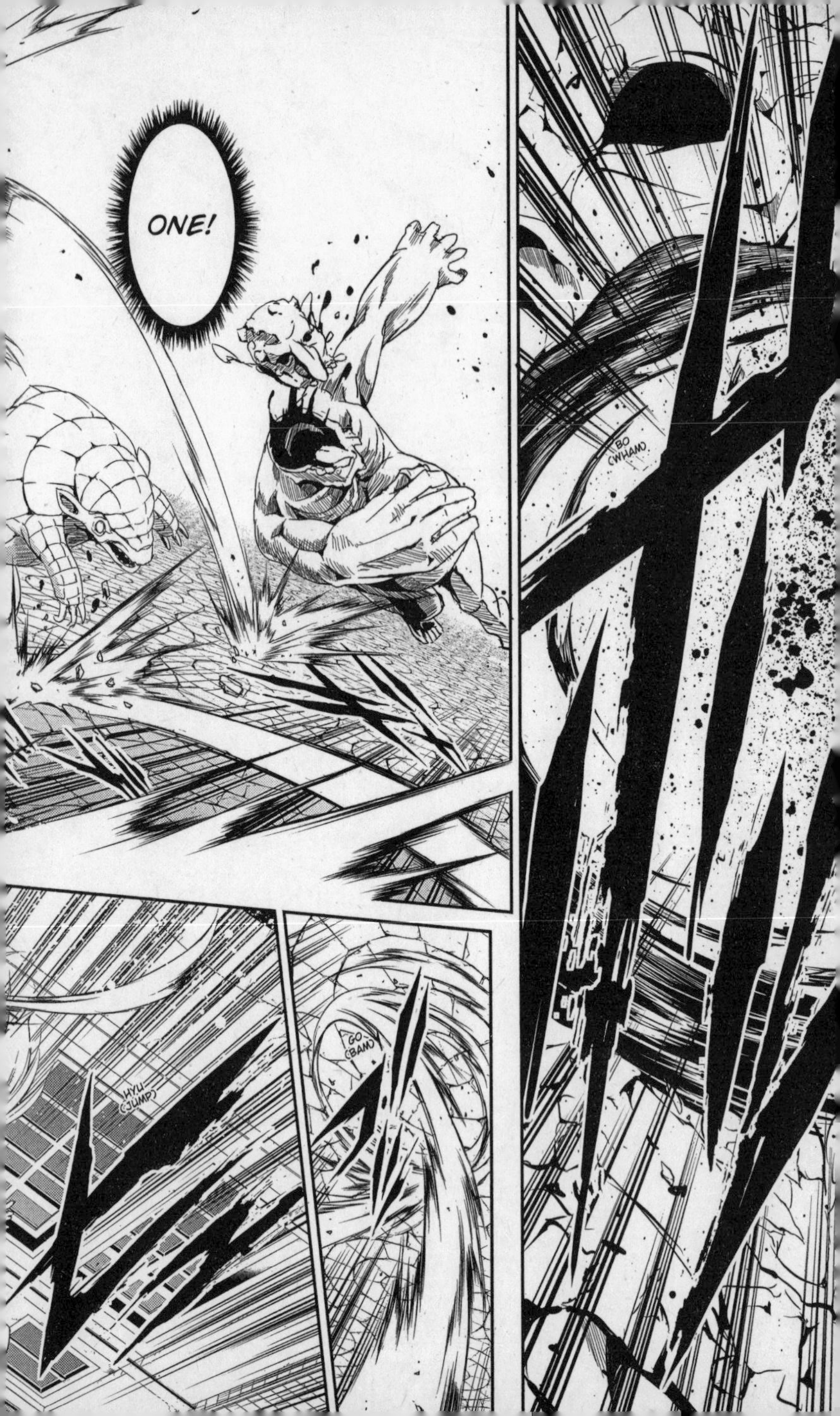
BO (WHAM)
ONE!
GO (BAM)
HYU (JUMP)

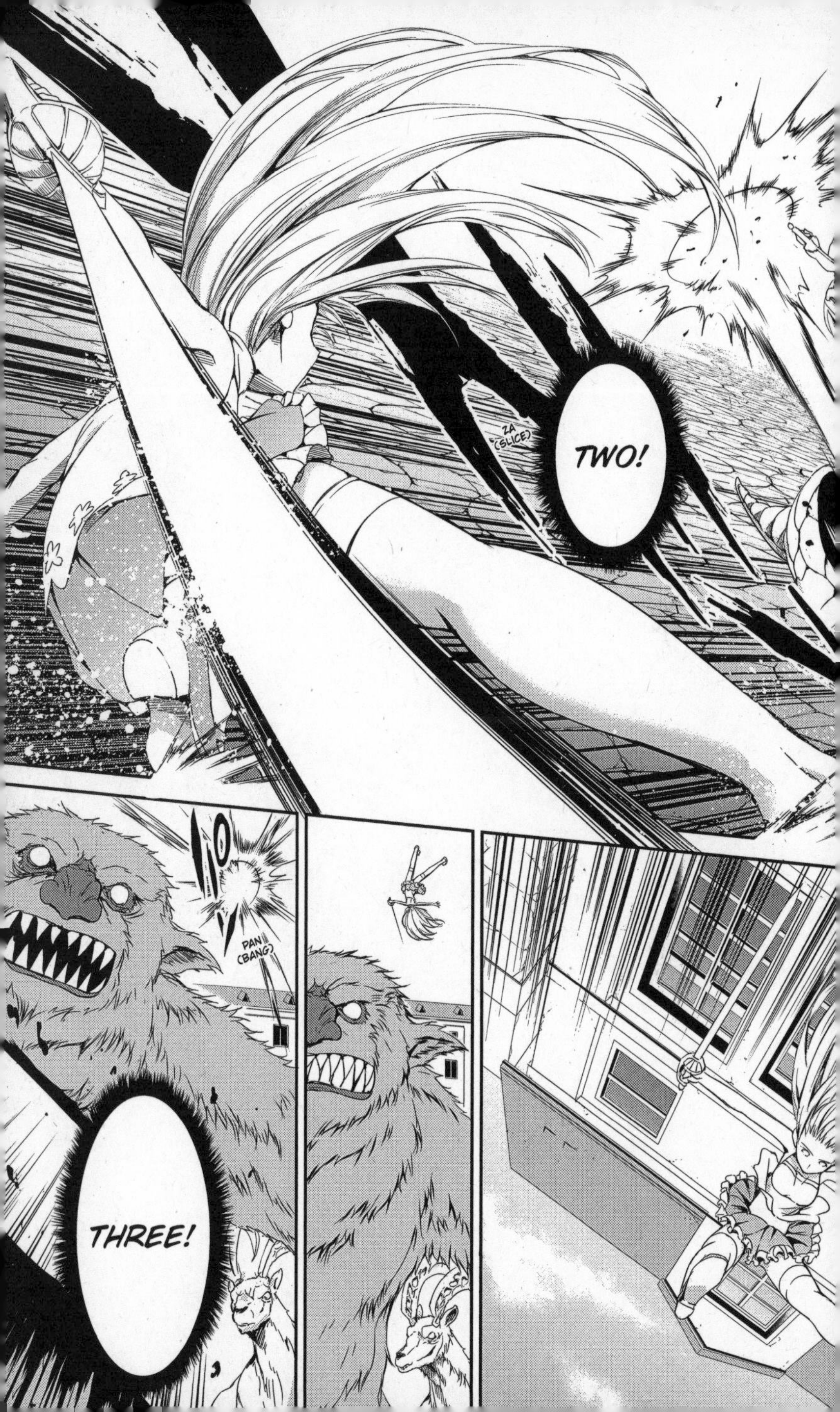
TWO!
ZA
(SLICE)
PAN
(BANG)
THREE!

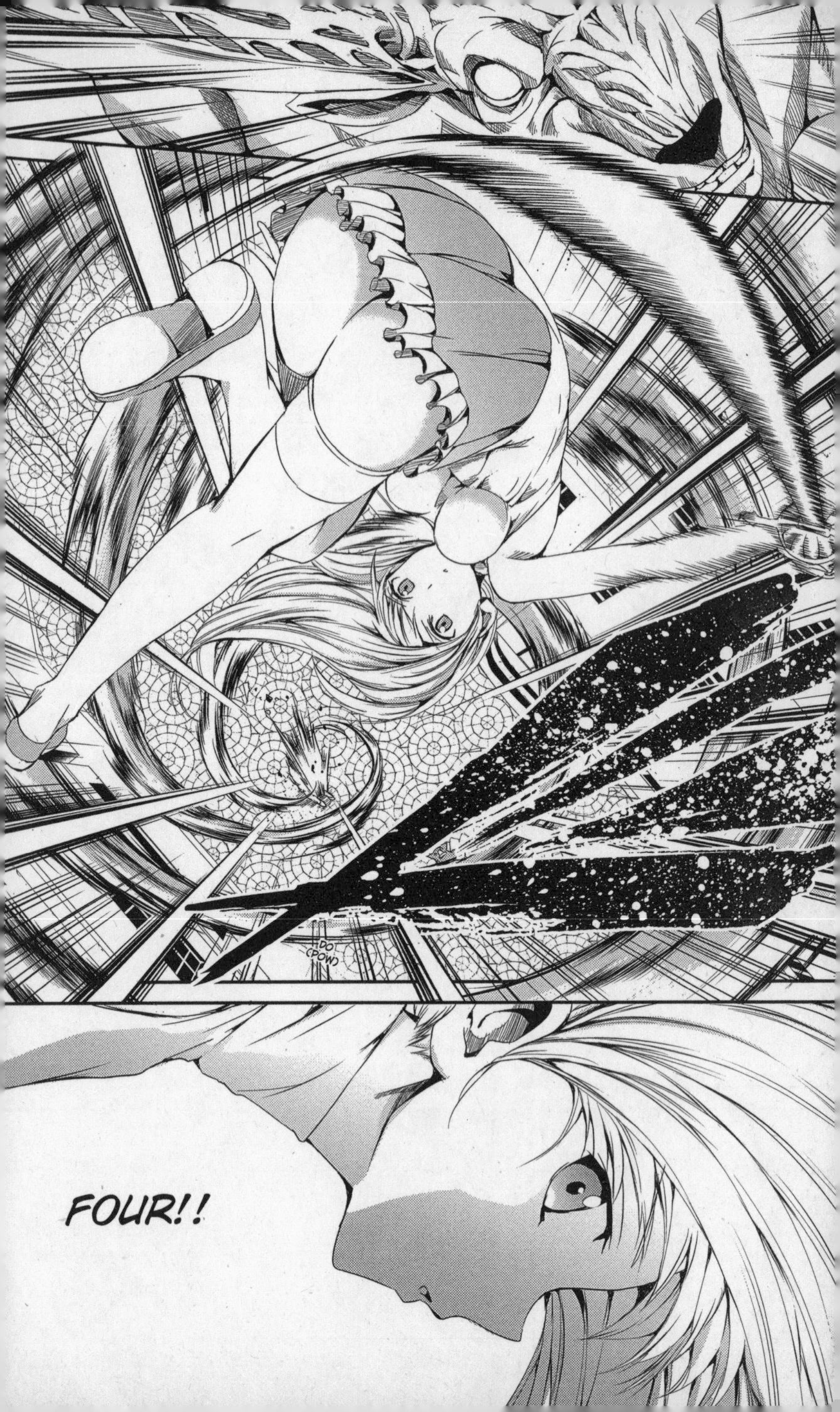
DO
(POW)
FOUR!!

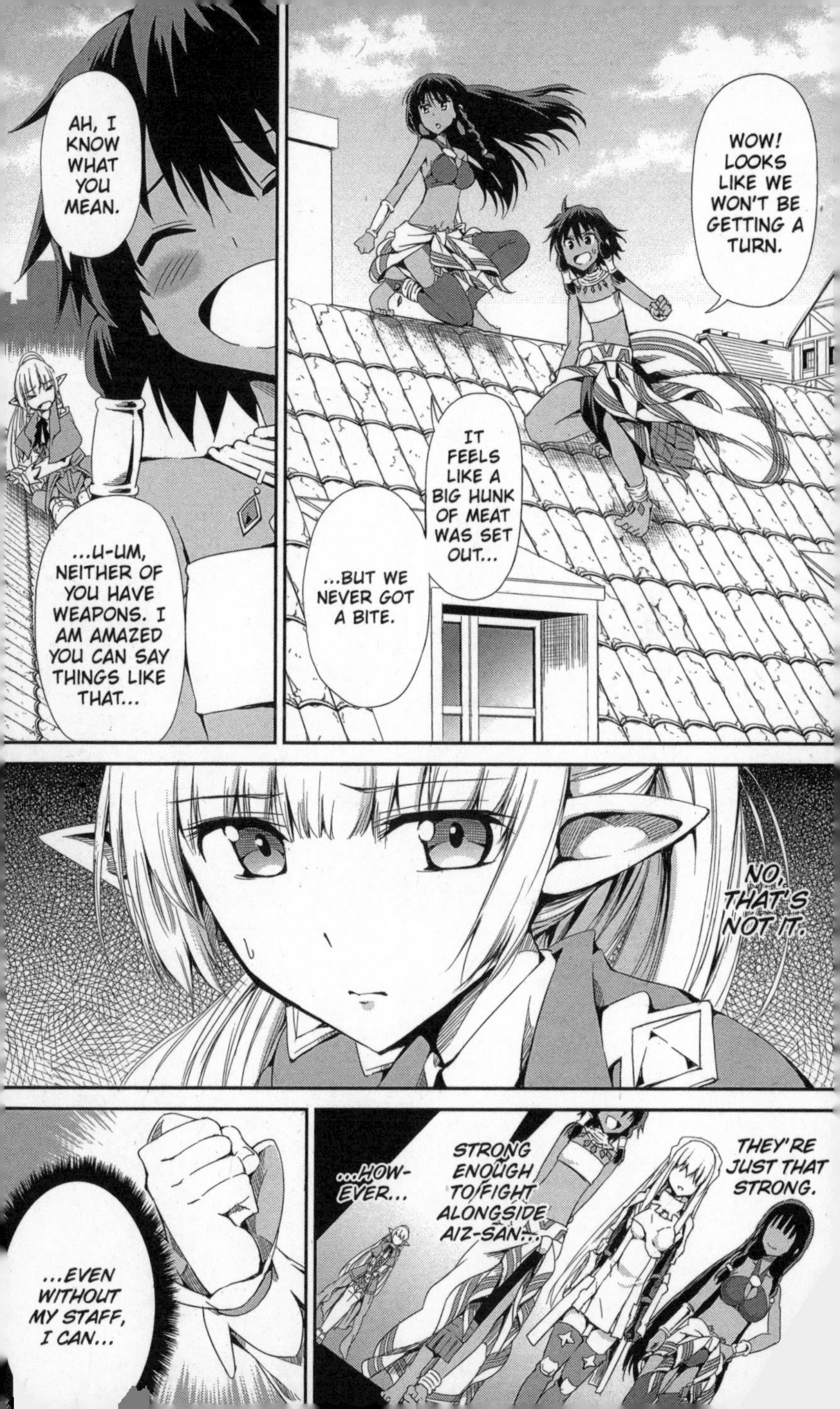
WOW! LOOKS LIKE WE WON'T BE GETTING A TURN.
IT FEELS LIKE A BIG HUNK OF MEAT WAS SET OUT...
...BUT WE NEVER GOT A BITE.
AH, I KNOW WHAT YOU MEAN.
...U-UM, NEITHER OF YOU HAVE WEAPONS. I AM AMAZED YOU CAN SAY THINGS LIKE THAT...
NO, THAT'S NOT IT.
THEY'RE JUST THAT STRONG.
STRONG ENOUGH TO FIGHT ALONGSIDE AIZ-SAN...
...HOW-EVER...
...EVEN WITHOUT MY STAFF, I CAN...

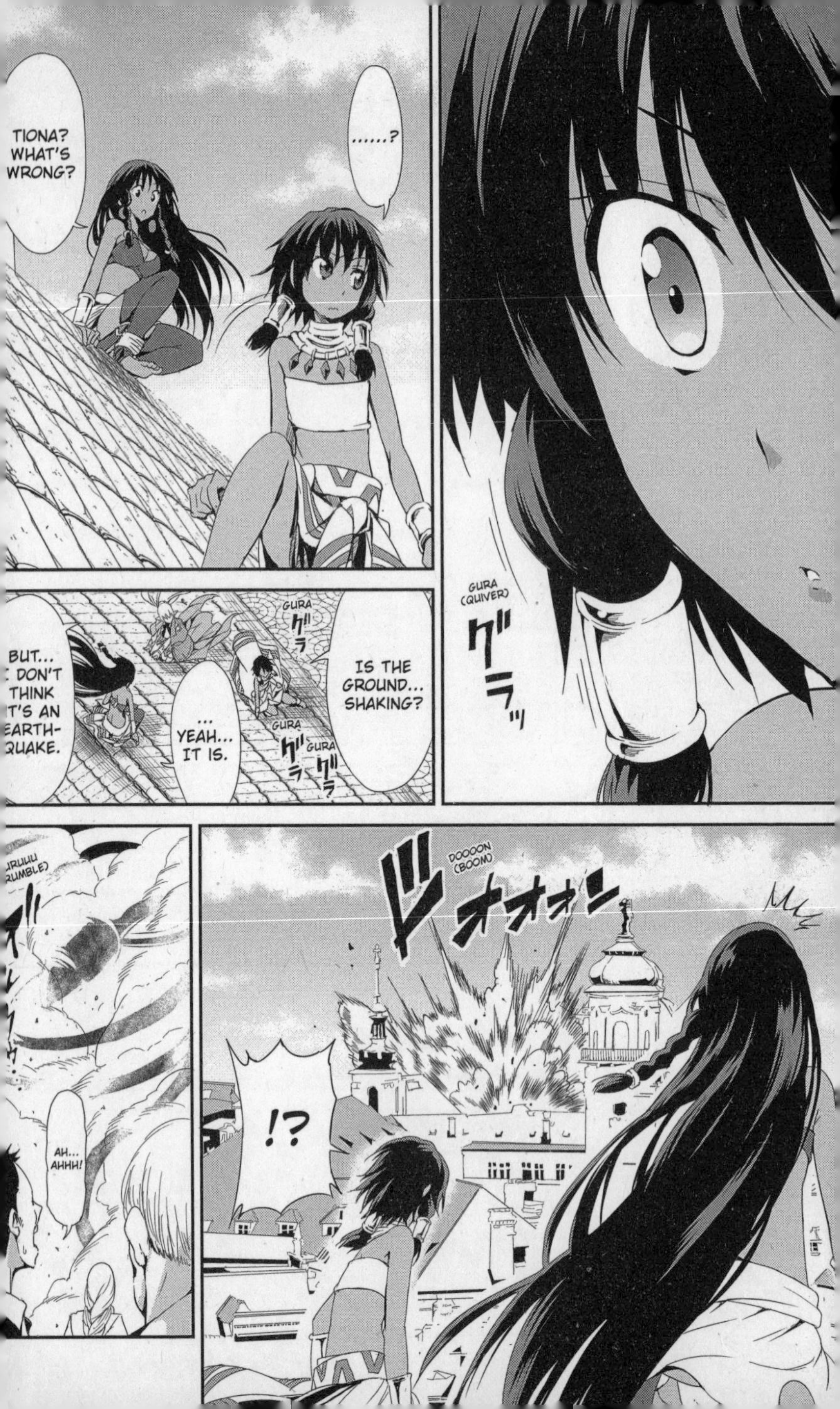
GURA (QUIVER)
グラッ
......?
TIONA? WHAT'S WRONG?
IS THE GROUND... SHAKING?
GURA
グラ
GURA
グラ
GURA
グラ
... YEAH... IT IS.
BUT... I DON'T THINK IT'S AN EARTH-QUAKE.
DOOOON (BOOM)
ドォオオン
!?
URUUU (RUMBLE)
AH... AHHH!

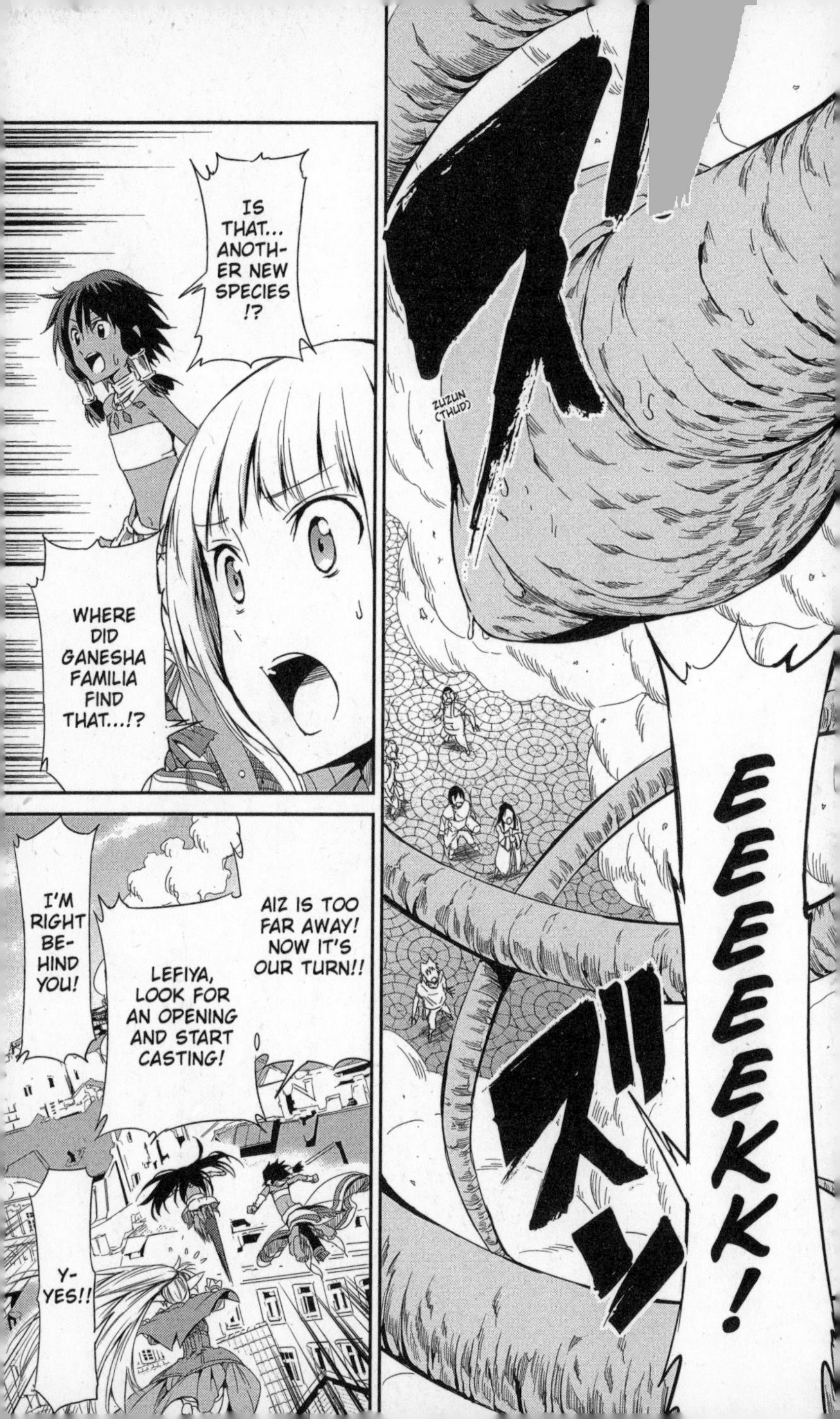
ZUZUN (THUD)
EEEEEEKK!
IS THAT... ANOTH-ER NEW SPECIES !?
WHERE DID GANESHA FAMILIA FIND THAT...!?
AIZ IS TOO FAR AWAY! NOW IT'S OUR TURN!!
LEFIYA, LOOK FOR AN OPENING AND START CASTING!
I'M RIGHT BE-HIND YOU!
Y-YES!!

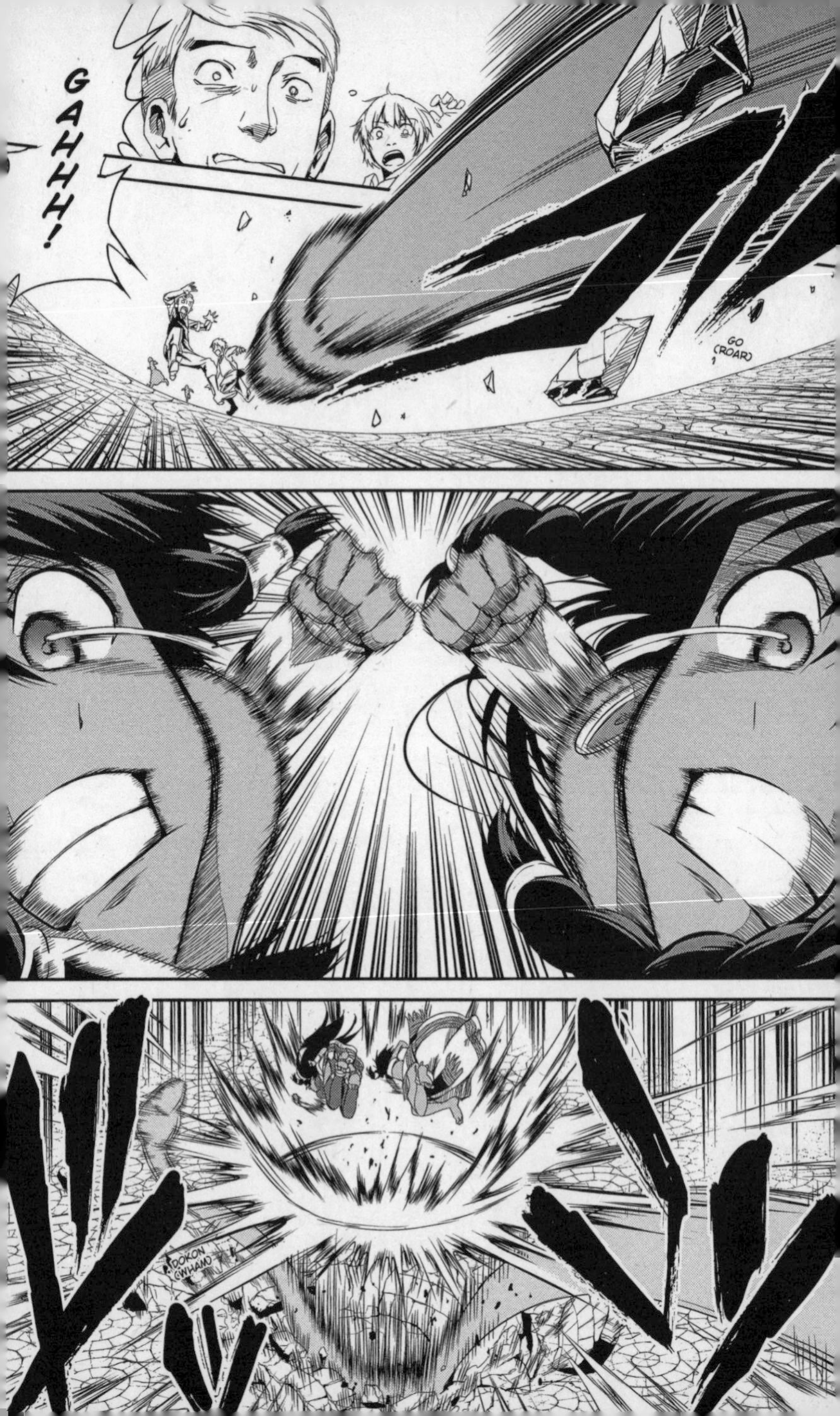
GO
(ROAR)
GAHHHH!
DOKON
(WHAM)

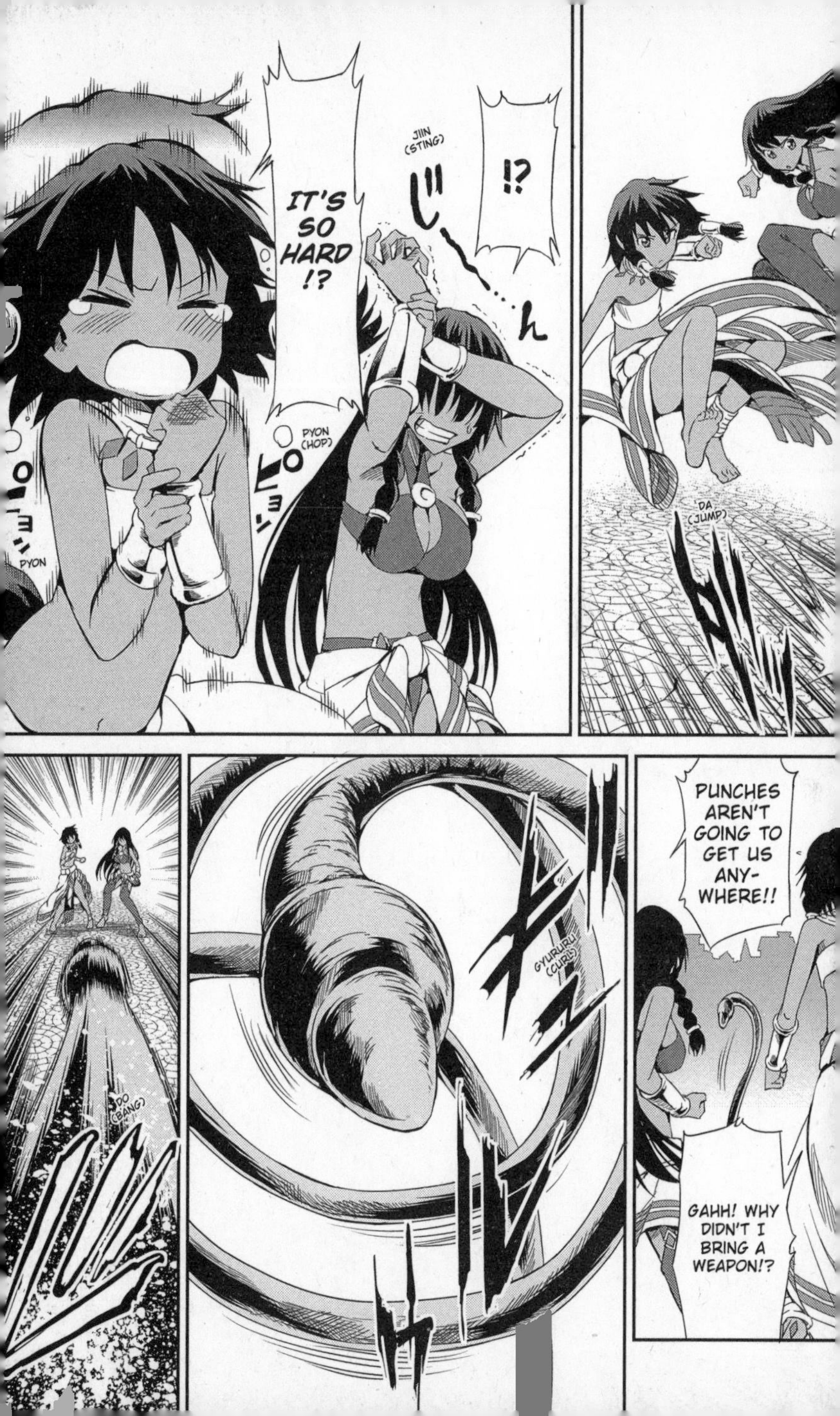

DA (JUMP)
!?
JIIN (STING)
じ～…ん
IT'S SO HARD !?
PYON (HOP)
PYON
PUNCHES AREN'T GOING TO GET US ANY-WHERE!!
GAHH! WHY DIDN'T I BRING A WEAPON!?
GYURURU (CURL)
DO (BANG)

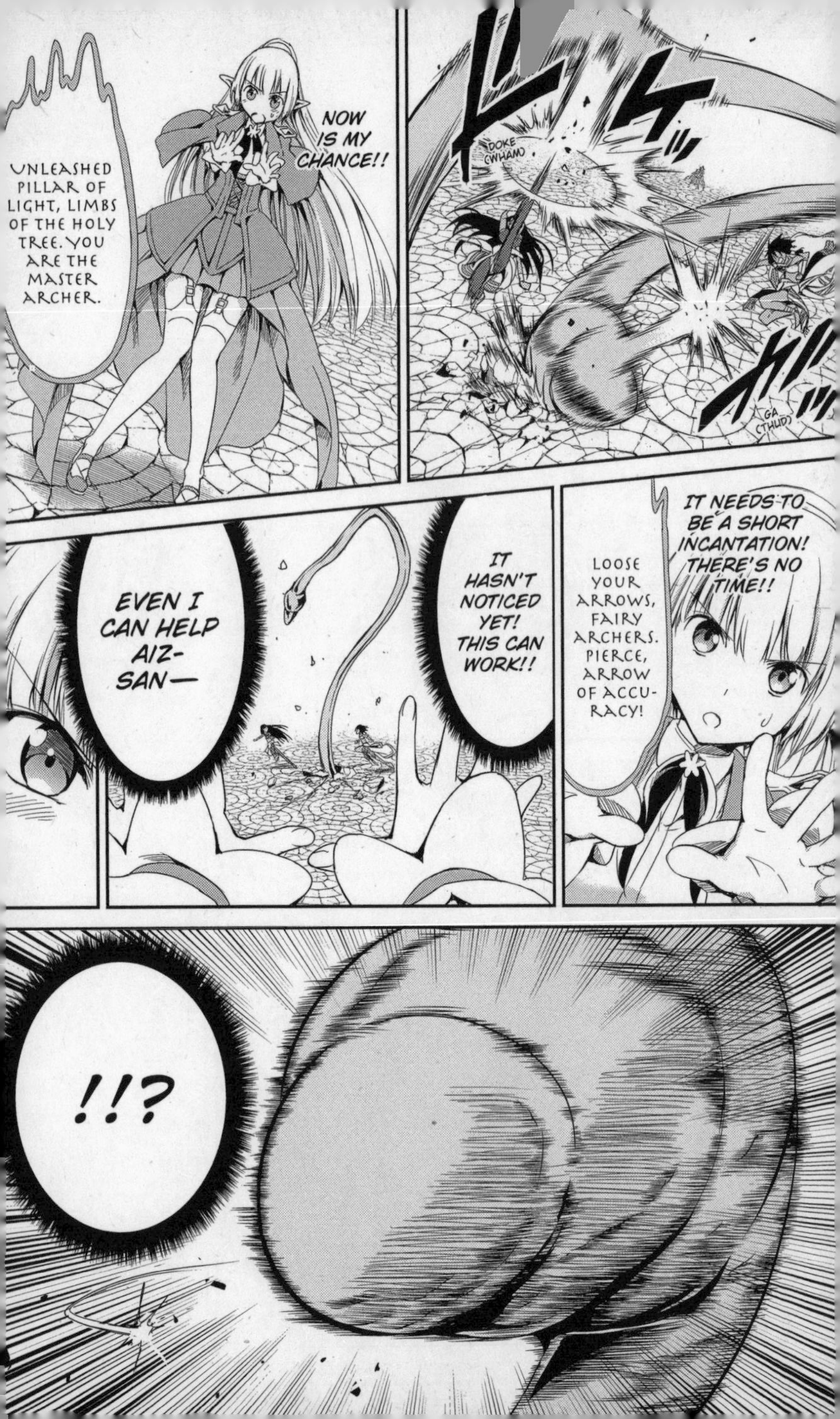
DOKE (WHAM)
GA (THUD)
NOW IS MY CHANCE!!
UNLEASHED PILLAR OF LIGHT, LIMBS OF THE HOLY TREE. YOU ARE THE MASTER ARCHER.
IT NEEDS TO BE A SHORT INCANTATION! THERE'S NO TIME!!
LOOSE YOUR ARROWS, FAIRY ARCHERS. PIERCE, ARROW OF ACCURACY!
IT HASN'T NOTICED YET! THIS CAN WORK!!
EVEN I CAN HELP AIZ-SAN—
!!?

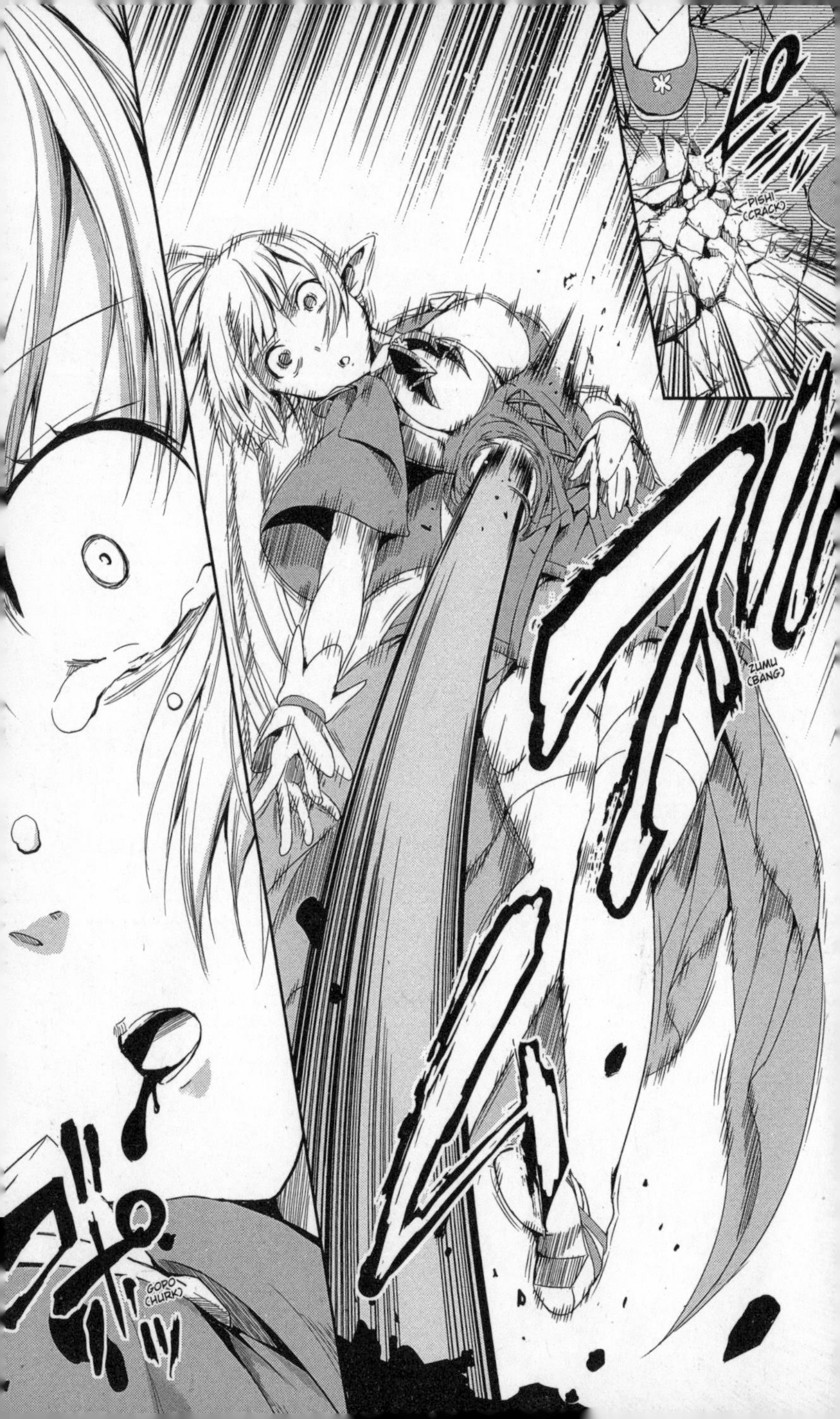
PISHI (CRACK)
ZUMU (BANG)
GOPO (CHURK)

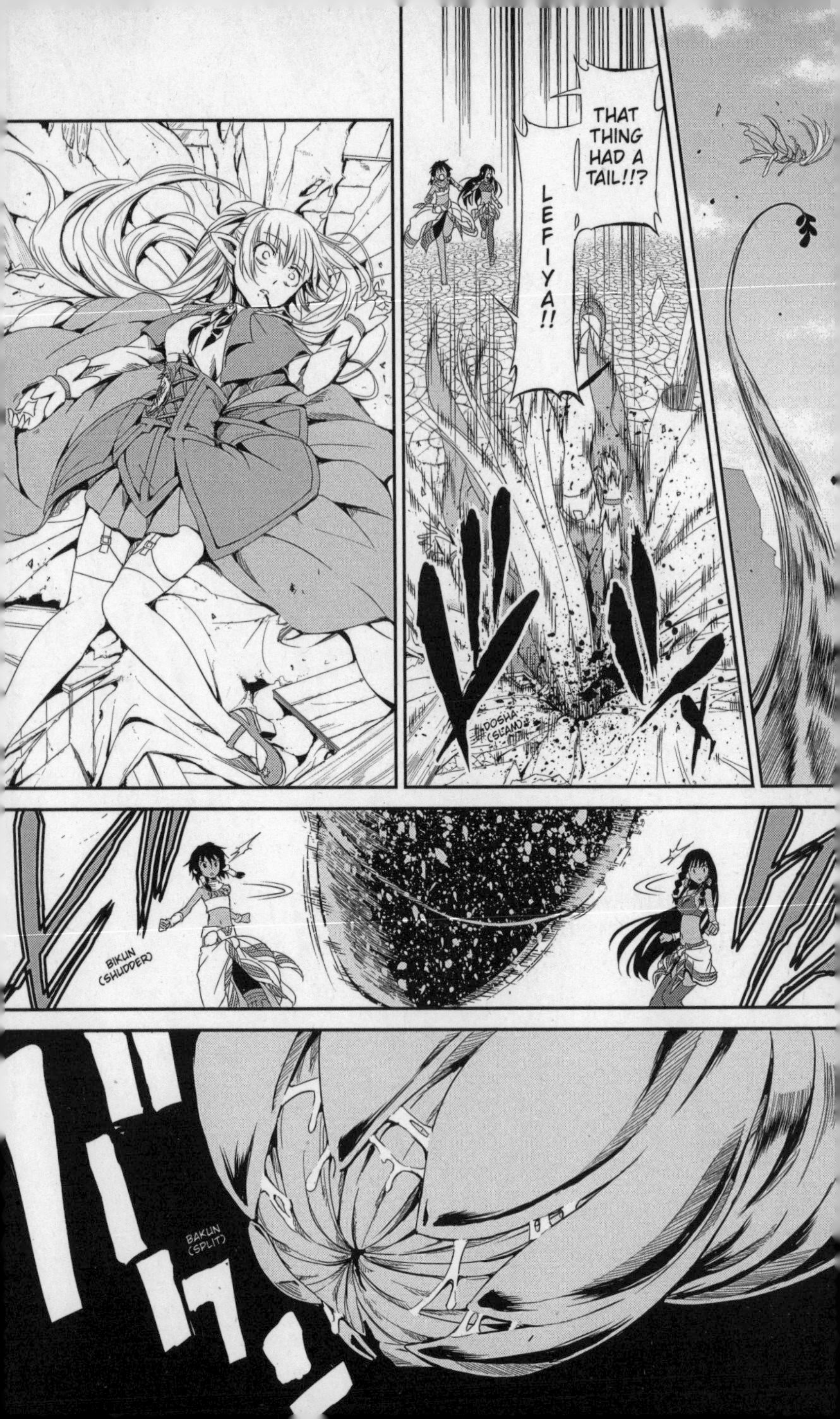
THAT THING HAD A TAIL!!?
LEFIYA!!
DOSHA (SLAM)
BIKUN (SHUDDER)
BAKUN (SPLIT)

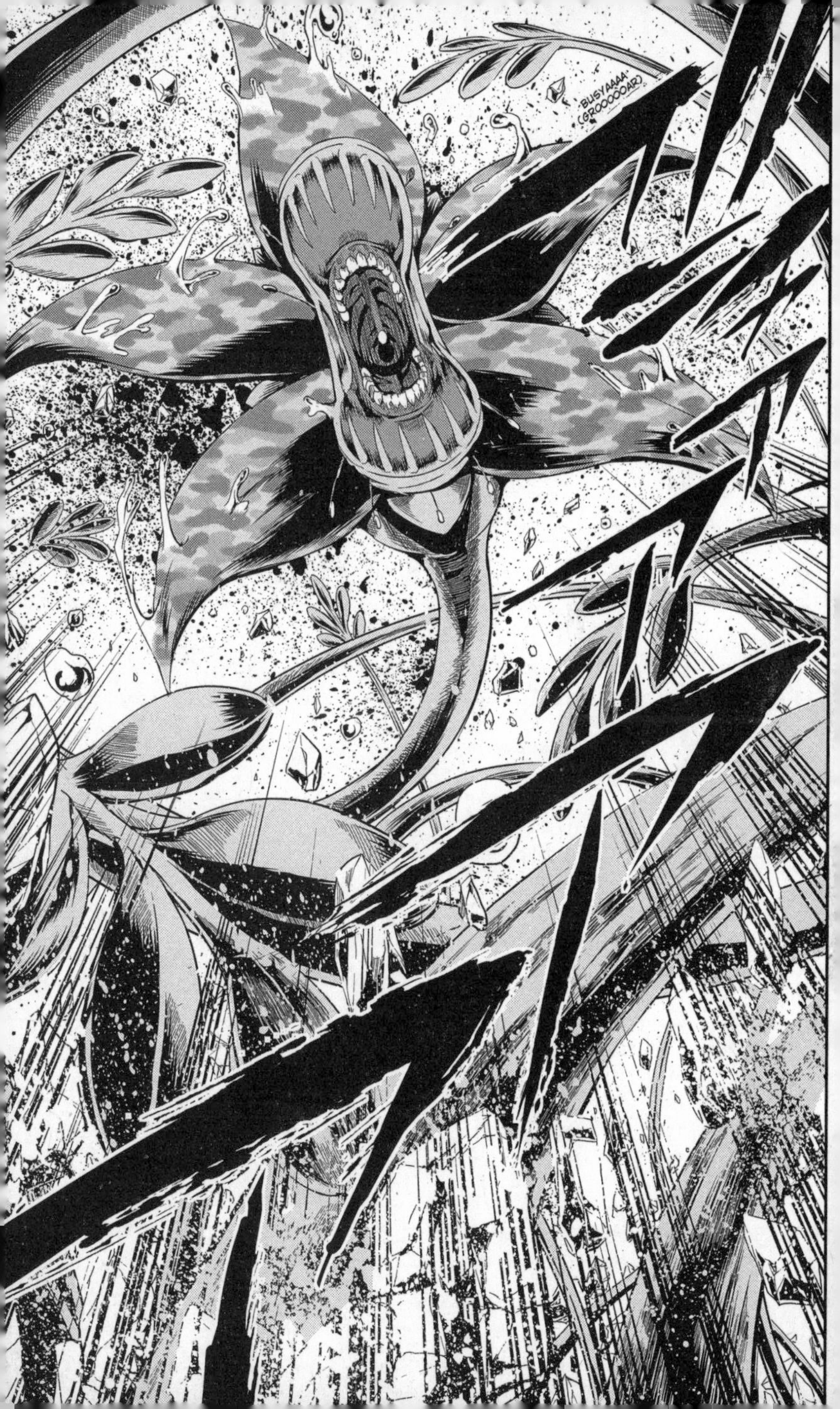
BUSYAAAA
(GROOOOOAR)

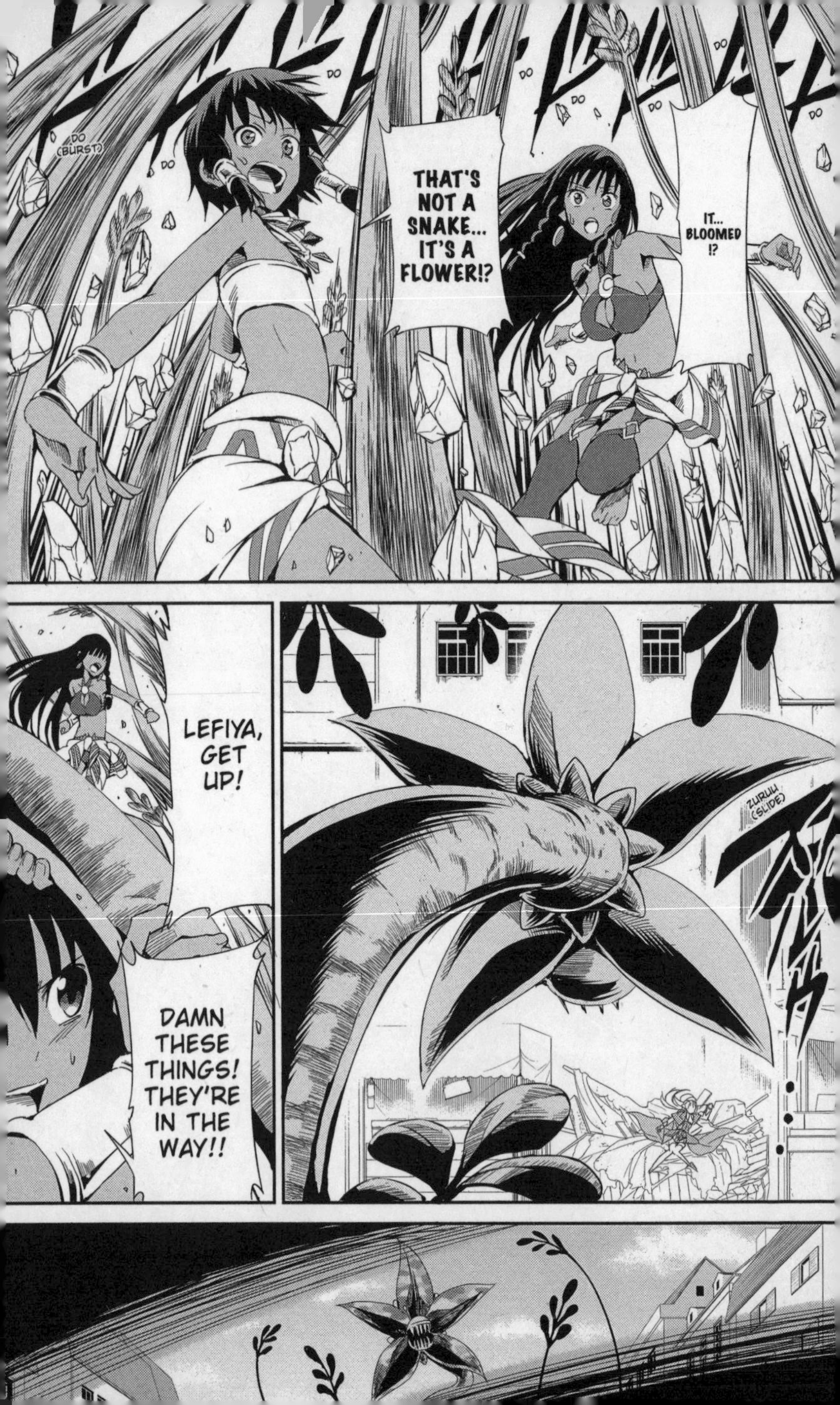
DO
IT... BLOOMED!?
THAT'S NOT A SNAKE... IT'S A FLOWER!?
DO (BURST)
ZURUU (SLIDE)
LEFIYA, GET UP!
DAMN THESE THINGS! THEY'RE IN THE WAY!!

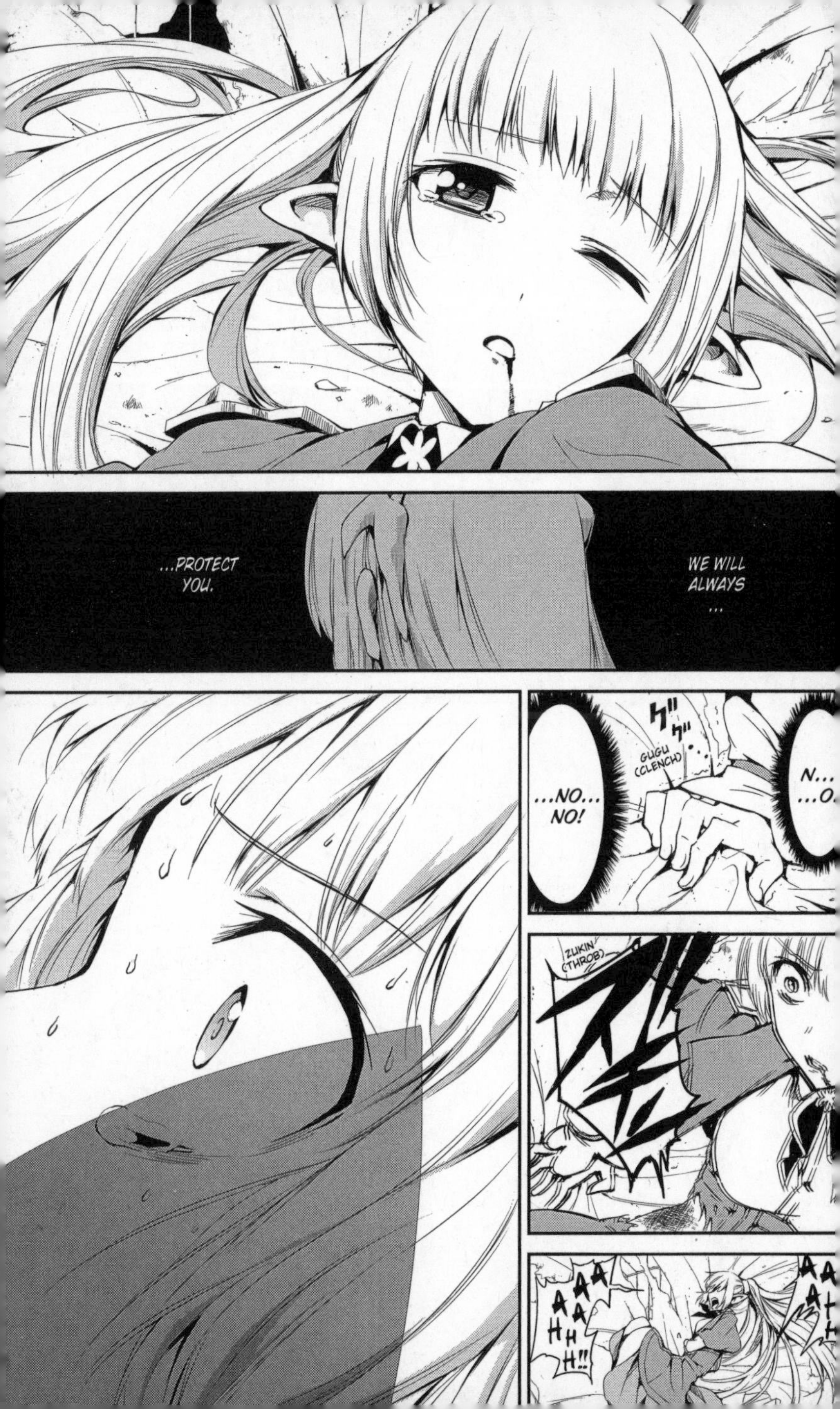
WE WILL ALWAYS ...
...PROTECT YOU.
N... ...O.
GUGU (CLENCH)
...NO... NO!
ZUKIN (THROB)
AAAAAHHH!!

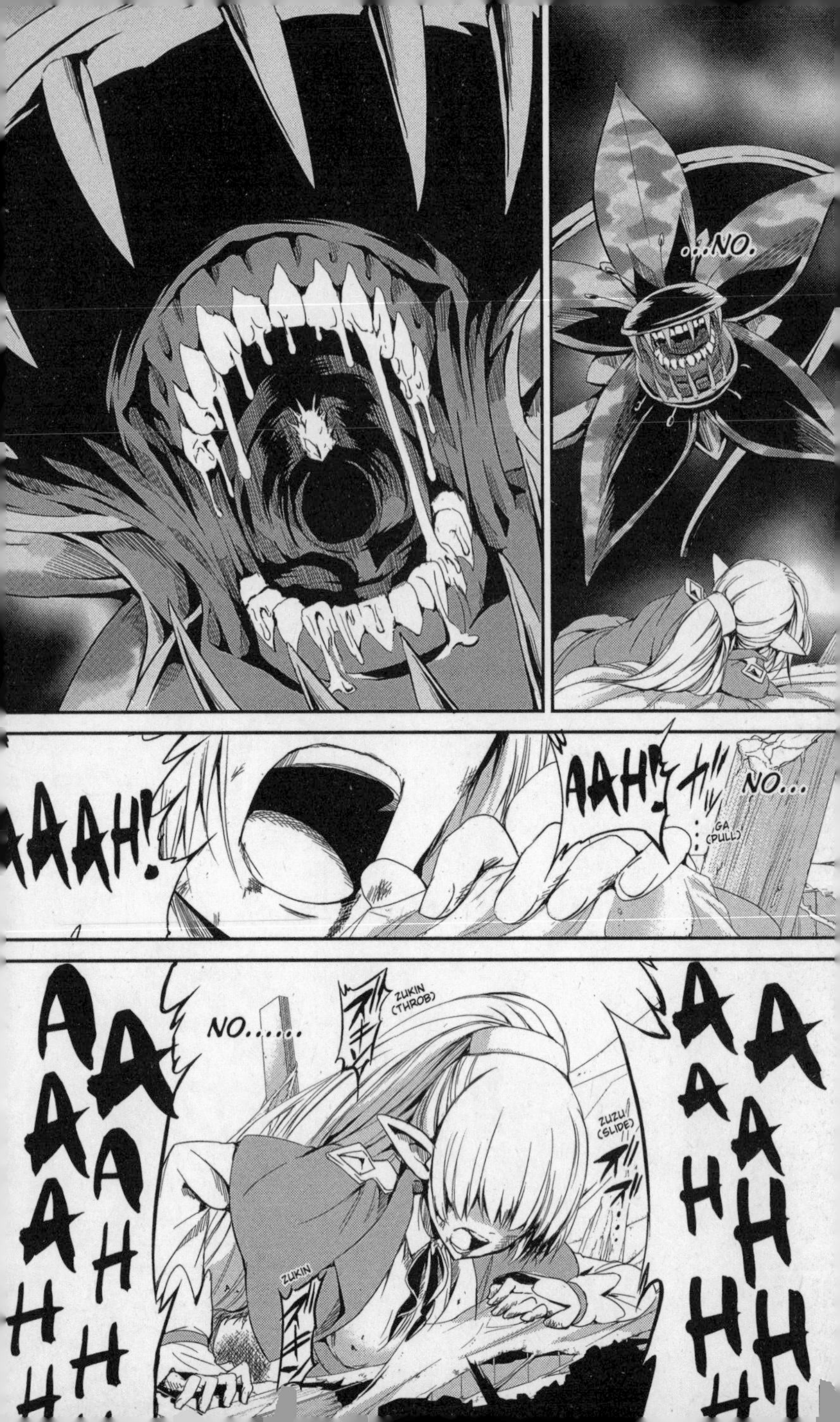
...NO.
NO...
GA (PULL)
AAH!
AAAH!
AAAAHHH!
ZUZU (SLIDE)
ZUKIN (THROB)
NO......
ZUKIN
AAAAHHH

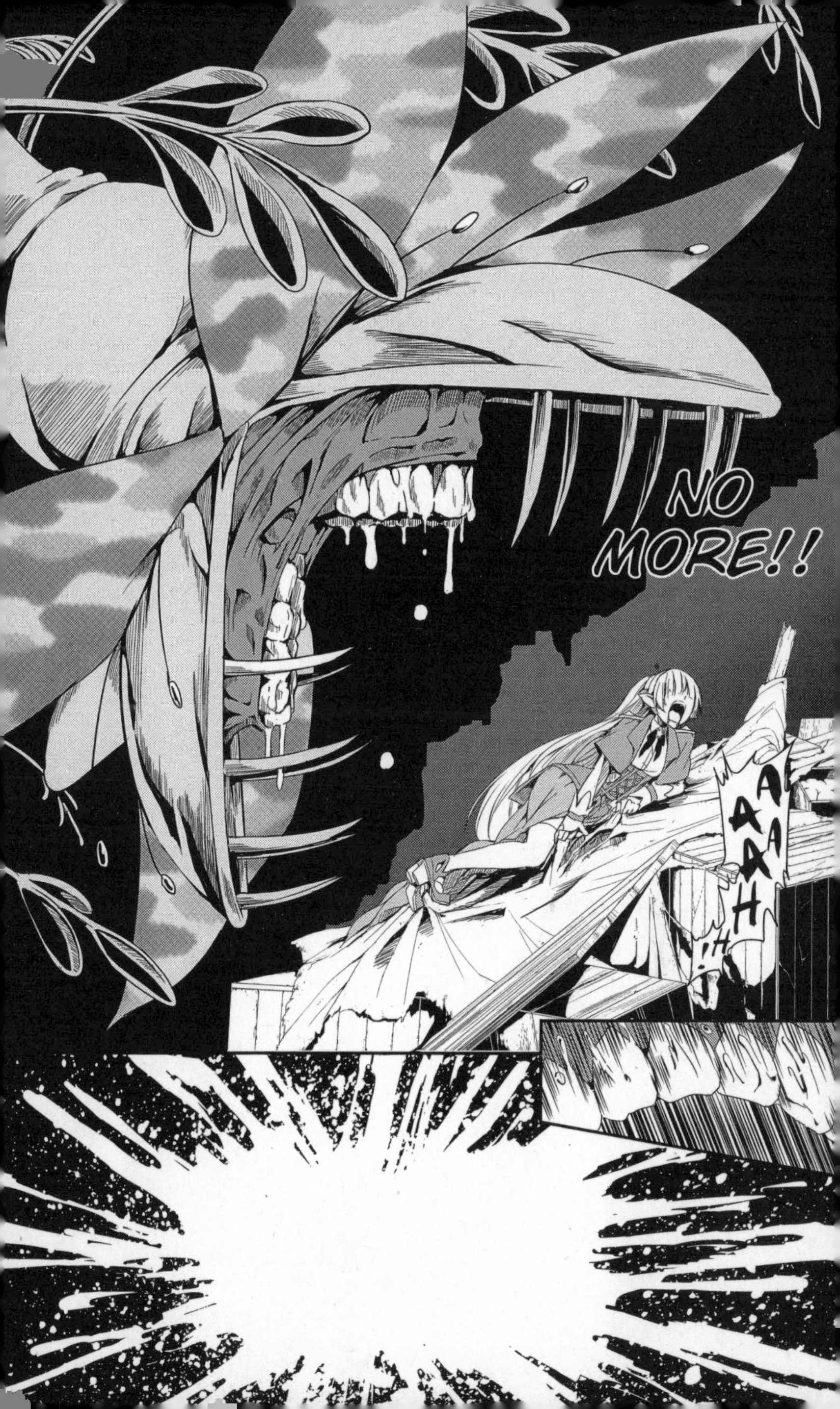
NO MORE!!
AAAAHH!!

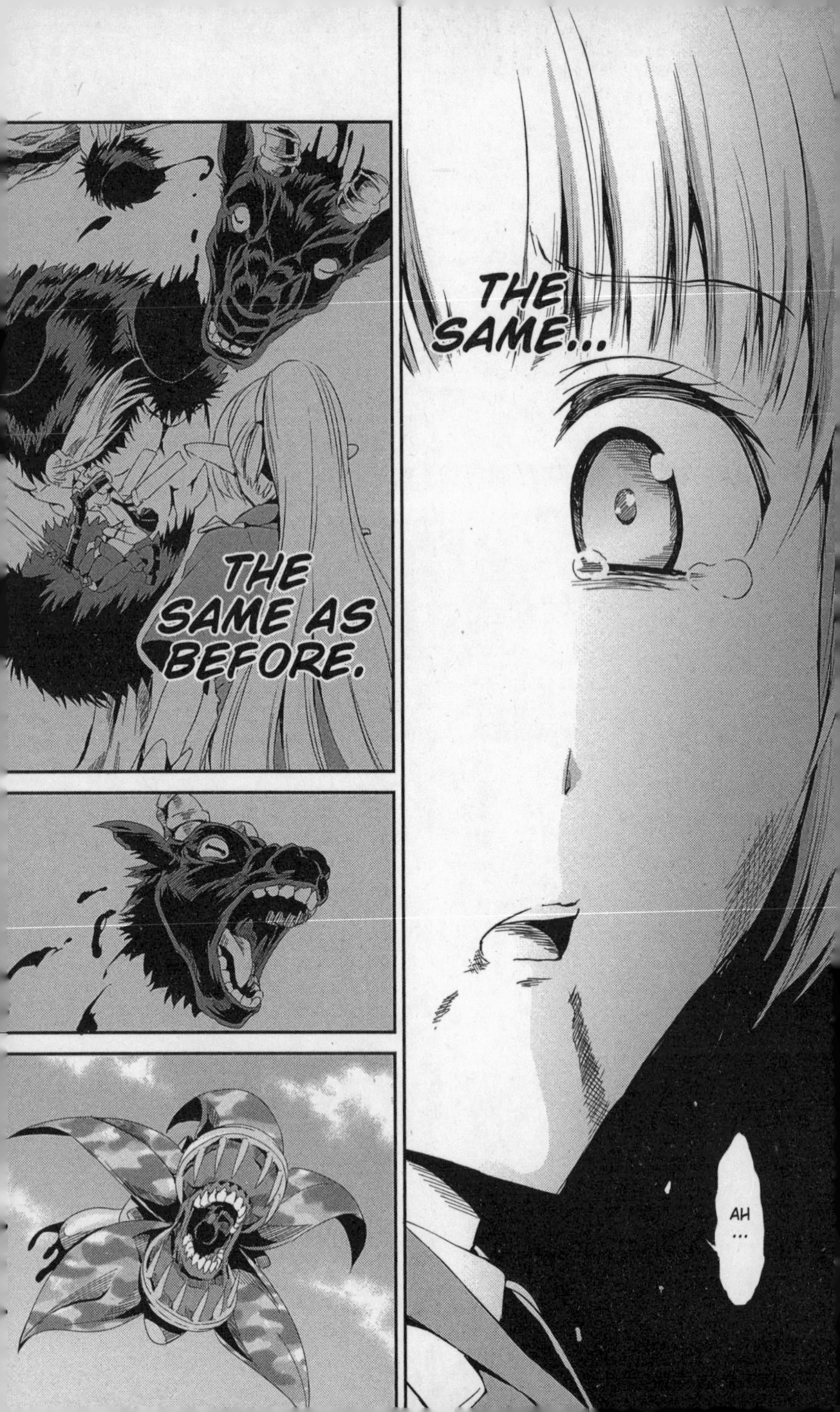
THE SAME...
AH ...
THE SAME AS BEFORE.

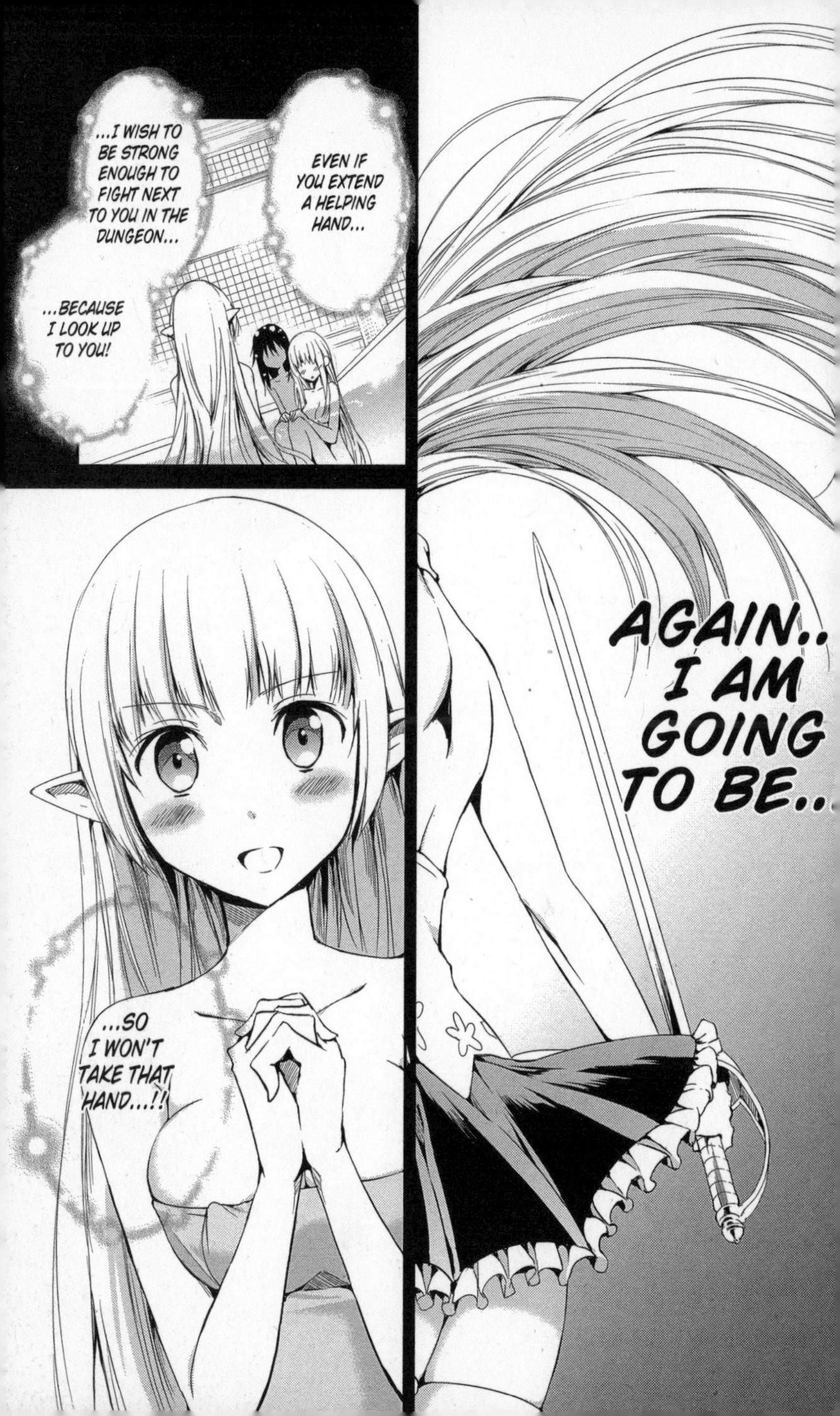
AGAIN.. I AM GOING TO BE..
EVEN IF YOU EXTEND A HELPING HAND...
...I WISH TO BE STRONG ENOUGH TO FIGHT NEXT TO YOU IN THE DUNGEON...
...BECAUSE I LOOK UP TO YOU!
...SO I WON'T TAKE THAT HAND...!!

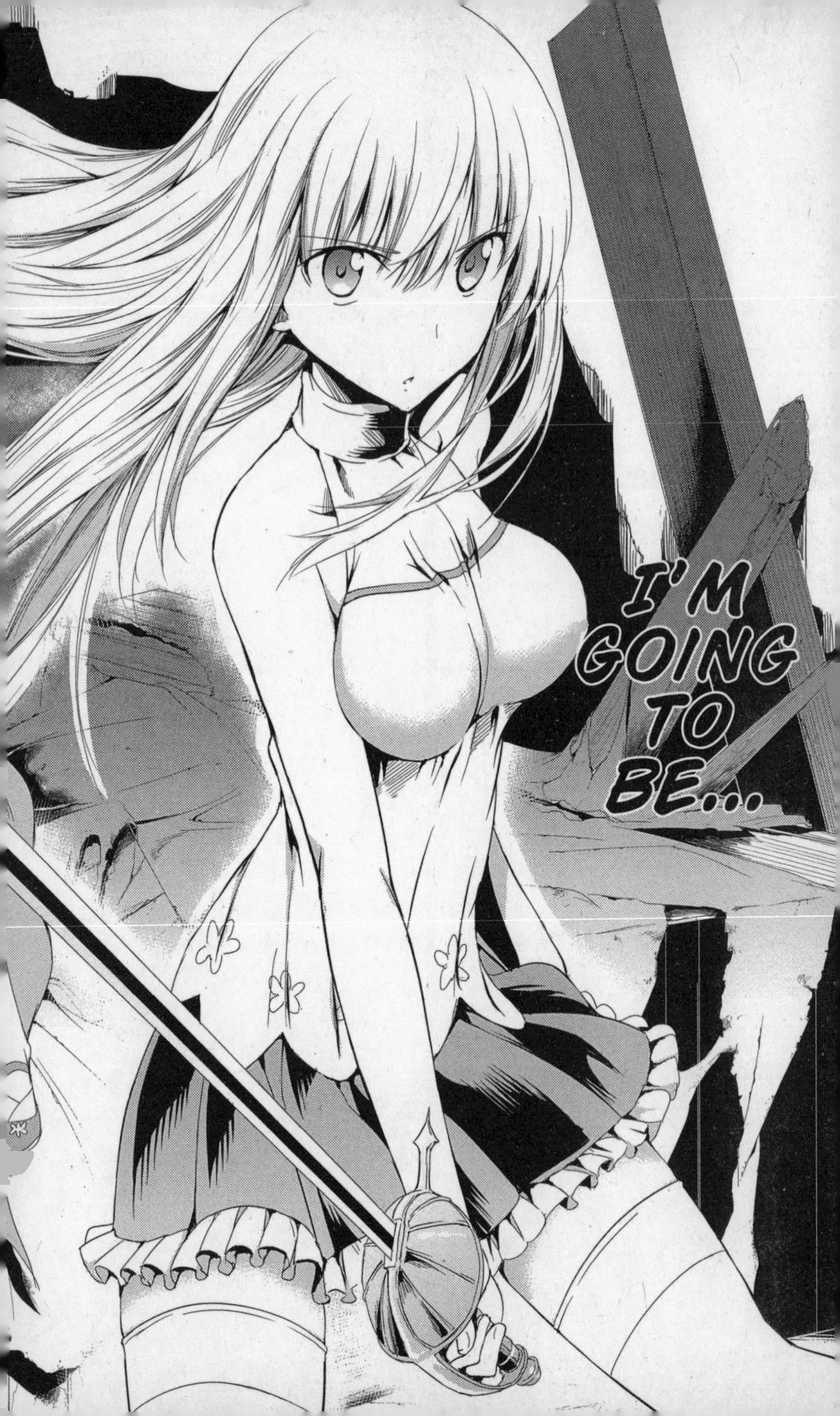
I'M GOING TO BE...

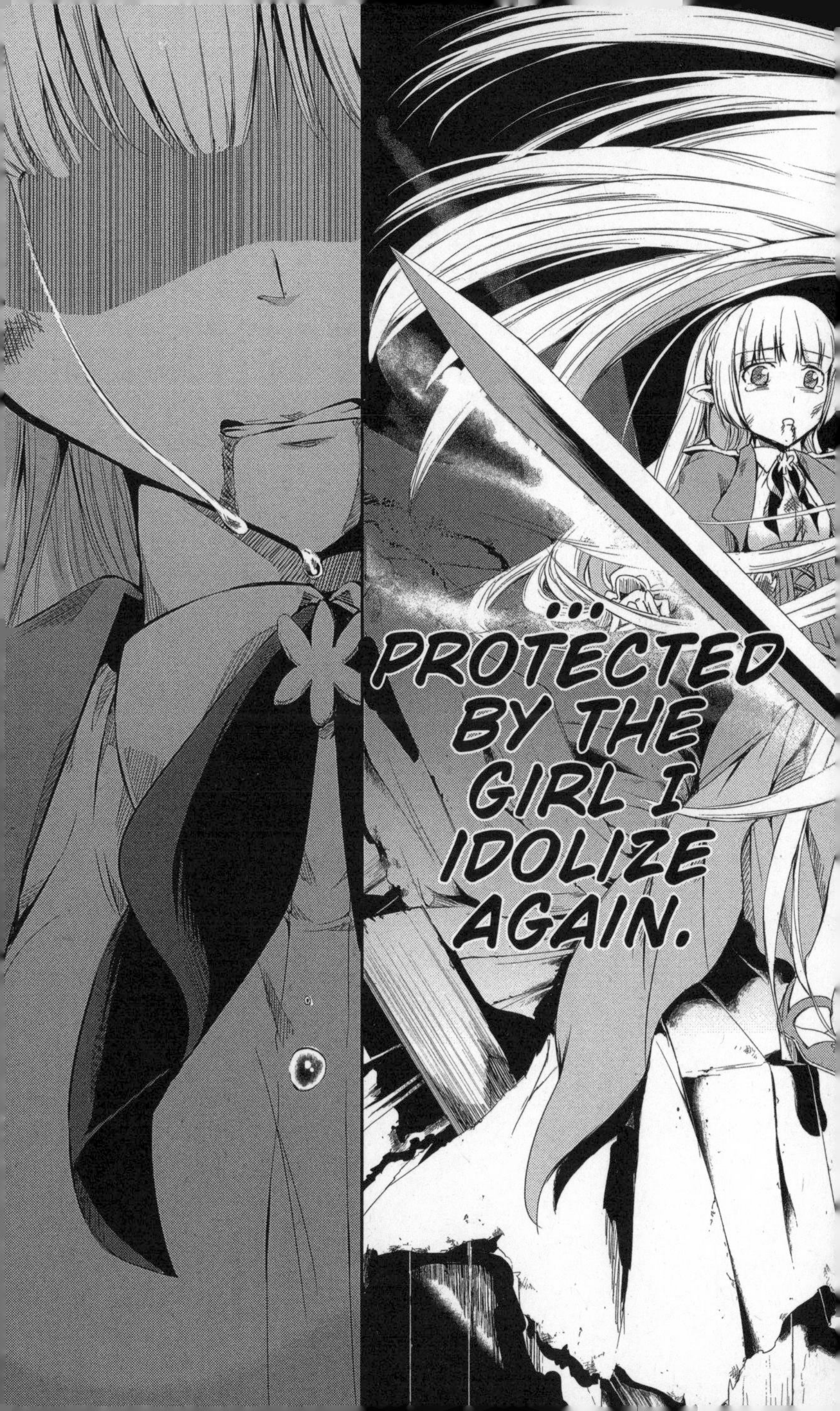
...PROTECTED BY THE GIRL I IDOLIZE AGAIN.

Is it WRONG to TRY to PICK-UP GIRLS IN A DUNGEON? ON THE SIDE

Sword Oratoria

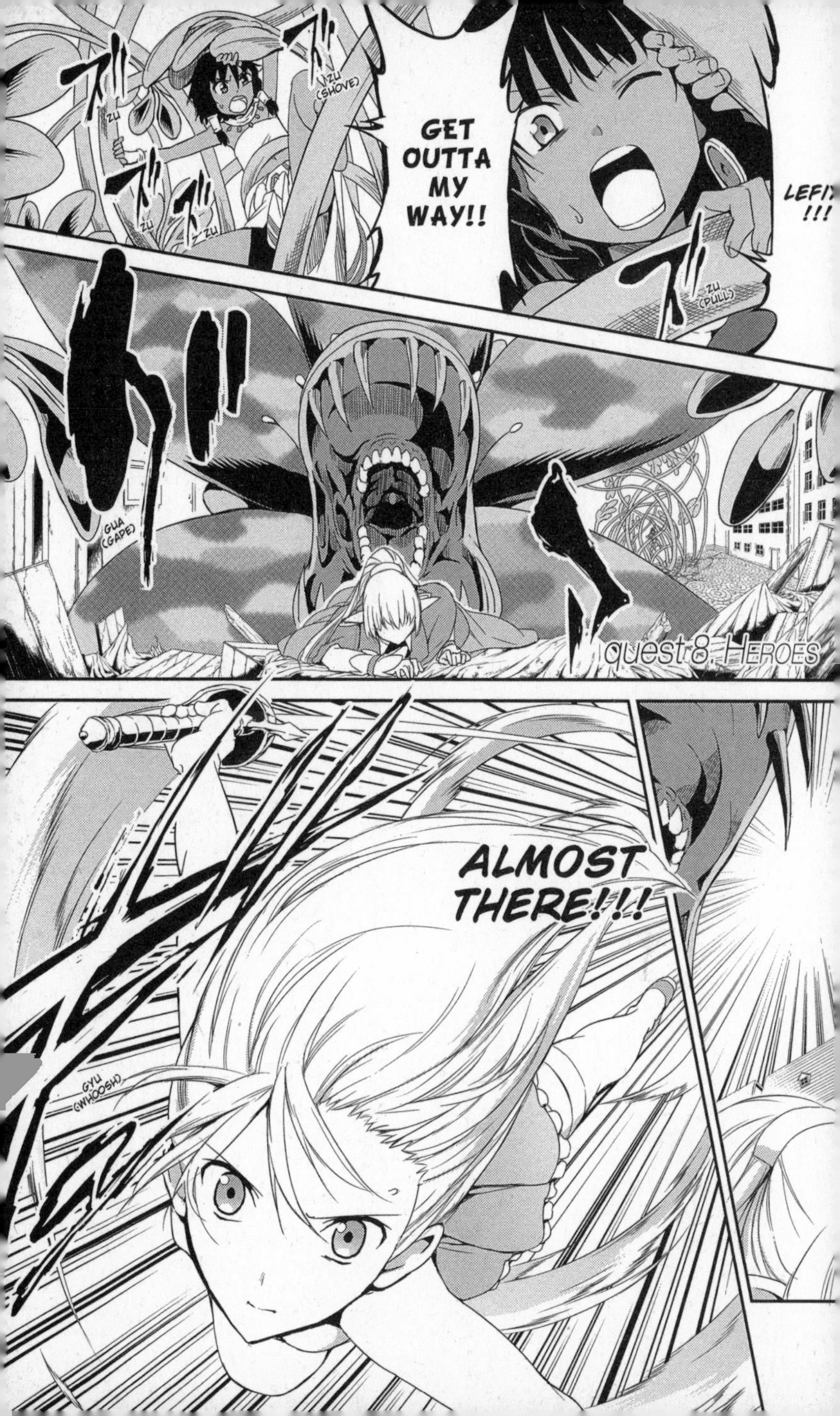

LEFI!!!
GET OUTTA MY WAY!!
ZU (PULL)
ZU (SHOVE)
ZU
ZU
ZU
GUA (GAPE)
quest 8: Heroes
ALMOST THERE!!!
GYU (WHOOSH)

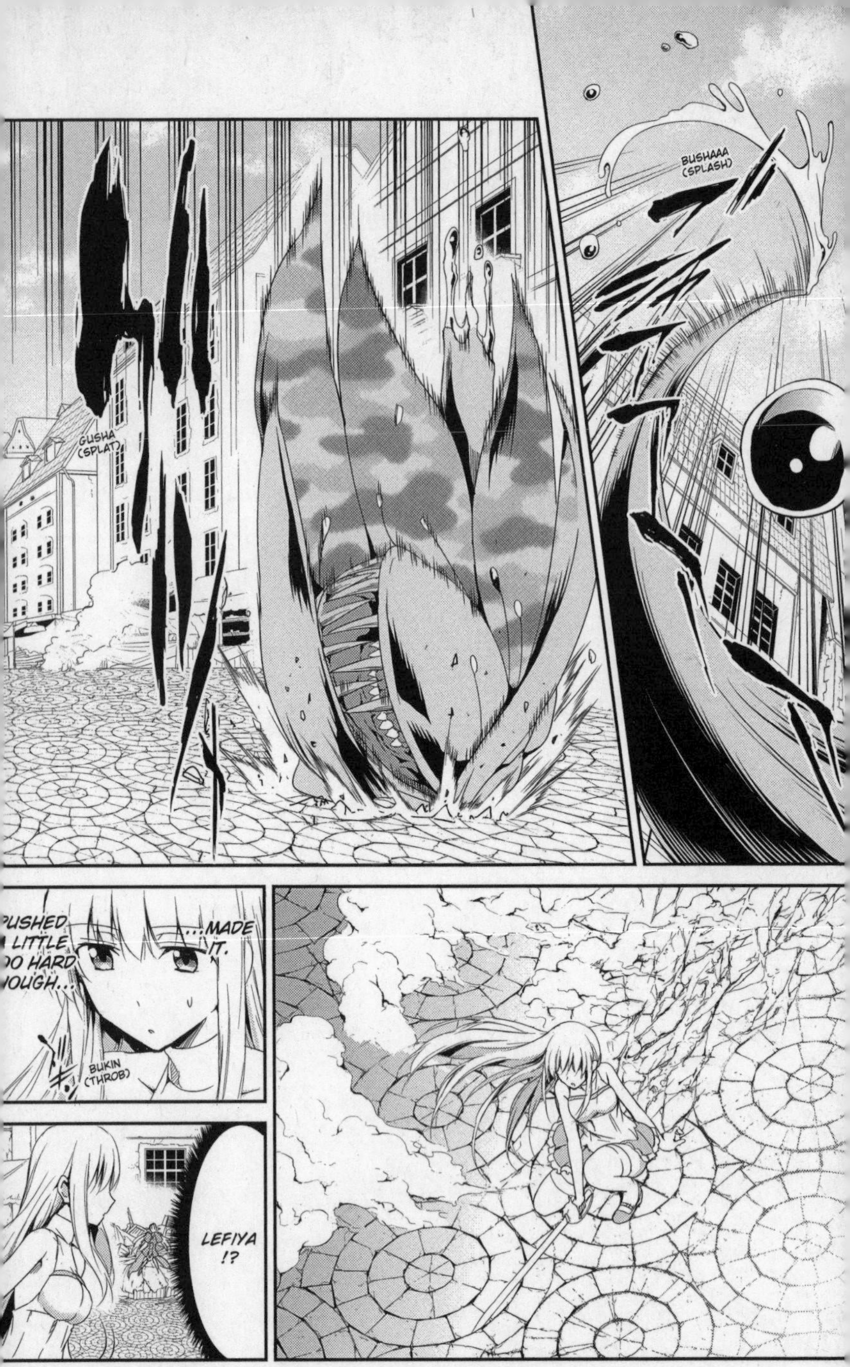
BUSHAAA (SPLASH)
GUSHA (SPLAT)
...MADE IT.
PUSHED A LITTLE TOO HARD THOUGH...
BUKIN (THROB)
LEFIYA !?

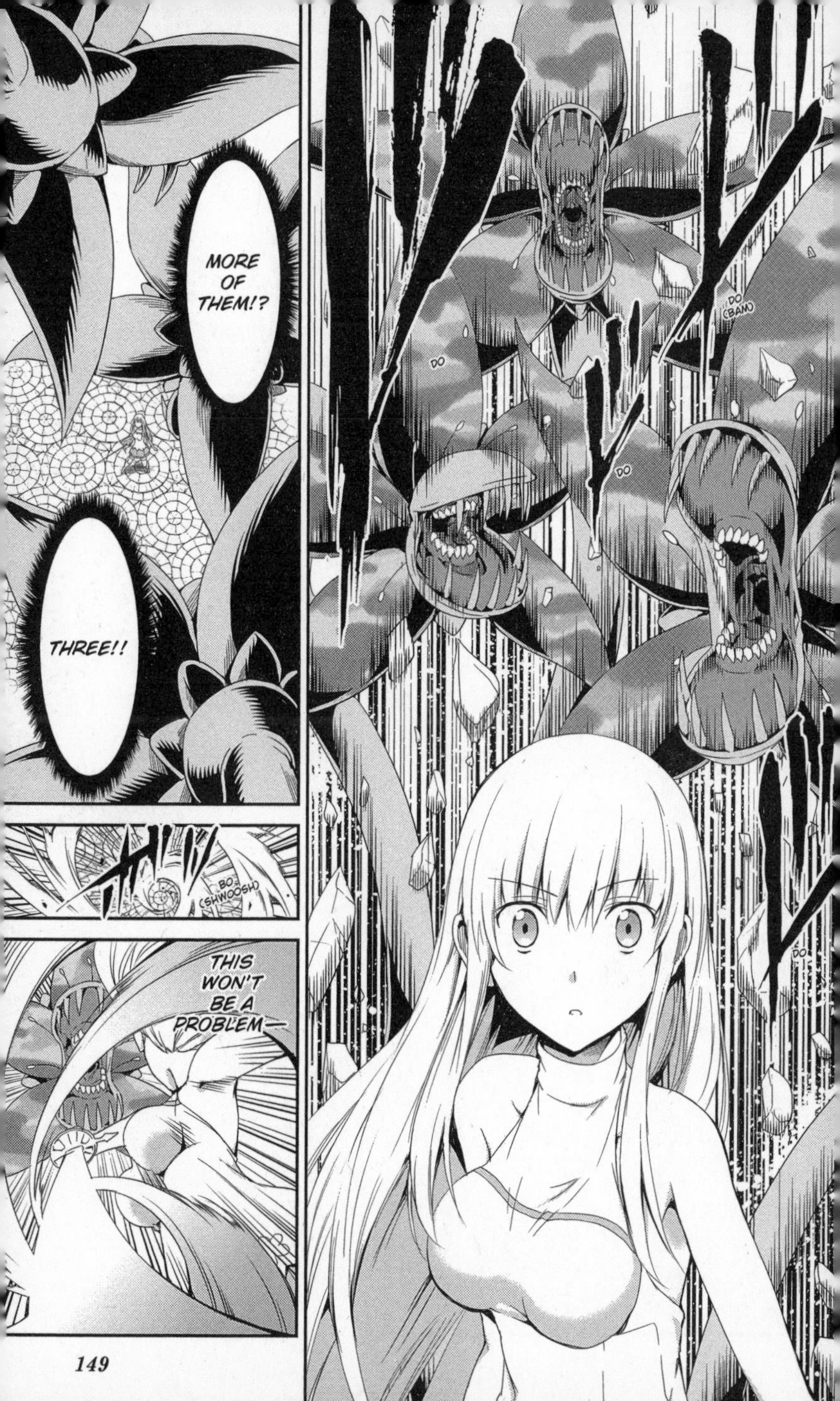
DO
(BAM)
DO
DO
DO
MORE OF THEM!?
THREE!!
BO
(SHWOOSH)
THIS WON'T BE A PROBLEM—

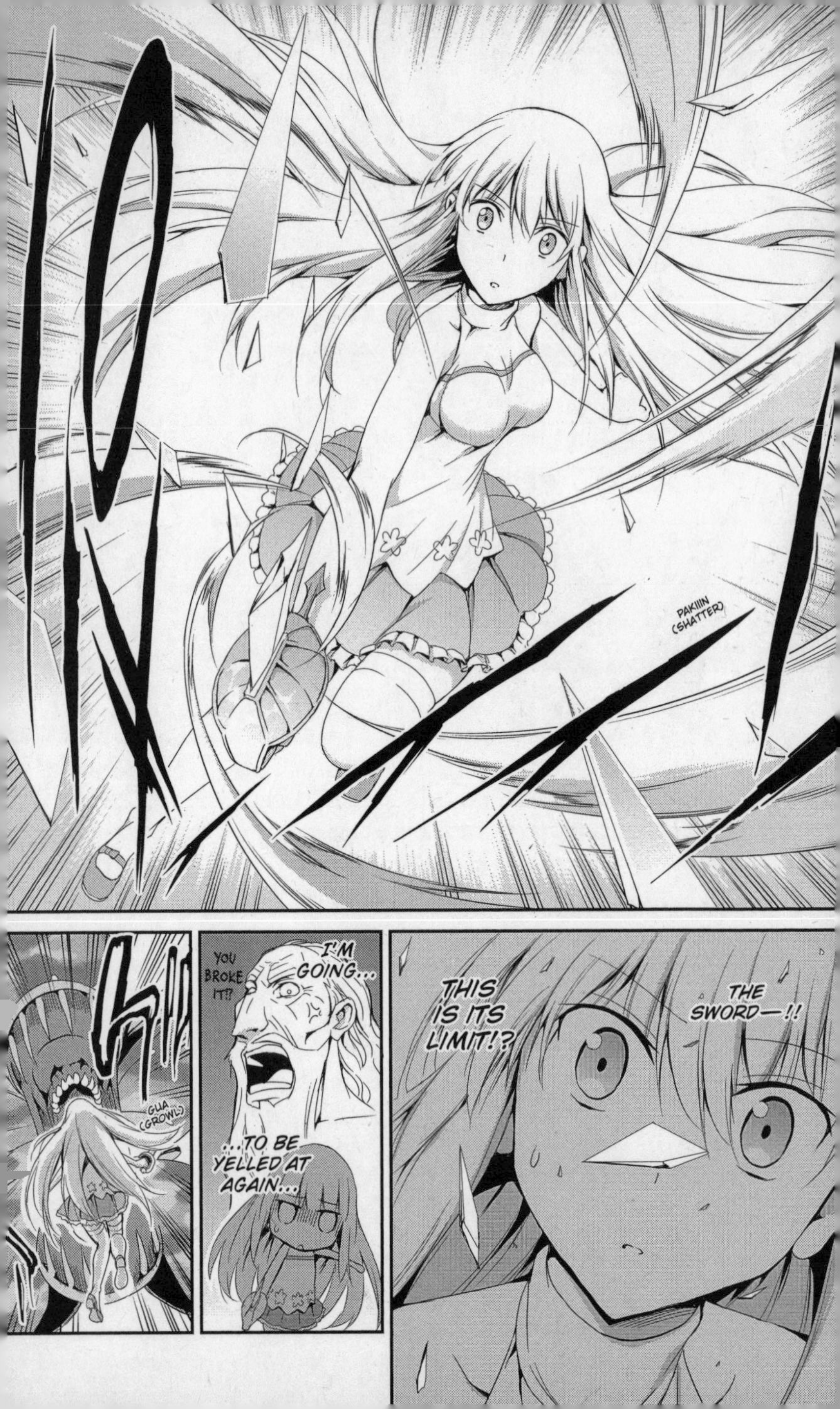
PAKIIIN (SHATTER)
THE SWORD—!!
THIS IS ITS LIMIT!?
YOU BROKE IT!?
I'M GOING...
...TO BE YELLED AT AGAIN...
GUA (GROWL)

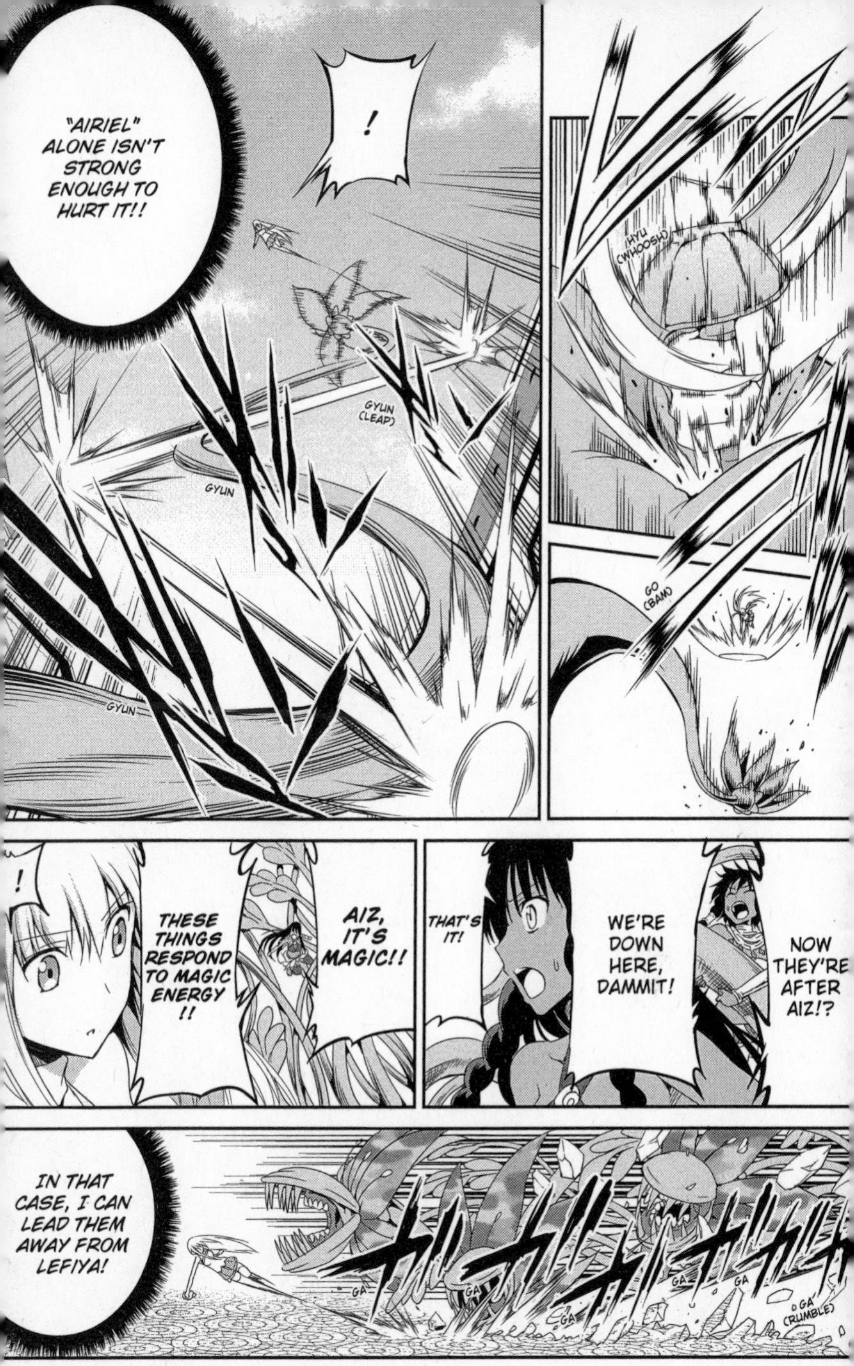
HYU
(WHOOSH)
GO
(BAM)
"AIRIEL" ALONE ISN'T STRONG ENOUGH TO HURT IT!!
!
GYUN
(LEAP)
GYUN
GYUN
NOW THEY'RE AFTER AIZ!?
WE'RE DOWN HERE, DAMMIT!
THAT'S IT!
AIZ, IT'S MAGIC!!
THESE THINGS RESPOND TO MAGIC ENERGY!!
!
GA
(RUMBLE)
GA
GA
GA
GA
GA
GA
IN THAT CASE, I CAN LEAD THEM AWAY FROM LEFIYA!

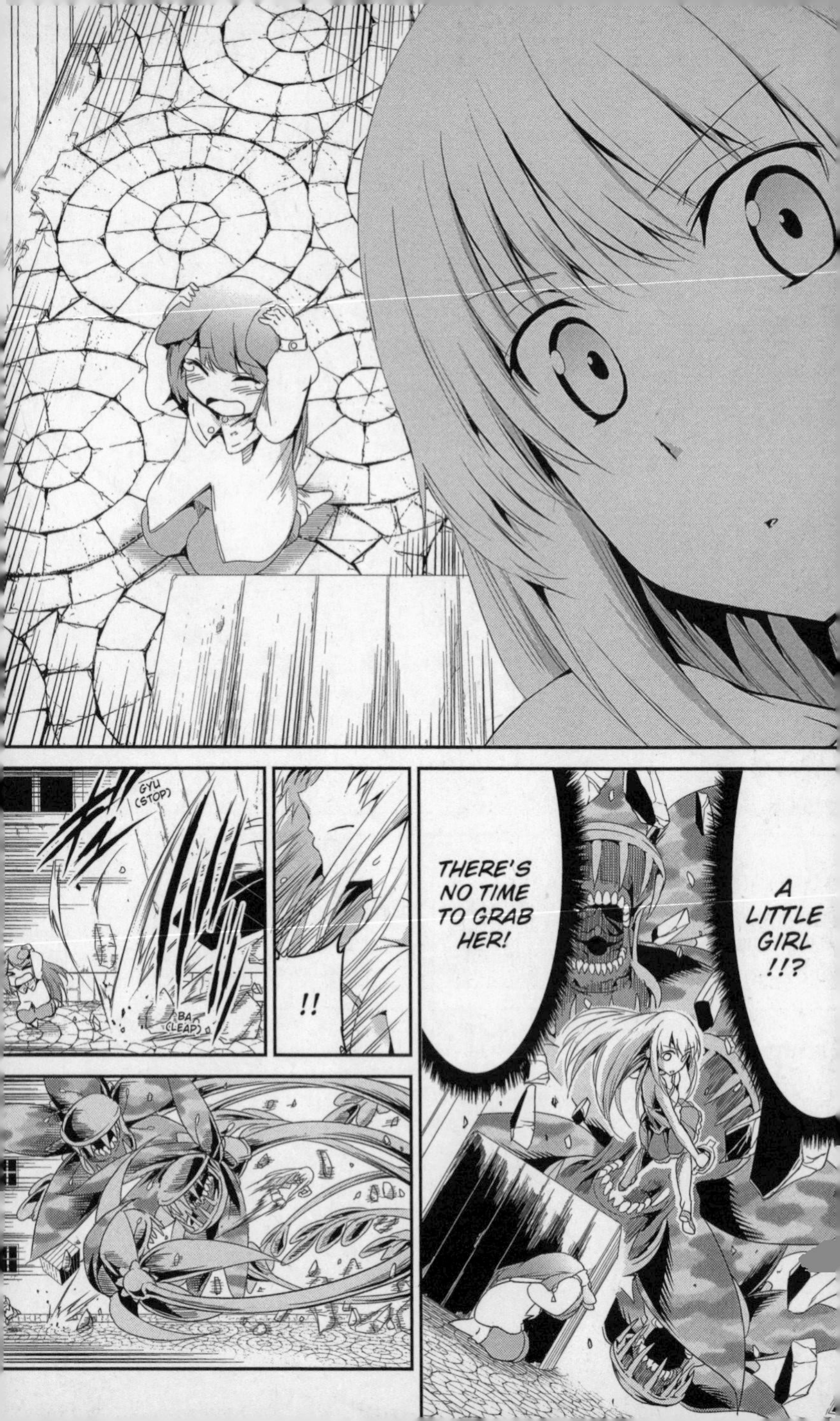
A LITTLE GIRL!!?
THERE'S NO TIME TO GRAB HER!
!!
GYU (STOP)
BA (LEAP)

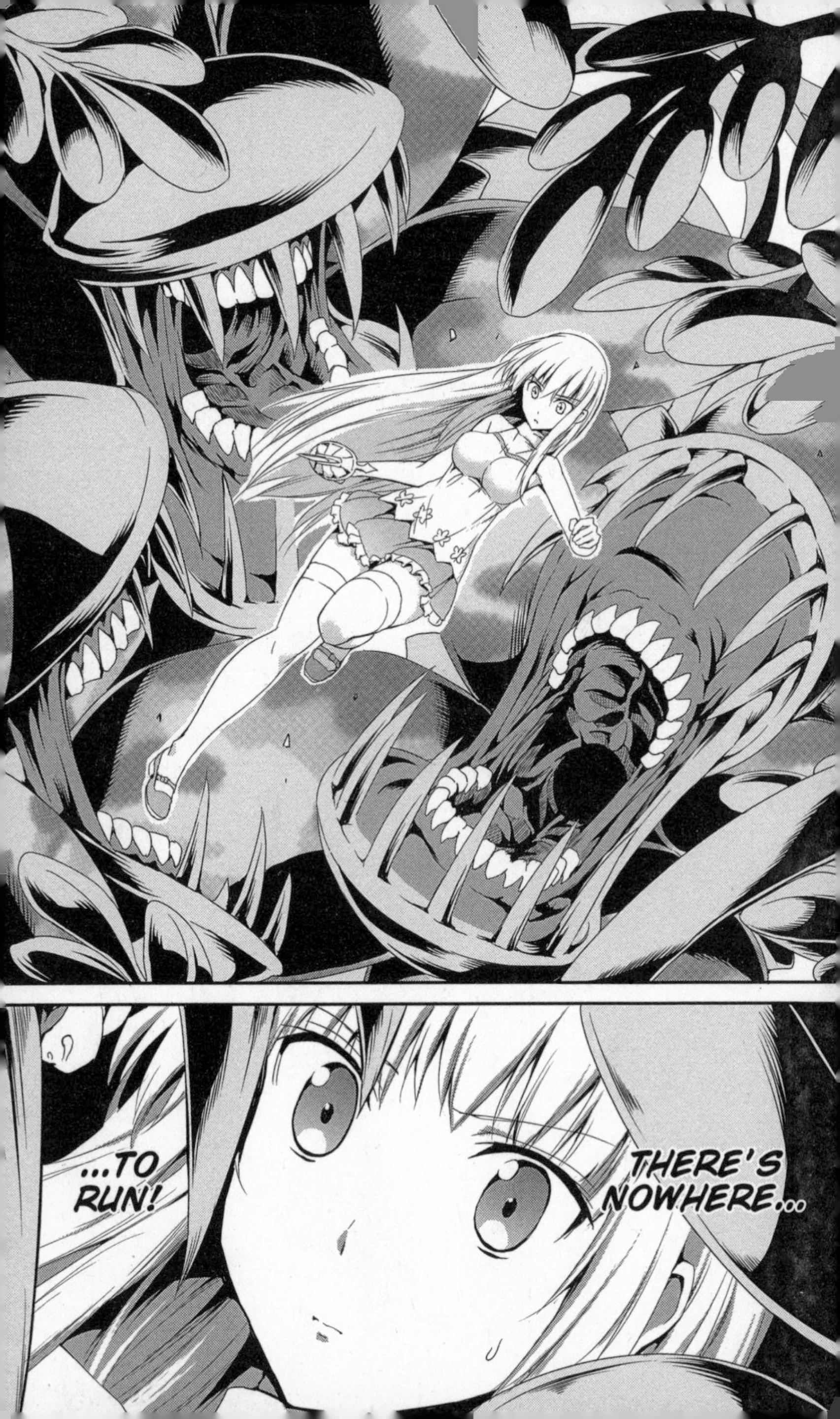
THERE'S NOWHERE...
...TO RUN!

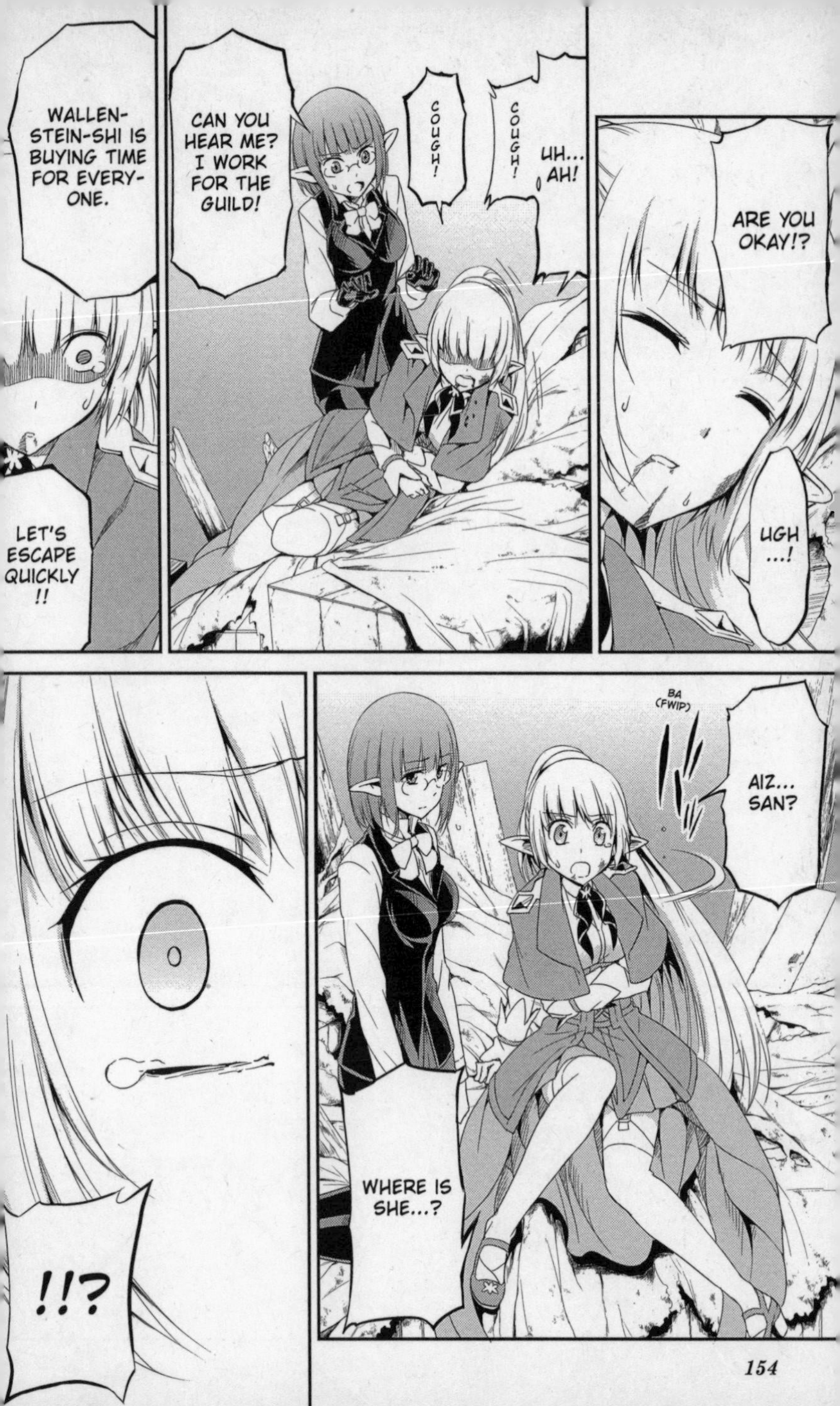
ARE YOU OKAY!?
UGH ...!
UH... AH!
COUGH!
COUGH!
CAN YOU HEAR ME? I WORK FOR THE GUILD!
WALLEN-STEIN-SHI IS BUYING TIME FOR EVERY-ONE.
LET'S ESCAPE QUICKLY !!
BA (FWIP)
AIZ... SAN?
WHERE IS SHE...?
!!?

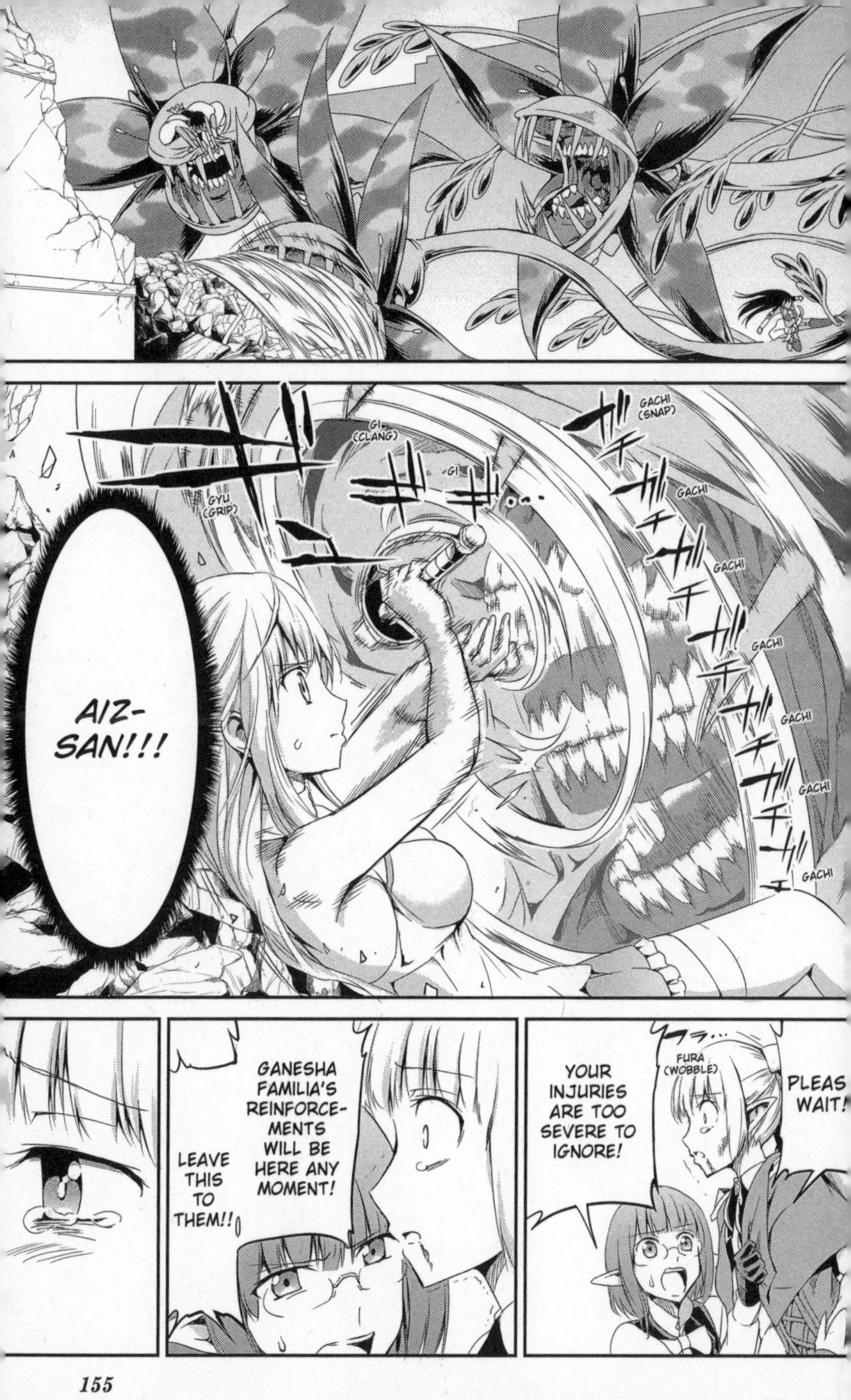
GACHI (SNAP)
GACHI
GACHI
GACHI
GACHI
GACHI
GACHI
GI (CLANG)
GI
GYU (GRIP)
AIZ-SAN!!!
PLEAS WAIT!
FURA (WOBBLE)
YOUR INJURIES ARE TOO SEVERE TO IGNORE!
GANESHA FAMILIA'S REINFORCEMENTS WILL BE HERE ANY MOMENT!
LEAVE THIS TO THEM!!

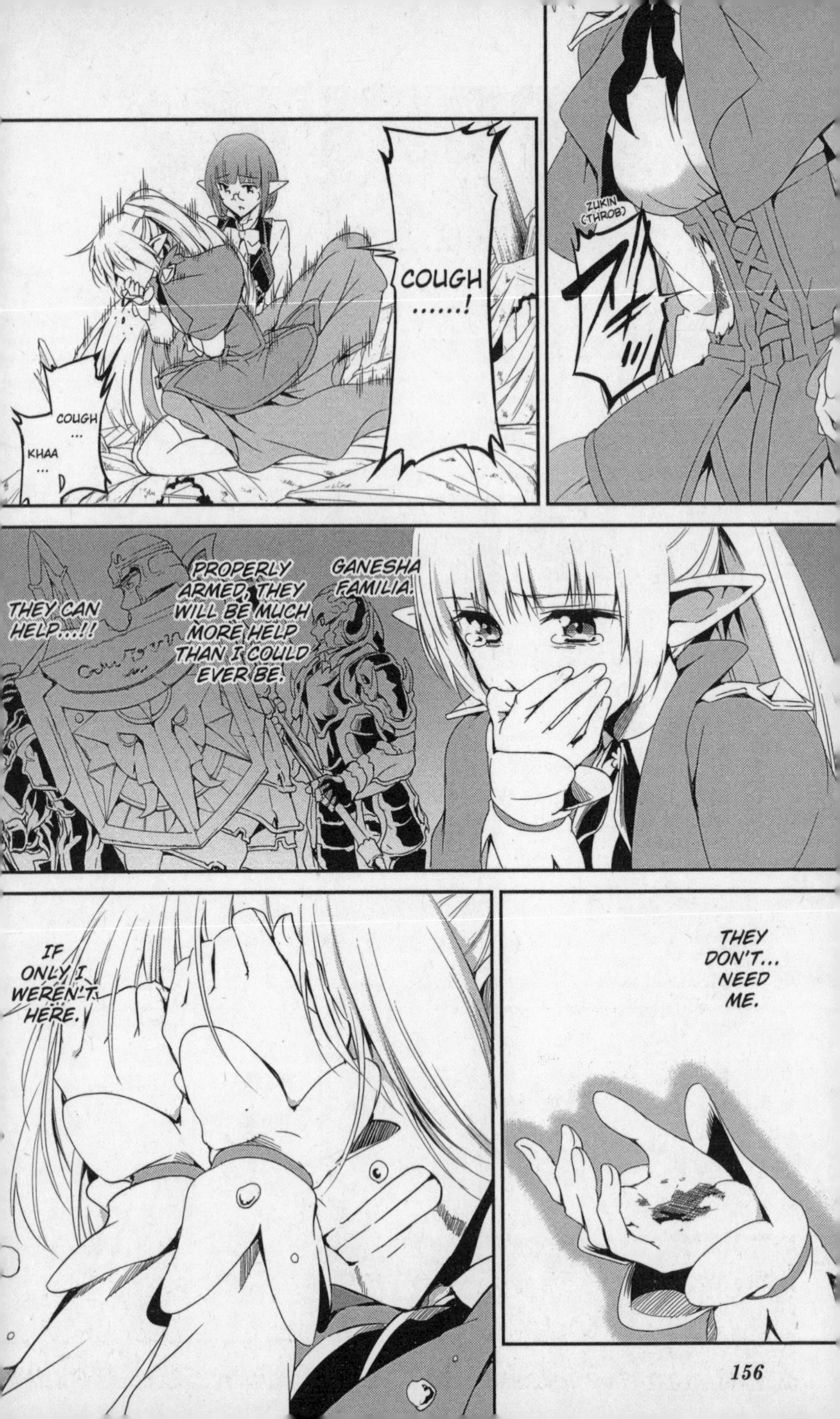
ZUKIN (THROB)
COUGH ......!
COUGH ... KHAA ...
GANESHA FAMILIA.
PROPERLY ARMED, THEY WILL BE MUCH MORE HELP THAN I COULD EVER BE.
THEY CAN HELP...!!
THEY DON'T... NEED ME.
IF ONLY I WEREN'T HERE.

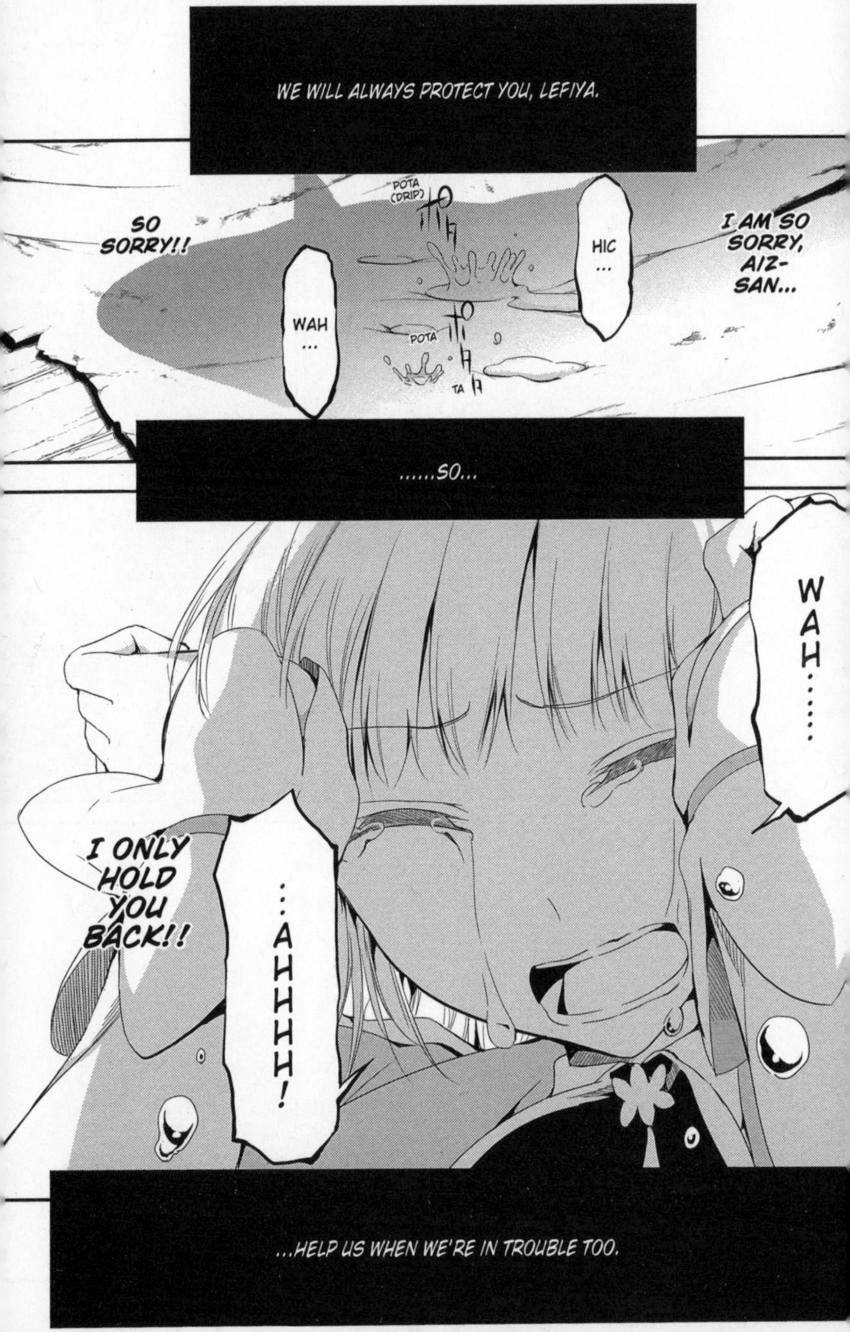

WE WILL ALWAYS PROTECT YOU, LEFIYA.
I AM SO SORRY, AIZ-SAN...
HIC...
POTA (DRIP)
WAH...
SO SORRY!!
POTA
TA
......SO...
WAH......
...AHHHHH!
I ONLY HOLD YOU BACK!!
...HELP US WHEN WE'RE IN TROUBLE TOO.

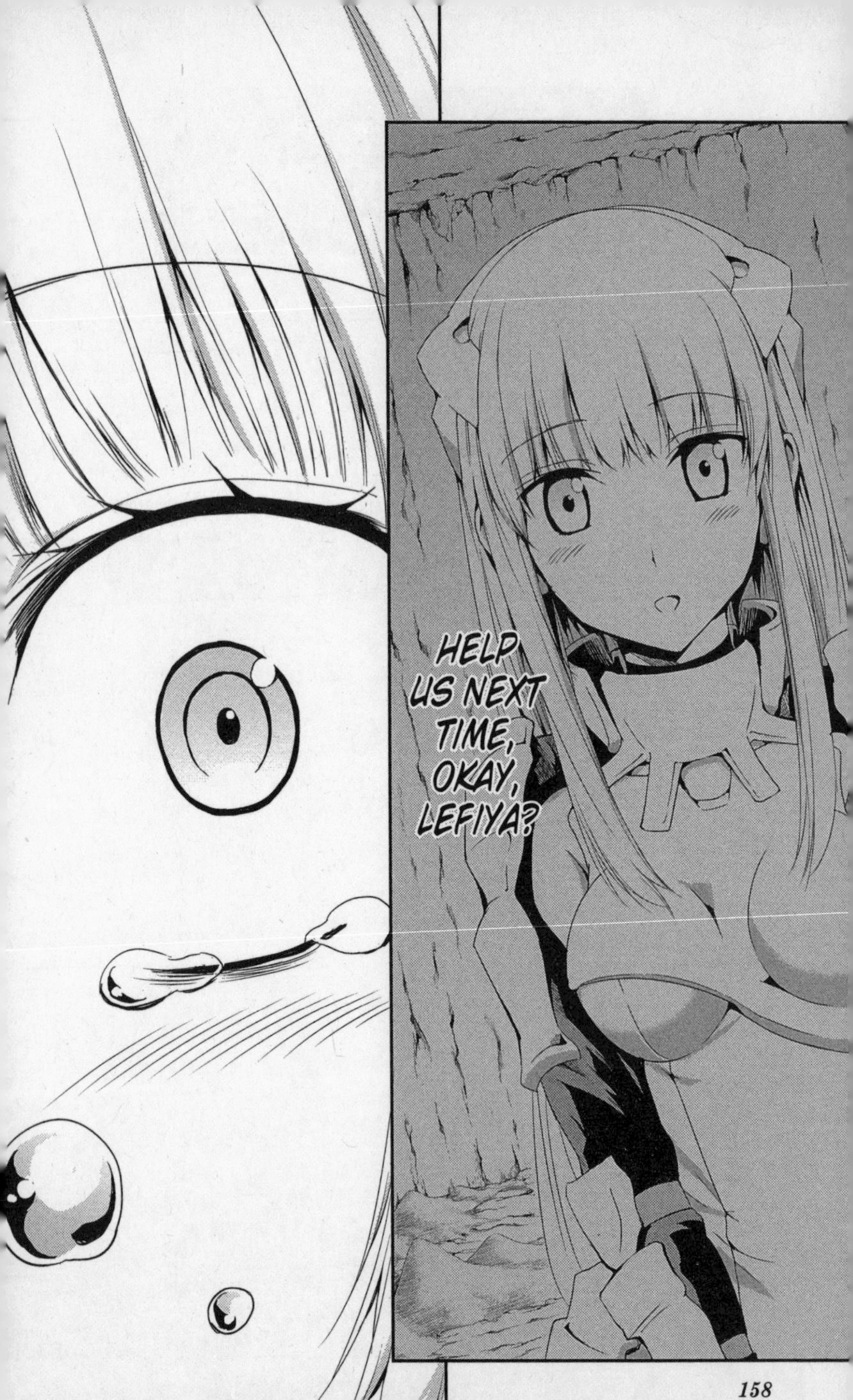
HELP US NEXT TIME, OKAY, LEFIYA?

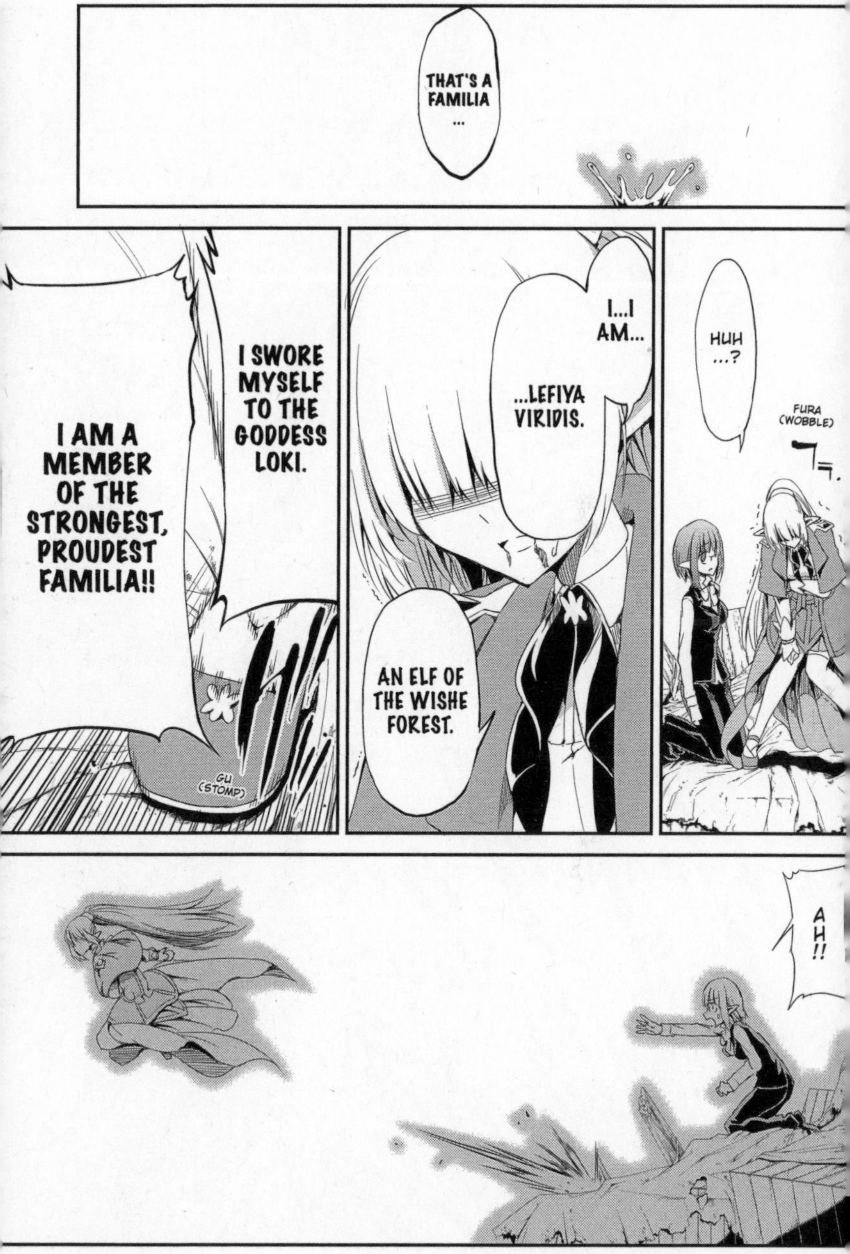
THAT'S A FAMILIA ...
HUH ...?
FURA (WOBBLE)
I...I AM...
...LEFIYA VIRIDIS.
AN ELF OF THE WISHE FOREST.
I SWORE MYSELF TO THE GODDESS LOKI.
I AM A MEMBER OF THE STRONGEST, PROUDEST FAMILIA!!
GU (STOMP)
AH!!

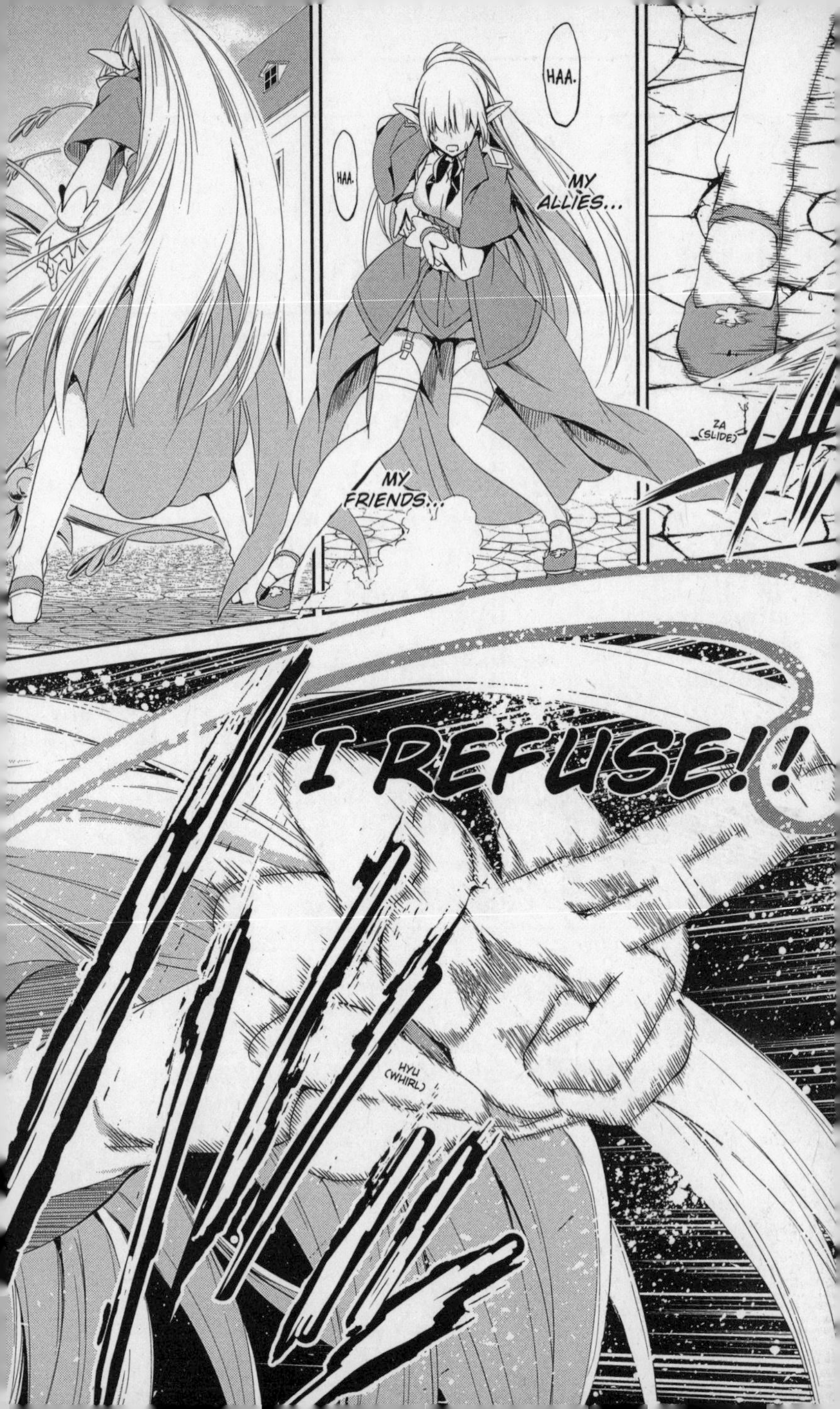
ZA
(SLIDE)
HAA.
HAA.
MY ALLIES...
MY FRIENDS...
I REFUSE!!
HYU
(WHIRL)

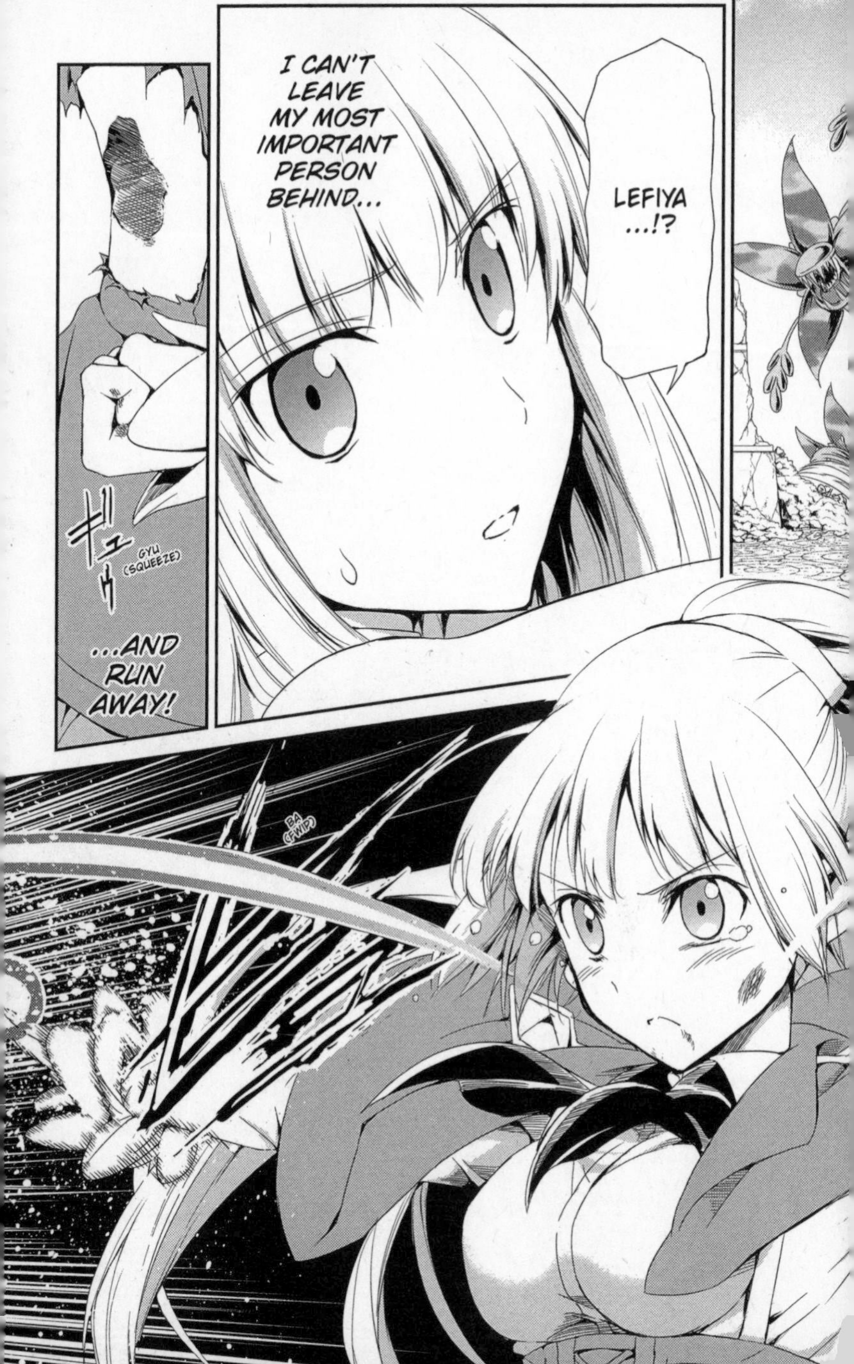
LEFIYA ...!?
I CAN'T LEAVE MY MOST IMPORTANT PERSON BEHIND...
GYU (SQUEEZE)
...AND RUN AWAY!
BA (FWIP)

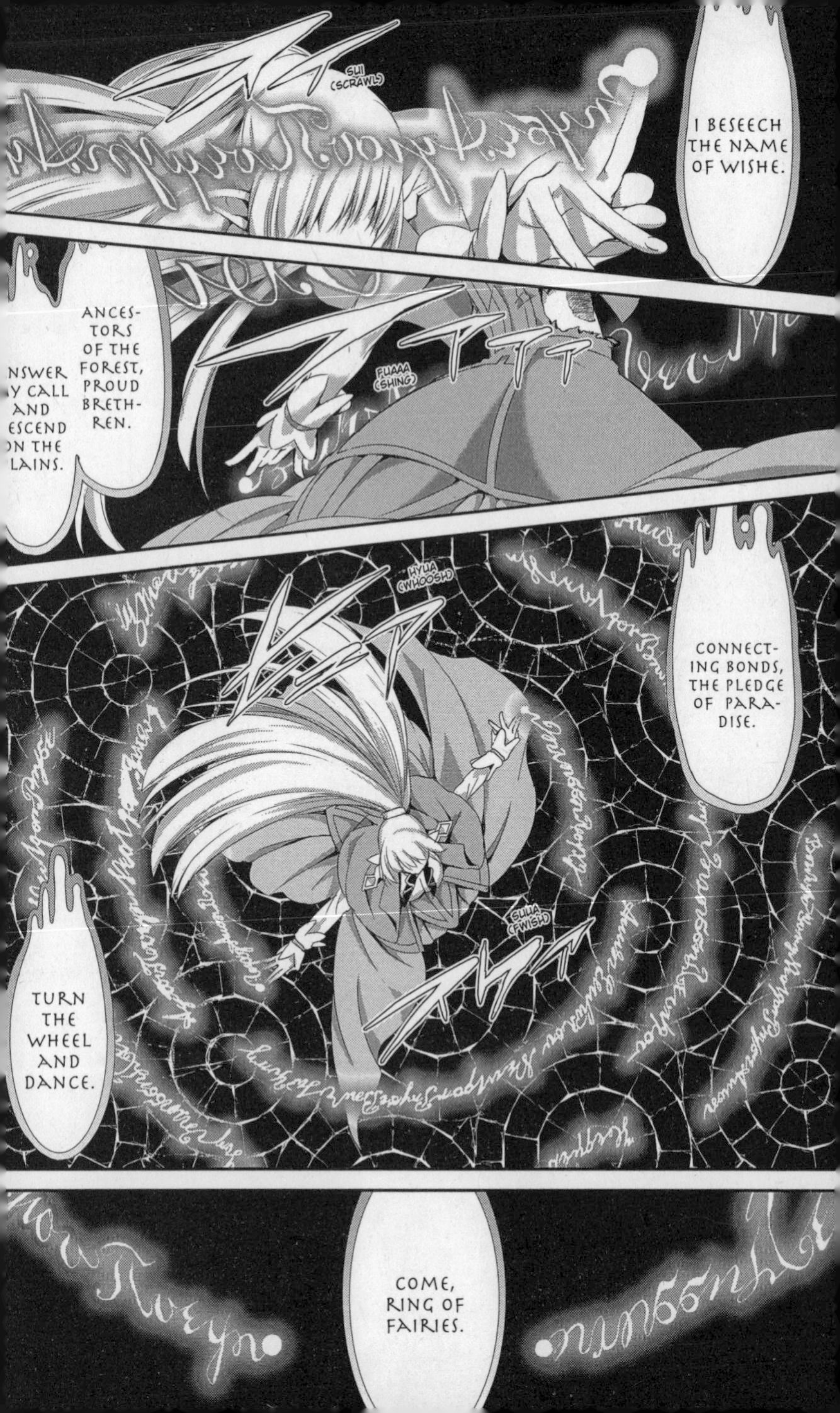
I BESEECH THE NAME OF WISHE.
SUI (SCRAWL)
ANCES-TORS OF THE FOREST, PROUD BRETH-REN.
NSWER Y CALL AND ESCEND ON THE LAINS.
FUAAA (SHING)
CONNECT-ING BONDS, THE PLEDGE OF PARA-DISE.
HYUA (WHOOSH)
SUUA (FWISH)
TURN THE WHEEL AND DANCE.
COME, RING OF FAIRIES.

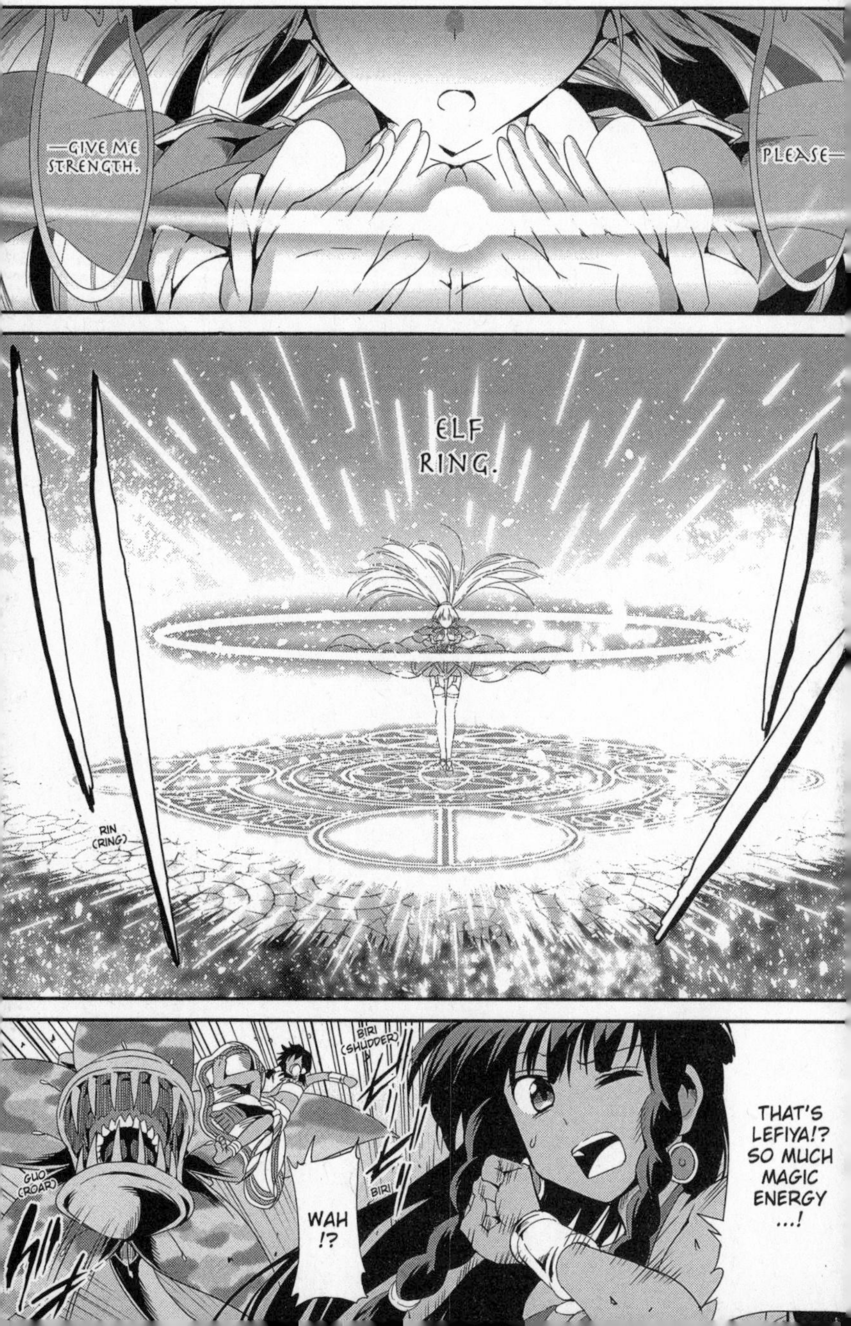
PLEASE—
—GIVE ME STRENGTH.
ELF RING.
RIN (RING)
THAT'S LEFIYA!? SO MUCH MAGIC ENERGY ...!
BIRI (SHUDDER)
BIRI
WAH !?
GUO (ROAR)

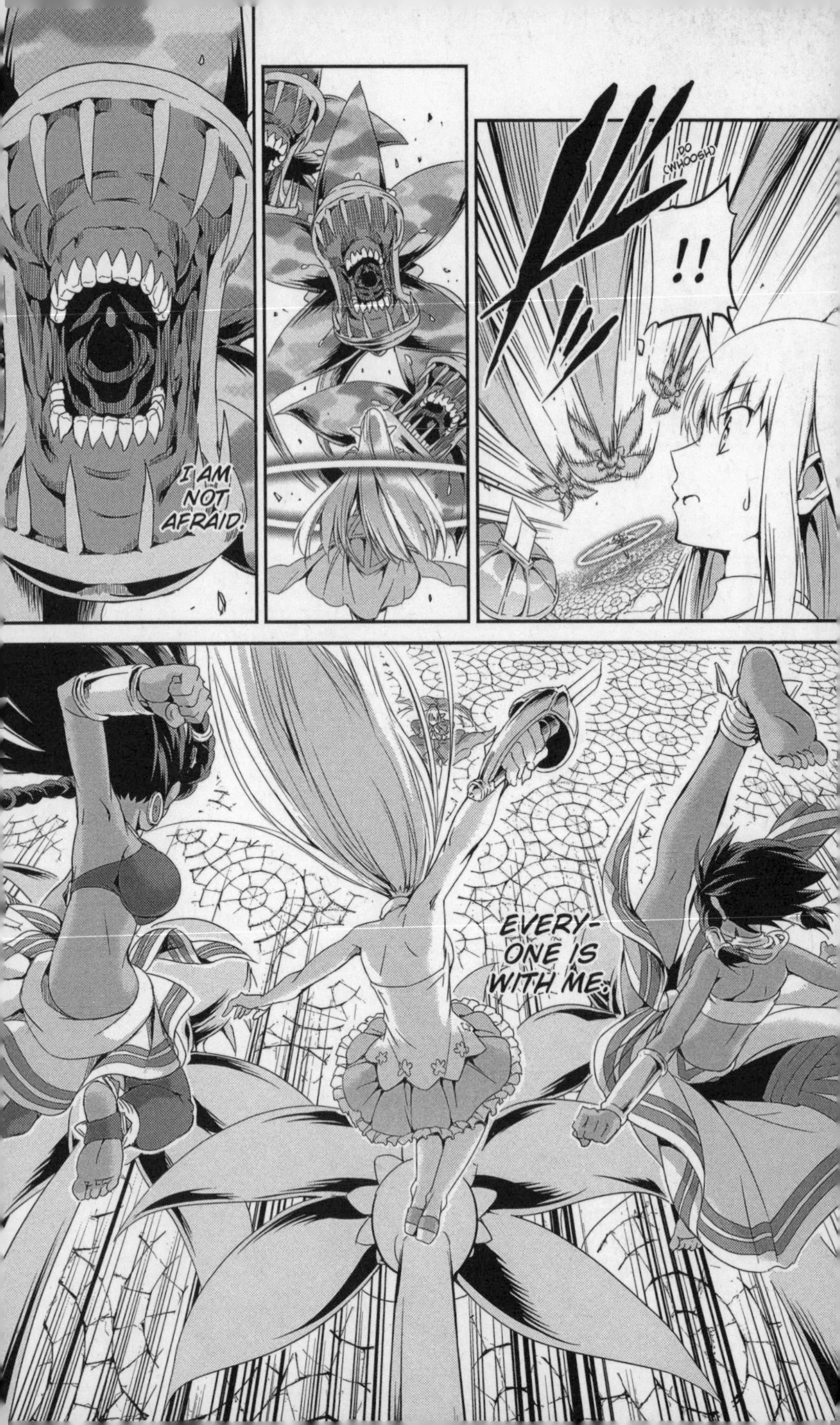
DO (WHOOSH)
!!
I AM NOT AFRAID!
EVERY-ONE IS WITH ME.

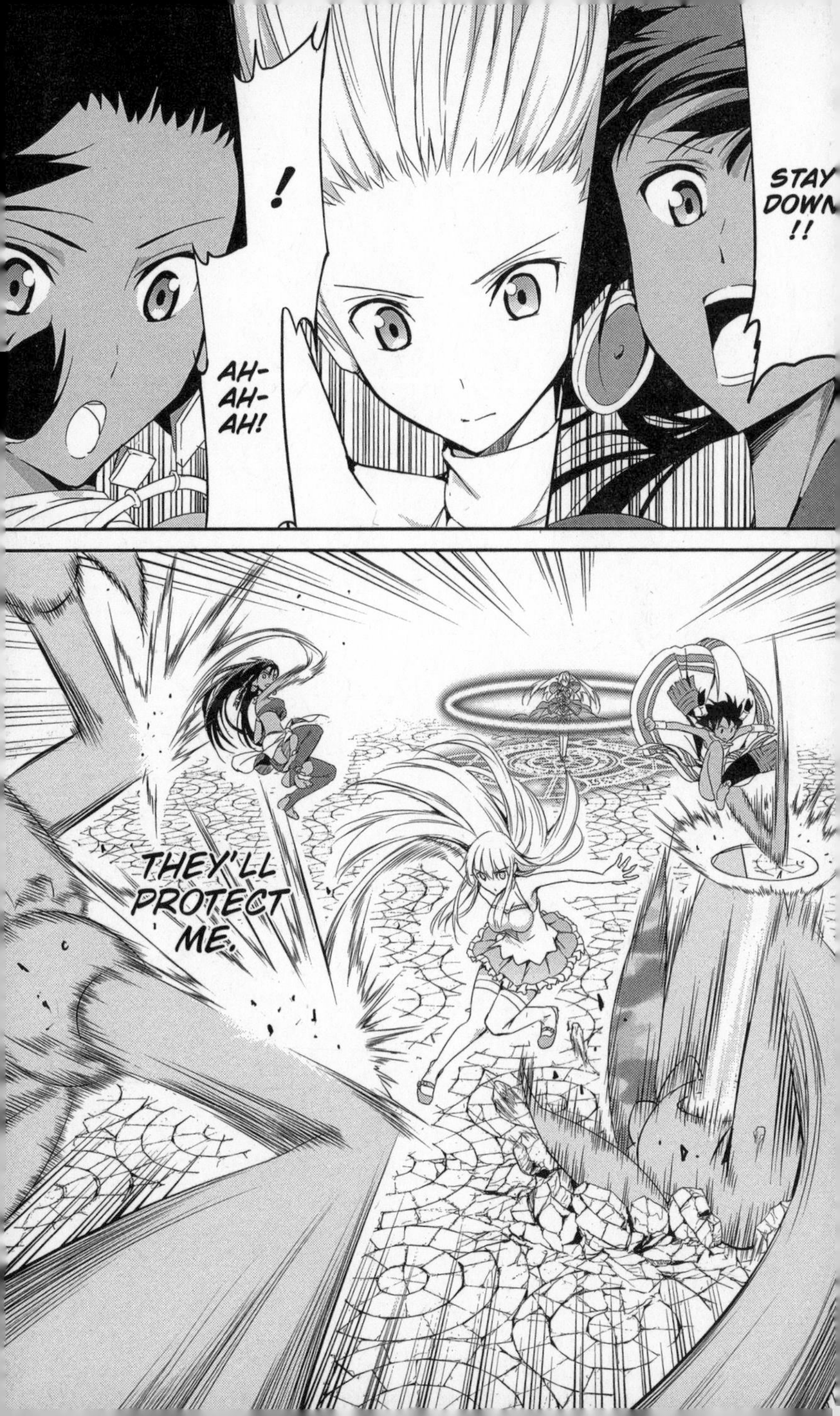
STAY DOWN !!
!
AH-AH-AH!
THEY'LL PROTECT ME.

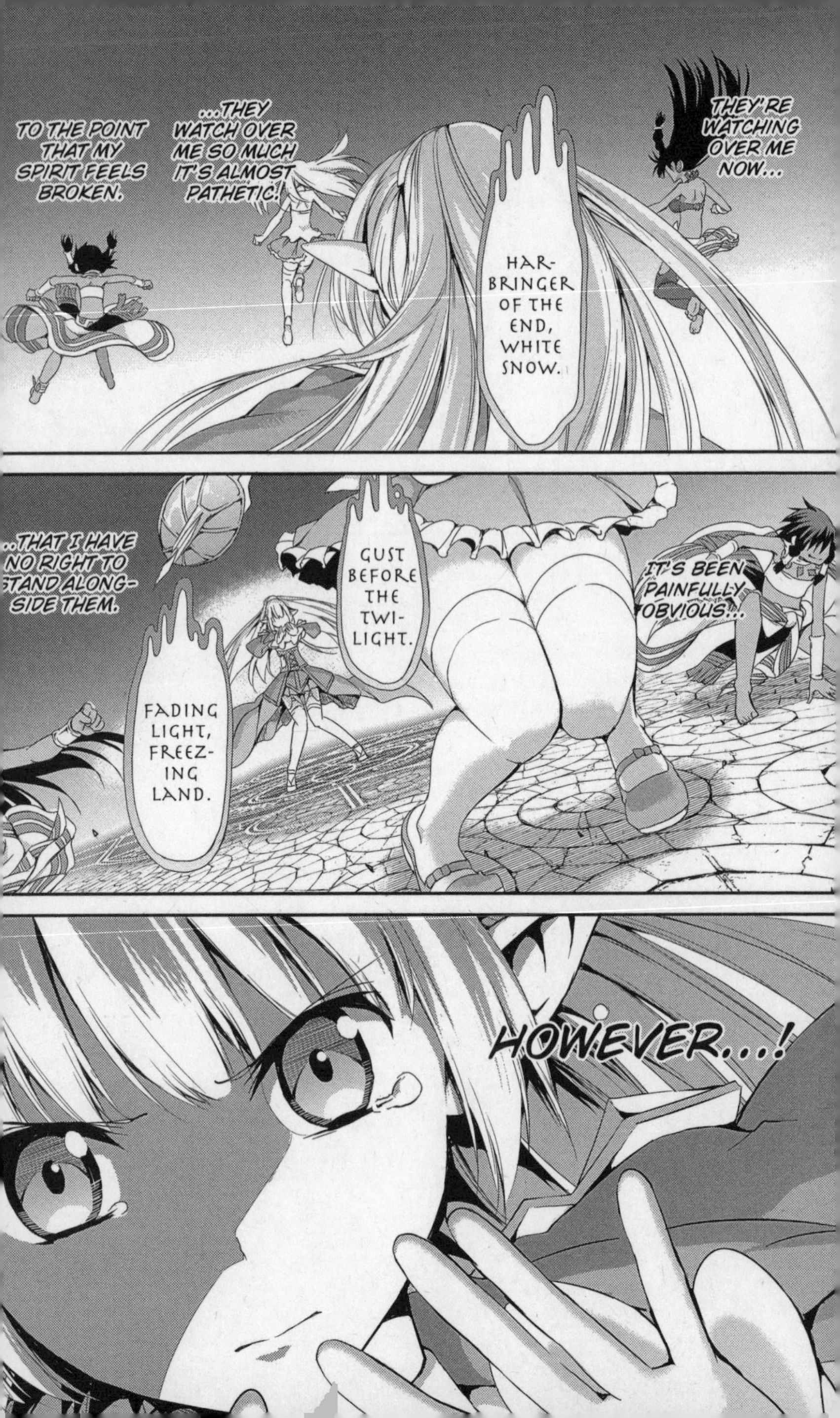
THEY'RE WATCHING OVER ME NOW...
HARBINGER OF THE END, WHITE SNOW.
...THEY WATCH OVER ME SO MUCH IT'S ALMOST PATHETIC!
TO THE POINT THAT MY SPIRIT FEELS BROKEN.
IT'S BEEN PAINFULLY OBVIOUS...
GUST BEFORE THE TWILIGHT.
FADING LIGHT, FREEZING LAND.
...THAT I HAVE NO RIGHT TO STAND ALONGSIDE THEM.
HOWEVER...!

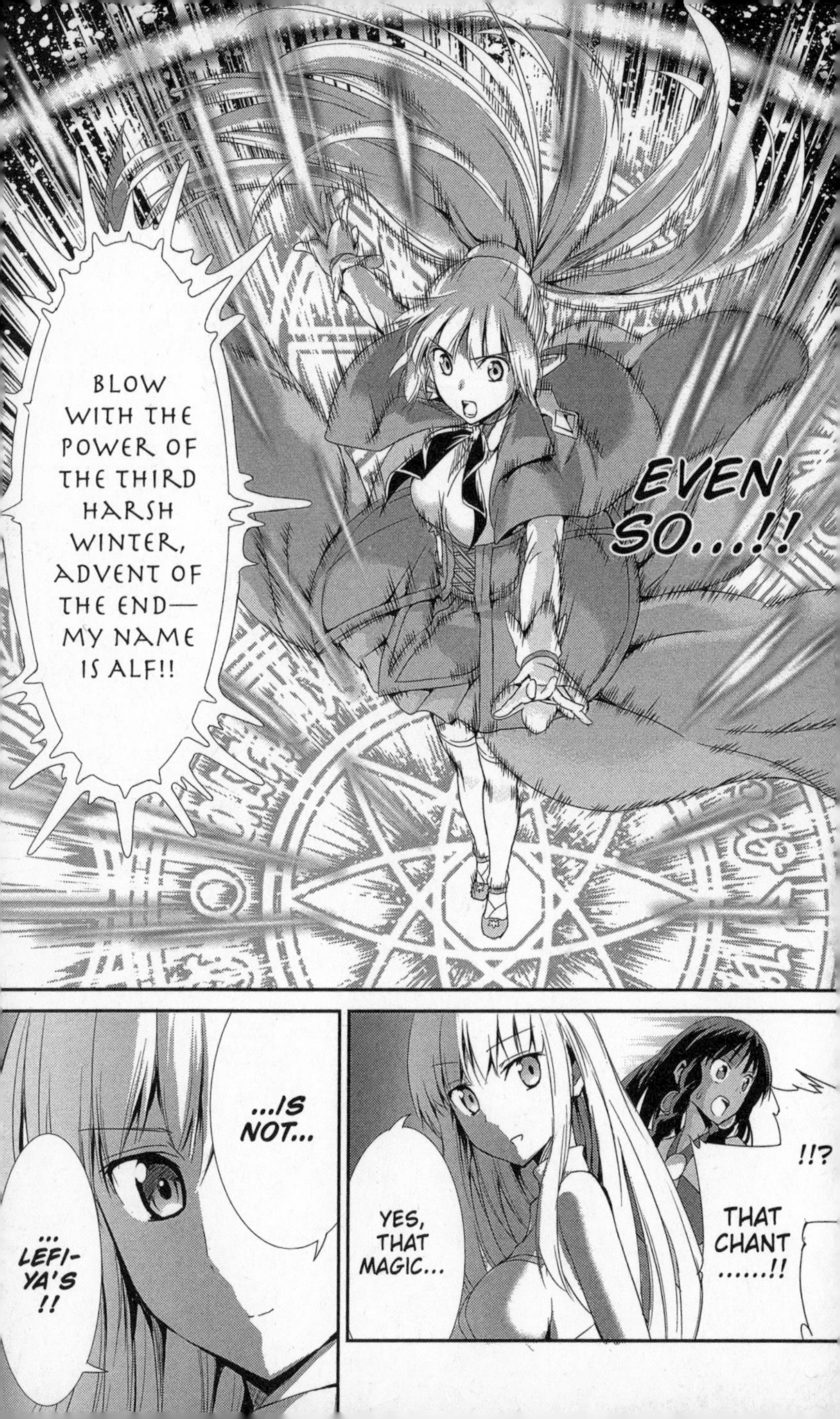
EVEN SO...!!
BLOW WITH THE POWER OF THE THIRD HARSH WINTER, ADVENT OF THE END—MY NAME IS ALF!!
!!?
THAT CHANT......!!
YES, THAT MAGIC...
...IS NOT...
...LEFI-YA'S!!

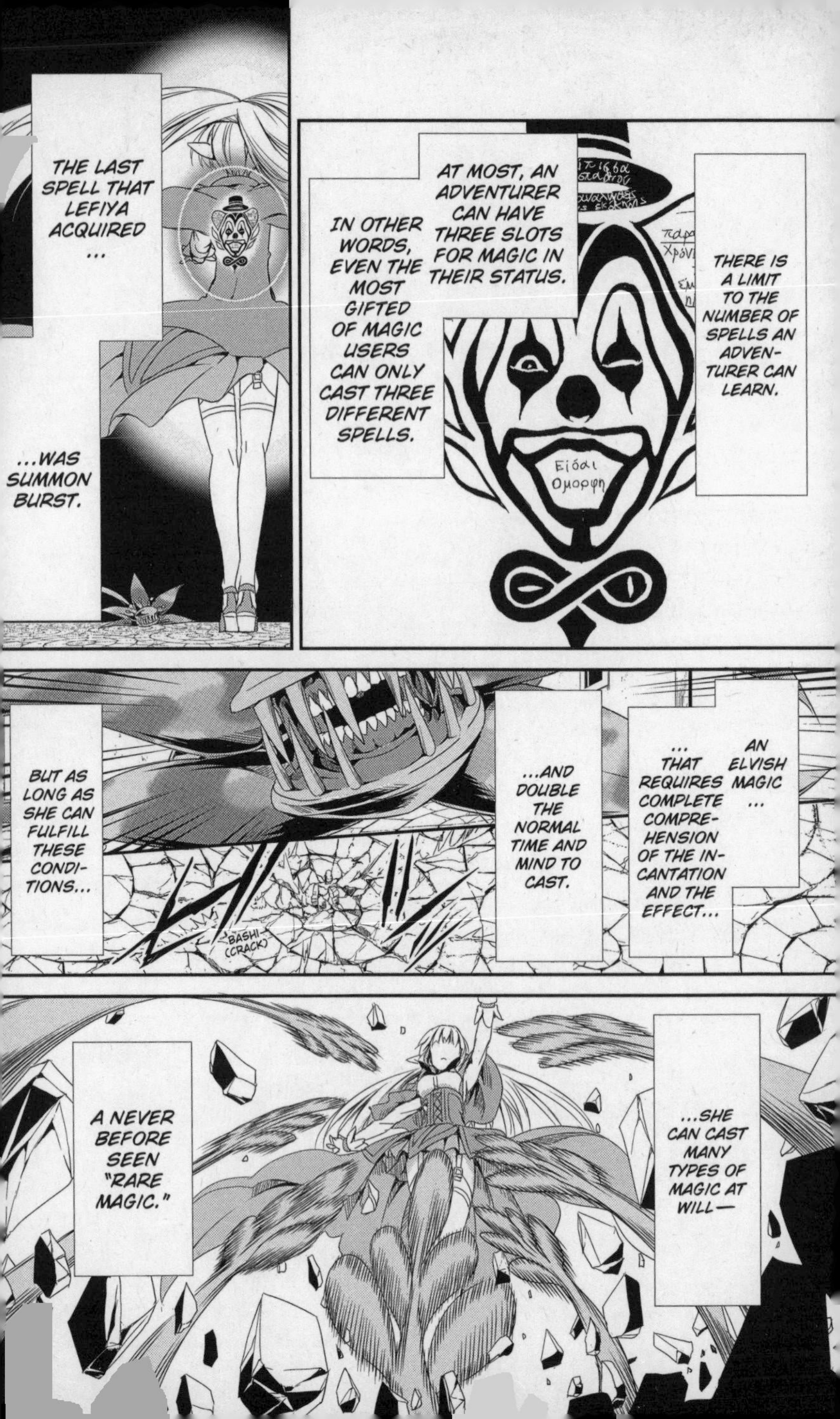
THERE IS A LIMIT TO THE NUMBER OF SPELLS AN ADVEN-TURER CAN LEARN.
AT MOST, AN ADVENTURER CAN HAVE THREE SLOTS FOR MAGIC IN THEIR STATUS.
IN OTHER WORDS, EVEN THE MOST GIFTED OF MAGIC USERS CAN ONLY CAST THREE DIFFERENT SPELLS.
THE LAST SPELL THAT LEFIYA ACQUIRED ...
...WAS SUMMON BURST.
AN ELVISH MAGIC ...
... THAT REQUIRES COMPLETE COMPRE-HENSION OF THE IN-CANTATION AND THE EFFECT...
...AND DOUBLE THE NORMAL TIME AND MIND TO CAST.
BASHI (CRACK)
BUT AS LONG AS SHE CAN FULFILL THESE CONDI-TIONS...
...SHE CAN CAST MANY TYPES OF MAGIC AT WILL—
A NEVER BEFORE SEEN "RARE MAGIC."

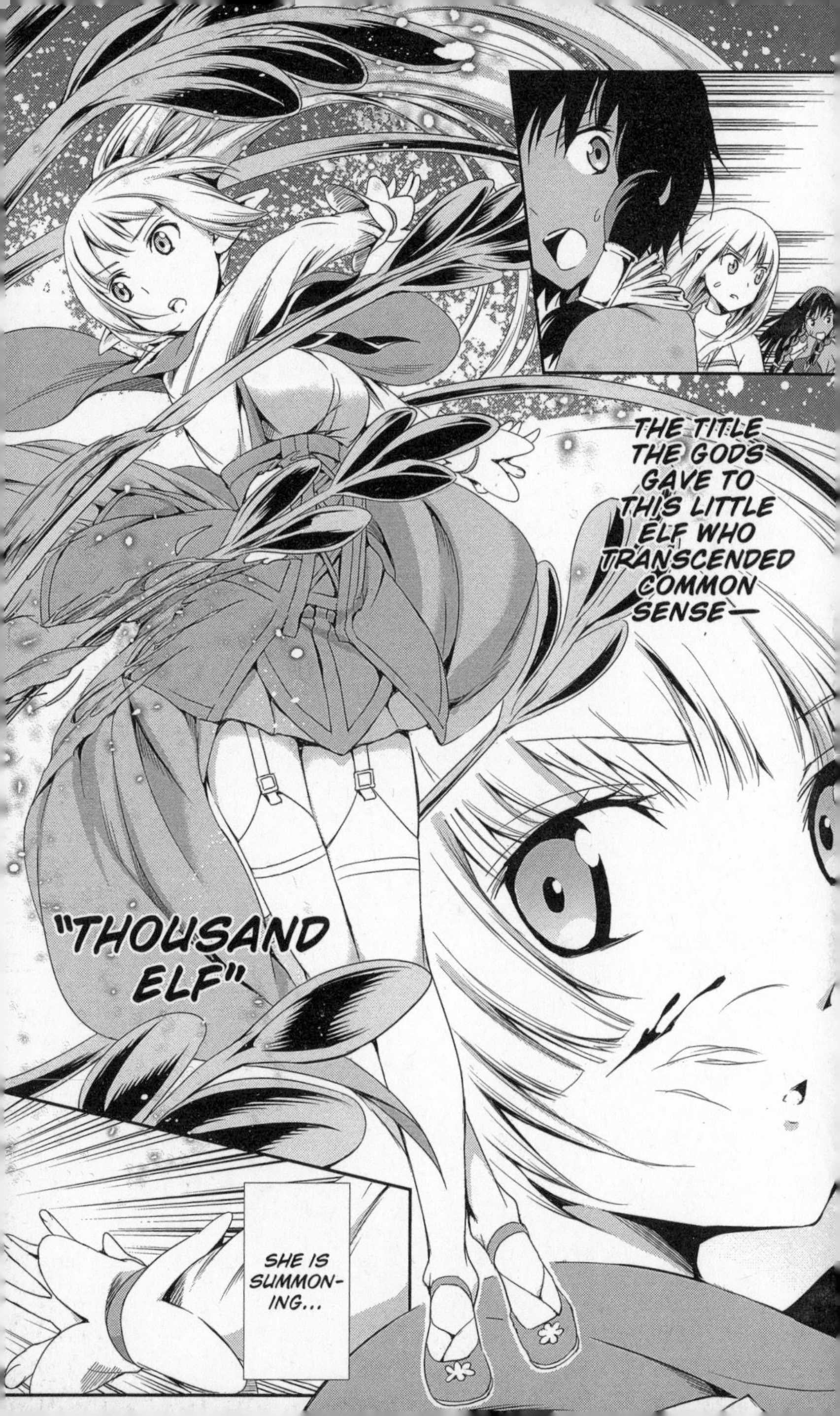
THE TITLE THE GODS GAVE TO THIS LITTLE ELF WHO TRANSCENDED COMMON SENSE—
"THOUSAND ELF"
SHE IS SUMMON-ING...

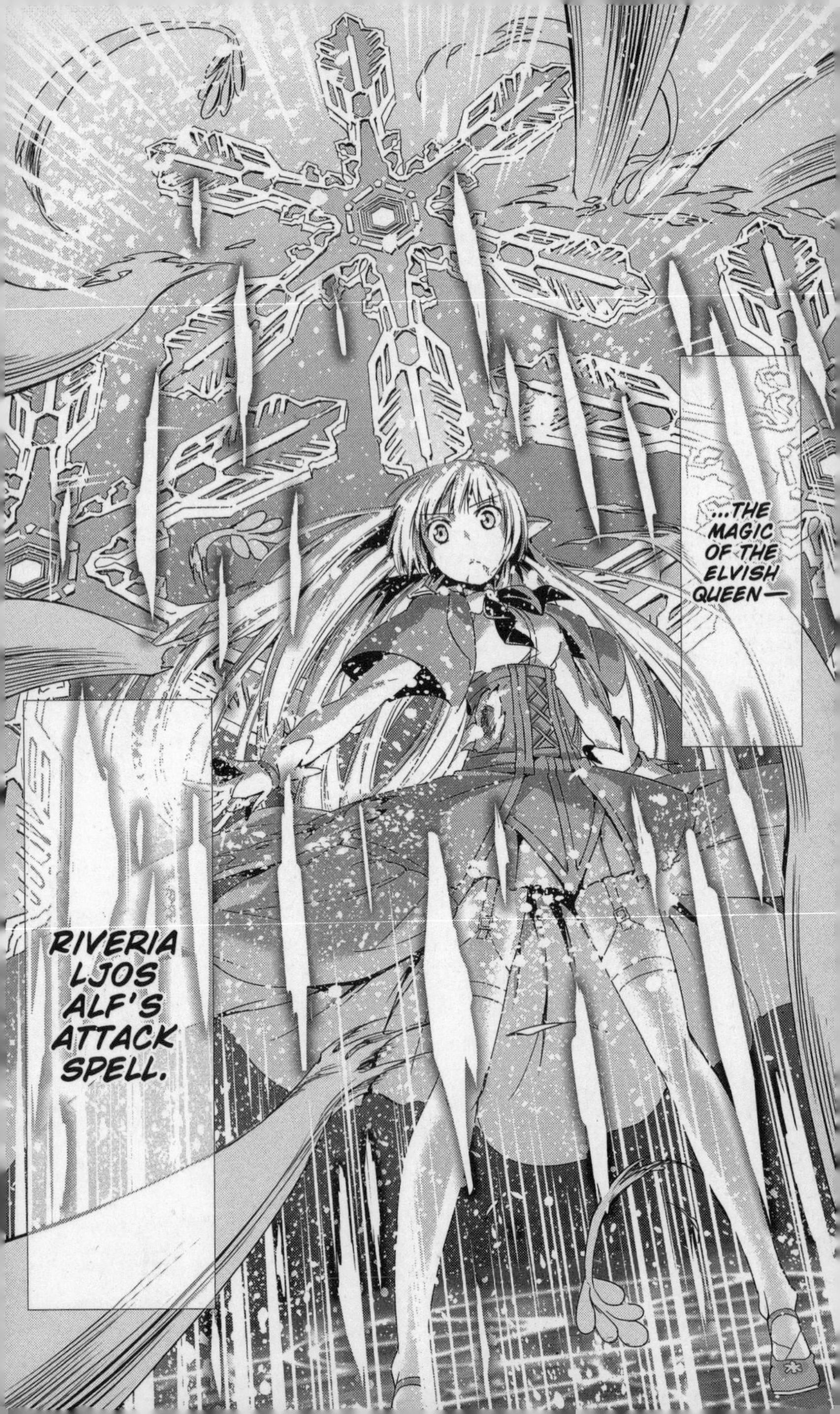
...THE MAGIC OF THE ELVISH QUEEN—
RIVERIA LJOS ALF'S ATTACK SPELL.

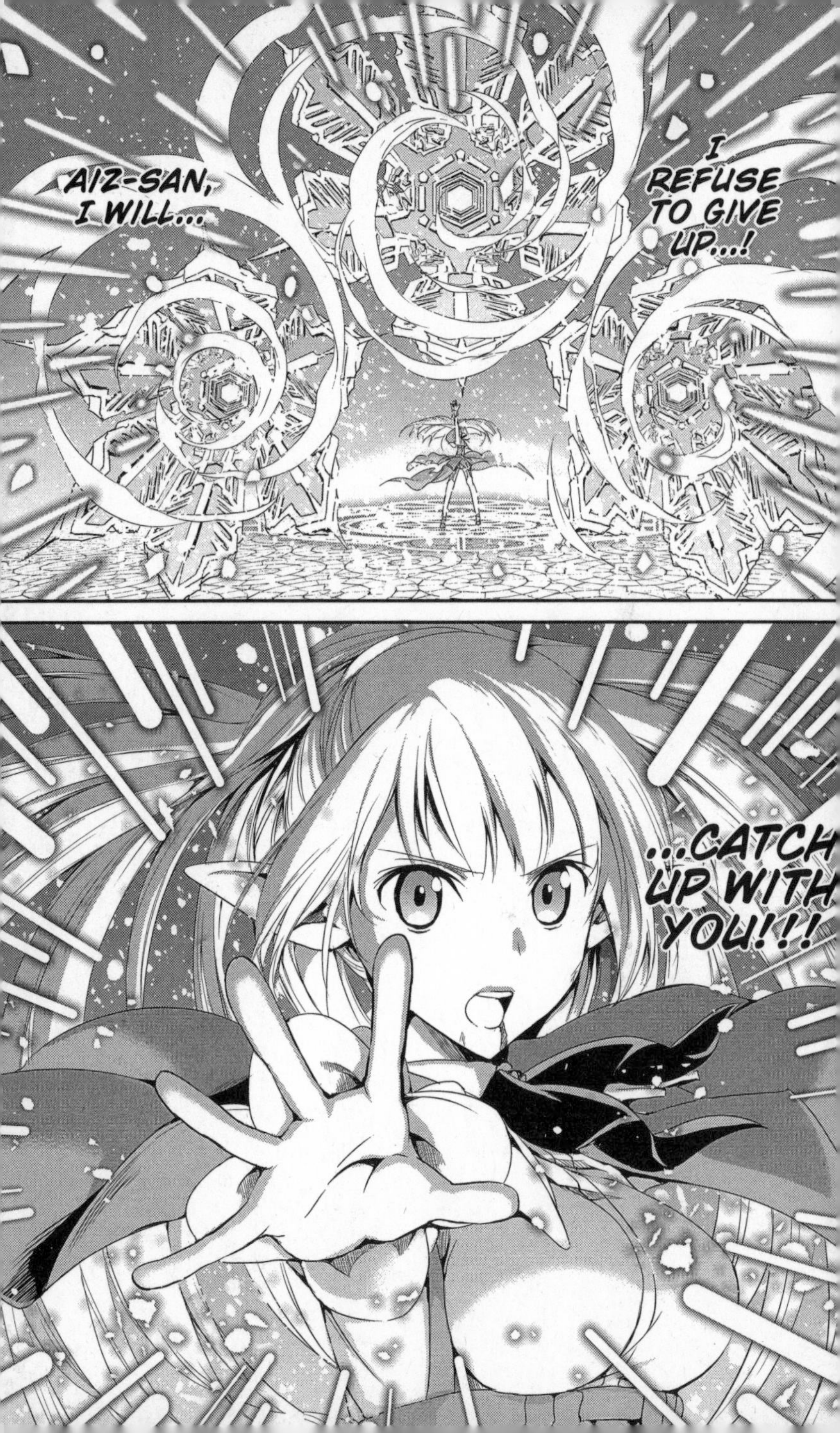
I REFUSE TO GIVE UP...!
AIZ-SAN, I WILL...
...CATCH UP WITH YOU!!!

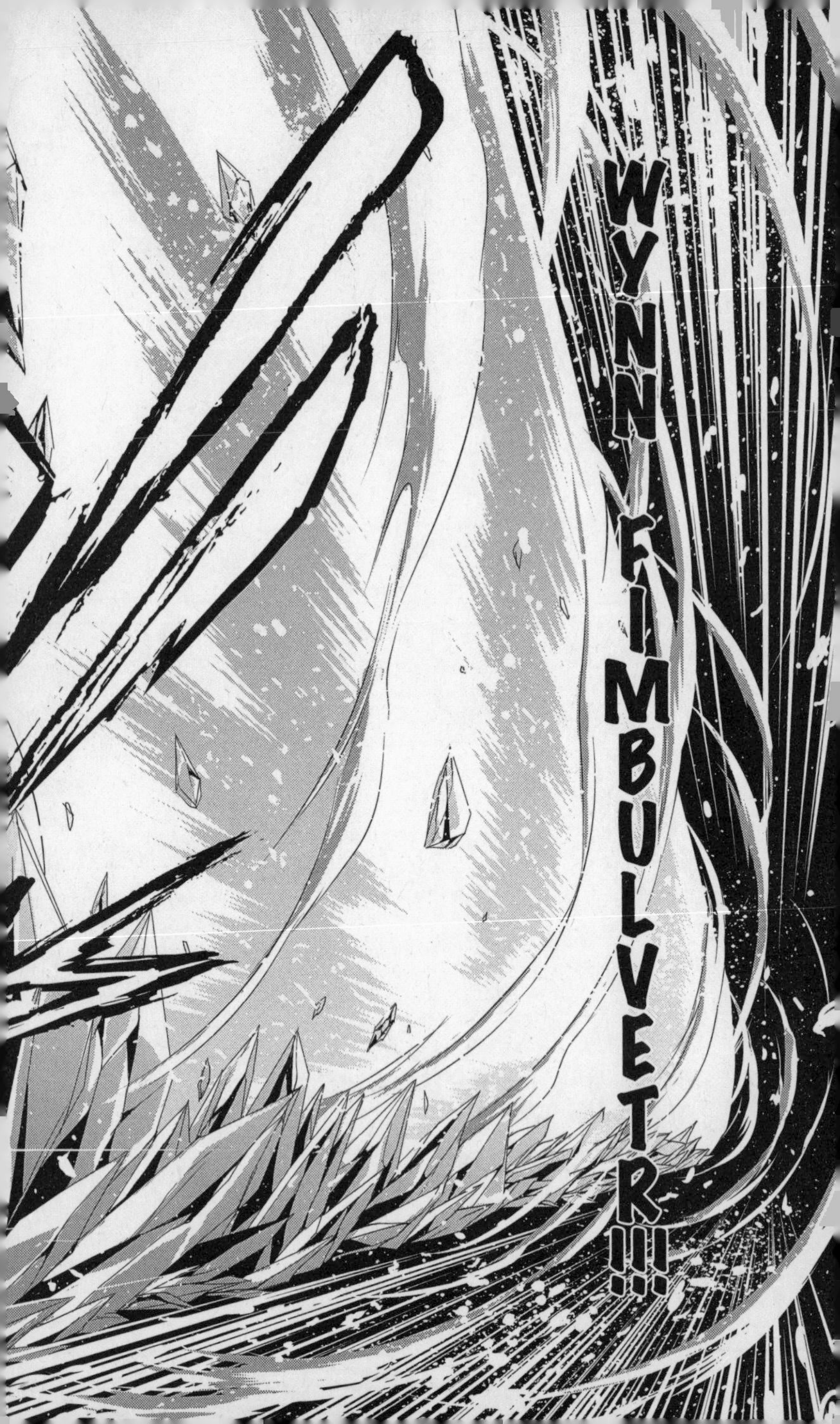
WYNN FIMBULVETR!!!

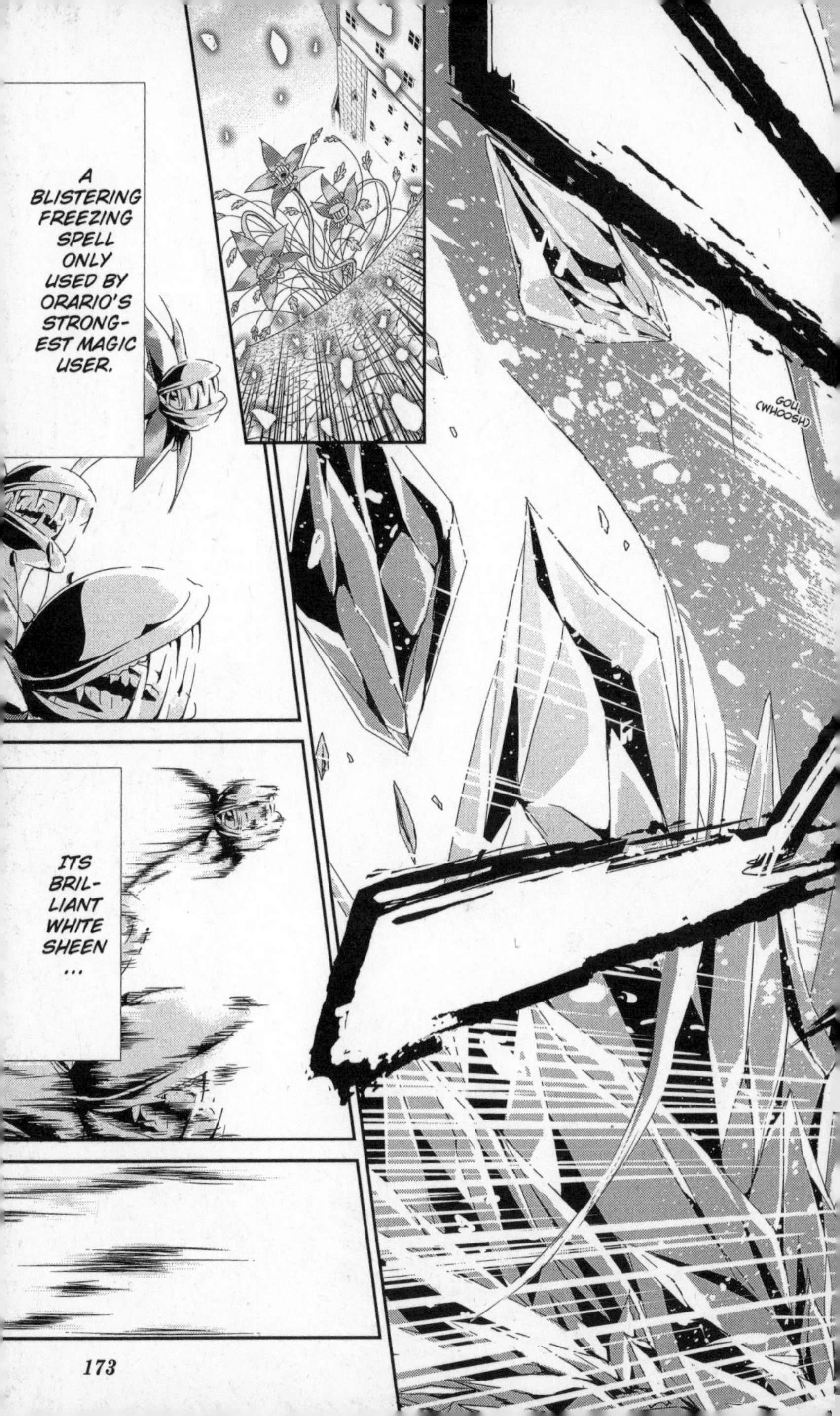
GOU (WHOOSH)
A BLISTERING FREEZING SPELL ONLY USED BY ORARIO'S STRONGEST MAGIC USER.
ITS BRILLIANT WHITE SHEEN ...

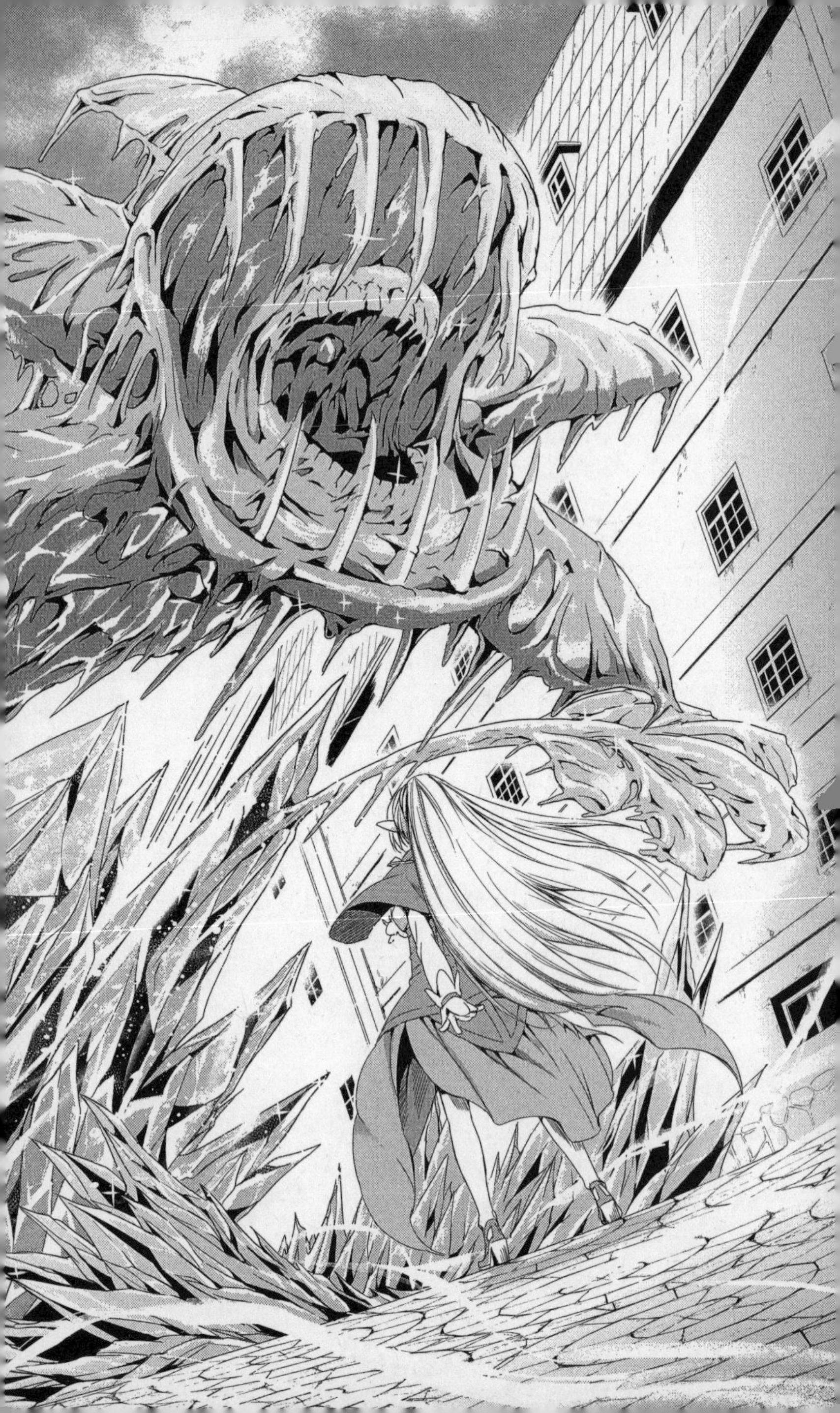

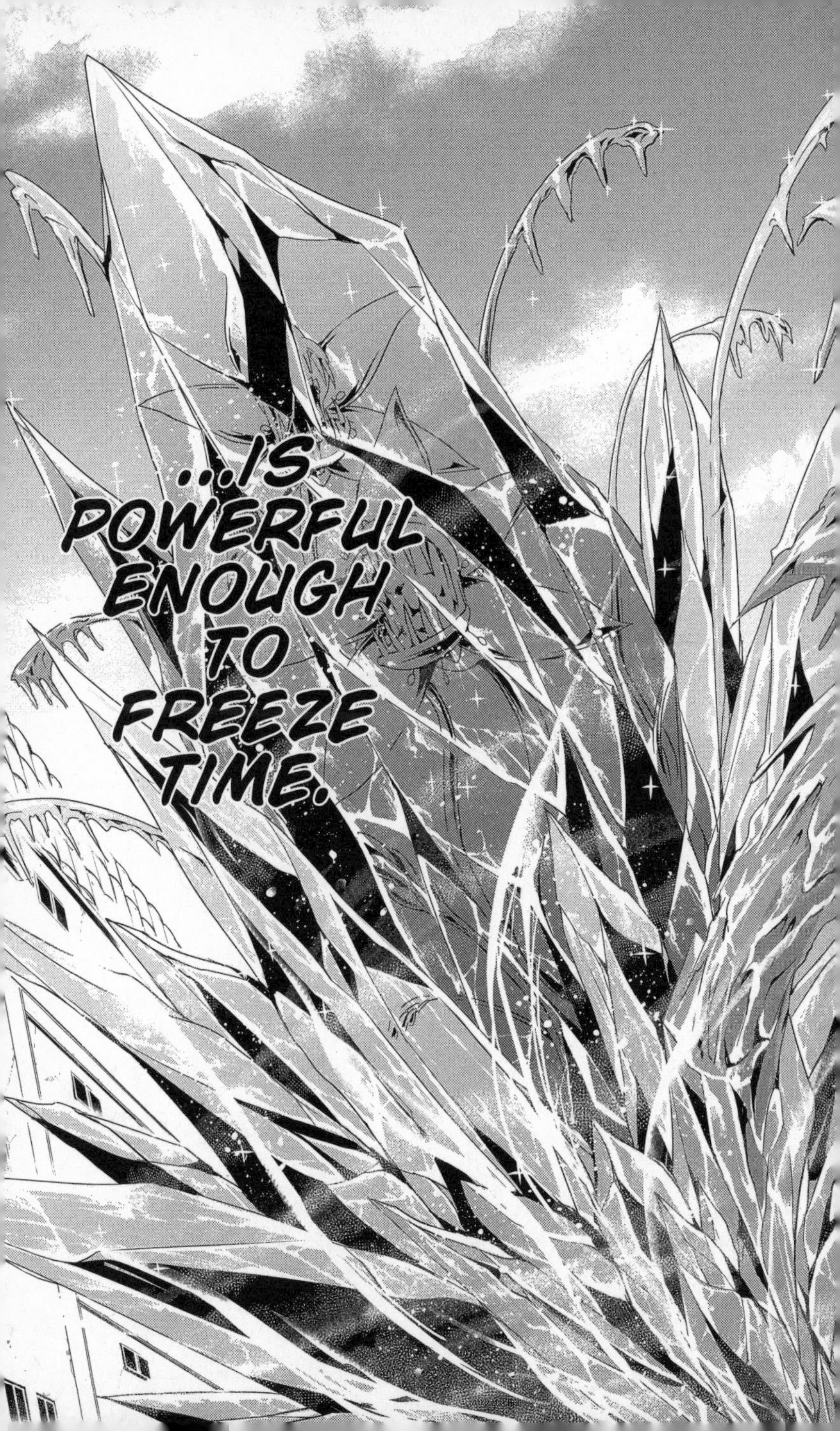
...IS POWERFUL ENOUGH TO FREEZE TIME.

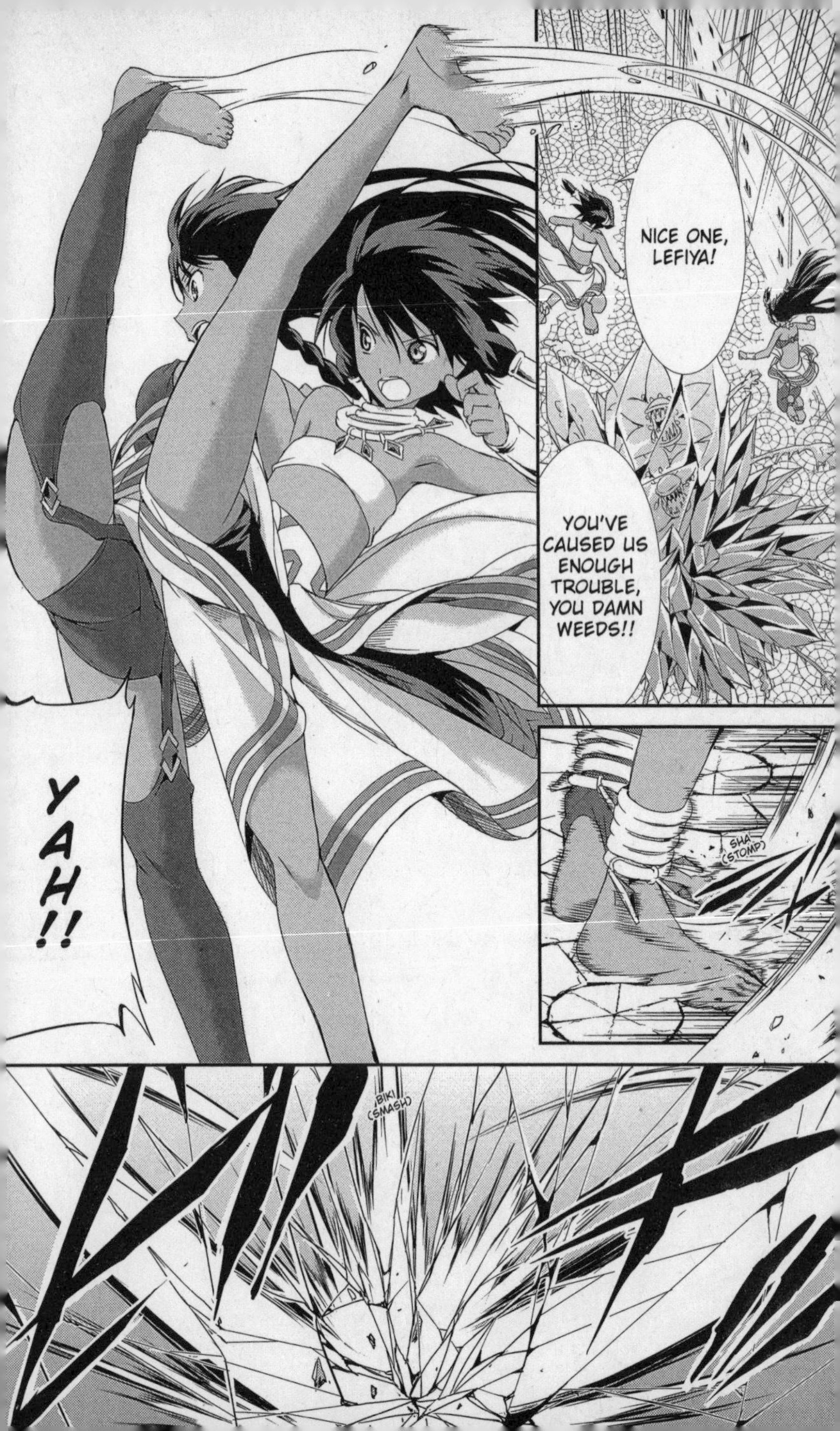
NICE ONE, LEFIYA!
YOU'VE CAUSED US ENOUGH TROUBLE, YOU DAMN WEEDS!!
SHA (STOMP)
YAH!!
BIKI (SMASH)

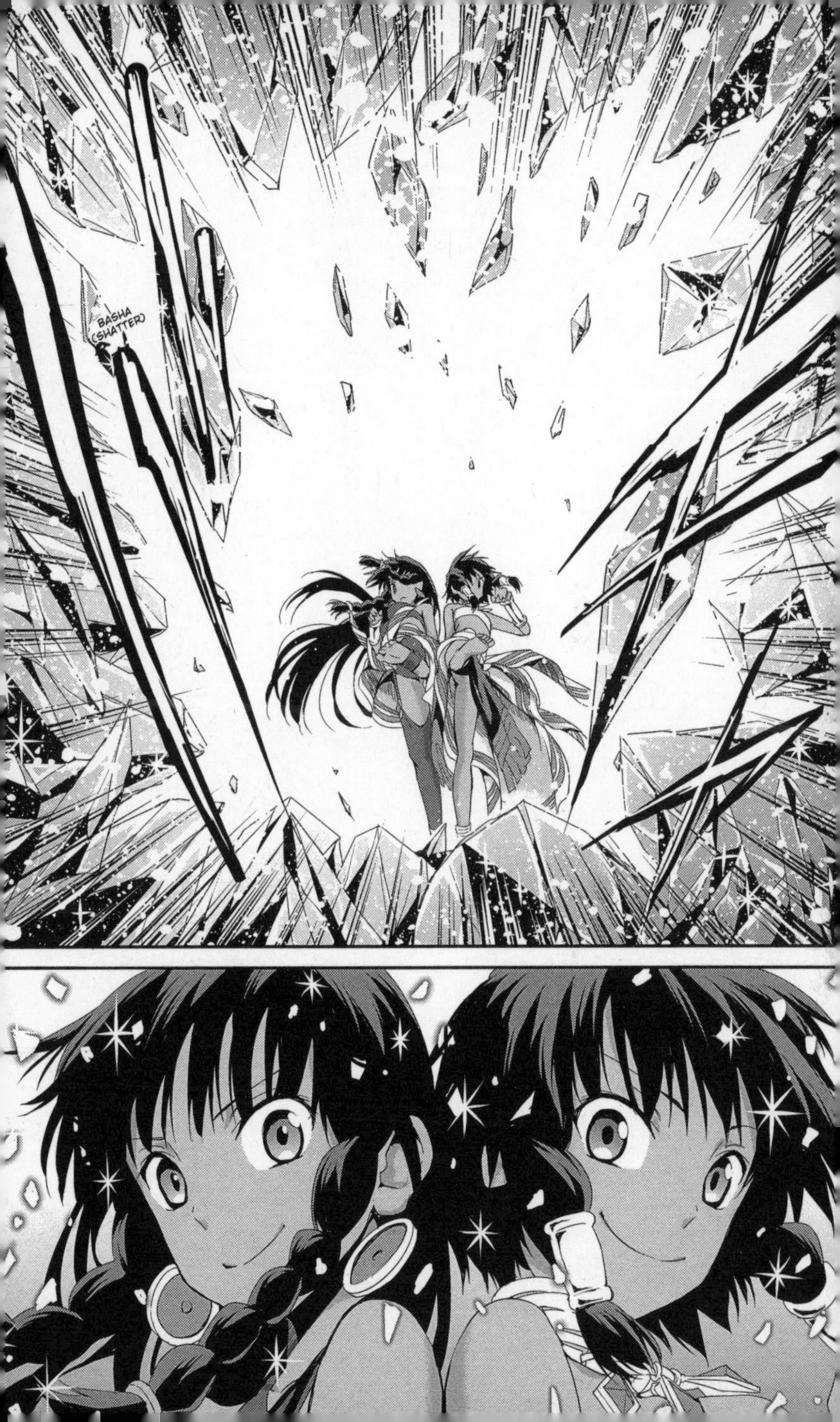
BASHA (SHATTER)

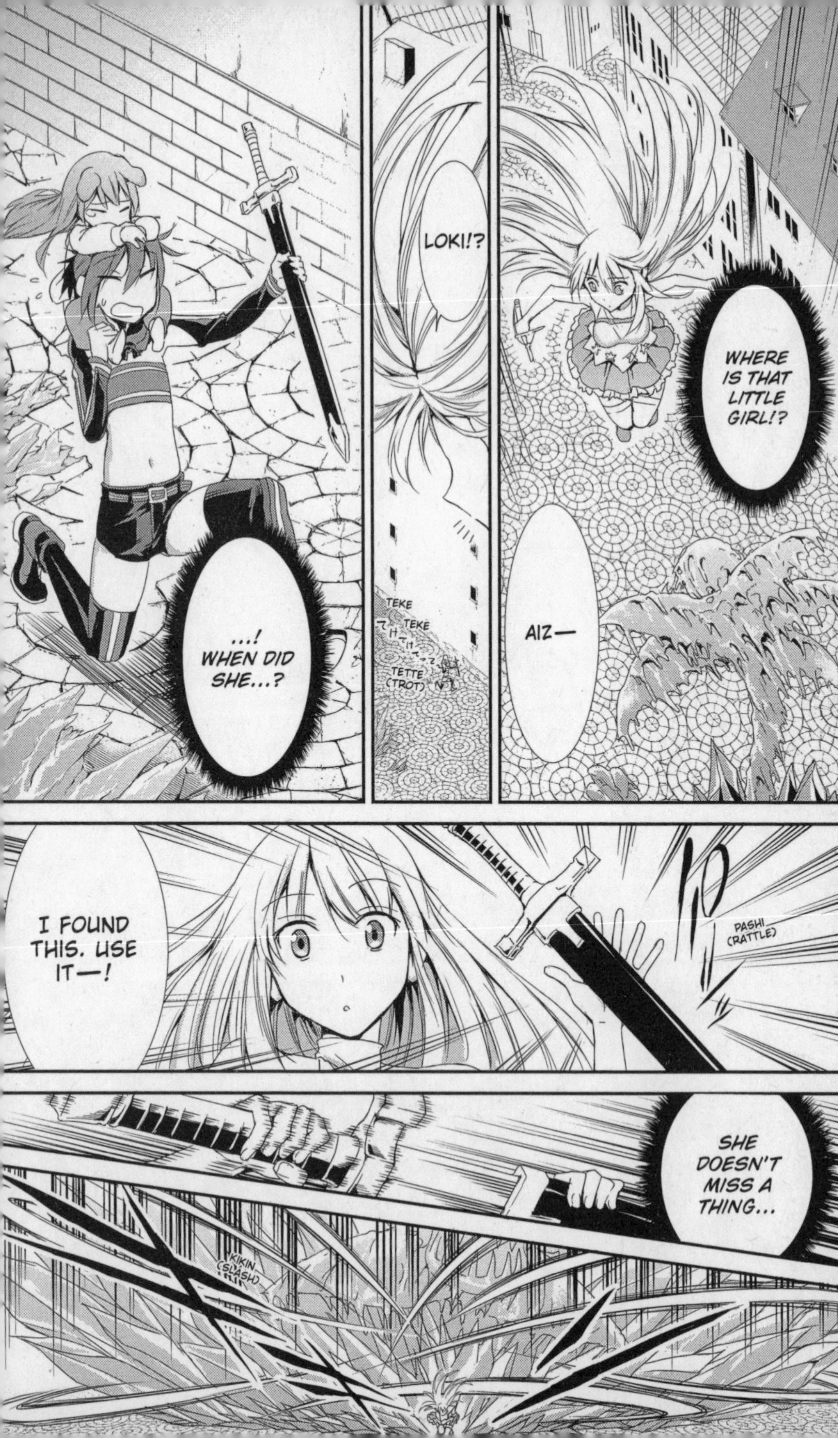
WHERE IS THAT LITTLE GIRL!?
AIZ—
LOKI!?
TEKE TEKE
TETTE (TROT)
...! WHEN DID SHE...?
PASHI (RATTLE)
I FOUND THIS. USE IT—!
SHE DOESN'T MISS A THING...
KIKIN (SLASH)

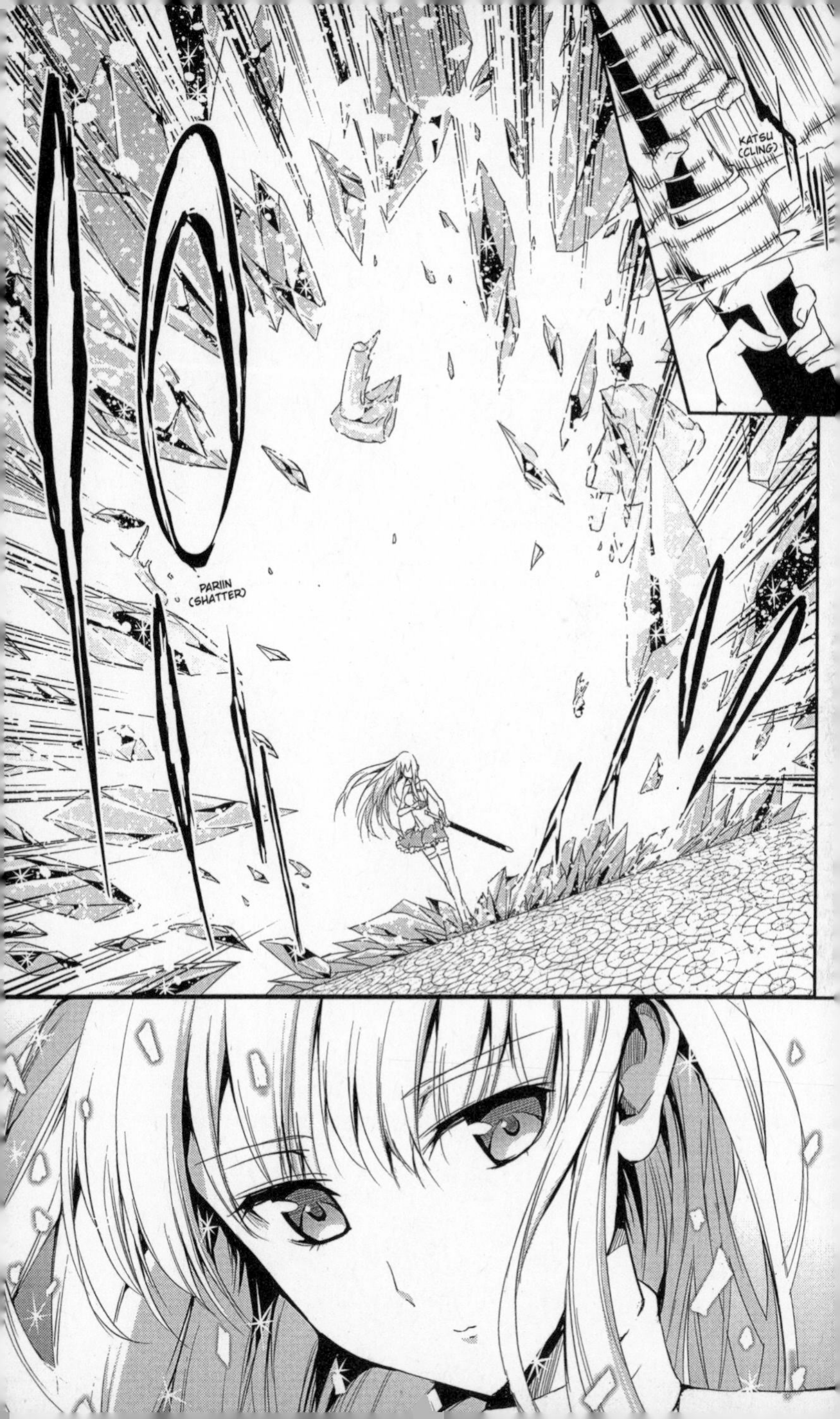
KATSU (CLING)
PARIIN (SHATTER)

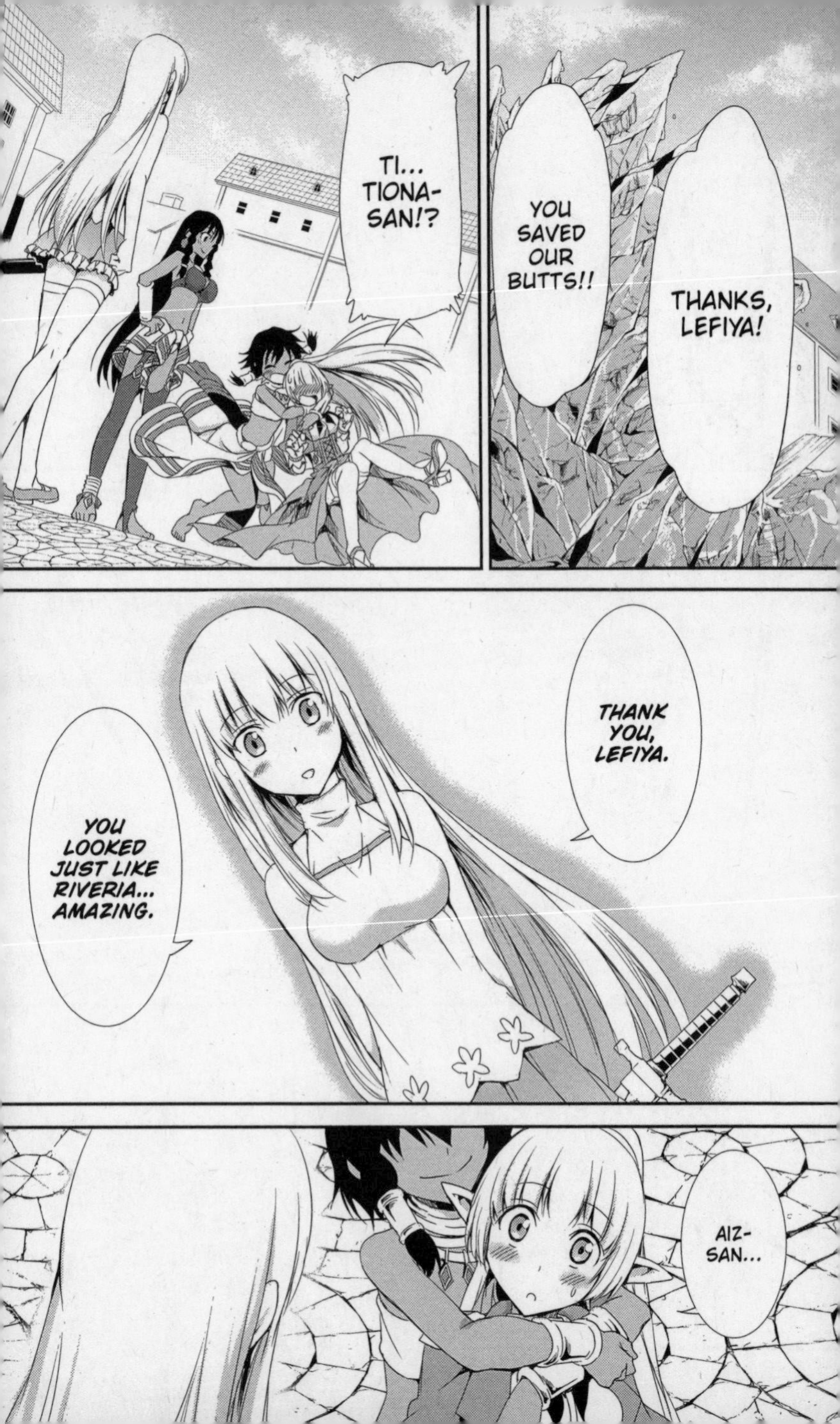
THANKS, LEFIYA!
YOU SAVED OUR BUTTS!!
TI... TIONA-SAN!?
THANK YOU, LEFIYA.
YOU LOOKED JUST LIKE RIVERIA... AMAZING.
AIZ-SAN...

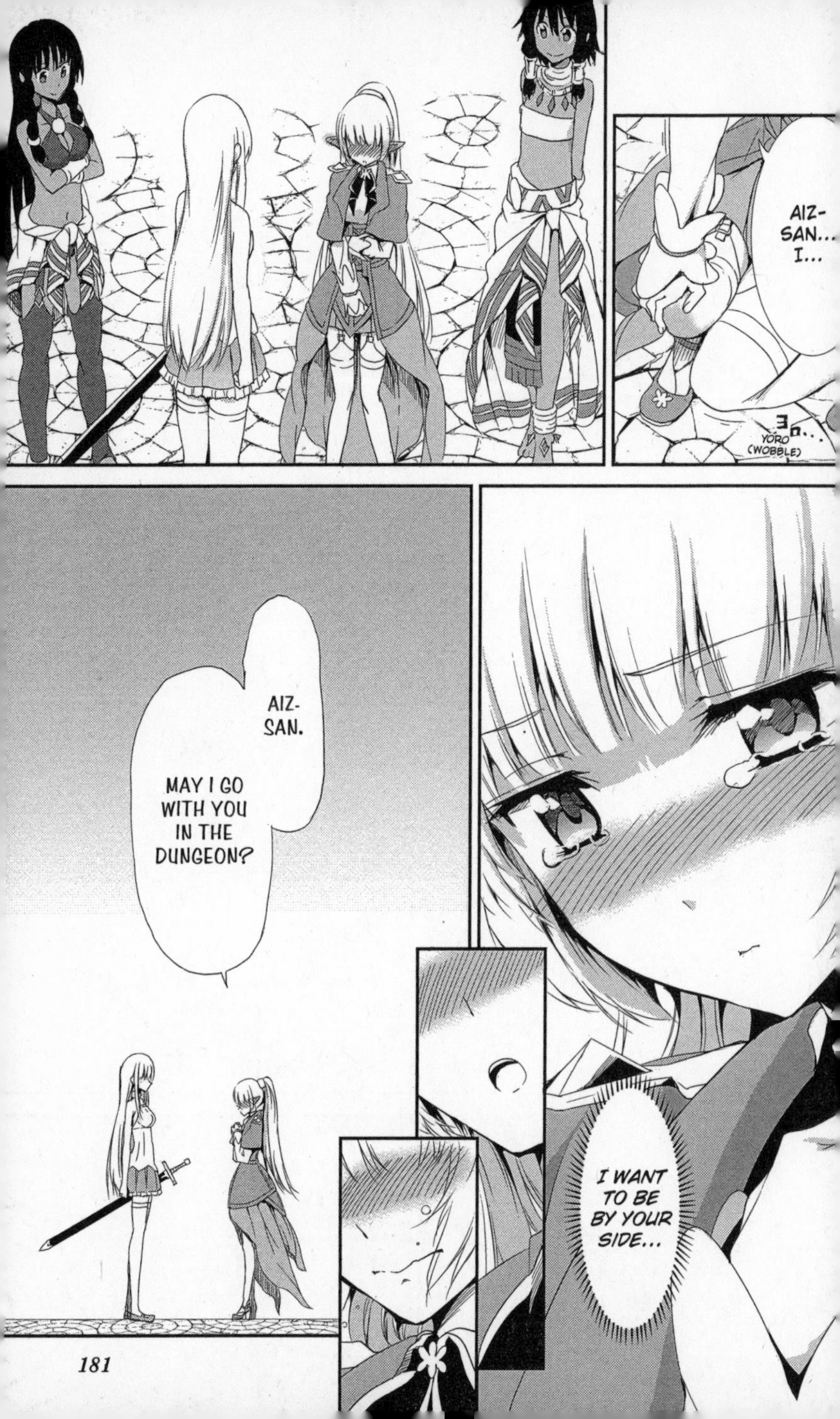
AIZ-SAN... I...
ヨロ... YORO (WOBBLE)
AIZ-SAN.
MAY I GO WITH YOU IN THE DUNGEON?
I WANT TO BE BY YOUR SIDE...

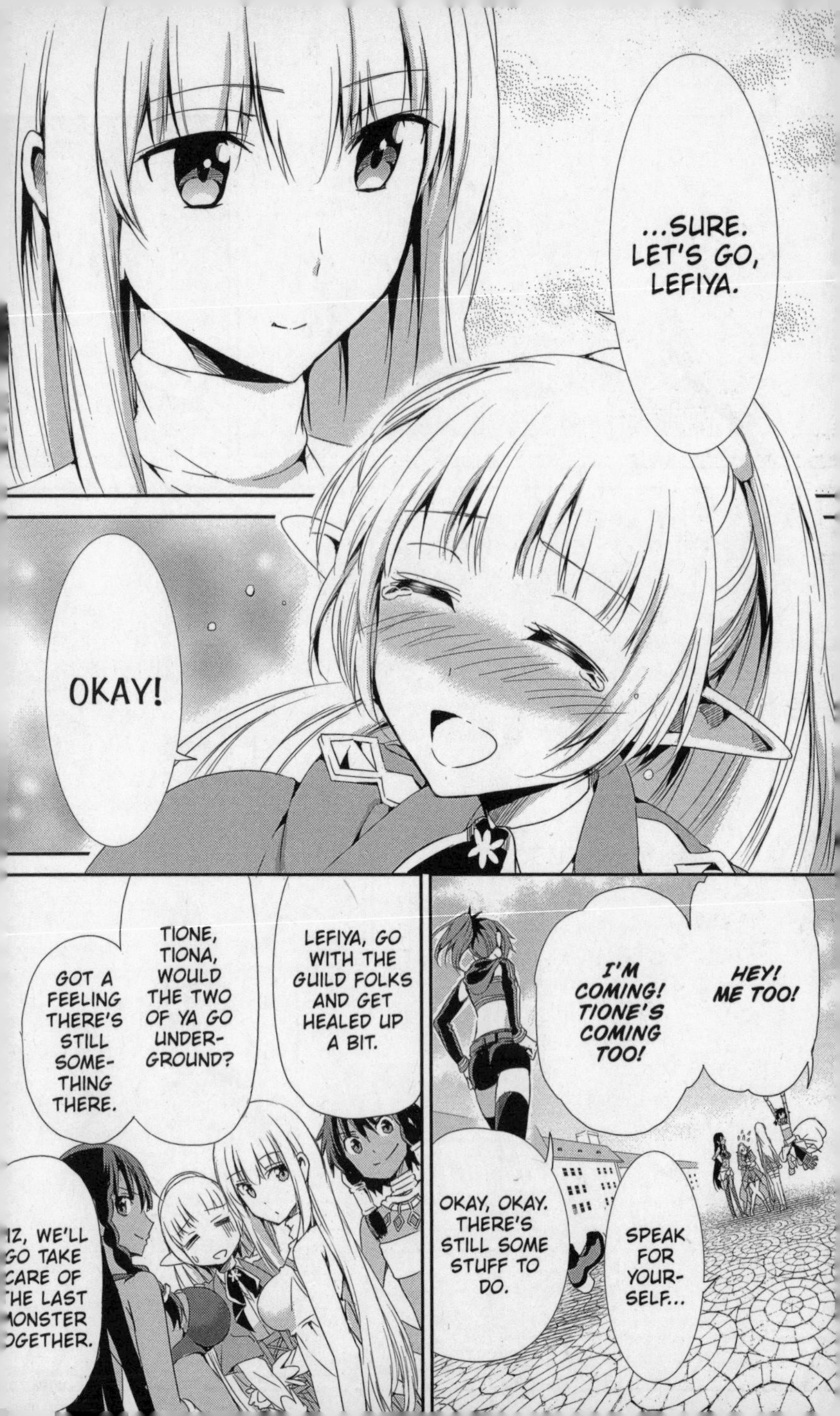

...SURE. LET'S GO, LEFIYA.
OKAY!
HEY! ME TOO!
I'M COMING! TIONE'S COMING TOO!
SPEAK FOR YOUR-SELF...
OKAY, OKAY. THERE'S STILL SOME STUFF TO DO.
LEFIYA, GO WITH THE GUILD FOLKS AND GET HEALED UP A BIT.
TIONE, TIONA, WOULD THE TWO OF YA GO UNDER-GROUND?
GOT A FEELING THERE'S STILL SOME-THING THERE.
IZ, WE'LL GO TAKE CARE OF THE LAST MONSTER OGETHER.

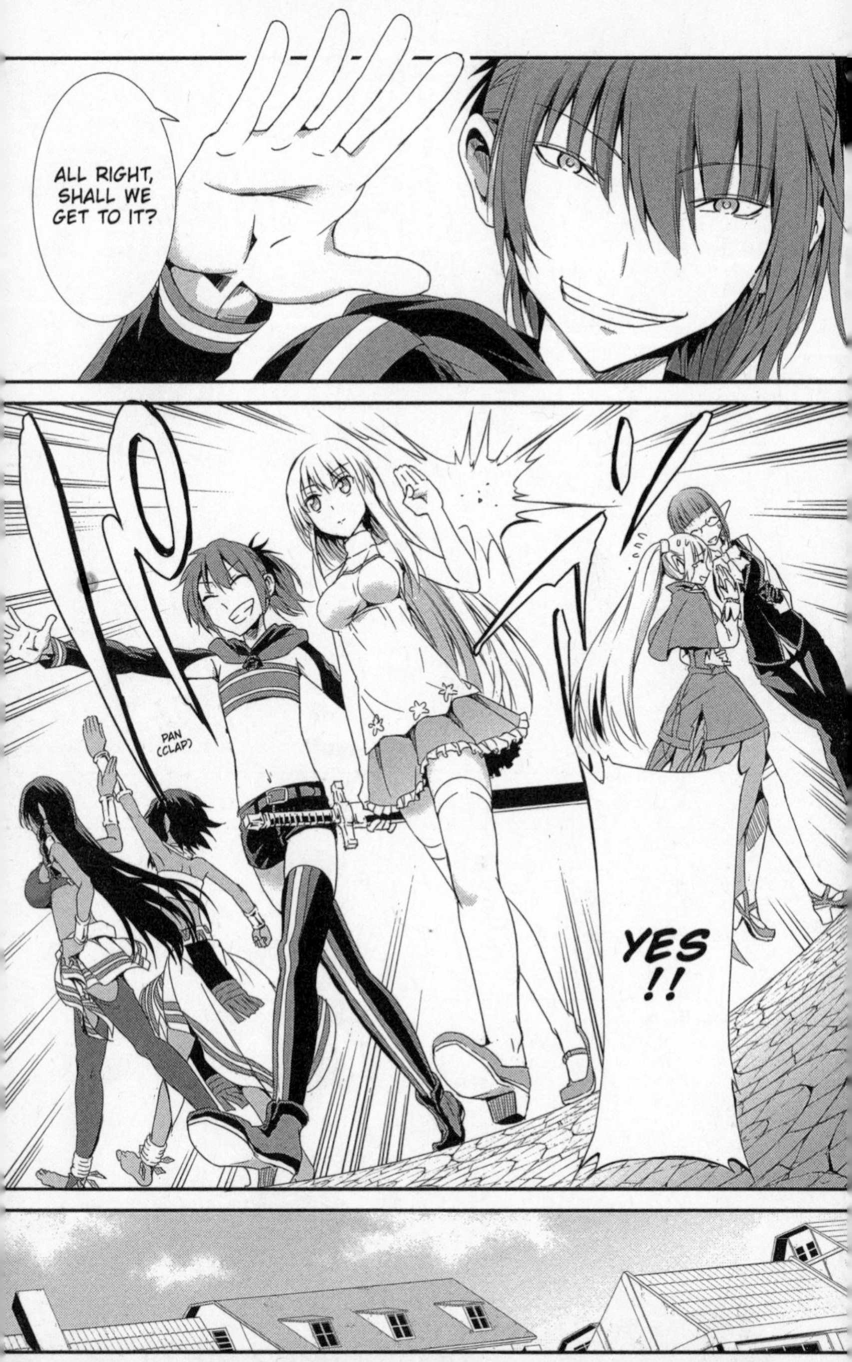
ALL RIGHT, SHALL WE GET TO IT?
PAN (CLAP)
YES!!

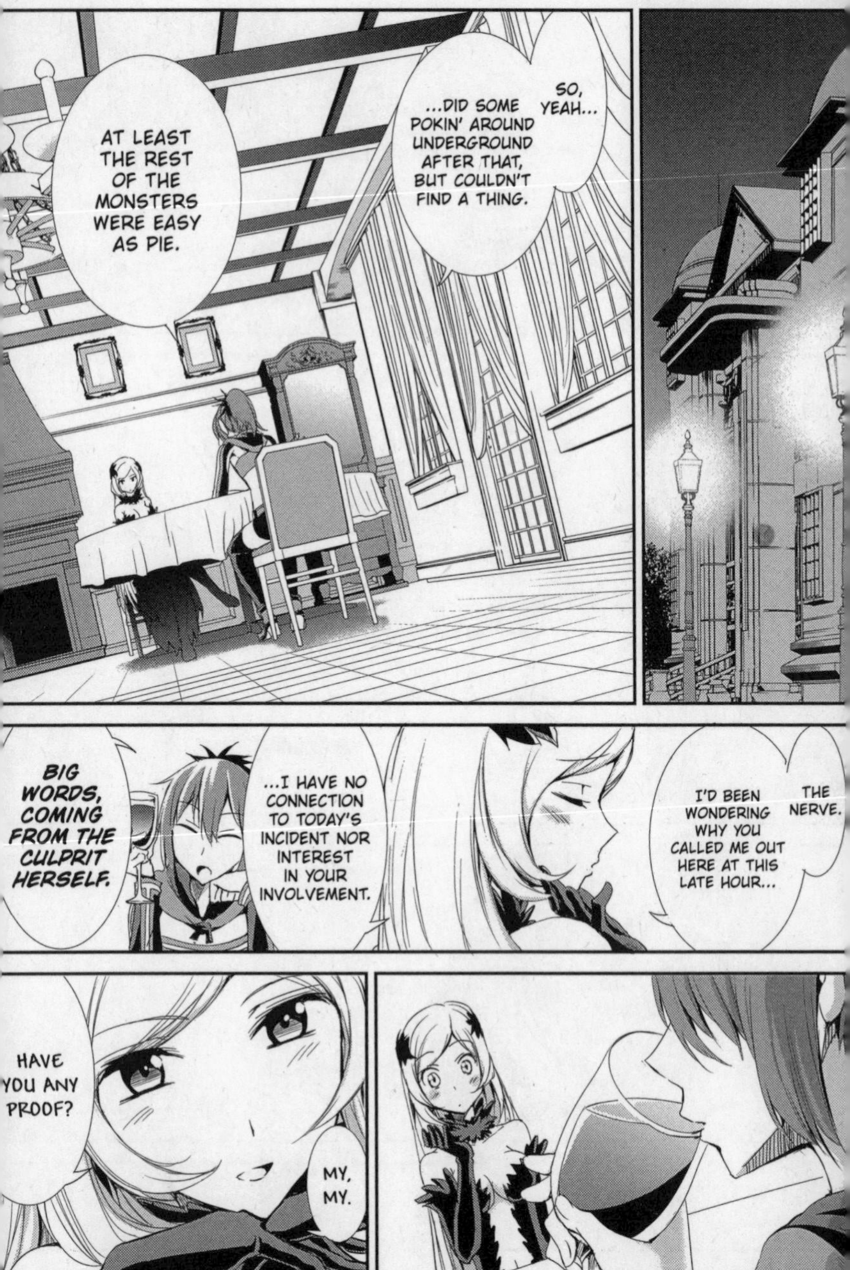
SO, YEAH...
...DID SOME POKIN' AROUND UNDERGROUND AFTER THAT, BUT COULDN'T FIND A THING.
AT LEAST THE REST OF THE MONSTERS WERE EASY AS PIE.
THE NERVE.
I'D BEEN WONDERING WHY YOU CALLED ME OUT HERE AT THIS LATE HOUR...
...I HAVE NO CONNECTION TO TODAY'S INCIDENT NOR INTEREST IN YOUR INVOLVEMENT.
BIG WORDS, COMING FROM THE CULPRIT HERSELF.
MY, MY.
HAVE YOU ANY PROOF?

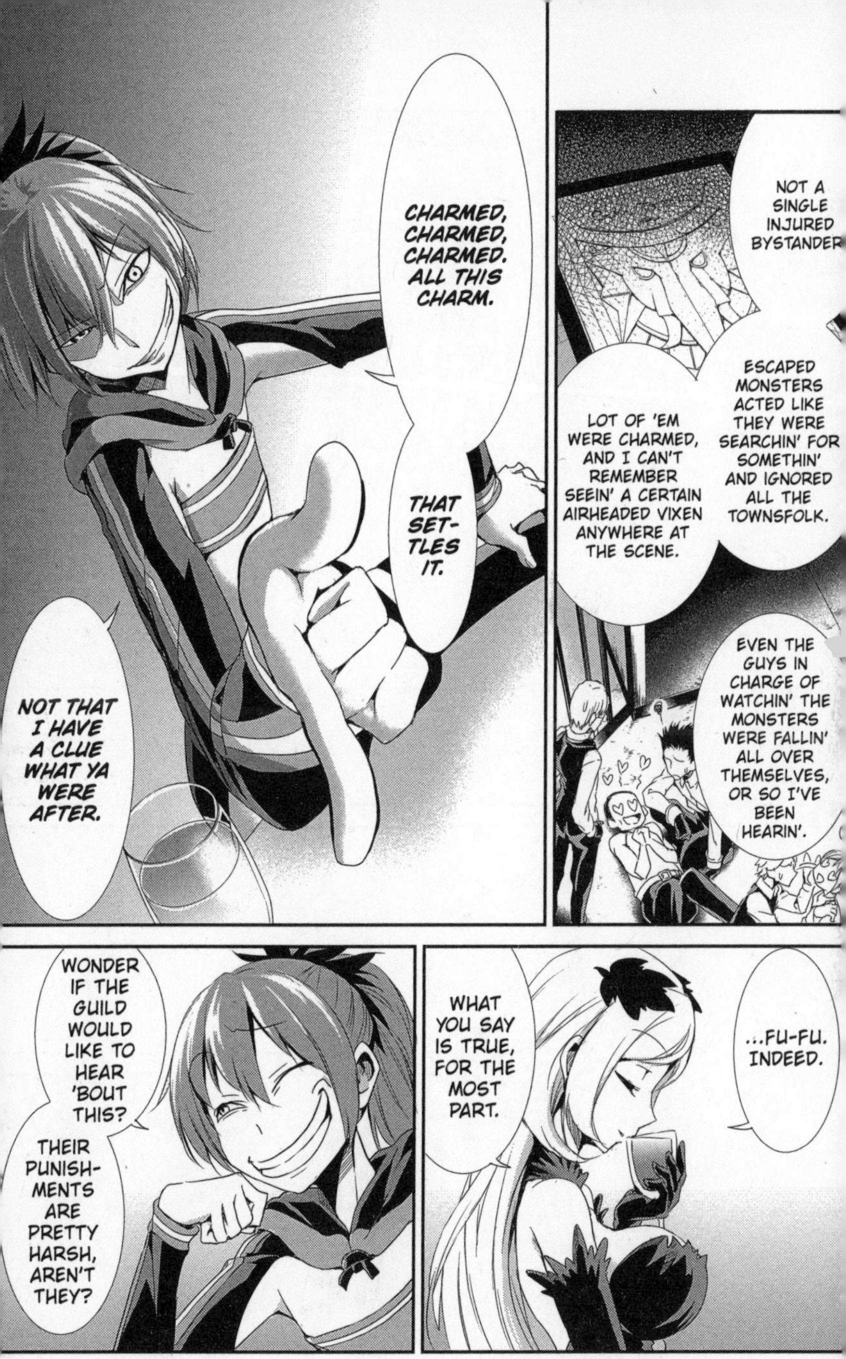
NOT A SINGLE INJURED BYSTANDER
ESCAPED MONSTERS ACTED LIKE THEY WERE SEARCHIN' FOR SOMETHIN' AND IGNORED ALL THE TOWNSFOLK.
LOT OF 'EM WERE CHARMED, AND I CAN'T REMEMBER SEEIN' A CERTAIN AIRHEADED VIXEN ANYWHERE AT THE SCENE.
EVEN THE GUYS IN CHARGE OF WATCHIN' THE MONSTERS WERE FALLIN' ALL OVER THEMSELVES, OR SO I'VE BEEN HEARIN'.
CHARMED, CHARMED, CHARMED. ALL THIS CHARM.
THAT SET-TLES IT.
NOT THAT I HAVE A CLUE WHAT YA WERE AFTER.
...FU-FU. INDEED.
WHAT YOU SAY IS TRUE, FOR THE MOST PART.
WONDER IF THE GUILD WOULD LIKE TO HEAR 'BOUT THIS?
THEIR PUNISH-MENTS ARE PRETTY HARSH, AREN'T THEY?

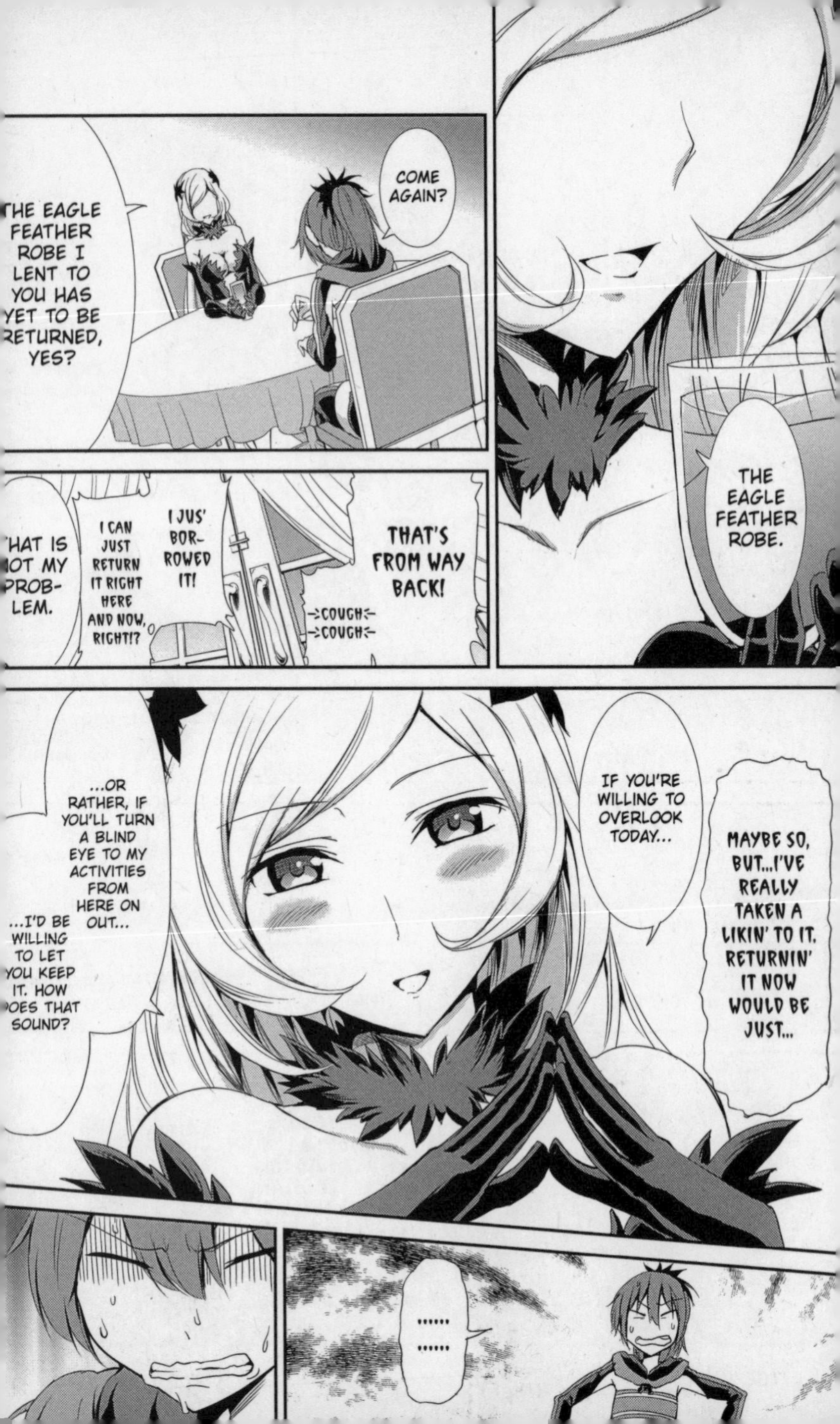
THE EAGLE FEATHER ROBE.
COME AGAIN?
THE EAGLE FEATHER ROBE I LENT TO YOU HAS YET TO BE RETURNED, YES?
THAT'S FROM WAY BACK!
-COUGH- -COUGH-
I JUS' BORROWED IT!
I CAN JUST RETURN IT RIGHT HERE AND NOW, RIGHT!?
HAT IS OT MY PROB-LEM.
MAYBE SO, BUT...I'VE REALLY TAKEN A LIKIN' TO IT. RETURNIN' IT NOW WOULD BE JUST...
IF YOU'RE WILLING TO OVERLOOK TODAY...
...OR RATHER, IF YOU'LL TURN A BLIND EYE TO MY ACTIVITIES FROM HERE ON OUT...
...I'D BE WILLING TO LET YOU KEEP IT. HOW OES THAT SOUND?
....

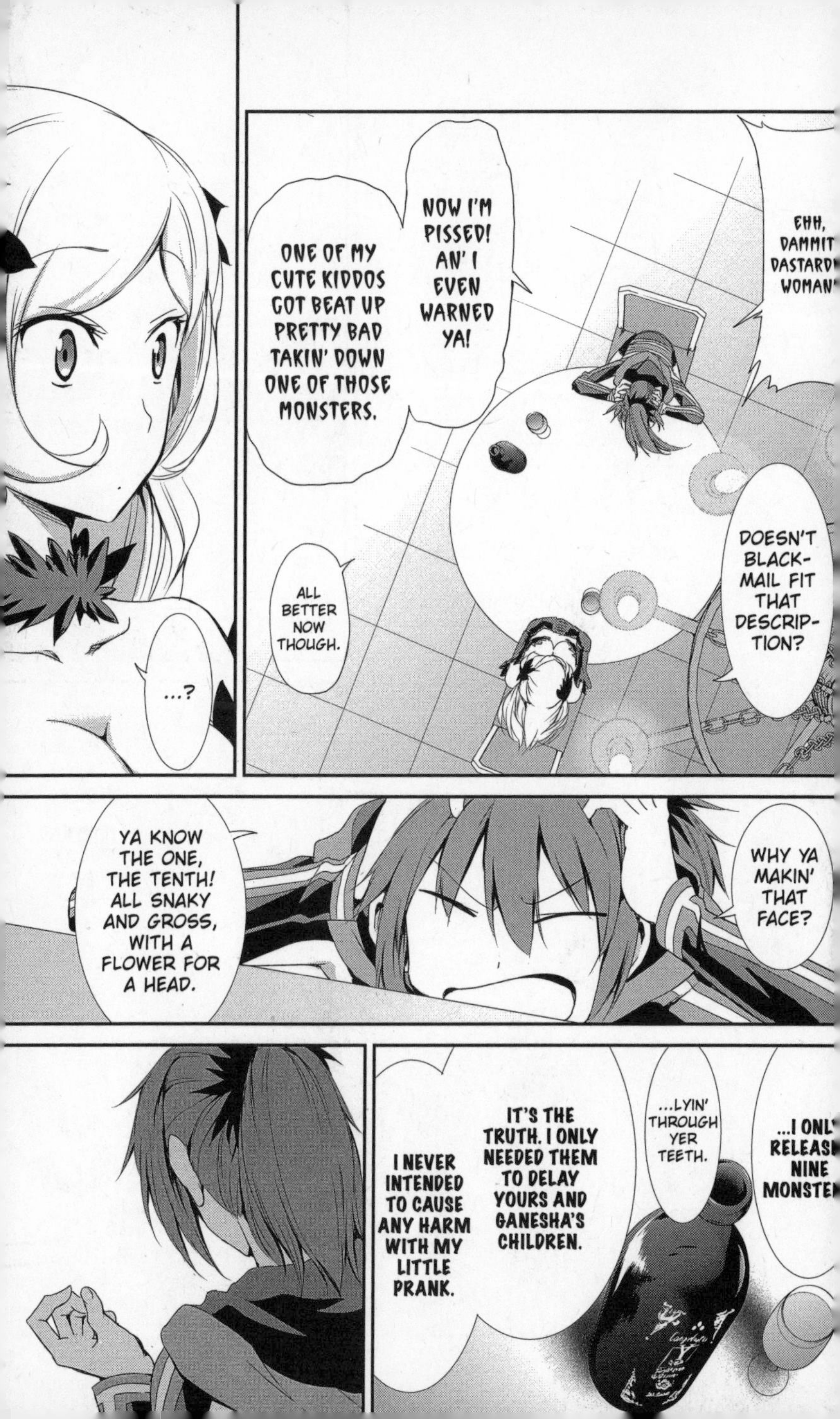
EHH, DAMMIT DASTARD WOMAN
NOW I'M PISSED! AN' I EVEN WARNED YA!
ONE OF MY CUTE KIDDOS GOT BEAT UP PRETTY BAD TAKIN' DOWN ONE OF THOSE MONSTERS.
DOESN'T BLACKMAIL FIT THAT DESCRIPTION?
ALL BETTER NOW THOUGH.
...?
WHY YA MAKIN' THAT FACE?
YA KNOW THE ONE, THE TENTH! ALL SNAKY AND GROSS, WITH A FLOWER FOR A HEAD.
...I ONL RELEAS NINE MONSTE
...LYIN' THROUGH YER TEETH.
IT'S THE TRUTH. I ONLY NEEDED THEM TO DELAY YOURS AND GANESHA'S CHILDREN.
I NEVER INTENDED TO CAUSE ANY HARM WITH MY LITTLE PRANK.

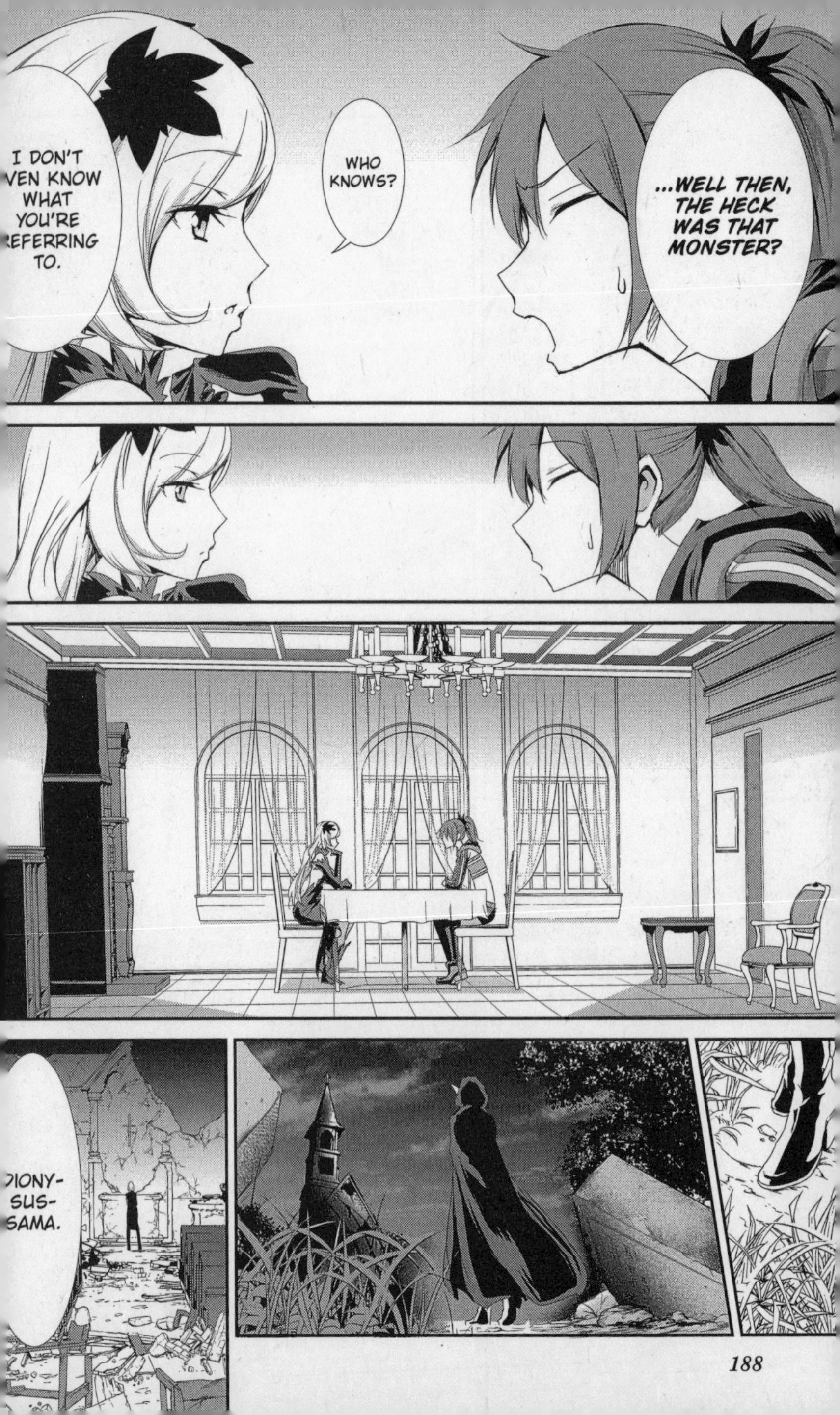
...WELL THEN, THE HECK WAS THAT MONSTER?
WHO KNOWS?
I DON'T VEN KNOW WHAT YOU'RE EFERRING TO.
IONY-SUS-SAMA.

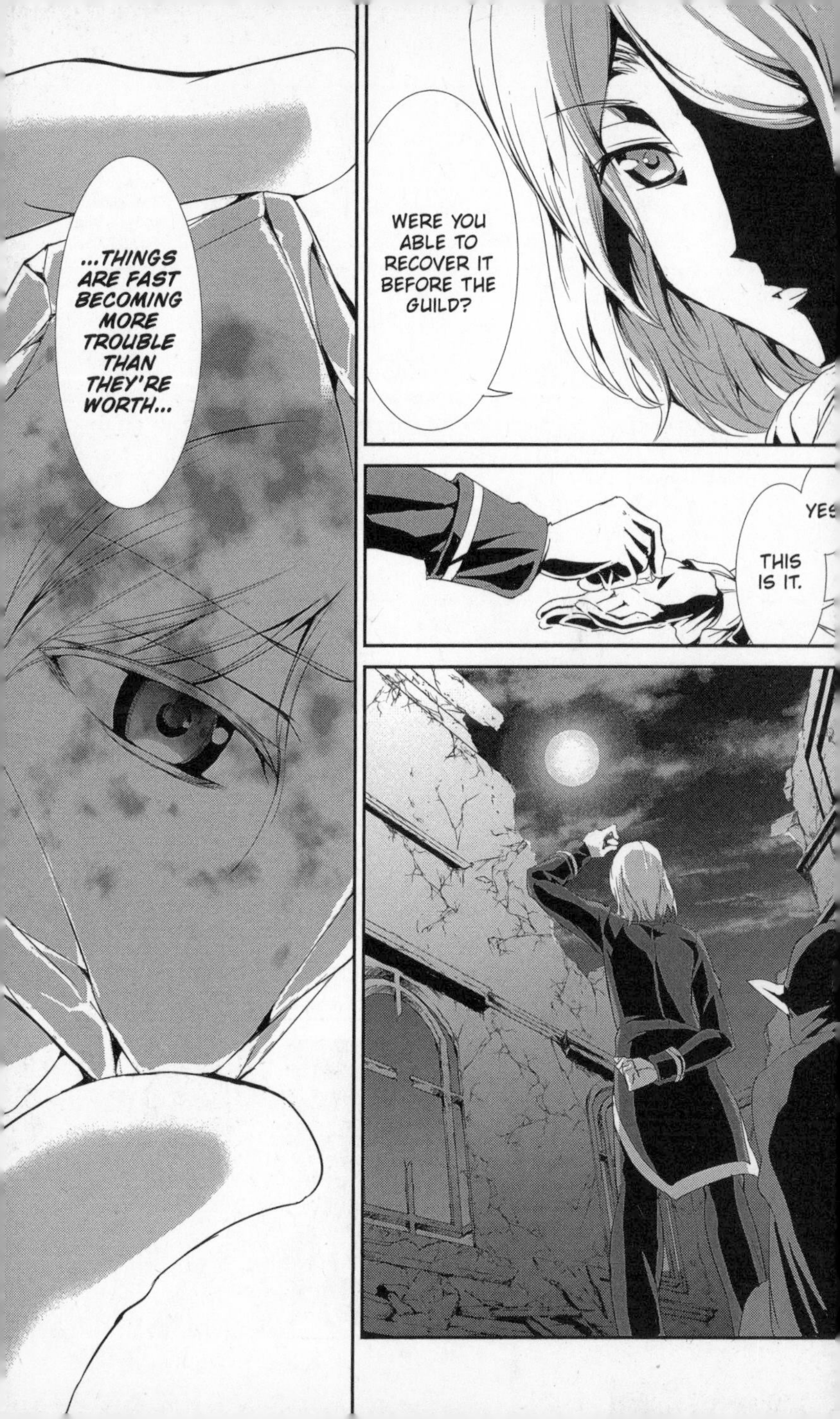
WERE YOU ABLE TO RECOVER IT BEFORE THE GUILD?
YES
THIS IS IT.
...THINGS ARE FAST BECOMING MORE TROUBLE THAN THEY'RE WORTH...

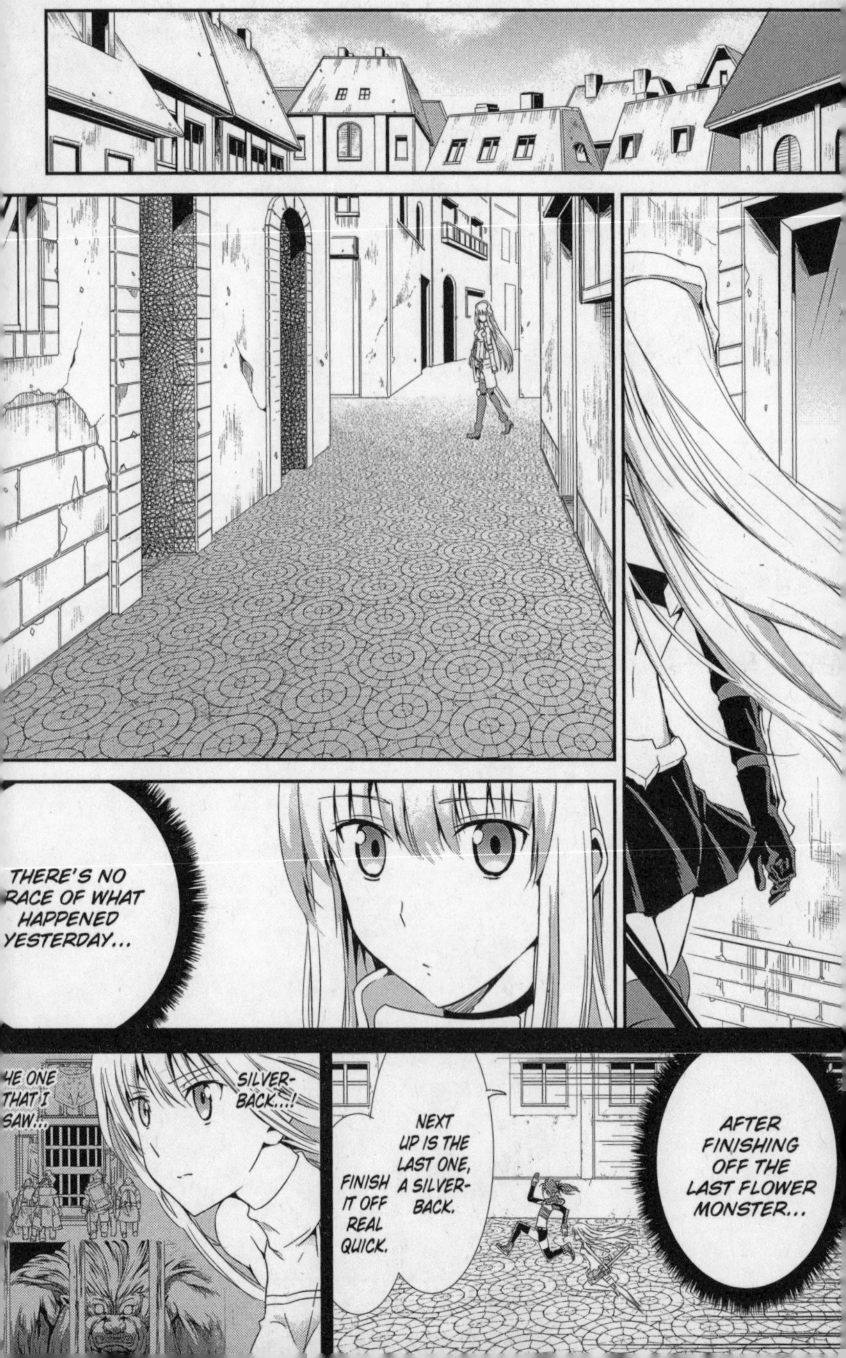
THERE'S NO RACE OF WHAT HAPPENED YESTERDAY...
AFTER FINISHING OFF THE LAST FLOWER MONSTER...
NEXT UP IS THE LAST ONE, A SILVER-BACK.
FINISH IT OFF REAL QUICK.
SILVER-BACK...!
HE ONE THAT I SAW...

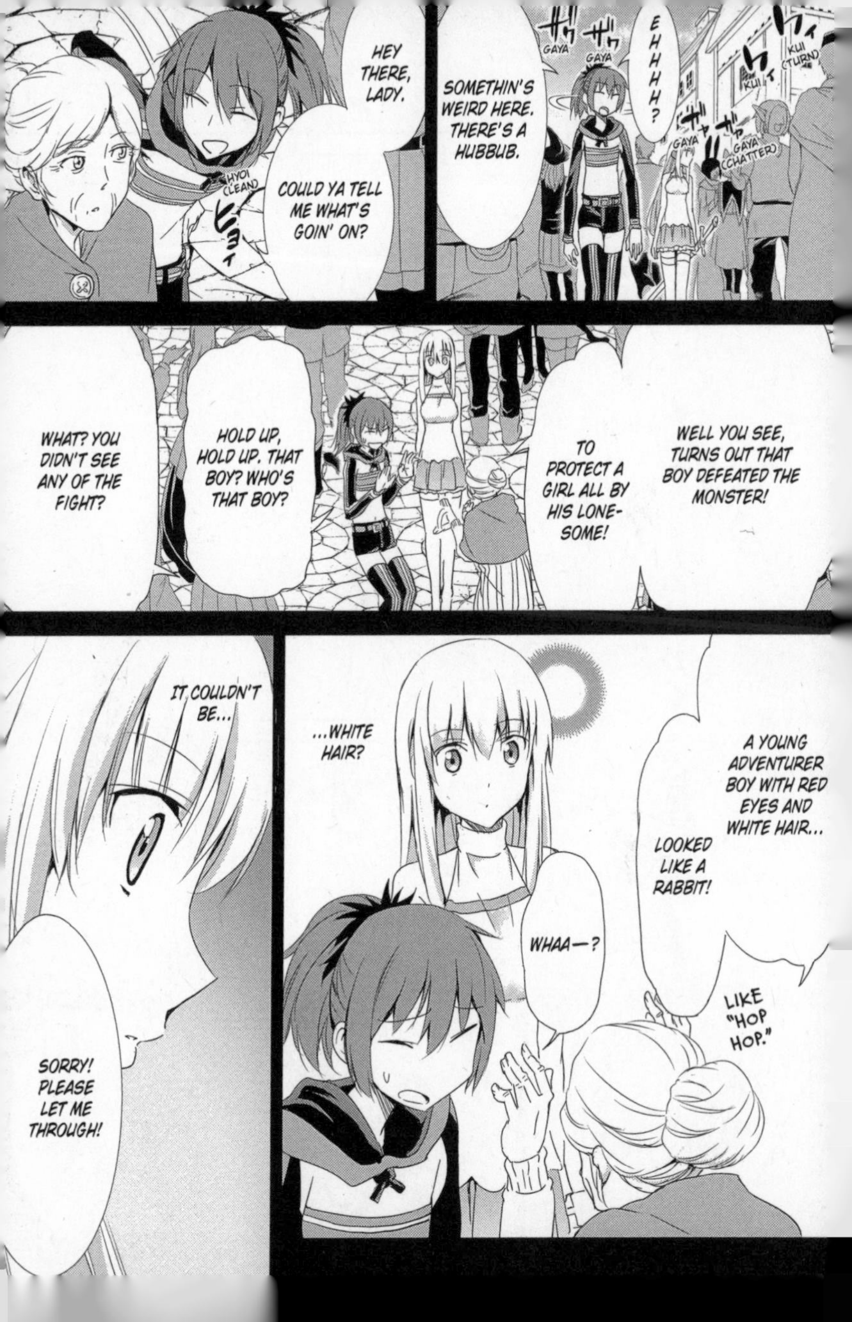
GAYA
GAYA
EHHHH?
SOMETHIN'S WEIRD HERE. THERE'S A HUBBUB.
KUI (TURN)
KUI
GAYA
GAYA (CHATTER)
HEY THERE, LADY.
HYOI (LEAN)
COULD YA TELL ME WHAT'S GOIN' ON?
WELL YOU SEE, TURNS OUT THAT BOY DEFEATED THE MONSTER!
TO PROTECT A GIRL ALL BY HIS LONE-SOME!
HOLD UP, HOLD UP. THAT BOY? WHO'S THAT BOY?
WHAT? YOU DIDN'T SEE ANY OF THE FIGHT?
A YOUNG ADVENTURER BOY WITH RED EYES AND WHITE HAIR...
LOOKED LIKE A RABBIT!
LIKE "HOP HOP."
WHAA—?
...WHITE HAIR?
IT COULDN'T BE...
SORRY! PLEASE LET ME THROUGH!

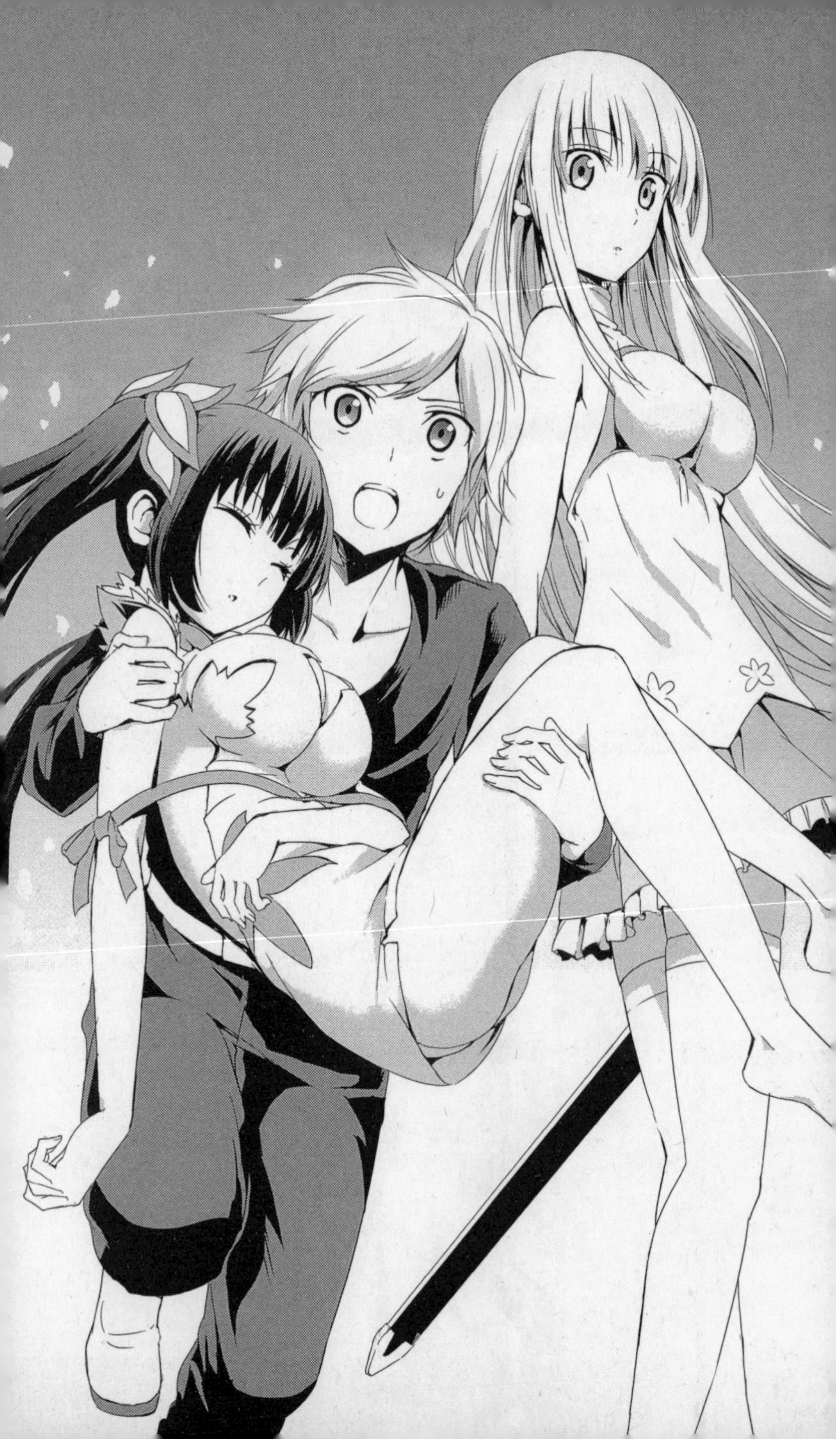

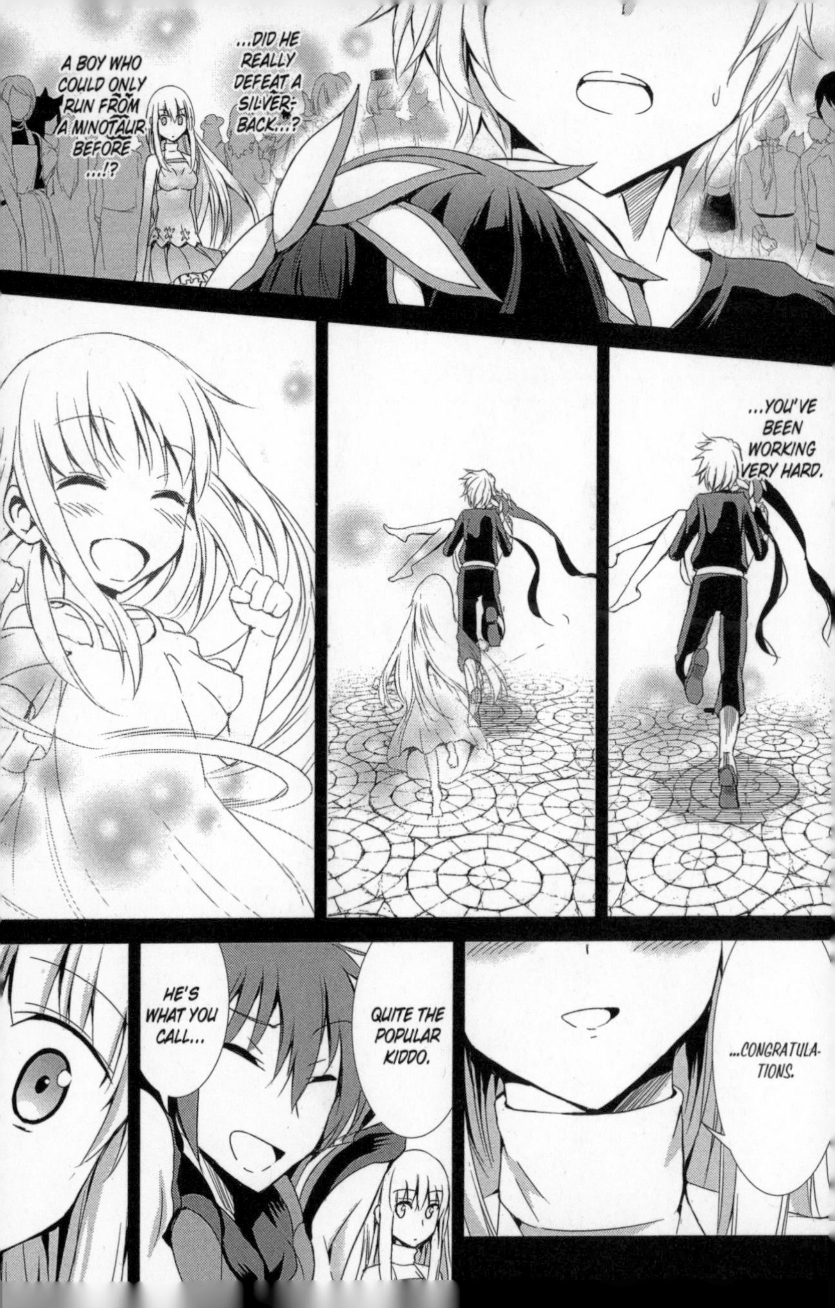
...DID HE REALLY DEFEAT A SILVER-BACK...?
A BOY WHO COULD ONLY RUN FROM A MINOTAUR BEFORE ...!?
...YOU'VE BEEN WORKING VERY HARD.
...CONGRATULA-TIONS.
HE'S WHAT YOU CALL...
QUITE THE POPULAR KIDDO.

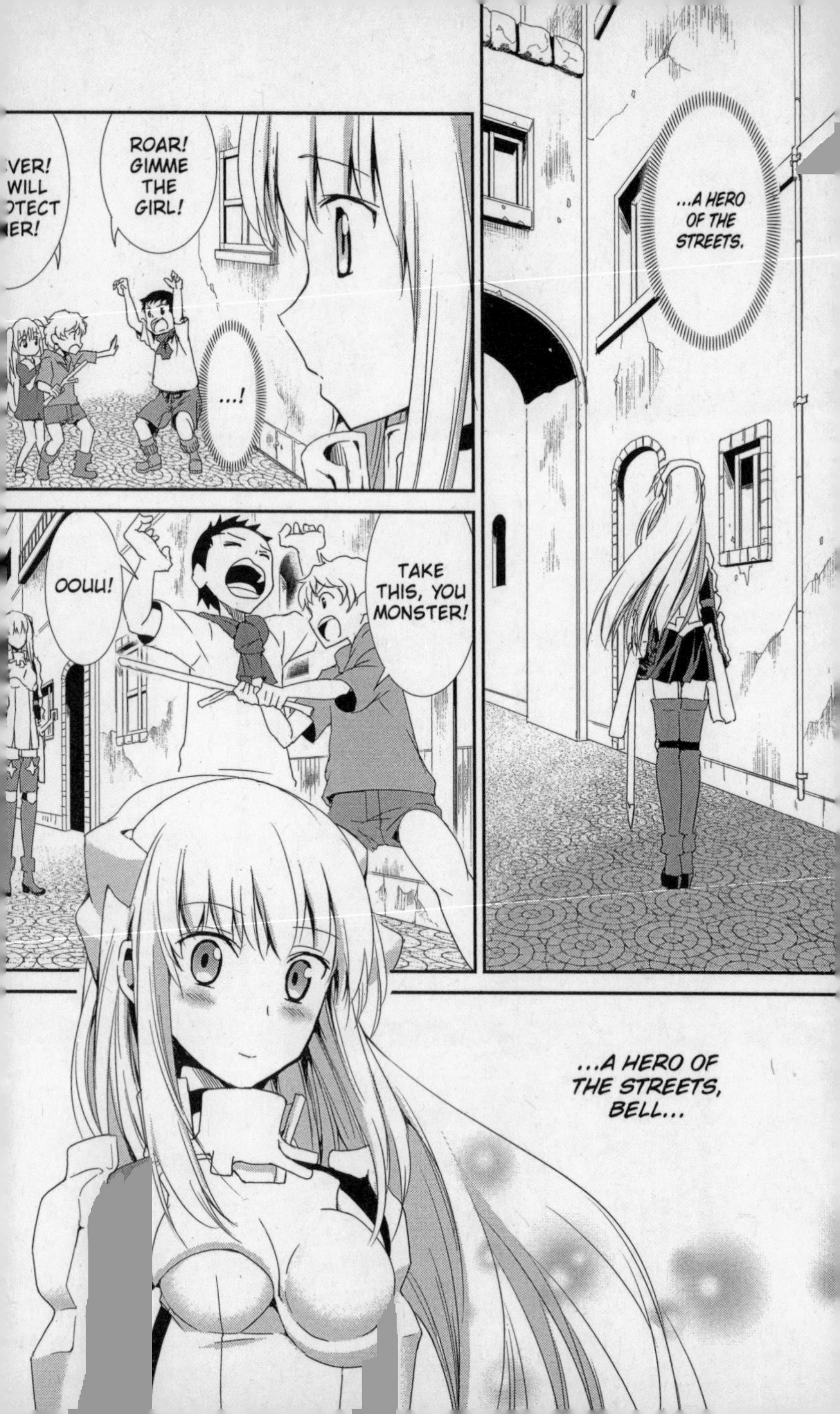
...A HERO OF THE STREETS.
ROAR! GIMME THE GIRL!
VER! WILL OTECT ER!
...!
TAKE THIS, YOU MONSTER!
OOUU!
...A HERO OF THE STREETS, BELL...

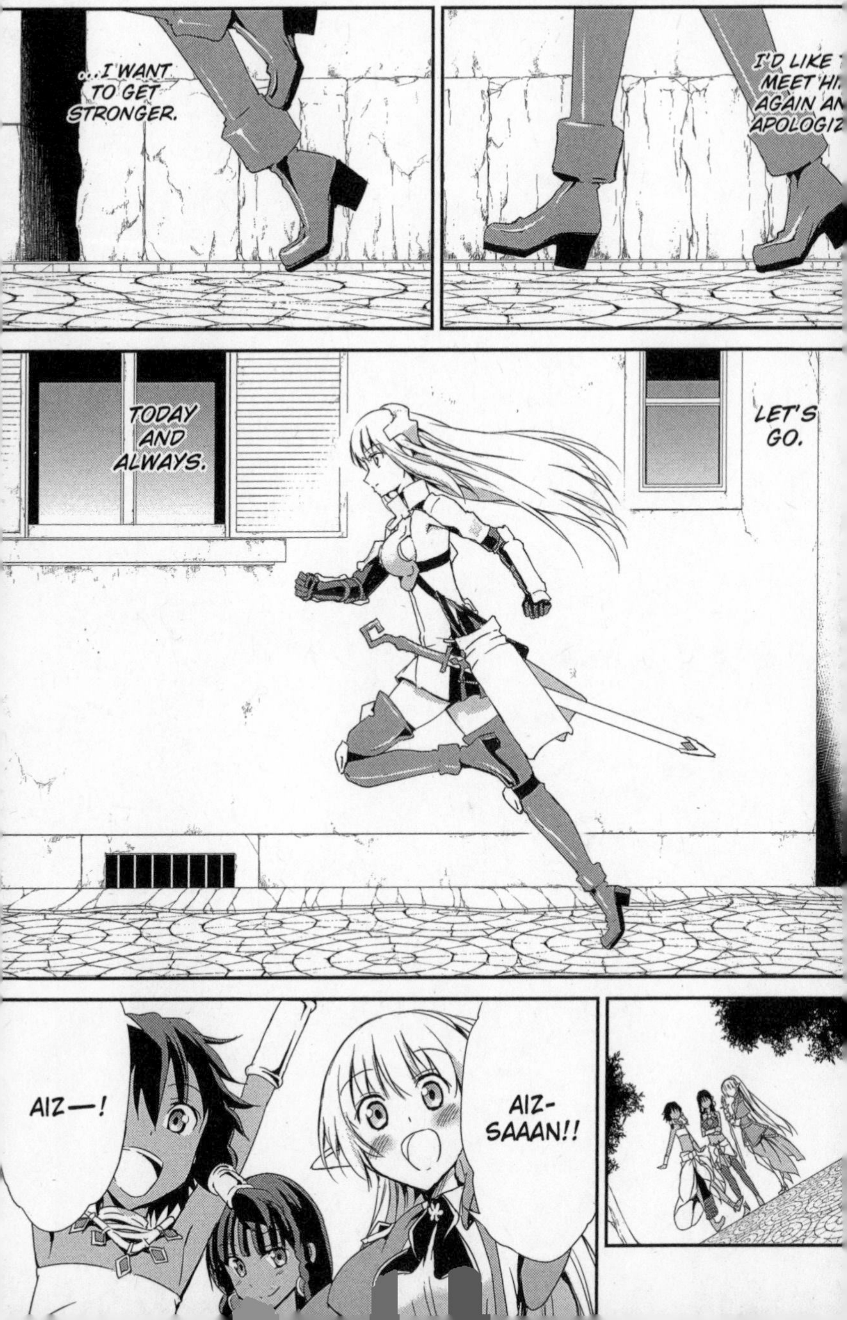

I'D LIKE MEET HI AGAIN AN APOLOGIZ
...I WANT TO GET STRONGER.
LET'S GO.
TODAY AND ALWAYS.
AIZ-SAAAN!!
AIZ—!

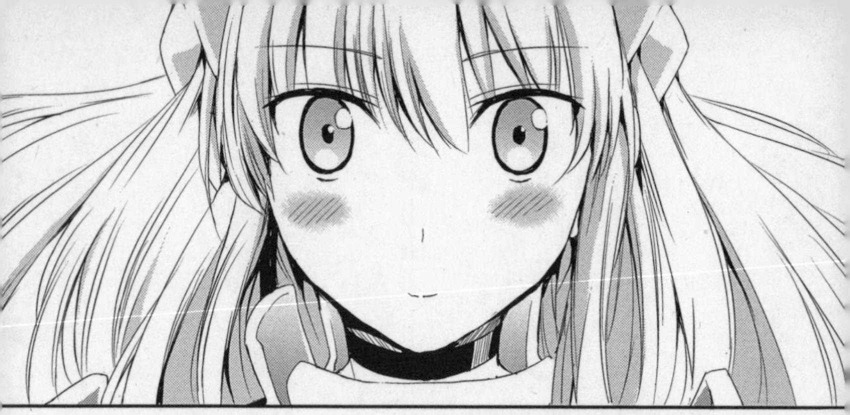

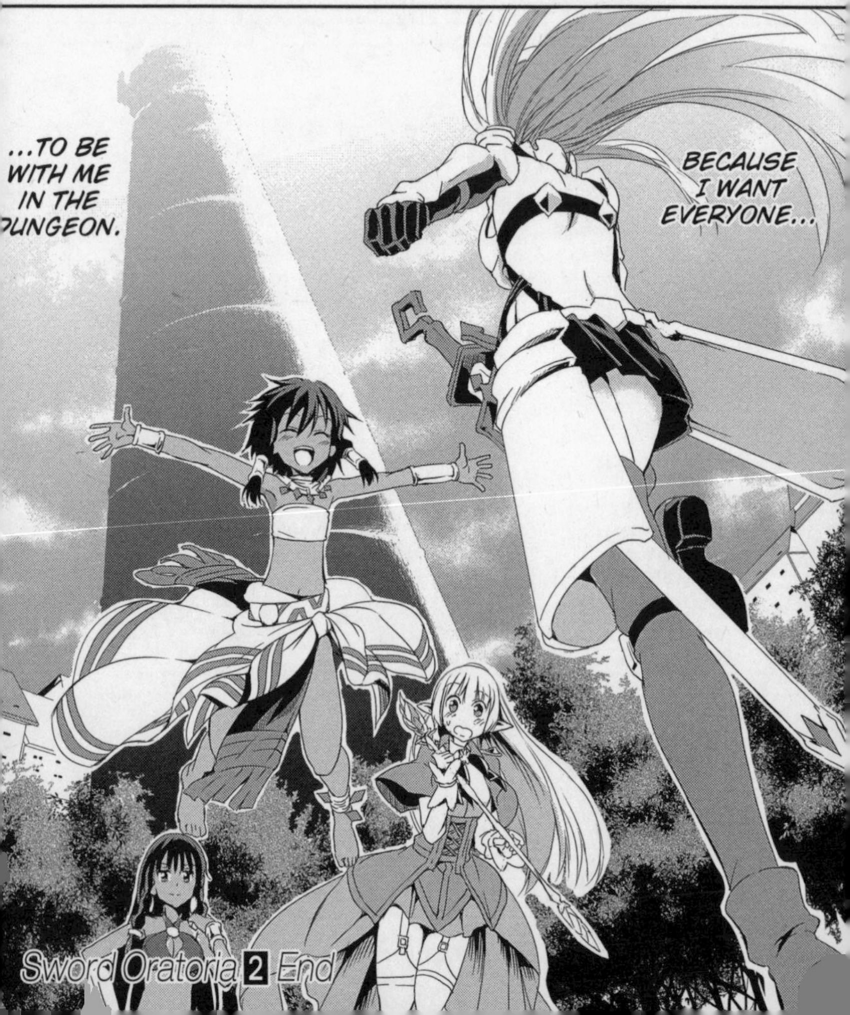
BECAUSE I WANT EVERYONE...
...TO BE WITH ME IN THE DUNGEON.
Sword Oratoria 2 End

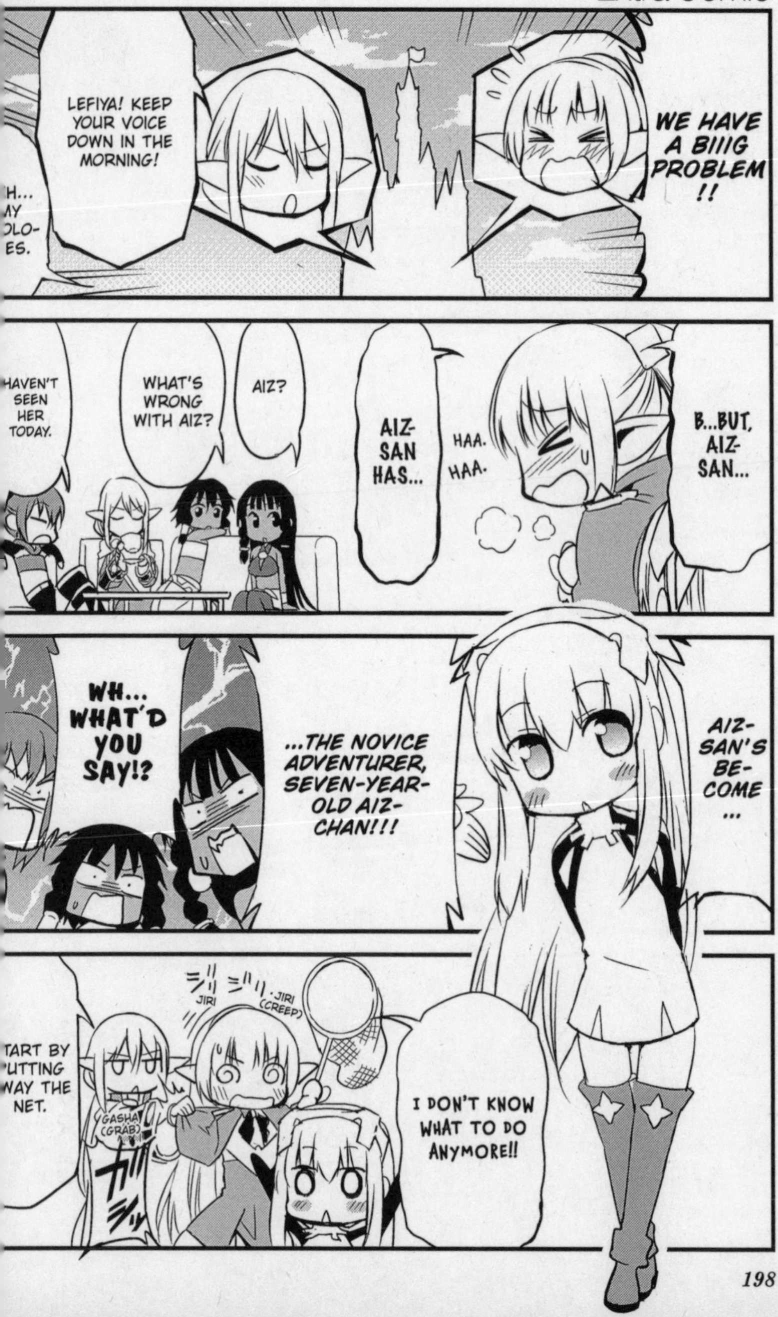
WE HAVE A BIIIG PROBLEM!!
LEFIYA! KEEP YOUR VOICE DOWN IN THE MORNING!
H... MY OLO- ES.
B...BUT, AIZ-SAN...
HAA. HAA.
AIZ-SAN HAS...
AIZ?
WHAT'S WRONG WITH AIZ?
HAVEN'T SEEN HER TODAY.
AIZ-SAN'S BE-COME ...
...THE NOVICE ADVENTURER, SEVEN-YEAR-OLD AIZ-CHAN!!!
WH... WHAT'D YOU SAY!?
I DON'T KNOW WHAT TO DO ANYMORE!!
JIRI
JIRI (CREEP)
GASHA (GRAB)
TART BY UTTING WAY THE NET.

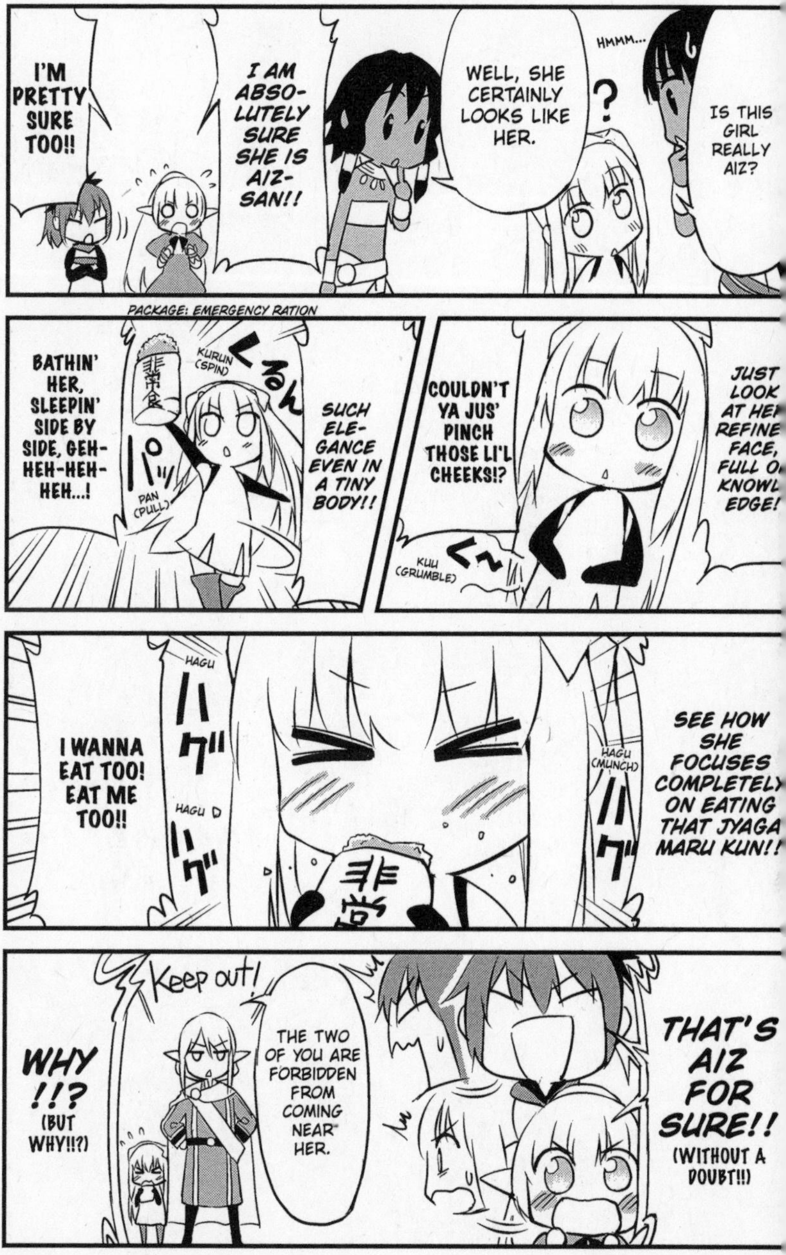
IS THIS GIRL REALLY AIZ?
HMMM...
?
WELL, SHE CERTAINLY LOOKS LIKE HER.
I AM ABSOLUTELY SURE SHE IS AIZ-SAN!!
I'M PRETTY SURE TOO!!
JUST LOOK AT HE REFINE FACE, FULL O KNOWL EDGE!
COULDN'T YA JUS' PINCH THOSE LI'L CHEEKS!?
くぅ
KUU (GRUMBLE)
PACKAGE: EMERGENCY RATION
SUCH ELEGANCE EVEN IN A TINY BODY!!
くるん
KURUN (SPIN)
非常食
パッ
PAN (PULL)
BATHIN' HER, SLEEPIN' SIDE BY SIDE, GEH-HEH-HEH-HEH...!
SEE HOW SHE FOCUSES COMPLETEL ON EATING THAT JYAGA MARU KUN!!
HAGU (MUNCH)
ハグ
非常
HAGU
ハグ
HAGU ♪
ハグ
I WANNA EAT TOO! EAT ME TOO!!
THAT'S AIZ FOR SURE!! (WITHOUT A DOUBT!!!)
THE TWO OF YOU ARE FORBIDDEN FROM COMING NEAR HER.
Keep out!
WHY!!? (BUT WHY!!?)

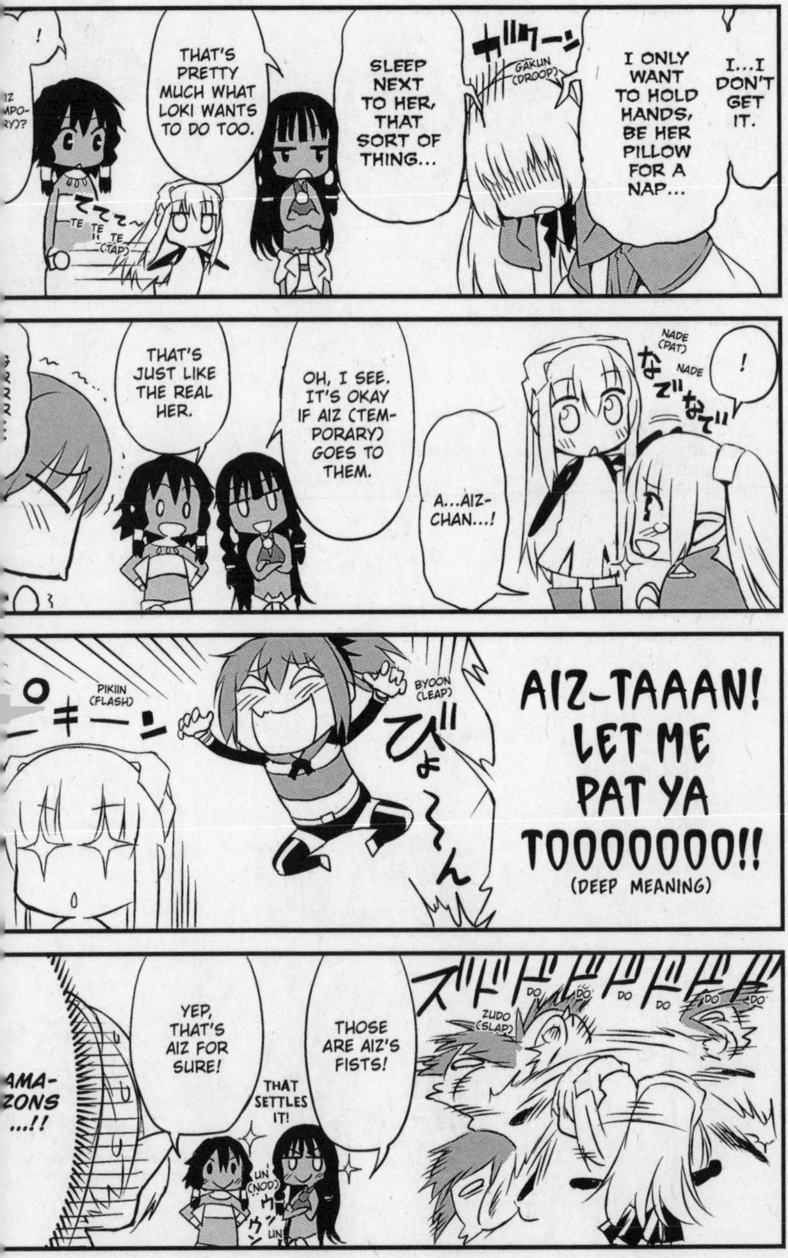
I...I DON'T GET IT.
I ONLY WANT TO HOLD HANDS, BE HER PILLOW FOR A NAP...
GAKUN (DROOP)
SLEEP NEXT TO HER, THAT SORT OF THING...
THAT'S PRETTY MUCH WHAT LOKI WANTS TO DO TOO.
TE TE TE (TAP)
!
!
NADE (PAT) NADE
A...AIZ-CHAN...!
OH, I SEE. IT'S OKAY IF AIZ (TEMPORARY) GOES TO THEM.
THAT'S JUST LIKE THE REAL HER.
AIZ-TAAAN! LET ME PAT YA TOOOOOOO!!
(DEEP MEANING)
BYOON (LEAP)
PIKIIN (FLASH)
DO DO DO DO DO DO
ZUDO (SLAP)
THOSE ARE AIZ'S FISTS!
YEP, THAT'S AIZ FOR SURE!
THAT SETTLES IT!
UN (NOD) UN
AMA-ZONS ...!!

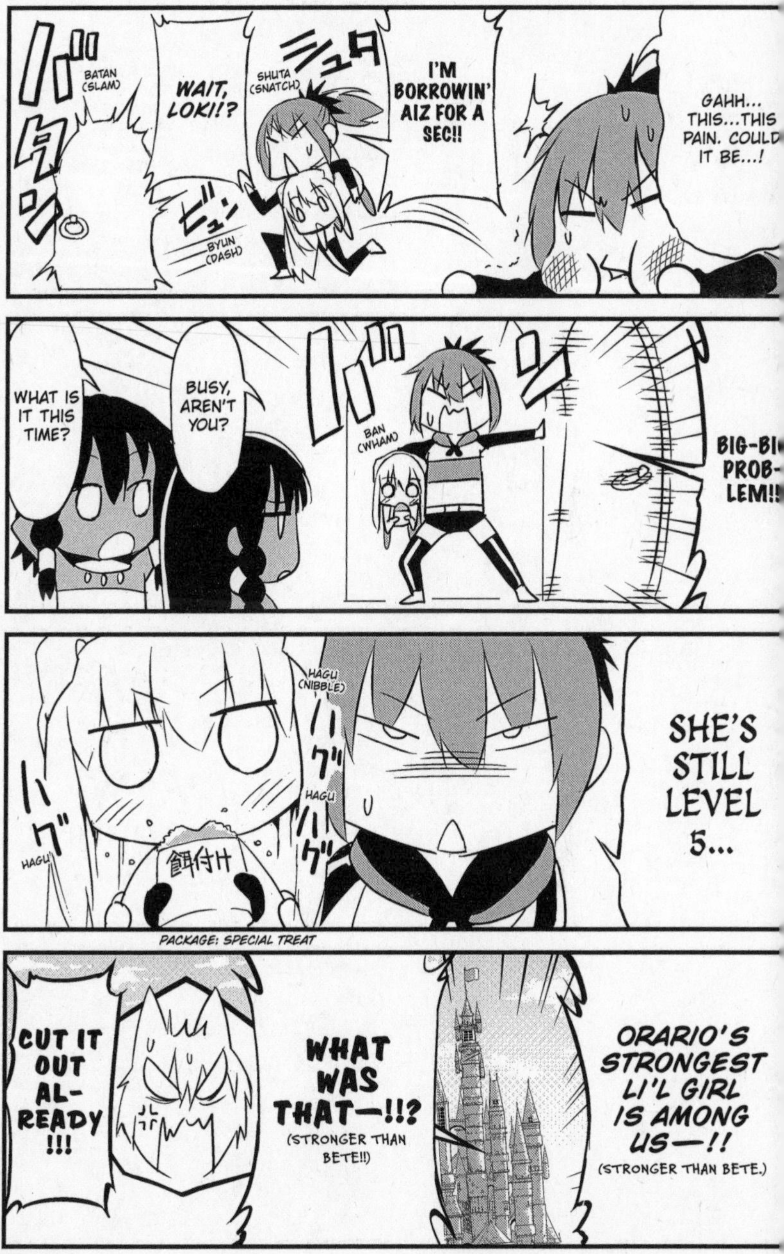
GAHH... THIS...THIS PAIN. COULD IT BE...!
I'M BORROWIN' AIZ FOR A SEC!!
シュタ
SHUTA (SNATCH)
WAIT, LOKI!?
ビュン
BYUN (DASH)
バタン
BATAN (SLAM)
BIG-BI PROB-LEM!!
バン
BAN (WHAM)
BUSY, AREN'T YOU?
WHAT IS IT THIS TIME?
SHE'S STILL LEVEL 5...
ハグ
HAGU (NIBBLE)
ハグ
HAGU
ハグ
HAGU
餌付け
PACKAGE: SPECIAL TREAT
ORARIO'S STRONGEST LI'L GIRL IS AMONG US—!!
(STRONGER THAN BETE.)
WHAT WAS THAT—!!?
(STRONGER THAN BETE!!)
CUT IT OUT AL-READY!!!

END

TRANSLATION NOTES

Common Honorifics
no honorific: Indicates familiarity or closeness; if used without permission or reason, addressing someone in this manner would constitute an insult.
-san: The Japanese equivalent of Mr./Mrs./Miss. If a situation calls for politeness, this is the fail-safe honorific.
-shi: Not unlike -san; the equivalent of Mr./Mrs./Miss but conveying a more official or bureaucratic mood
-sama: Conveys great respect; may also indicate that the social status of the speaker is lower than that of the addressee.
-kun: Used most often when referring to boys, this indicates affection or familiarity. Occasionally used by older men among their peers, but it may also be used by anyone referring to a person of lower standing.
-chan: An affectionate honorific indicating familiarity used mostly in reference to girls; also used in reference to cute persons or animals of either gender.

PAGE 13
Kenki: "Sword princess." The nickname Aiz Wallenstein's feats have earned her.

PAGE 114
Jyaga maru kun: Fried potato puffs sold at a popular stall from the *Is it Wrong to Try to Pick Up Girls in a Dungeon* original series.

Is it Wrong to Try to Pick Up Girls in a Dungeon? On the Side

Sword Oratoria

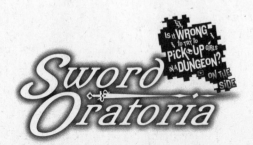

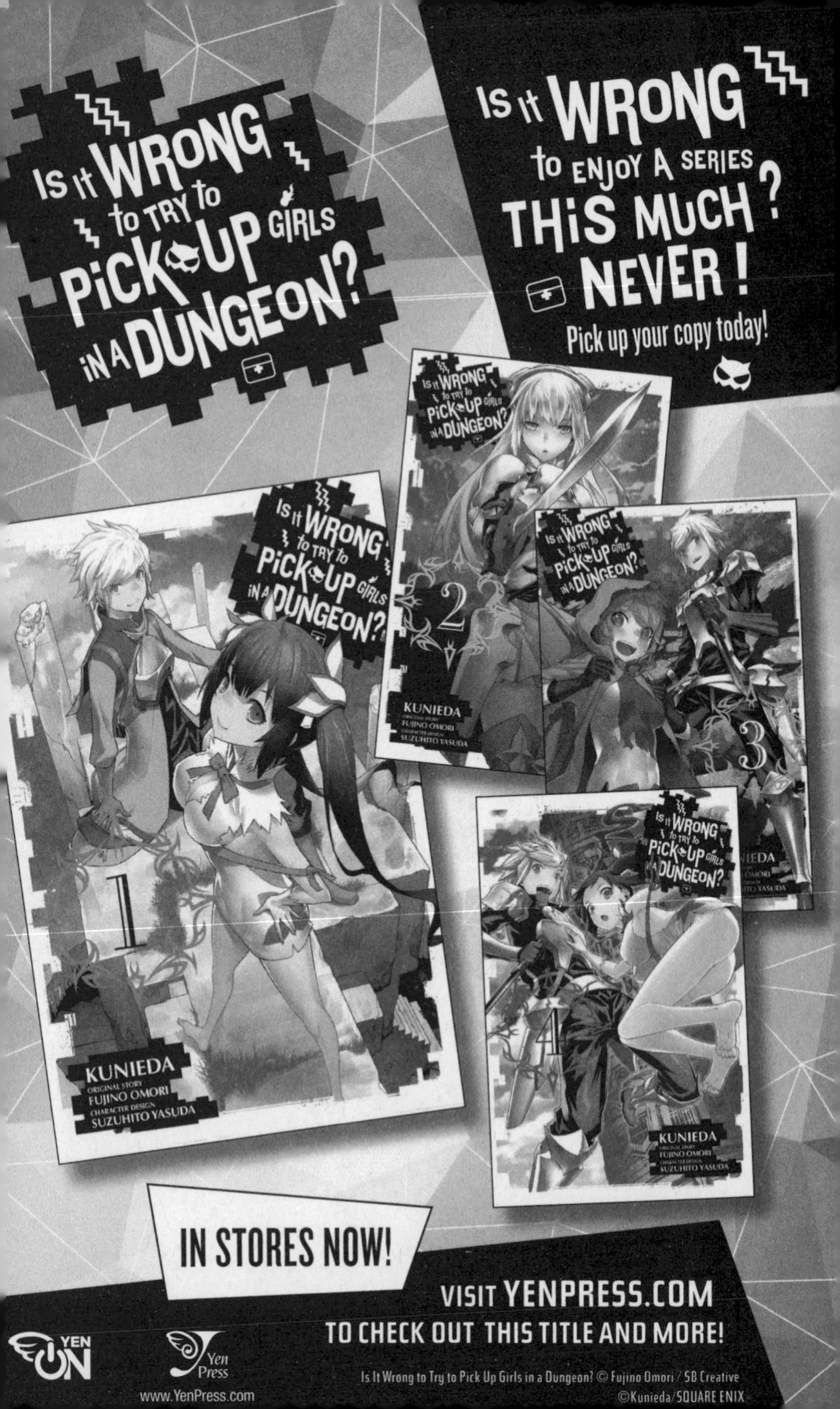
Is it WRONG to Try to PiCK UP GIRLS iN A DUNGEON?
Is it WRONG to ENJOY A SERIES THIS MUCH?
NEVER!
Pick up your copy today!
Is it WRONG to Try to PiCK UP GIRLS iN A DUNGEON?
1
KUNIEDA
ORIGINAL STORY FUJINO OMORI
CHARACTER DESIGN SUZUHITO YASUDA
Is it WRONG to Try to PiCK UP GIRLS iN A DUNGEON?
2
KUNIEDA
ORIGINAL STORY FUJINO OMORI
CHARACTER DESIGN SUZUHITO YASUDA
Is it WRONG to Try to PiCK UP GIRLS iN A DUNGEON?
3
Is it WRONG to Try to PiCK UP GIRLS iN A DUNGEON?
4
KUNIEDA
ORIGINAL STORY FUJINO OMORI
CHARACTER DESIGN SUZUHITO YASUDA
IN STORES NOW!
VISIT YENPRESS.COM
TO CHECK OUT THIS TITLE AND MORE!
YEN ON
Yen Press
www.YenPress.com
Is It Wrong to Try to Pick Up Girls in a Dungeon? © Fujino Omori / SB Creative
©Kunieda/SQUARE ENIX

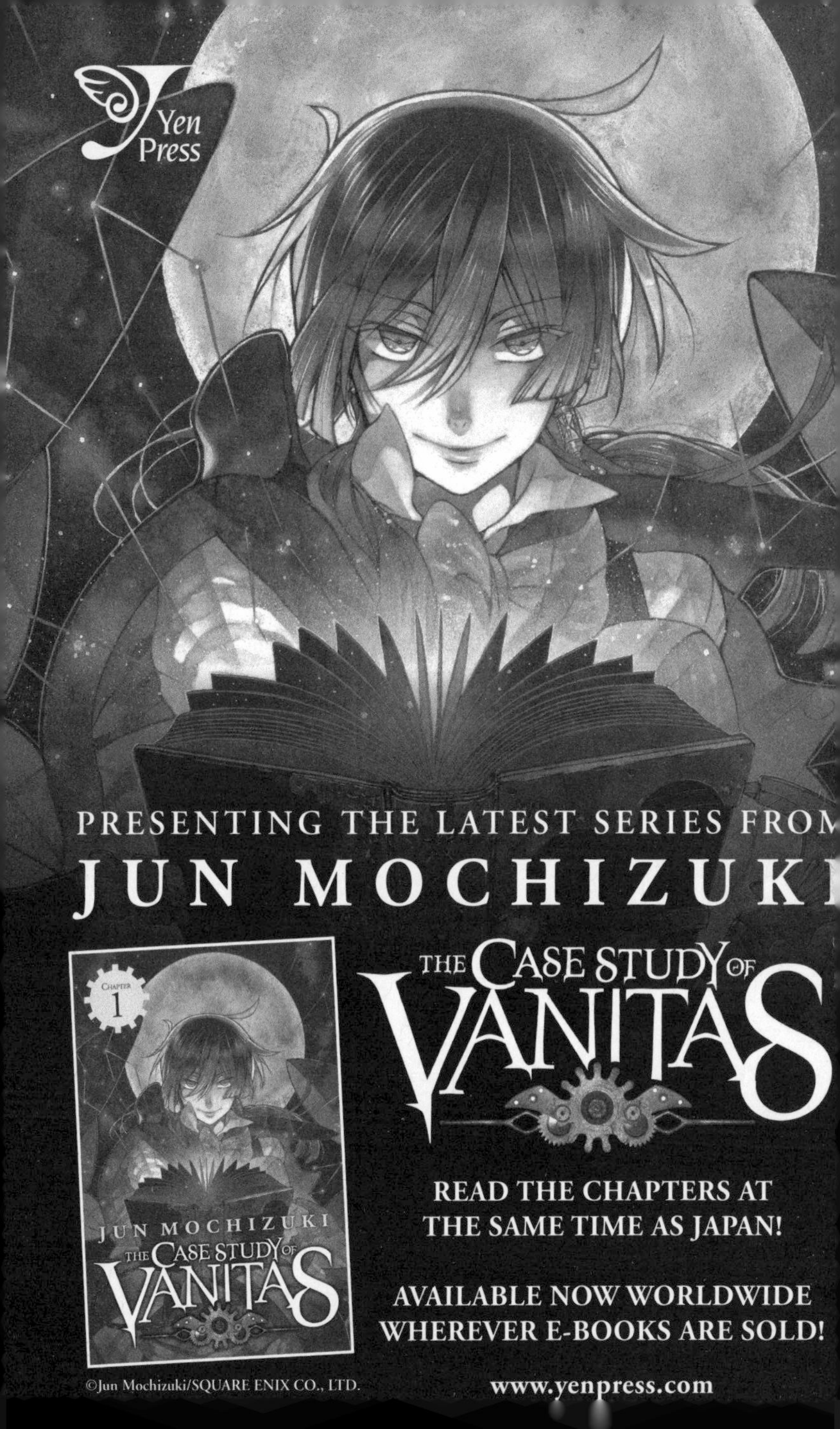

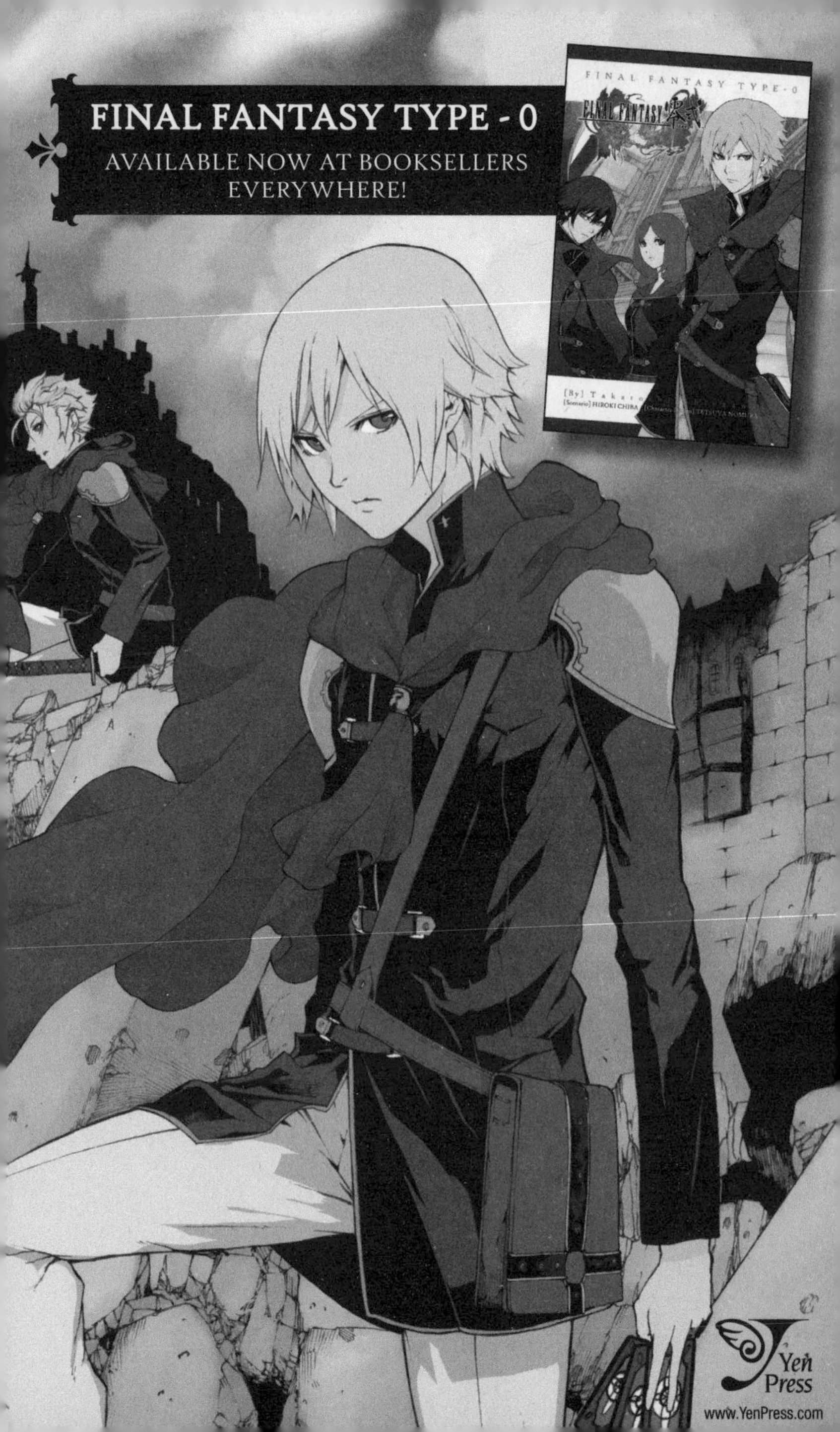
FINAL FANTASY TYPE - 0
AVAILABLE NOW AT BOOKSELLERS
EVERYWHERE!
FINAL FANTASY TYPE-0
[Scenario] HIROKI CHIBA
Yen Press
www.YenPress.com

FINAL FANTASY 零式 TYPE-0

FINAL FANTASY TYPE-0
©2012 Takatoshi Shiozawa / SQUARE ENI
©2011 SQUARE ENIX CO.,LTD.
All Rights Reserved.

Art: TAKATOSHI SHIOZAWA
Character Design: TETSUYA NOMUR
Scenario: HIROKI CHIBA

The cadets of Akademeia's Class Zero are legends, with strength and magic unrivaled, an crimson capes symbolizing the great Vermilion Bird of the Dominion. But will their elite traini be enough to keep them alive when a war breaks out and the Class Zero cadets find themselves the front and center of a bloody political battlefield?!

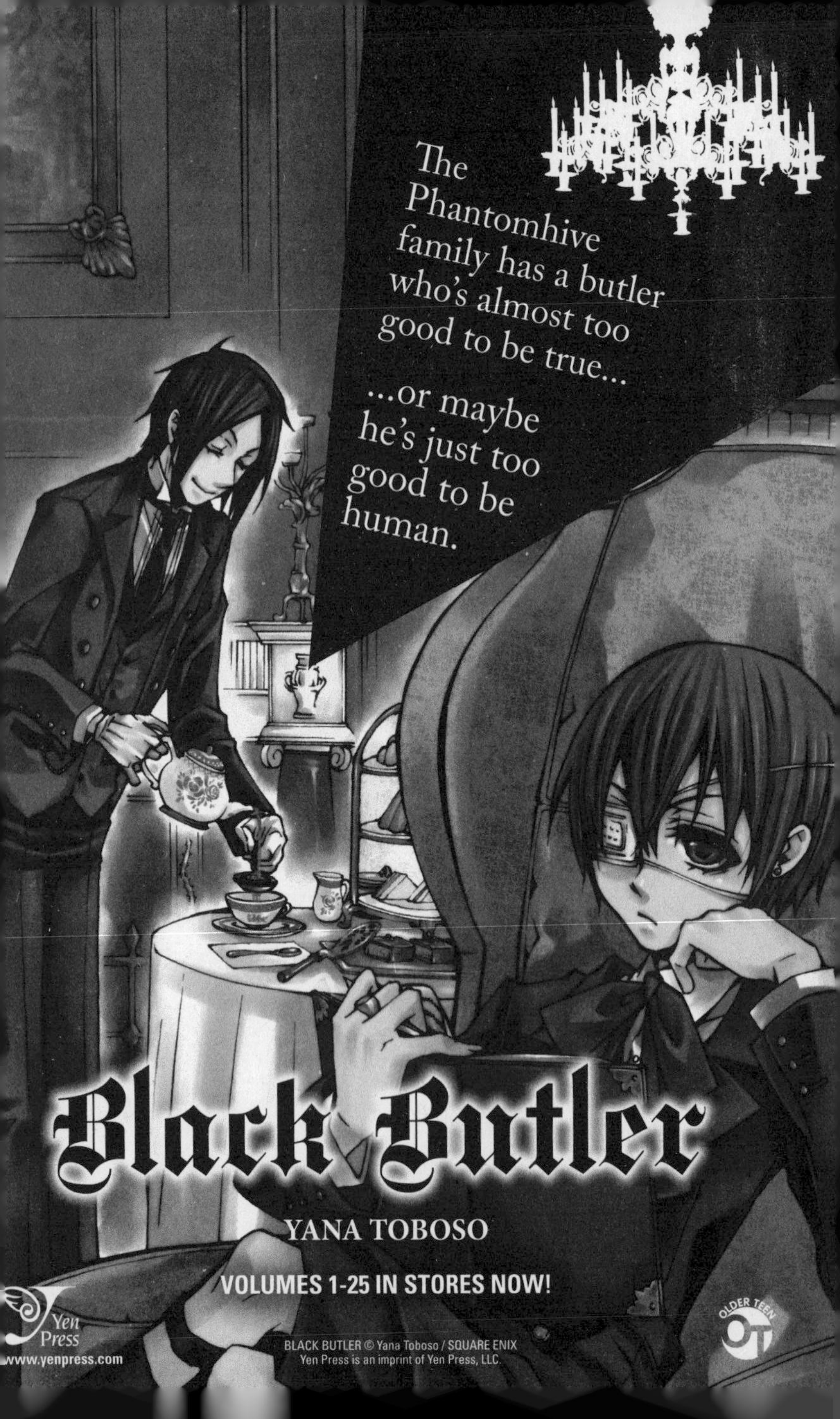

The Phantomhive family has a butler who's almost too good to be true...
...or maybe he's just too good to be human.
Black Butler
YANA TOBOSO
VOLUMES 1-25 IN STORES NOW!
Yen Press
www.yenpress.com
BLACK BUTLER © Yana Toboso / SQUARE ENIX
Yen Press is an imprint of Yen Press, LLC.
OLDER TEEN
OT

HE DOES NOT LET ANYONE ROLL THE DICE.

A young Priestess joins her first adventuring party, but blind to the dangers, they almost immediately find themselves in trouble. It's Goblin Slayer who comes to their rescue—a man who has dedicated his life to the extermination of all goblins by any means necessary. A dangerous, dirty, and thankless job, but he does it better than anyone. And when rumors of his feats begin to circulate, there's no telling who might come calling next...

Light Novel
V. 1-2
Available
Now!

Check out the simul-pub manga chapters every month!

Goblin Slayer © Kumo Kagyu / Noboru Kannatuki / SB Creative Corp.

Yen Press   Yen ON

www.yenpress.com

IS IT WRONG TO TRY TO PICK UP GIRLS IN A DUNGEON? ON THE SIDE: SWORD ORATORIA ❷

Fujino Omori
Takashi Yagi
Haimura Kiyotaka, Yasuda Suzuhito

Translation: Andrew Gaippe • Lettering: Brndn Blakeslee

DUNGEON NI DEAI WO MOTOMERU NO WA MACHIGATTEIRUDAROUKA GAIDEN SWORD ORATORIA vol. 2
© Fujino Omori / SB Creative Corp. Character design: Haimura Kiyotaka, Yasuda Suzuhito
© 2015 Takashi Yagi / SQUARE ENIX CO., LTD.
First published in Japan in 2015 by SQUARE ENIX CO., LTD.
English translation rights arranged with SQUARE ENIX CO., LTD. and Yen Press, LLC through Tuttle-Mori Agency, Inc.

English translation © 2018 SQUARE ENIX CO., LTD.

Yen Press
1290 Avenue of the Americas
New York, NY 10104

Visit us at yenpress.com
facebook.com/yenpress
twitter.com/yenpress
yenpress.tumblr.com
instagram.com/yenpress

First Yen Press Edition: January 2018

Yen Press is an imprint of Yen Press, LLC.
The Yen Press name and logo are trademarks of Yen Press, LLC.

Library of Congress Control Number: 2016946068

ISBNs: 978-0-316-55864-8 (paperback)
        978-0-316-44794-2 (ebook)

10 9 8 7 6 5 4 3 2 1

BVG

Printed in the United States of America